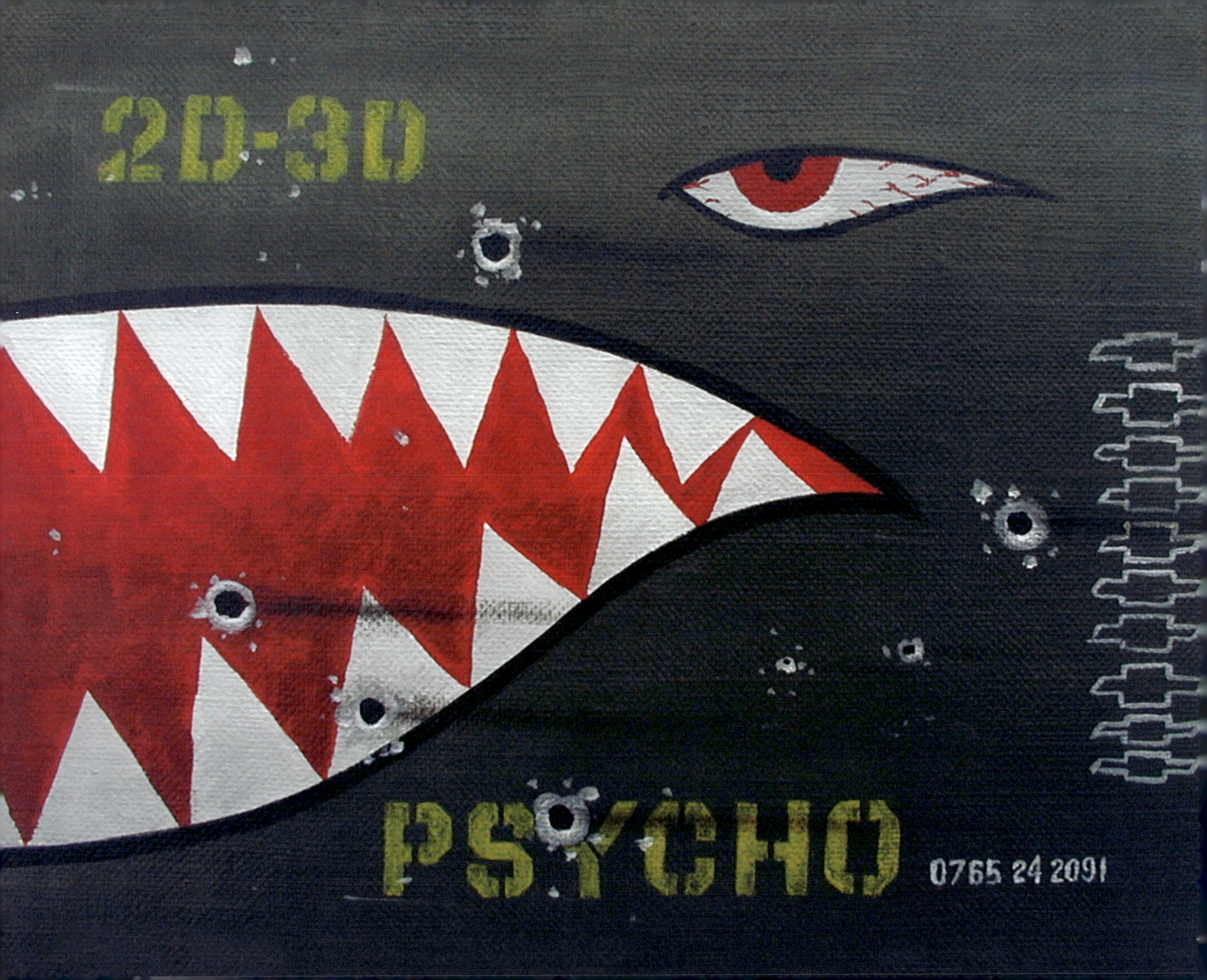
2D-3D
PSYCHO
0765 24 2091

Kustom Japan

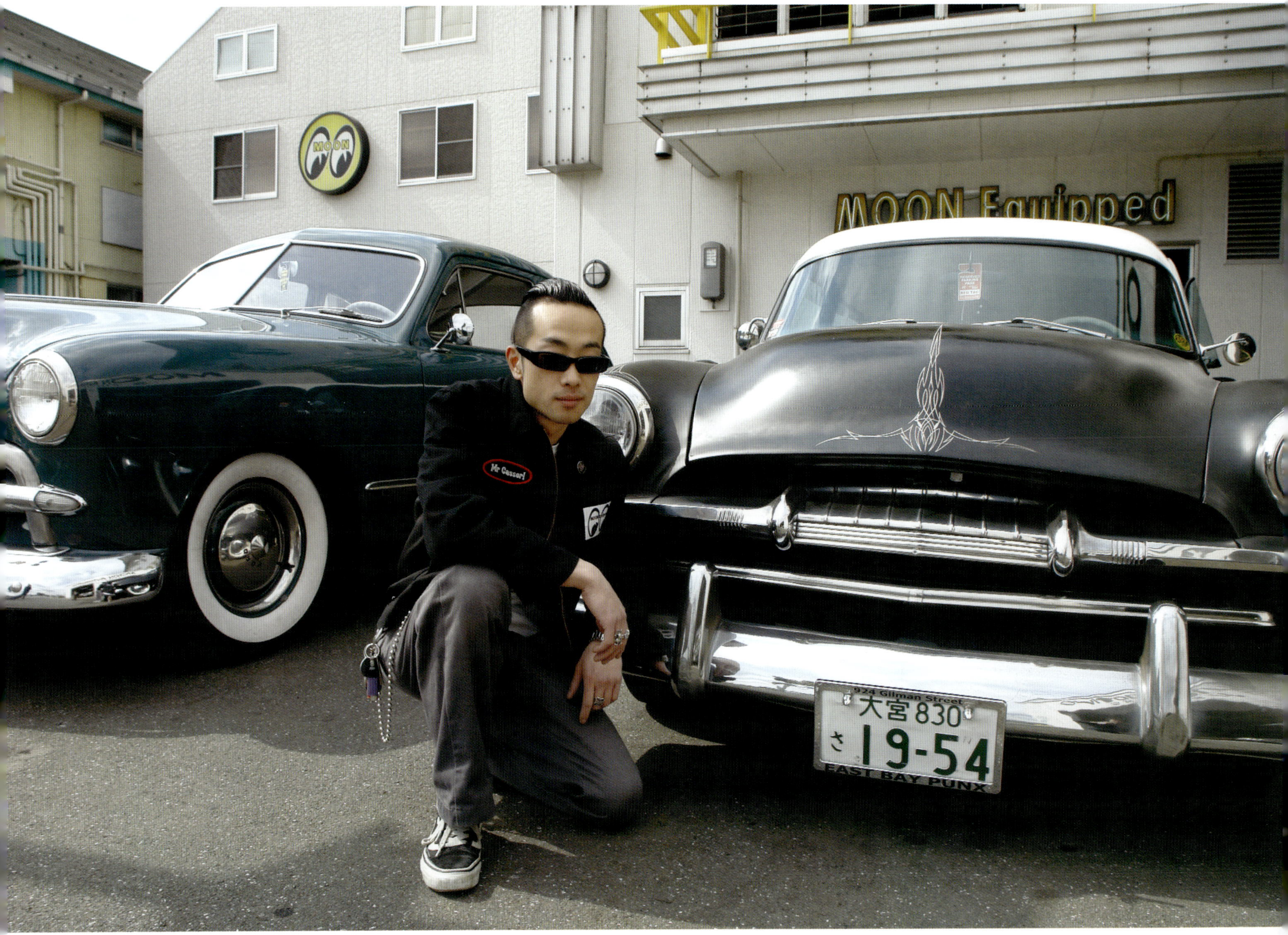
MOON
MOON Equipped
924 Gilman Street
大宮830
さ 19-54
EAST BAY PUNX

Kustom Japan

Text and Photographs by

Michael McCabe

with a forward by

Don Ed Hardy

HM

HARDY MARKS PUBLICATIONS

注記：

• ほとんどのインタビューは英語が母国語でない人と英語で、あるいは通訳を介して行われたものです。インタビューの内容は、読みやすくするよう、ある程度の編集がなされています。
• インタビューされた人はほとんどが日本人ですが、翻訳は英語の原稿をもとにしています。したがって、インタビューされた人が日本語で話したときの実際の方言や言い回しなどを反映しないことがあります。
• 日本語の原稿は、英語で執筆された原稿の翻訳ですので、日本語では一般的に使われない用語や表現があります。
• 日本語の個人名は英語の原稿に記載された内容と使用法を反映するもので、日本語の原稿にそのままの形で表されています（日本での標準的な姓名の順序や漢字が使用されていないことがあります）。
• 日本語の翻訳は、本書制作の後期に追加された変更を反映しないことがあります。

Notes on the text:

• Most interviews were conducted through an interpreter or in English with non-native English speakers, and editorial license was used to make the interviews read more smoothly.
• Though the interviewees are mostly Japanese, the translation of their interviews is based on the English text, so the language may not reflect the interviewees' actual dialect or speaking style in Japanese.
• The Japanese is a translation reflecting the original English work, and as such may use terms and phrasing not typical in Japanese writing.
• The handling of Japanese personal names reflects the information available from and usage in the English text, and is represented as such in the Japanese text (standard name order and use of *kanji* characters may not apply in the Japanese translation).
• The Japanese translation may not reflect English editorial changes made later in the book production process.

Design: Craig Okino, Okino Graphics, Honolulu
D. E. Hardy

Translation: Hitoshi Shigeta
Lisa Louis
TechArt, San Francisco

Editors: D. E. Hardy
Francesca Passalacqua

Front Cover: Syu Merk tail, pinstriping by Makoto

Back Cover: Masato with T-Bucket Toy T

Frontispiece: Toshi Endo, Mooneyes staff

Endpapers: Painting by Psycho

Page 192: On the road (Photo: Hiroki Natsume, Greaser Original Wear)

Hardy Marks Publications
700 Lombard Street
San Francisco, CA 94133

ISBN 978-0-945367-35-2

Printed and bound by Prolong Press, China

Acknowledgments

There are many people who I would like to thank. A book project like this is a complicated undertaking and, without interest and help from insider people, impossible. In many ways, the sensibility surrounding Kustom Kulture is nuanced and private, fueled by strong appreciation that keeps the flame burning about a unique collection of ideas, aesthetics and objects. In Japan, Kustom Kulture takes on added mystery as devotees there measure and sift through layers of historical association from a foreign place. For an outsider, making sense of this process is impossible without guidance.

First, I wish to thank Shige Suganuma at Mooneyes for his generous assistance and guidance and invaluable help and suggestions. Shige rearranged his busy schedule and allowed me to photograph freely at his impressive Yokohama Mooneyes building complex. Also at Mooneyes I wish to thank Goshu Okita for his generous assistance. His translation skills were also invaluable, particularly with the Wildman interview, and I appreciate the time he took to explain the nuances of Yokohama car culture. Thank you also to the guys at Mooneyes for moving and re-parking their cars a dozen times for the photos.

I also wish to thank Nash Yoshii of *Burn Out Magazine* for his constant help. His effort to answer questions as well as invite and include me in his *Kustom Kulture Now* events was extremely generous and important. Conversations with Nash about the Kustom Kulture sensibility helped point me in the right direction, and I appreciate his time. I am especially appreciative of Nash's help translating my interviews with Shorty of Pumpkin Sally and Mr. G. Rei Mizushima, Izumi Akiba and Hata Ryosuki of INKRAT TATTOO in the Koenji section of Tokyo were also very helpful. Izumi made countless phone calls, translated, and was very generous with her time. INKRAT became a home away from home, and I appreciate their hospitality very much. Yushi Ichinohe of Scratch Addiction tattoo in Tokyo was also very generous with his time and assistance. He made important connections with people in the Harajuku district and talked with me about the unique postwar cross-cultural process between Japan and America. .

In the Nagoya area, Yoshiki Miyagawa and Rei of ViSE Clothing were very important to this project. Yoshiki's generosity and efforts are deeply appreciated. He made appointments with important builders in the Nagoya area and then drove me around to meet with them. I also wish to thank Hiroki Natsume of Greaser clothing for his generous assistance.

Junichi Shimodaira of Paradise Road, Hideki Kato of Border's and Akira Tokita of Vannuys Automotive were very generous to invite me into their shops and talk about the development of Kustom Kulture in Japan. I am thankful to all the Nagoya builders for their openness and generosity. Dice Kobayashi and Masashi Fukaya of the Strongers Car Club were always generous with their time and advice, as was photographer and friend Mattias Westfalk, who helped me sort through a long list of photographic mysteries.

Thank you to my publisher and editor, Ed Hardy, for this opportunity to pursue my interest in cultural discovery. His knowledge about Japan and awareness of the subtle cultural layers there was critical. His personal sensibility of Kustom Kulture helped to focus my intentions about my research.

Finally, I would like to thank my wife, Tzyy Jye Chang, for her constant support and guidance throughout this project. I traveled to Japan numerous times and was living in unfamiliar places away from my native language. At times, everything became a bit strange, lonely, and overwhelming; and Tzyy Jye's phone calls of support encouraged and grounded me. Thank you, Tzyy Jye.

謝辞

この本の出版にあたりお礼を述べたい方々がたくさんいる。このような執筆プロジェクトは複雑な仕事であり、事情に通じた方々の影響力と援助なしには不可能なものだ。色々な意味でカスタム・カルチャーに関連する感性は微妙でプライベートなものであり、ユニークなアイデア、美的感覚および造形の集合体への絶え間ない情熱によって支えられている。日本においては、車愛好家がこの外来の何層にもなった過去からの連想を測り、より分けることよって、カスタム・カルチャーの謎はさらに深まっている。部外者にとって、何らかの指導なしにこのプロセスの意味を理解することは不可能である。

まず、惜しみない援助と指導、そして貴重な助力と提案をくださったムーンアイズのシゲ菅沼氏にお礼を申し上げたい。同氏は多忙なスケジュールを変更して、印象的な横浜のムーンアイズ・ビルで私が自由に撮影できるようにしてくださった。また、ムーンアイズでは、色々と援助をくださったGoshu大喜多氏にもお礼を申し上げる。同氏の通訳は計り知れないほど貴重で、特にワイルドマンとのインタビューではずいぶん助けていただいたばかりでなく、横浜のカー・カルチャーのニュアンスについて時間をかけて説明していただいたことに感謝したい。さらに、写真撮影のために何度も車を移動していただいたムーンアイズの皆様にも心からお礼を申し上げる。

そして、絶え間なく助力をくださったBurnout Magazineの Nash吉井氏にもお礼を申し上げたい。質問にお答えいただいた尽力に加えて、寛大にもカスタム・カルチャー・ナウのイベントにご招待・参加させていただいたことは非常に重要だった。Nash氏とのカスタム・カルチャーの感性についての対談は、私を正しい方向に導いてくれた。貴重な時間を割いていただいたことに感謝したい。さらに、パンプキン・サリーのショーティ氏、Mr.G氏とのインタビューでもNash氏に助けていたことに特にお礼を申し上げたい。東京高円寺INKRAT TATTOOの水島レイ氏、秋庭イズミ氏、ハタ・リョウスケ氏にもずいぶんご援助いただいた。イズミ氏には数え切れないほどの電話と通訳をしていただき、多大な時間をかけていただいた。INKRATは私にとって我が家のような場所になった。その温かいおもてなしに心より感謝したい。また、東京Scratch AddictionタトゥーのYushiイノウエ氏には惜しみないお時間とご援助をいただいた。同氏は原宿地区の人々との大切なつながりを作ってくださり、戦後日米間のユニークな異文化交流について語っていただいた。

名古屋地域では、ViSE衣料店の宮川佳己氏とレイ氏は、この執筆プロジェクトにとって非常に重要な存在だった。佳己氏のご親切・ご尽力に心から感謝を申し上げる。同氏は名古屋地域の重要なビルダーに会えるよう手配してくださり、車で連れて行っていただいた。また、Greaser衣料店の夏目広樹氏にも多大なご援助をいただいたことにお礼を申し上げる。

Paradise Roadの下平純一氏、Border'sの加藤秀樹氏、Vannuys Automotiveの時田彰氏には、私を温かくショップにお招きいただき、日本のカスタム・カルチャーの展開について語っていただいた。名古屋のビルダー全員に、その率直さと寛大な対応に感謝の気持ちを述べたい。Strongersカー・クラブのダイス小林氏と深谷昌史氏には惜しみない時間とアドバイスいただき、また、写真家で友人のマティアス・ウェストフォーク氏には山積みの写真からの大変なより分けをお手伝いいただいた。

出版元・編集者のエド・ハーディ氏には、文化的発見に対する私の興味追求に機会を与えてくださったことにお礼を申し上げる。日本についての同氏の知識と、微妙な文化的構造に対する認識は、重要な役割を果たした。また、同氏のカスタム・カルチャーに対する個人的な感性が、調査についての私の趣旨に的確な視点を与えてくれた。

最後に、このプロジェクト全体にわたって常に支援と指導をくれた妻のツィ・ジェ・チャンに感謝したい。何度も訪日し、母国語の通じない不案内な場所に住みながら、ときにはすべてが奇妙で心細く、圧倒されるような気分になることもあった。そんなとき、ツィ・ジェの電話での支援は、私を励まし落ち着かせてくれた。ありがとう、ツィ・ジェ。

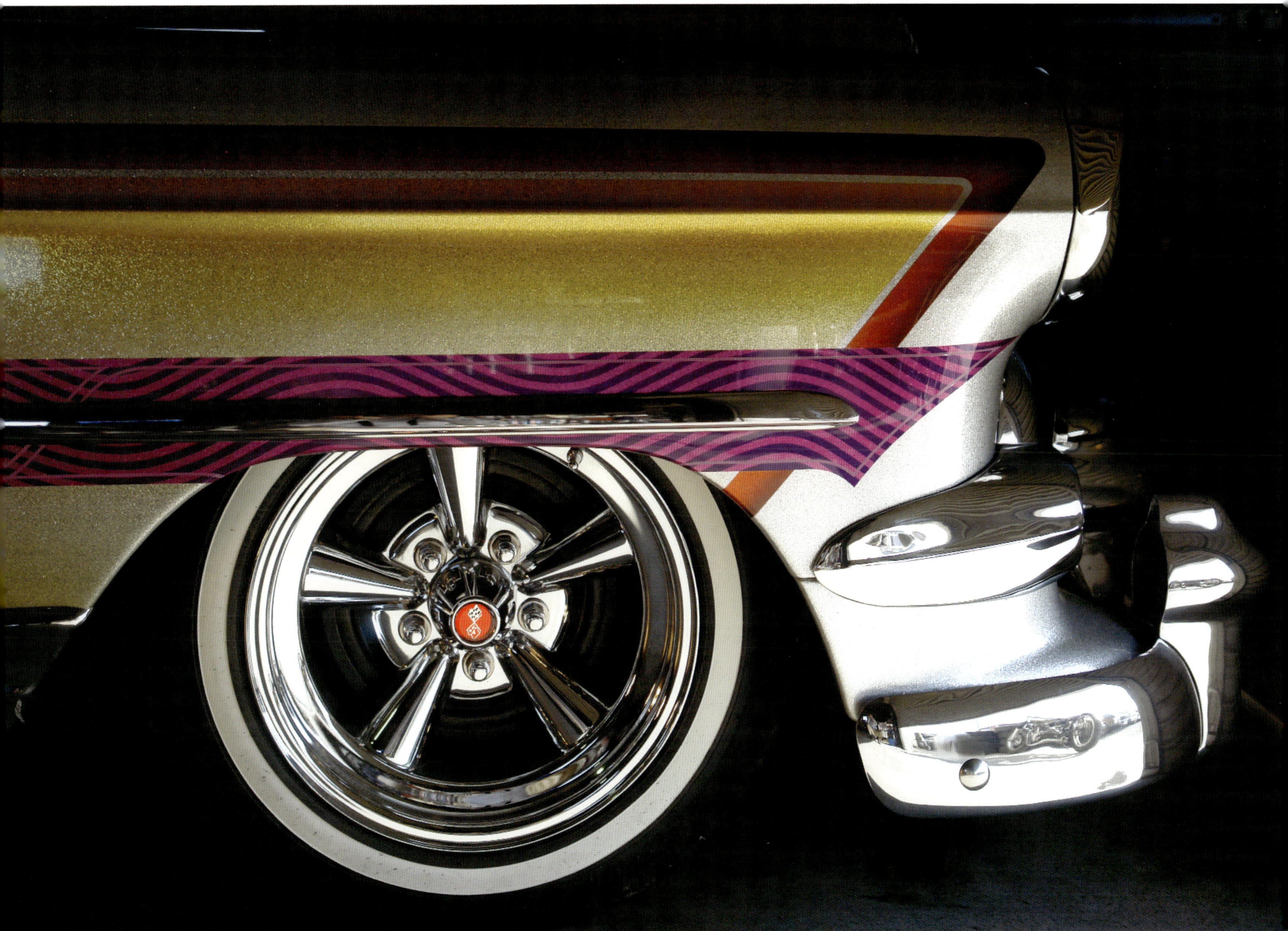

まえがき

長年にわたる仕事仲間であり、アジア通であるマイク・マッケイブが日本のカスタム・カーやホットロッド・シーンについての本を執筆していると言ってきたとき、私はぜひとも出版したいと思った。このサブカルチャーの存在は知りつつも、その情熱と複雑な深遠さには気づいていなかった。個人レベルでは、その原点は、南カリフォルニアのビーチタウンで過ごした私自身の青年期の初期にきわめて重要なものであり、タトゥーやサーフィンと共に、これら３つを合わせたスタイルは、今も私の心に共鳴するものがある。

1950 年代中頃、家からすぐ近くのハイウェイ 101 では、大胆に改造され、念入りに塗装された車がクルージングし、その壮観をビッグ・コロナ・ビーチの駐車場で誇示していた。そこに集まった我々若者は、夏の日のすべての瞬間を惜しみなく味わったものだった。そこでは車のボディや内装、クラブの刻板、トップに君臨するヴォンダッチ、エド・ロス、ディーン“キッド・ジェフ”ジェフリーズらの手による驚くべきピンストライピング、炎のパターン、そして「ウィアドー（変人）」ペインティングのニュアンスを食い入るようにじっくり観察することができた。

さらに、初めて認可を受けたナショナル・ホットロッド協会のドラッグレース・コースが、約３マイル内陸のサンタアナ飛行場にあった。友人のレン・ジョーンズと私は、ものすごい車とバイクのタイムトライアル・アクションを日曜日ごとに見ることができた。タトゥーパーラーや巨大なニューパイク遊園地をのぞきに、海岸に沿って 25 マイルほど上がったロングビーチへもよく行き、大規模なカー・ショーに参加できることもたびたびあった。そこで、初めてピンストライパーの実演や、エド・ロス（そのころはまだ“ビッグダディ”とは呼ばれていなかった）がトレーナーなどにエアブラシで「クレイジー・ペインティング」を描くのを見た。それに刺激されて、1957 年、コンプレッサーとエアブラシを購入し、それほど洗練された作品ではなかったが、地元の友達らのために短期間、同様のことをやってみた。

1960 年代後期、本気で日本美術史の勉強を始め、精緻かつ催眠術的な炎を描いた 900 年前の仏教地獄絵を発見した。はっと驚いて、車のペインターらは、このような原型的作品を知っていたのかと思いを巡らした。さらに、地獄に生息する「餓鬼」は、太鼓腹と干からびた腕や足で描かれており、ディーン・ジェフリーズが 1950 年代に創作した変な小人（彼の作品の代表的要素）の直接的先祖とも言えるものだった。同氏と 2005 年に電話で話したとき、そのことを尋ねると、彼はそんな日本の作品についてはまったく知らないようだったが、その類似性に不思議な何かを感じた。

カリフォルニアのポップカルチャーは 20 世紀全体にわたって世界中に深い影響を与えた。そして日本のさまざまな側面は私の人生にも影響を与え、さらに東西の対話は、今も尽きることのないインスピレーションの基盤を提供してくれる。本書に登場する日本のビジョナリーや車愛好家は、今もパワフルな表現の本流・支流を取り込んで吸収し、マスターし、変貌させ続けている。マイク・マッケイブの写真と言葉は、この改変プロセスの斬新かつ見事な証である。

ドン・エド・ハーディ
2008 年 1 月
ホノルルにて

Foreward

When my longtime associate and savvy Asia expat Mike McCabe told me he was working on a book about the custom and hot rod scene in Japan, I was eager to publish it. I was aware of this subculture, but not the passion and depth of its complexity. On a personal level, its origins were crucial to my early youth in a Southern California beach town and, along with tattooing and wave riding, formed a triumvirate of style that resonates with me to this day.

In the mid-1950s, radically modified and elaborately painted cars cruised Highway 101 (a few doors from my house) and were poised in all their glory in the parking lot of Big Corona beach, where my crowd spent every possible waking summer moment. There we could scrutinize nuances of the bodies and interiors, club plaques, and amazing pinstriping, flames, and "weirdo" painting by the reigning masters—Von Dutch, Ed Roth, Dean "Kid Jeff" Jeffries, and others.

Additionally, the first sanctioned National Hot Rod Association drag strip was at the Santa Ana Air Field, about 3 miles inland. There, on Sundays, my friend, Len Jones, and I could see amazing cars and bikes in time-trial action. On forays to Long Beach, 25 miles up the coast, to hang out in tattoo parlors and dig the scene at the giant Nu-Pike amusement park, we were often able to attend huge car shows. There, we first saw stripers at work and Ed (not yet "Big Daddy") Roth airbrush sweatshirts with "Krazy Painting." Inspired, in 1957 I bought a compressor and airbrush and briefly pursued a similar, though less polished, career for local friends.

In the late 1960s I began studying Japanese art history in earnest and discovered 900-year-old Japanese paintings of Buddhist hells featuring elaborate and hypnotic flames. Startled, I began to wonder if the car painters were aware of these prototypical works. Moreover, scenarios of "hungry ghosts" populating the infernal zones, with their potbellies and shriveled limbs, were direct forebears of the weird little men (a signature element) of Dean Jeffries' 1950s creations. When I questioned him about this in a 2005 phone conversation, he denied any knowledge of the Japanese works, though the resemblance is uncanny.

California popular culture has deeply impacted the world throughout the 20th century. Myriad aspects of Japan have influenced my life, and the East/West dialog still provides inexhaustible ground for inspiration. The Japanese visionaries and enthusiasts in this book continue to embrace, digest, perfect and transform powerful sub- and mainstream realms of expression. Mike McCabe's pictures and words are a fresh and amazing testament to this process of reinvention.

Don Ed Hardy
Honolulu
January, 2008

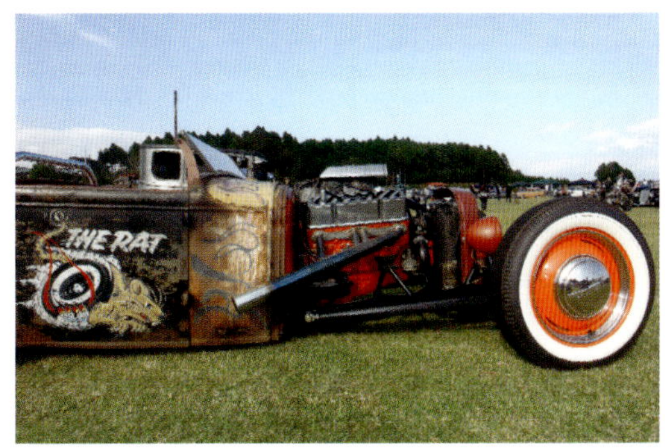

"Sal, we gotta go and never stop going till we get there."
"Where we going man?"
"I don't know but we gotta go."

Jack Kerouac – *On the Road*

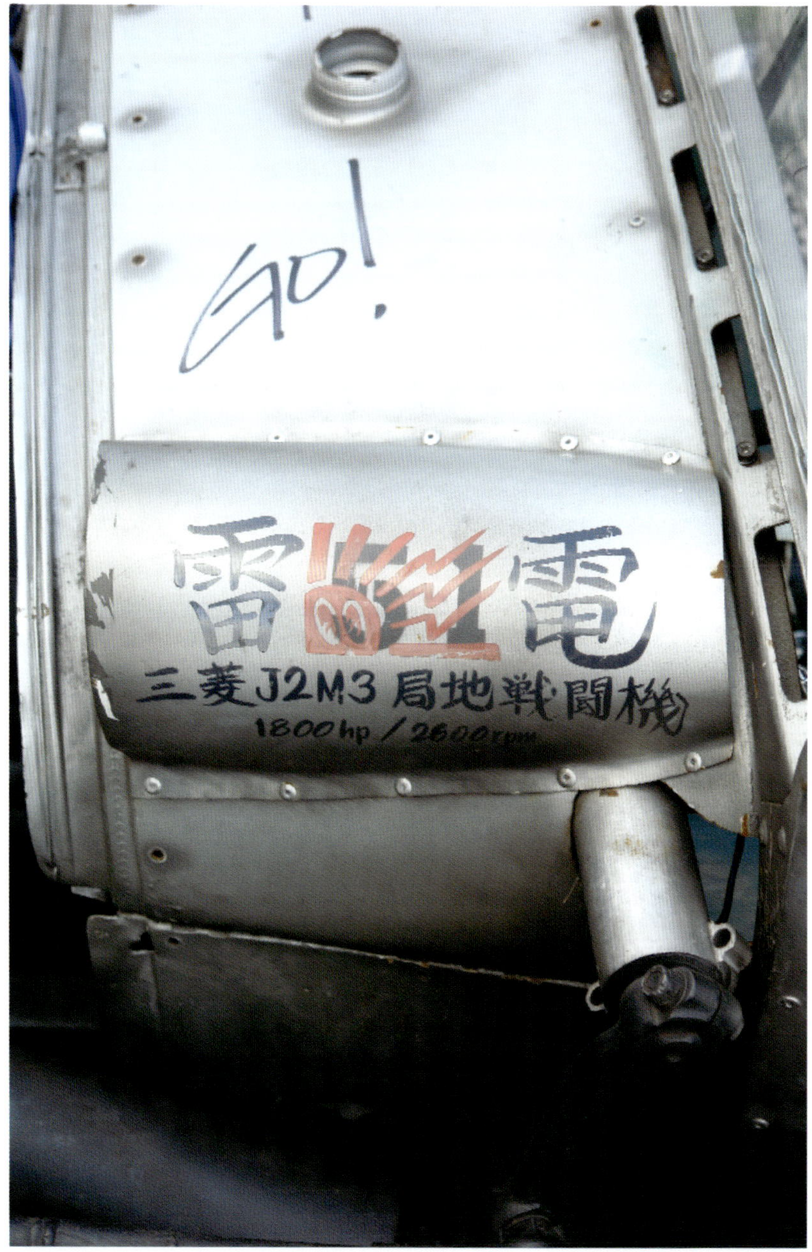

Chapter One: The Kustom Road

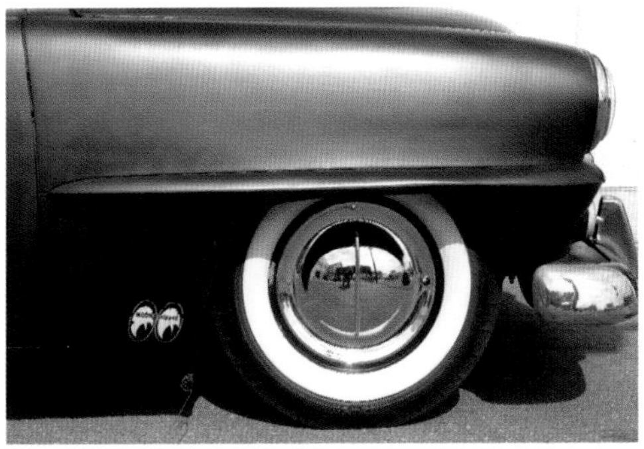

Above: 1954 Plaza Suburban, owner, Toshi Endo

As an East Coast teenager in the early 1970s I did a lot of hitchhiking around the northern and western United States. The mythos of adventure and rebirth along the American trail, characterized first by pioneers, cowboys and railroad men then by Steinbeck during the Depression and Jack Kerouac during the 1950s, was magnetic. The trail evolved from dirt to steel to pavement; and with this, themes of freedom and rebirth ran deeply into the American psyche. Throughout America's history, the mystique of the road was repackaged several times for different purposes by a society that seemed perpetually on the move. This cultural fascination with travel as a process of personal expansion was mysterious but also poignant for many young people like myself, and the automobile was the delivery system that could take you where you wanted to go.

Very late one night in Arizona, standing at the edge of Route 66 in the middle of the Mojave Desert, I remember feeling overwhelmed by the expanse of the endless American landscape. An impressive starry sky hung over an empty flatness that went forever in both directions and then faded into the darkness. The narrow strip of two-lane pavement I stood on seemed resilient with a sense of accumulated importance that struck a balance with the spaciousness of the land. I had no idea where I was, but I had a sense that I had fulfilled something and arrived someplace.

Finally there were headlights, and a white Cadillac Eldorado pulled over to give me a lift. The driver was a middle-aged salesman; and, as I climbed in, he asked if I had a driver's license and could I take the wheel? He had an early morning meeting in Bakersfield and needed some sleep. There was a pole stretching between the windows in the back crowded with suit jackets and shirts, and I figured the guy posed no risk. As I settled into the leather

カスタムロード

1970年代の初め、東海岸に住むティーンエイジャーだった私は、アメリカの北部や西部でよくヒッチハイクをしたものだった。アメリカ史初期の西部開拓者やカウボーイや鉄道労働者、また大恐慌時代にはスタインベック、1950年代にはジャック・ケルアックが形作ったアメリカン・トレイルの冒険や復活の神話は、私にとって大いに魅力があった。そのトレイルは、土から線路、アスファルトの舗装道へと進化していき、それに伴って自由と復活のテーマはアメリカ人の心理の中に深く根ざしていった。アメリカの歴史全体にわたり、絶え間なく変化を続けるように思える社会の中で、道に対する神話はさまざまな目的に合わせて何度も組み直されてきた。この個人の成長プロセスとしての旅についての社会的魅惑は、神秘であると同時に、私のような多くの若者にはしびれるほど感動的であった。そして車とは自分の望む場所へ連れて行ってくれる運搬システムだったのだ。

ある深夜、私はアリゾナ州モハーヴェ砂漠のど真ん中、ルート66の道路わきに立っていた。果てしないアメリカの砂漠の景観の広がりに圧倒されたことを憶えている。印象的な満天の星がうつろな大地を覆い、その地面は両方向に延々と続き、やがて闇の中に消えていった。私が立っていた細い2車線の車道は、この広大な大地とその上に積み重ねられた道の大切さをバランスよく調和し、まるで生き生きと輝いているように感じられた。その時自分がどこにいるかさえ分からなかったにもかかわらず、ある充実感があり、どこかに到達したような気さえした。

ようやくヘッドライトが見え、白いキャデラック・エルドラドが道路わきに停まった。ドライバーは中年のセールスマンで、私が車に乗り込むと運転免許を持っているか、代わりに運転してくれるかなどと聞いてきた。ベーカーズフィールドで早朝にミーティングがあったので、しばらく居眠りしたいと言うのだ。車の後部座席には左右の窓から窓に棒が延びていて、スーツやシャツがたくさんかかっていた。危険な人物ではないと感じた。革のシートに体を沈め、内側からライトに照らされたダッシュボードの機器を学ぼうとしていると、彼はこの車が500立方インチ・エンジンの馬力だから気をつけるようにと忠告した。「夜の砂漠ではついついスピードが出てしまうからね。」高級車をいとも簡単に他人に運転させる彼に驚いたが、車に乗せてもらえたのがうれしかった。ときどきトラックが通過する以外、ルート66には何もなく、パワフルな8気筒エンジンを噴かすと車は楽に時速90マイルを超えた。障害物はどこにもなく、あるのは地平線の彼方へ消えていく何百マイルものまっすぐな車道だけ。助手席から聞こえる彼のいびきと、窓のシーリングからヒューヒューと漏れる風の音を今も憶えている。

ヘンリー・フォードの貢献は、手頃な価格の車を量産しただけではなかった。パワフルな技術を、それを使いこなす能力のある社会のために普及させたこと、そして景観と一体になりたいという自己的決断の深層心理とマシンとをつなぐ一連の機会を生み出したのだ。やがてこのクリエイティブな構造物は、ユニークで影響力のある精神的感性を生み出し、それに意義を与え、拍車をかけた。つまりそれはアメリカ文化の特徴を成形したのだった。

第二次大戦後、下取りに出され売れ残ったT型やA型フォードが改造され、後に「ホットロッド」と呼ばれる車になった。このような車は、当時アメリカで人口が急増していた若者の間で人気が沸騰し、社会のいくつものレベルで反響を起こした明確なアメリカ文化の象徴となった。車は速く、騒々しく、クールで、危ない…。それはサブカルチャー、カウンターカ

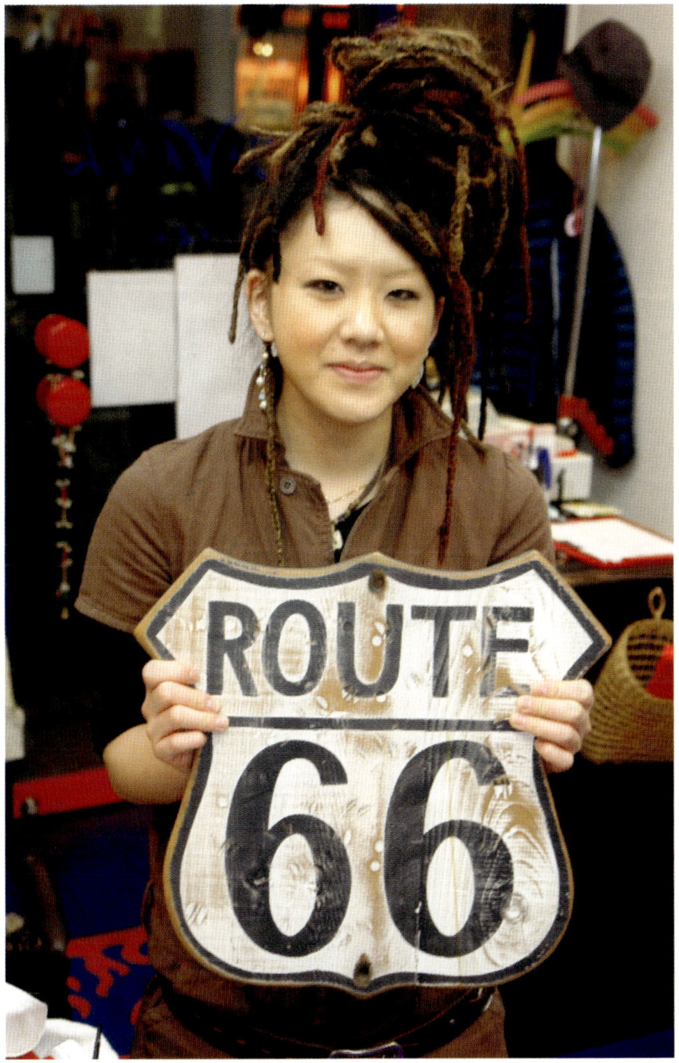

Koenji, Tokyo Hair Braiding shop
Route 66

upholstery and familiarized myself with the glowing dashboard, he told me to mind the power of the 500 cubic inch engine. “At night in the desert it can get away from you,” he said. I was shocked that he had given me control of his expensive car but was happy for the lift. Route 66 was empty except for an occasional truck, and I took the powerful V8 easily over 90mph. There was nothing to run into, just the vanishing point of straight pavement for hundreds of miles ahead of me into space. I remember the window seals whistled gently as the man snored.

Henry Ford did more than mass-produce an affordable automobile. He popularized a powerful technology for a culture that was capable of discovering how to use it and put into motion a process of opportunities that intersected a machine with a deep psychological sense of self-determined access to a landscape. Over time, this creative construct produced a unique and influential mindset that gained momentum and significance as it shaped America’s personality.

After World War II, a surplus of stock Ford Model A and T trade-ins were innovated into what came to be called hot rods. They became distinguishing metaphors that resonated on a number of different levels with the ballooning population of young men and women in the United States. The cars were fast, noisy, cool and dangerous, and represented a mixture of age-sensitive strategies of reinvention that articulated sub and counter-cultural codes of style, language and behavior: rarefied mechanical aptitude and aesthetic specialization which evolved into Kustom Kulture.

Today these cultural stylizations are a part of a nostalgic mystique that is being adopted by a growing number of young people in Japan who see Kustom Kulture as transcendent, powerful and most importantly, defining. Kustom Kulture is about more than redesigning stock model automobiles. The history of the cultural

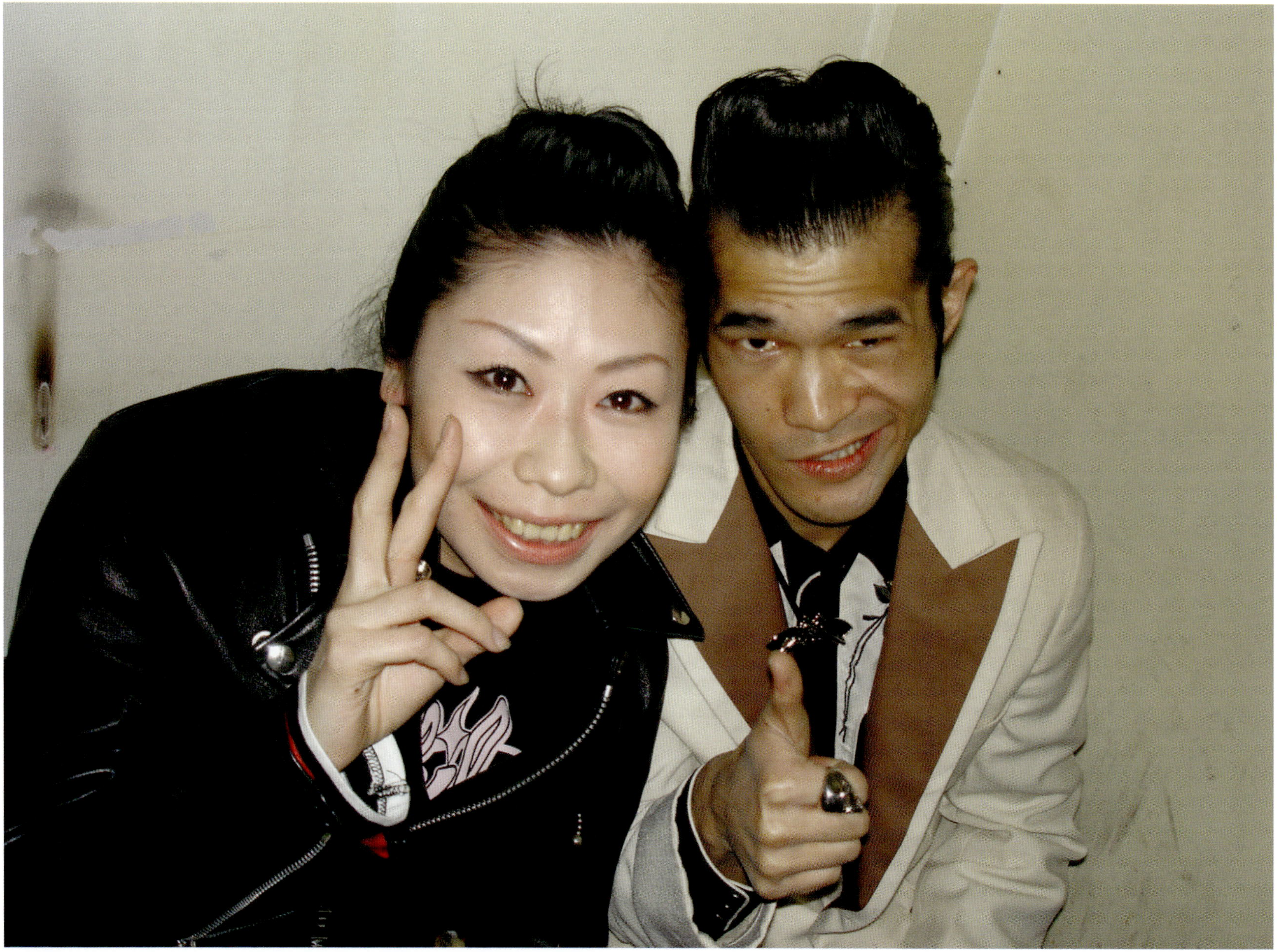

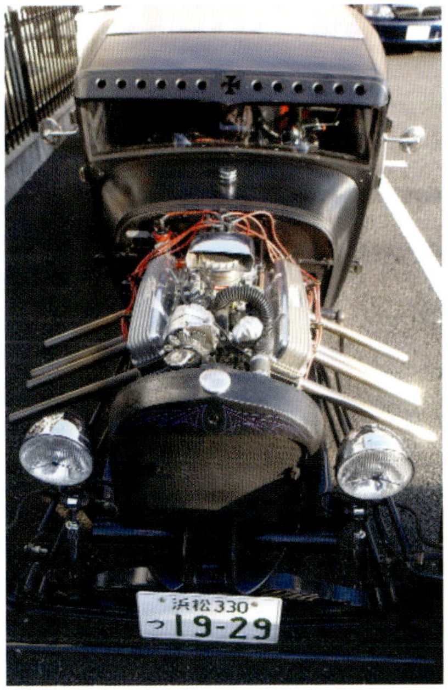

Above: '29 Ford two door sedan
Built by Shorty, Pumpkin Sally
Owner: Kitajima

Left: Shibuya retro

movement is connected to the ascendancy of youth identity and the power associated with this realization. During the postwar period into the 1950s and '60s, Southern California youth embraced hot rods and custom cars as iconic representations that expressed the nuanced but raw power of youth. Rods and customs and the creative values that surrounded them empowered young people to oppose the formal symbols of adulthood that encroached on their lives.

Young urban Japanese adults are sensitive to the reality of the boundaries in their culture. As an island nation, Japan is a relatively small and compact place. It is experienced by many as a safe, finite space with strict limitations of behavior and attitude, directed by stiff historical codes and traditions. Today, for many young urban Japanese, this collection of old codes is being reshaped to accommodate a shrinking world. Postwar Japanese youth have turned increasingly to influential images of the United States that project a spaciousness of possibility and personal opportunity—a place of wide boundaries characterized by liberating values.

Japanese youth culture represents a curious system of fascination. The young people who stroll the narrow Tokyo streets of Shibuya, Shinjuku and Shimokitazawa become swept up into trends and fads. Clothing, music, and vocabulary are increasingly influenced by the vast construct of the United States. The youth-based pop culture produced in America defines a recognizable space that projects a special brand of power for young people everywhere, but particularly in a place like Japan where urban youth feel a sense of limitation.

The essence of Kustom Kulture combined the automobile with the expansive, innovative spirit that had always framed life in America. Postwar young people capitalized on a unique historical moment and followed cultural impulses to reshape the variables of their lives. The ascendancy of the automobile intersected seamlessly with the rise of youth power during the 1950s. The intuitive acts of young

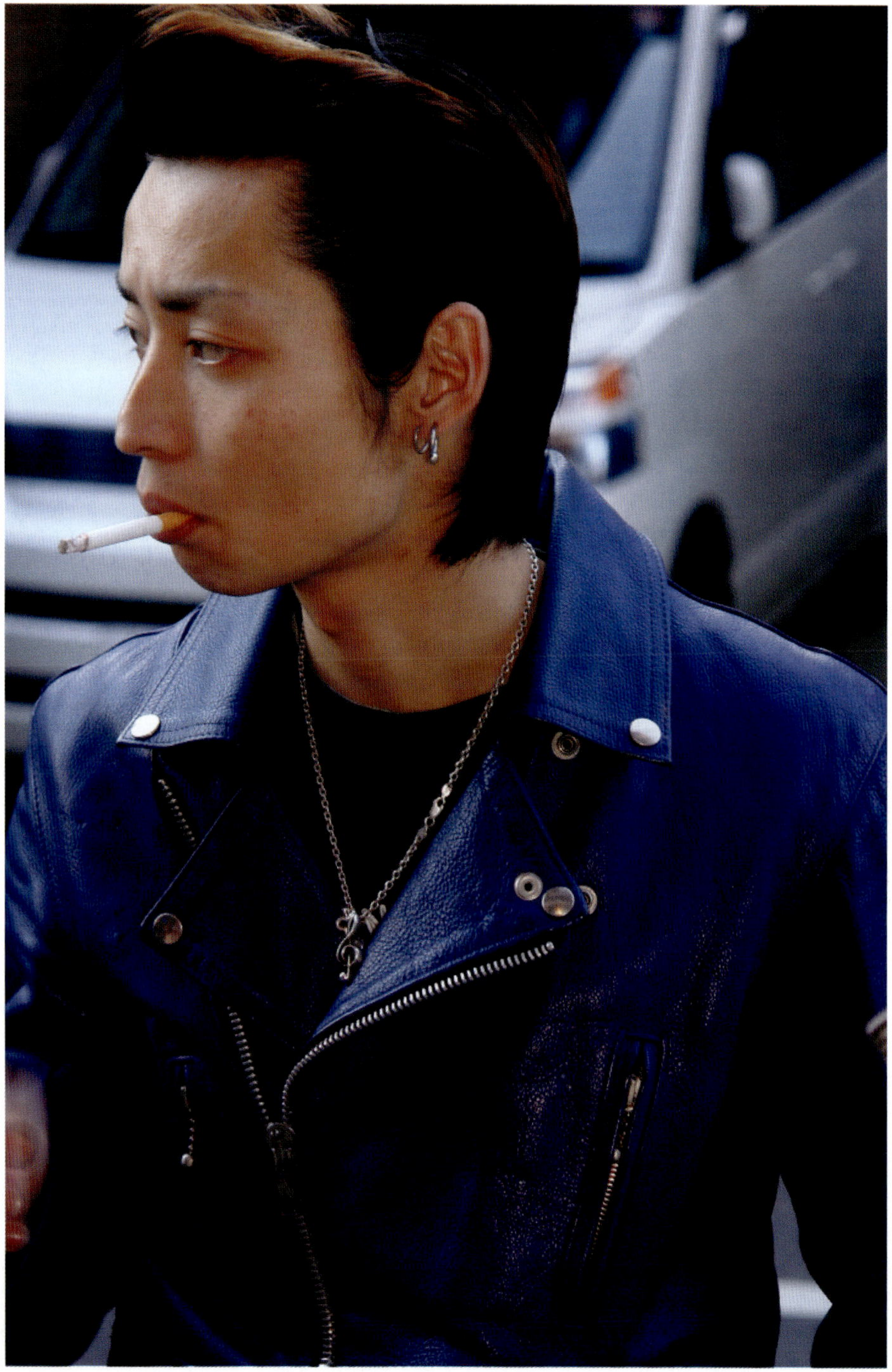

ルチャーの規範を成形する、年齢に敏感なスタイルや言葉、行動の変革を意味した。それはまた機械に対する適性と美的感性の特化の精錬であり、後に「Kustom Kulture＝カスタム・カルチャー」へと進化していった。

今日、こうしてスタイル化された文化は、カスタム・カルチャーを超越的かつパワフル、そして最も重要なこと—つまり自己を定義するものと見なす日本の若者に受け入れられ、ノスタルジックな神話の一部として引き継がれている。カスタム・カルチャーは市販の車を再設計する以上のことを意味する。この文化的な動きの歴史は、若者のアイデンティティとパワーの上昇、そしてホットロッドを通したその具体化と関連している。1950年代から60年代の戦後時代、南カリフォルニアの若者は、そのパワーを粗野かつ微妙に象徴してくれるアイコンとして、ホットロッドやカスタム車を受け入れた。ロッドやカスタム、そしてそれを取り巻くクリエイティブな価値観は若者に力を与え、彼らの生活を侵害する格式ばった大人の象徴に反抗するものだった。

都会に住む日本の若者は、彼らの文化に存在する境界という現実に敏感だ。島国である日本は比較的小さくコンパクトな場所である。多くの若者は、日本が安全ながら限られた空間であり、堅苦しい歴史的規律や伝統が定めた行動や態度という厳しい制限があると感じている。今日、都会に住む多くの若い日本人は、縮小していく世界に適応できるよう、この古い規律の数々を再定義している。戦後の日本の若者は、影響力の強くなっていったアメリカの可能性の大きさ、個人的なチャンス等を投影したイメージをますます求めるようになった。それは自由になることを特徴とした、幅広い境界を持った場所だった。

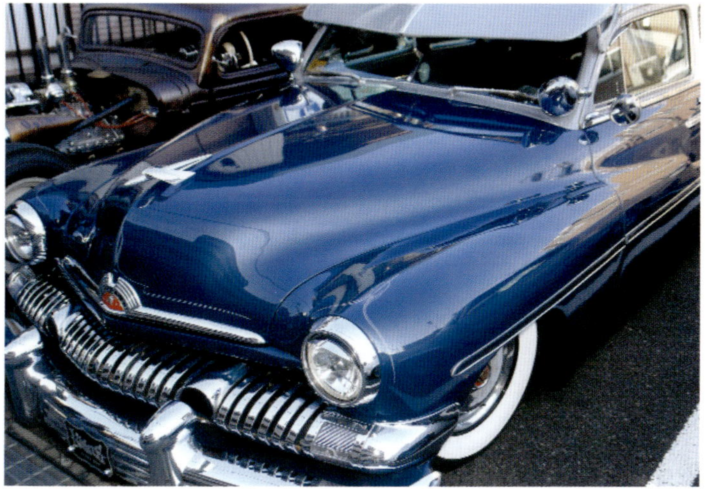

Above: Mayashiro's '51 Merc

Left: Tokyo Kustom Style

hot-rodders were informed by a historically unique American experience that stretched back into time. This guided their creative impulse in a very natural process. Today, young Japanese people are captivated by the exotic pop results of this intuitive and expansive American decision-making ability.

The sympathetic relationship that developed in America between automobiles and the mystique of the road—to continent's edge and beyond—is a prime component of the influential American continuum. The addition of velocity (wagons to trains to autos) permanently changed the meaning of "covering ground." Technology created by human intelligence and then put to good use has always been seen in America as a validation of the unique combination of innovation and endeavor.

Steinbeck's "Mother Road" (the term he coined for Route 66 in *Grapes of Wrath*) and Kerouac's later writings were references to a distinctive American passage: an ability to create change through movement, toil and risk, knowing that without it there is no life. The distance traveled became a physical metaphor of experiential change but also internal, spiritual growth. Travel across the continent was always discussed with a vocabulary of trepidation and danger—survival through the wilderness, life threatening exchanges with hostiles, or being killed in a high-speed car crash. All represented a mystique of covering ground, described in terms of surrender to irrational risk and a reckless lack of control. Emerging at the other end in one piece was a sign of cleverness and character and was seen as transforming.

The combination of risk and transformation is at the core of the American ethos. It is experienced in the practicality of movement—of leaving some part of you behind in an effort to experience something new. The brashness of this realization is coupled with a naive unwillingness to accept any other result. The simultaneous process

日本の若者文化は、自分の興味を不思議な形で表そうとする。東京の渋谷や新宿、下北沢の狭い道をぶらつく若者は、トレンドや一時的流行に巻き込まれている。彼らの服装や音楽、そして使用する言葉は、アメリカの膨大な影響を受けている。若者を基盤とするアメリカのポップカルチャーは、世界各地の若者にとって独自の力を投影する、認識可能な特殊な空間を定義している。都会の若者が制限を感じている日本などでは特に…。

カスタム・カルチャーの本質は、これまでずっとアメリカを構成してきた発展的・革新的な精神と車を組み合わせたことである。戦後の若者は、ユニークな歴史的瞬間を利用し、社会的衝動に従って、彼らの人生の可変的要素を作り直した。1950 年代における車の台頭は、若者パワーの上昇とスムーズにつながっていった。歴史的にユニークなアメリカ的体験に鼓舞された若いホットロッダーの直感的行動は、自然とそのクリエイティブな衝動を導いて行った。そして今日、日本の若者は、エギゾチックなアメリカの直感的・発展的な意思決定能力、またそこから生まれたもののとりこになっている。

アメリカで生まれ、大陸の境界を越えてつながる道路の神話と車との間の共鳴関係は、影響力の強いアメリカ文化のパワフルな要素だ。単なる歩行より速い移動法が、幌馬車から列車、そして車へと変遷し加速していったことは、「走破」の意味を永久的に変えてしまった。人間の知能が生み出したテクノロジーとそれを有益に利用することの意義とは、アメリカにおいては、革新と努力のユニークな組み合わせに対する正当性だと見られてきた。

スタインベックの「マザー・ロード (『怒りの葡萄』に出てくるルート 66 のニックネーム)」や、ケルアックの後期の執筆は、アメリカ特有の「旅」について言及している。「旅」は移動、労苦、リスクを通して変化を起こす能力、そして変化を促すための努力の過程にともなうリスクを要求する。だがそんなリスクがなければ人生は存在しない。移動した距離は経験的変化の象徴であると同時に、内部的かつ精神的成長をも意味する。大陸横断の旅は、荒野での生き残りや敵意を抱く人たちとの命がけの遭遇、高速での自動車事故など、常に不安と危険の言葉をもって語られてきた。「走破」の神話とは、不合理なリスクと無謀なコントロールの欠如をあえて受け入れるということなのだ。無事に反対側にたどり着くことは、知恵と人格を有する証であり、また人生を変貌させてしまう経験であると見なされた。

リスクと変貌の組み合わせは、アメリカ的気質の核である。この気質は、実際に新しい何かを体験するために、自分のある部分を置き去っていくことによって体験できる。このアメリカの向こう見ずな認識は、他のどんな結果も受け入れないというナイーブな意思と組み合わされた。「放棄することによって獲得する」というプロセスには危険がともなうが、その報酬を思えば旅する価値は十分にあるという考え方である。そのような旅に自ら挑むアメリカ人の気質は、他の社会の人々にとっては非常に魅惑的なのである。

1950 年代、アメリカの若者が車をカスタマイズしたときに体験した感覚は、変化と変貌のプロセスに対する傾倒と魅惑を反映したものだった。それは時間とともに進化し、それ自身の推進力と神話を生み出した。西洋とその力強さを歴史的にはいくぶん冷笑的に見てきた社会に育つ日本の若者にとって、カスタム・カルチャーの「変貌」という中核テーマ自体の印象は強烈だ。日本でのアメリカン・ホットロッドのイメージは海外を意味するものであり、神秘、危険、運命のテーマで満ちている。1950 年代のアメリカでは、ホットロッドはさまざまな感情をないまぜに呼び起こす魅惑的な象徴だった。今日の日本においても、若者が自由、そして人生の方向は自らで決めるという斬新な概念を試みるにあたり、このシンボリズムは強い印象を与え、漠然とした目的を果たしている。彼らは、クラシックなアメリカ映画で見た、または影響力の

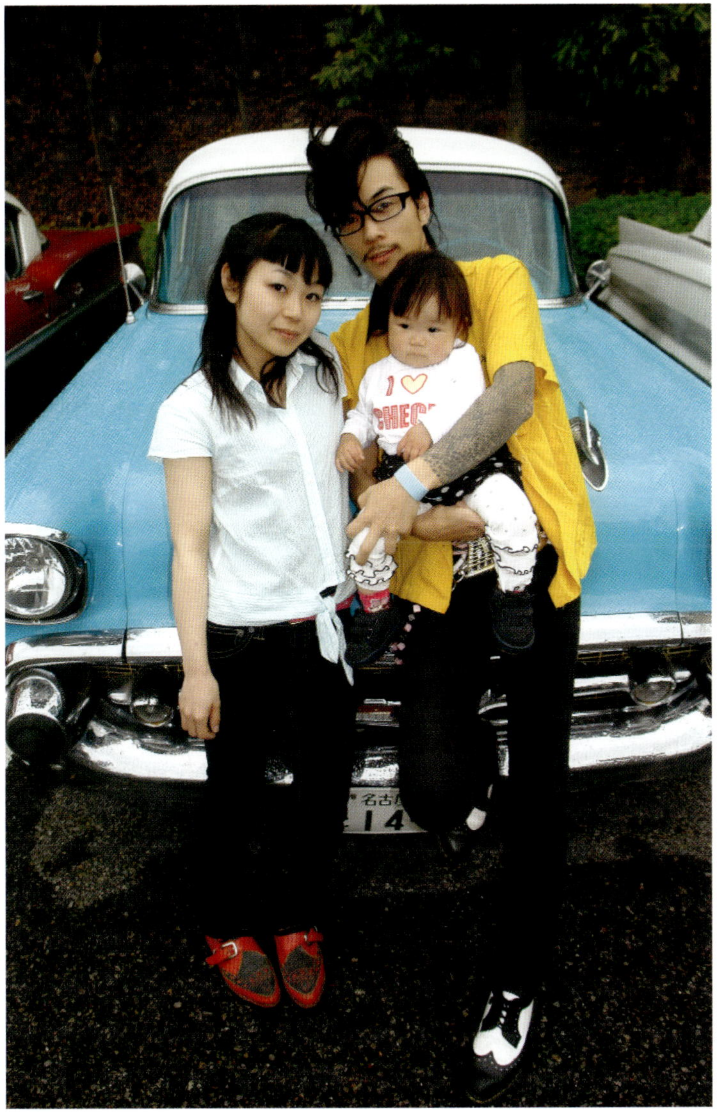

Dead Heat Mikawa
Nagoya area

of surrender and acquisition is risky but the payoff is worth the trip. Americans are willing to make such a trip, and people from different cultures find it fascinating.

The sense of opportunity young Americans experienced during the 1950s as they customized their cars reflected a bias and fascination with this process of change and transformation. It evolved over time and generated its own momentum and mystique. For young Japanese who live in a culture that has historically viewed the West and its dynamism somewhat cynically, the core transforming theme of Kustom Kulture is in itself impressive. The image of an American hot rod in Japan is an offshore signifier, loaded with themes of mystery, danger and uncontrollable eventuality. During the 1950s in America, hot rods were exotic symbols with powerful associations that stirred a mixture of ambiguous emotions. In Japan today, this symbolism continues to impress and serve a similar purpose among young people. They borrow from the associations that surround it as they experiment with novel notions of freedom and self-determination. They wear American working class Carhartt and Dickies clothing and trucker hats with Von Dutch logos as a way to flirt with an impressive mythology they have seen in classic American films and heard in American rock and roll music.

America is characterized by its unique brand of danger and crudity—a roll-up-your-sleeves, dirt-under-your-fingernails mythology that frightens but also impresses and inspires others. Cultural information creates its own momentum that can point the people who use it in certain directions. Others from different groups on different cultural trajectories can put this exotic information to use for a mixture of purposes. Today, the matrix of behaviors and tastes that surround Kustom Kulture, hot rod cars and the mythic roads they traveled are symbols and tools with transcendent significance. For many young Japanese, these have opened a large psychological space.

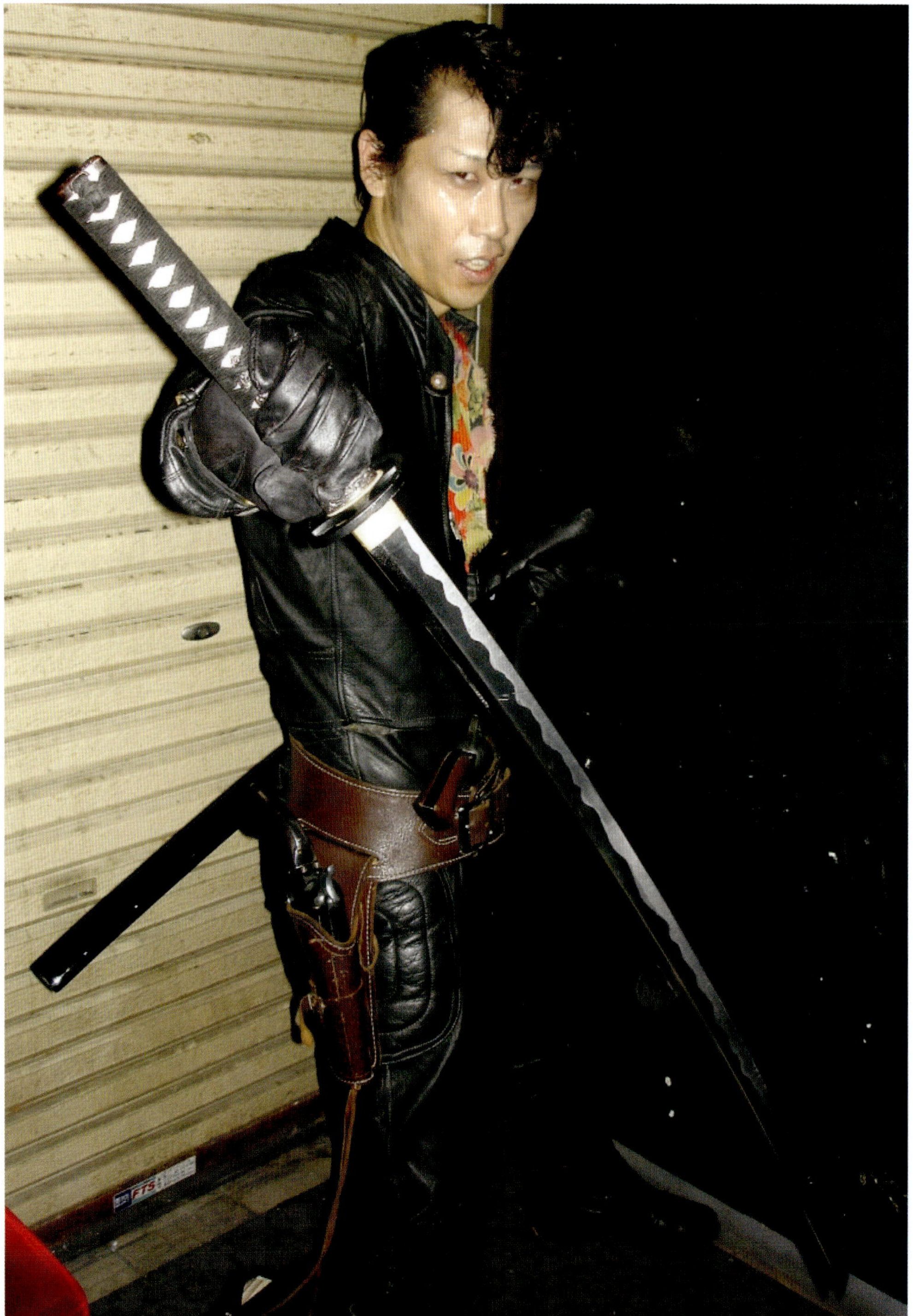

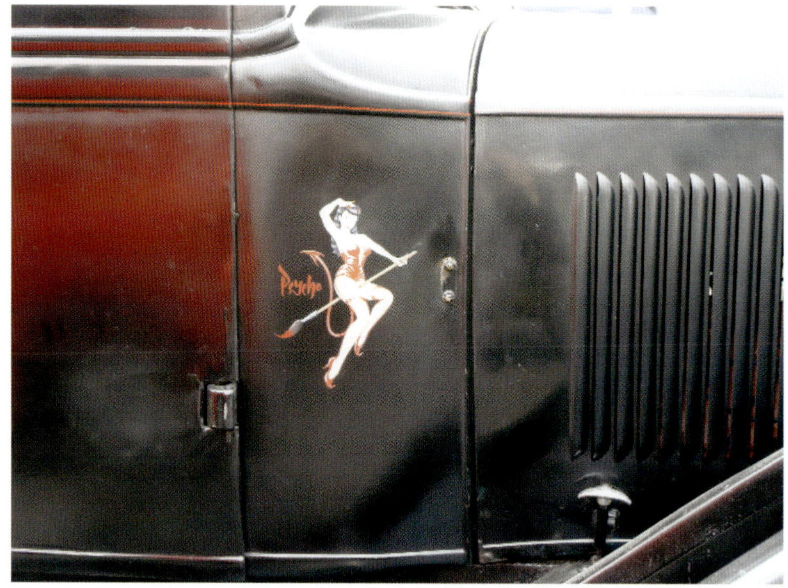

Left: Shibuya retro, six-shooter, biker, samurai

Right: Tokyo Style
INKRAT

Far right: Syu Merk
Owner: Syu Chan, Nagoya
Pinstriping: Makoto

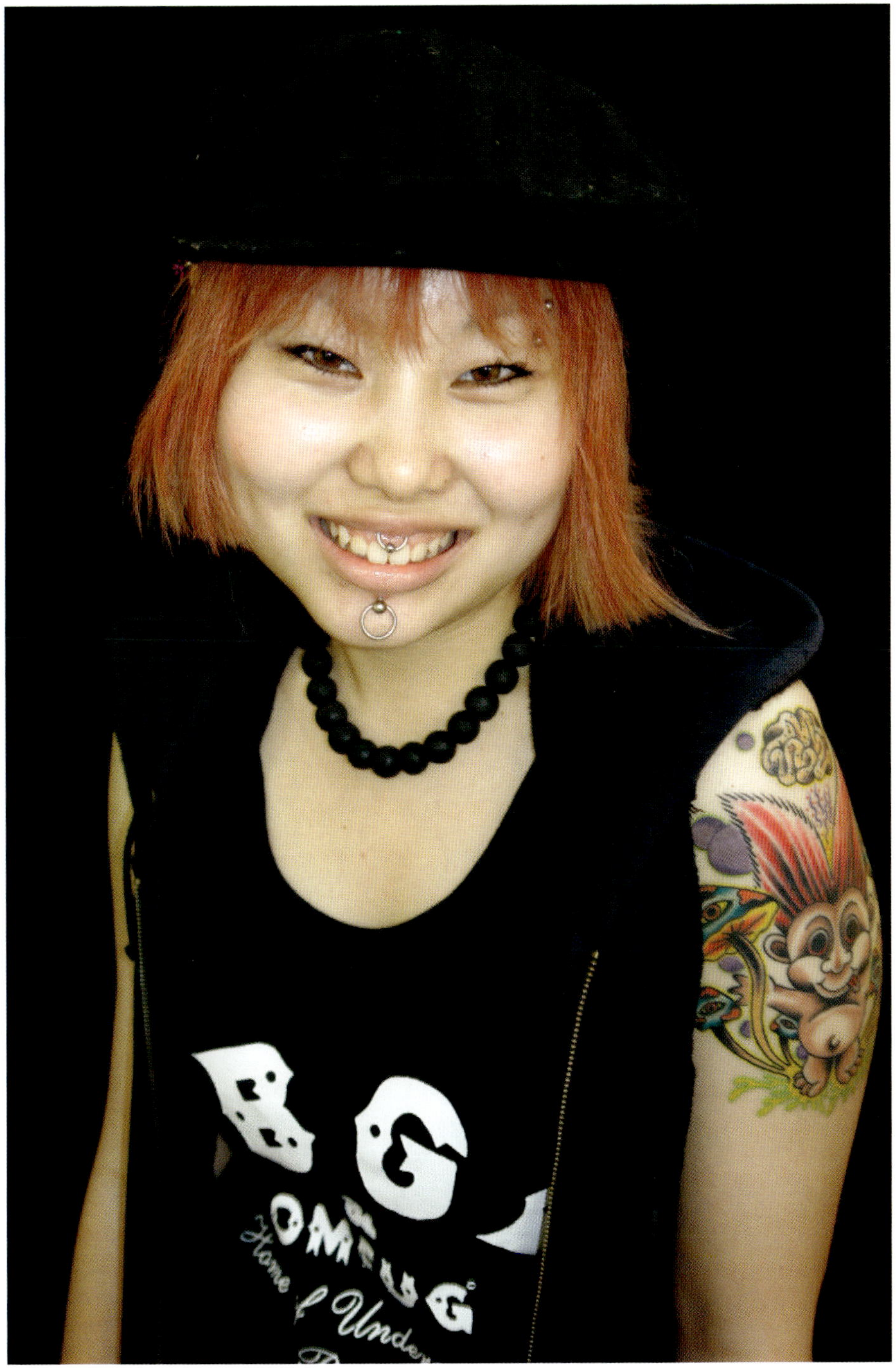

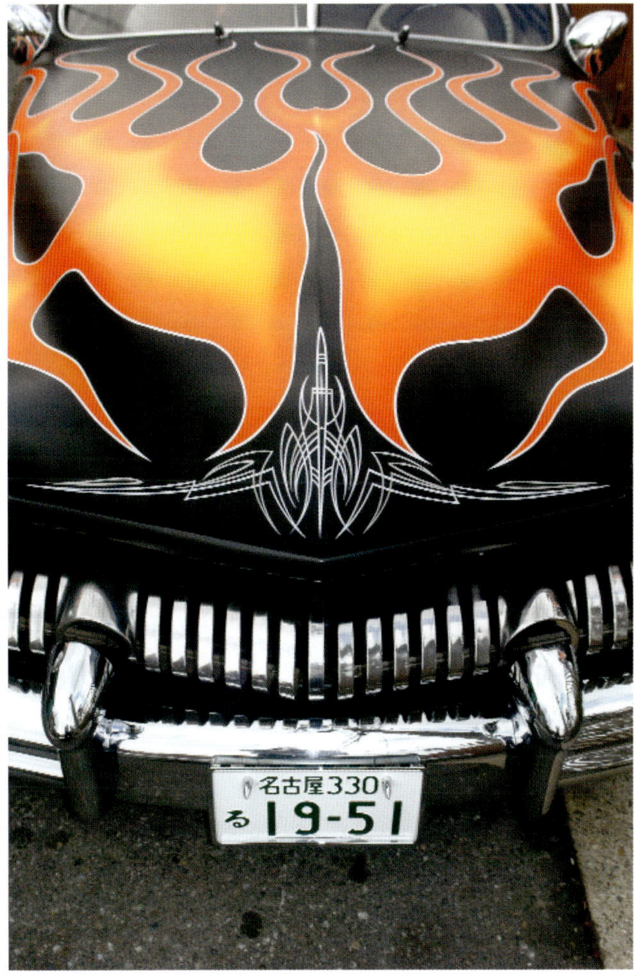
名古屋330
る 19-51

あるアメリカのロックンロール・ミュージックで聞いた、印象深いアメリカ神話と戯れる手段として、労働者階級のカーハートやディッキーズのアメリカ衣料、ヴォンダッチのロゴが付いたトラッカー・ハットを着用する。

アメリカはユニークな形の危険性や粗野さを特徴とする。まくり上げた袖、泥の詰まった指爪などの神話は、人々に恐怖のみならず、強い印象とインスピレーションを与える。文化的な情報は、それ自体が勢いを生み出し、それを利用する人々に特定の方向を指し示す。異なる文化的軌道にある異なるグループの人々は、この外来の情報をさまざまな目的に利用することができる。カスタム・カルチャー、ホットロッド、そしてそれらが旅した神秘の道を取り巻く行動と嗜好のマトリクスは、多くの日本の若者に大きな心理的スペースを与える超越的で重要なシンボルであり、ツールだと言える。

アメリカの1950年代、60年代にホットロッダーを活気づけた若者の正当性、そして伝統的権力に対する反抗という元々のテーマは、今日の日本において懐古的な形で再利用されている。若い日本人にとって、スタイルの再定義の詳細を知る必要などない。重要なことはその情報を利用し、それが彼らの人生の意味を理解するためにどう役立てるかだ。その中核において、カスタム・カルチャーは、ものを改造、再設計、変更することについての魅力を体現している。これらの変更の効果は、全体として個々の変更の合計を上回る。カスタマイザーは、部分そして全体がどのように見えるかを変えるための選択を行う。単にスタイルを目的とし、機能を損なう選択もあるが、最終的には変貌したものが投影するメッセージの力が重要なのだ。

トレンディな渋谷、下北沢、新宿の若者は、白黒のチェッカー模様のフィニッシュフラッグのデザインが付いたスニーカーで歩き回り、ヴォンダッチのトラッカー・ハットや、英語が書かれたTシャツを着用している。Tシャツには“GO FASTS、THE LAKES、

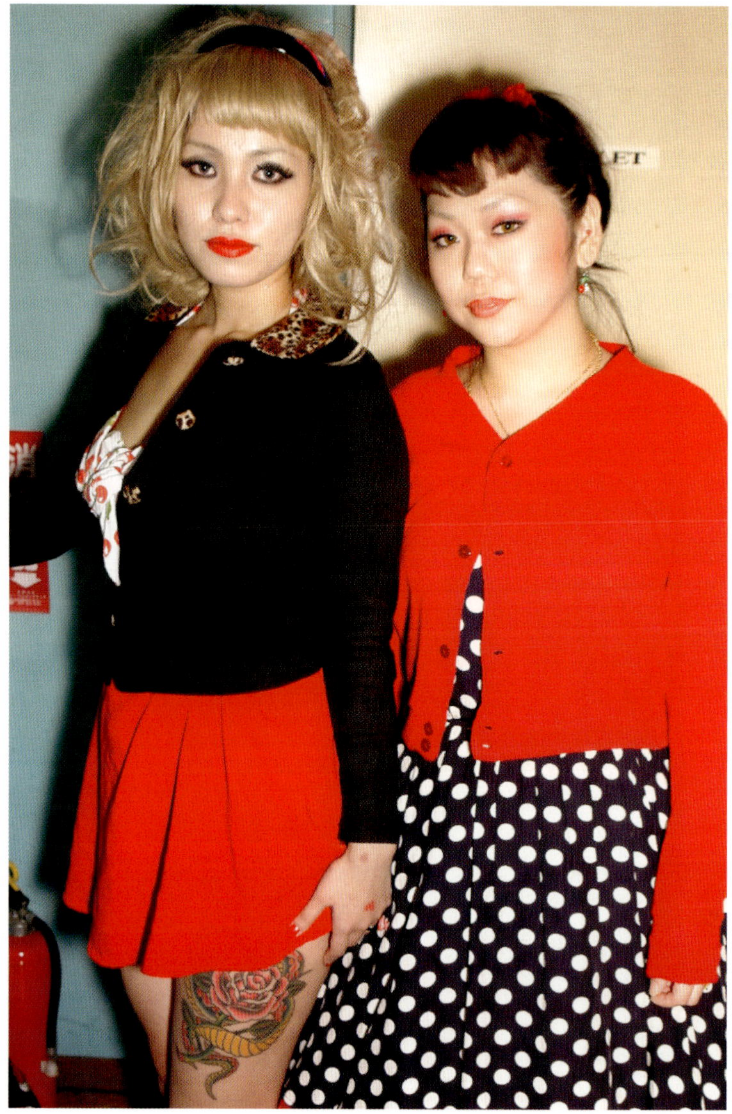

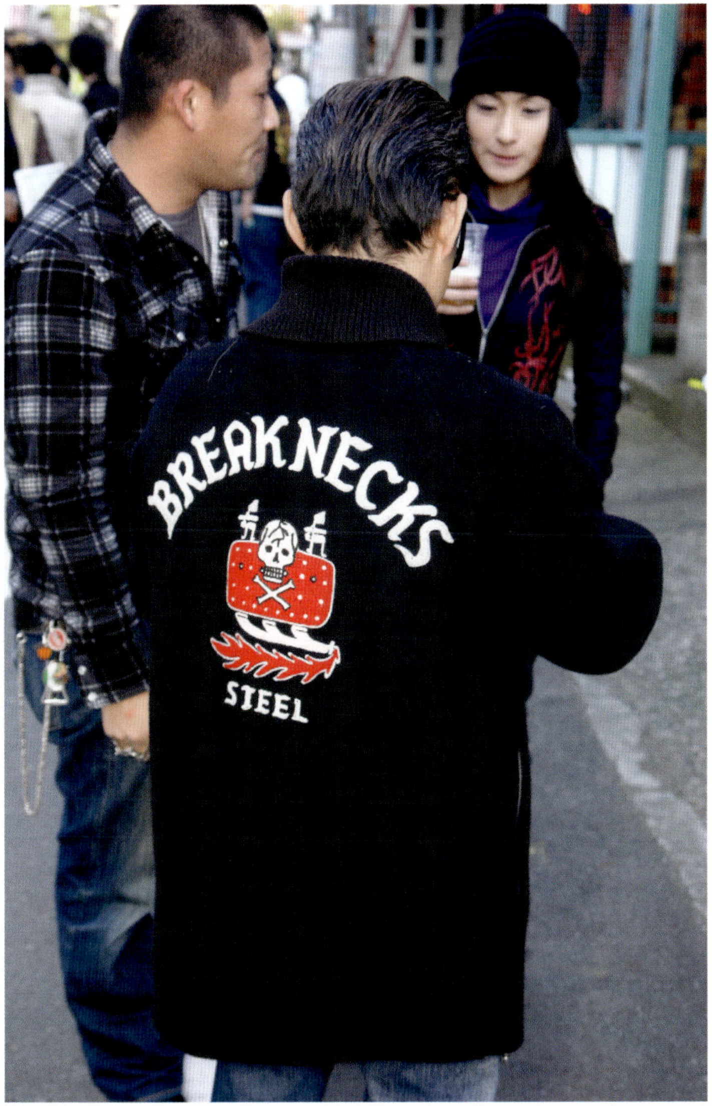

Above: Breaknecks

Left: Kustom beauties
Atsugi, Kustom Kulture Now event

It is not necessary for young Japanese to know all the particulars of their stylistic reinterpretations. The importance lies in the use of the information and how it can help them make sense of their lives. At its core, Kustom Kulture embodies a fascination about altering, redesigning and changing things. The effect of these changes adds up to more than the sum total of the parts. By making choices, the customizer changes how the parts and the whole are seen. Some choices are purely stylistic and may undermine function, but ultimately the significance lies in the power of the messages projected by what has been transformed.

Trendy Shibuya, Shimokitazawa and Shinjuku kids walk along pinch-toed in black and white checkered "finish flag" designed sneakers, Von Dutch trucker hats and t-shirts reading: GO FASTS, THE LAKES, HOTS RODDER, GEARSHEAD, MOON EYES and I LOVES FLATHEAD 8. The grammar is a little off but they have grabbed onto a growing fascination among young people everywhere with Kustom Kulture.

There is an interesting preoccupation among young urban Japanese about postwar American culture. It is not so much reproduction, but more creative reinvention. This theme of acquisition, assimilation and redesign runs deep into Japan's historical past. Also, there is a nuanced quality to life in Japan; a lot of what goes on between people is undeclared or intangible, which creates a cerebral guessing game of daily deciphering and decoding of the unspoken. Japanese people live in a culture that is thick with layers of subtle meaning, and sifting through it all is an endless preoccupation.

Young style kids moving along Tokyo sidewalks wear retro American clothing and tattoos and now Kustom Kulture iconography to evoke an intangible but powerful exotic mystique. Like young people everywhere, they have borrowed and redefined all of it as contemporary representations of themselves, but with a completely

HOTS RODDER、GEARSHEAD、MOON EYES、I LOVES FLATHEAD 8"などと書かれている。英語の文法は多少間違ってはいるが、カスタム・カルチャーと呼ばれるものへの、若者の間で増大する強い興味を掴んでいる。

戦後のアメリカ文化について、都会に住む日本の若者が没頭している興味深いことがある。それは模写と言うよりは、むしろクリエイティブな改変とでも呼べるものだ。このような習得、吸収、再設計のテーマは、日本の歴史的過去に深く根ざしている。また日本での生活には「ニュアンス」が存在する。それは人と人との間に、公表していない漠然としたコミュニケーションが実は多く行き来し、これによって、言葉にして表明されたなかったことは何だったのかを解読・復号化する推測ゲームを毎日のように果たしているということだ。日本人は何層にも重なった微妙な意味合いの社会の中で生活しており、人生においてこれをふるい分けることに終始している。

東京の歩道を歩き回るスタイリッシュな若者は、レトロなアメリカの服を着用し、タトゥーを入れ、そして今度はカスタム・カルチャーの象徴を取り入れて、実体はないながらもパワフルかつエキゾチックな神秘性を喚起する。どこにでもいる若者と同様に、彼らはそれらすべてを借りて自分自身を現代的に描写・再定義しているが、そこにはまったくユニークな流暢さと美的感覚が備わっているのだ。

20世紀半ばの南カリフォルニアとその他の地域のホットロッダーは、当時の自由奔放なカウンターカルチャリストだった。彼らは車を個人的なアート・オブジェとして再設計し、企業・産業によるホワイトカラーの豊かさと権力のシンボルである車を、速く、美しく、個人的でユニークなものに作り変えた。それは、それ以前の成熟したアメリカ社会に挑戦した、新しい「ベビーブーム世代」のヤングパワーを体現する人口推移の始まりだった。1955年にはアメリカの人口が逆転した。史上初めて年配者よりも若者の数が上回ったのだ。ティーンエイジャーの男の子がみすぼらしい白いTシャツと汚れたジーンズを着用し、髪にはグリースを付けて、チョップド、レイクド、チャネルドにした高速デュース・ローボーイの横に立っている姿にワクワクした人もいれば、ゾッとした人たちもいた。ホットロッドは、繊細で深く、美的感性の高いものであると同時に、無謀かつ命を脅かす気ままなものという、両義性を持った象徴となった。スタイル化されたアメリカのシンボル、「無謀かつ命を脅かす気ままなもの」との触れ合いは、安全かつ過度に衛生的で都会化された環境に住む今日の日本の若者にとって、想像を絶する素晴しい意味を持っている。

日本ではカスタム・カルチャー・スタイルのテーマに焦点を合わせたイベントがますます増えている。イベントに参加する大勢の人たちが、車、音楽、タトゥー、ファッション、アートワークを共に楽しんでいる。2006年6月、東京の高円寺で「Rock of Ages」ショーを企画したINKRAT TATTOOのタトゥー・アーティストの水島レイと妻のイズミは、このショーが500人を超える観衆であふれたことに驚いた。

「ショーを準備するのに1年以上かかりました」とレイは説明する。「普通、日本のイベントは規模が小さくて、ロックバンドやバイカー、ヒップホップをやる連中、セクシーな女の子がいるくらいで、アングラ的な感じがするんです。私たちはタトゥーやアートに重点を置くことがより大切だと思ったのです。」

「今のところ日本ではまだカスタム・カルチャーはあまり知られていません」とレイは続ける。「タトゥーをやっている人で、カスタム・カルチャーとかサーフィンとかスケートボードとか、ピンストライピング、ホットロッド、50年代ファッションに個別に重点を置く人はいますが、こういうものがまとめられたことはありませんでした。ロック・オブ・エイジズ・ショーでは、日本で初めてこういうものすべてを結集させたのです。カスタム・カルチャーはすべてを包括するものなの

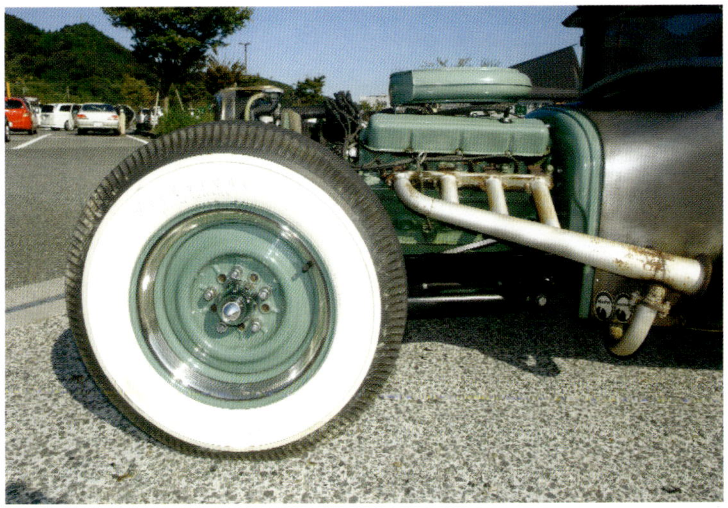

unique sense of fluency and refined aesthetic.

The mid-20th century hot-rodders of Southern California and elsewhere were the bohemian counterculturists of their day. They redesigned machines as personal objects of art; reshaping the corporate-industrial symbols of white-collar affluence and power into something personal and unique, fast, and beautiful. It was the beginning of a demographic shift embodied in the Baby Boomer youth power that challenged a previously maturing American society. In 1955 the population of America flipped. For the first time there were more young than older people, and the image of a teenage boy wearing a ratty white t-shirt and dirty jeans, hair greased back, standing next to his very fast, chopped, raked and channeled Deuce Lowboy thrilled some while it terrified others. Hot rods became ambiguous, simultaneous symbols of both a nuanced, rarefied aesthetic and reckless, life-threatening abandon. Today, for young Japanese living in a safe, overly sanitized and urbanized environment, interaction with stylized American symbols that represent "life-threatening total abandon" is too good to be true.

There are a growing number of events taking place in Japan that focus on themes of Kustom Kulture style. Cars, music, tattoos, fashion and artwork are shared and enjoyed by the growing number of people who attend. Tattoo artist Rei Mizushima and his wife Izumi Akiba of INKRAT TATTOO organized the Rock of Ages show in June 2006 in their Tokyo neighborhood, Koenji, and were surprised by the overflow crowd of more than 500 people.

Rei explained: "It took more than one year to organize the show. Usually Japanese events are very small with rock bands and bikers, hip hop guys and sexy girls. These events look underground. We felt it was more important to focus on tattoos and art." Right now, Kustom Kulture is not widely known about in Japan. Some Japanese tattoo people focus individually on Kustom Kulture or surfing or

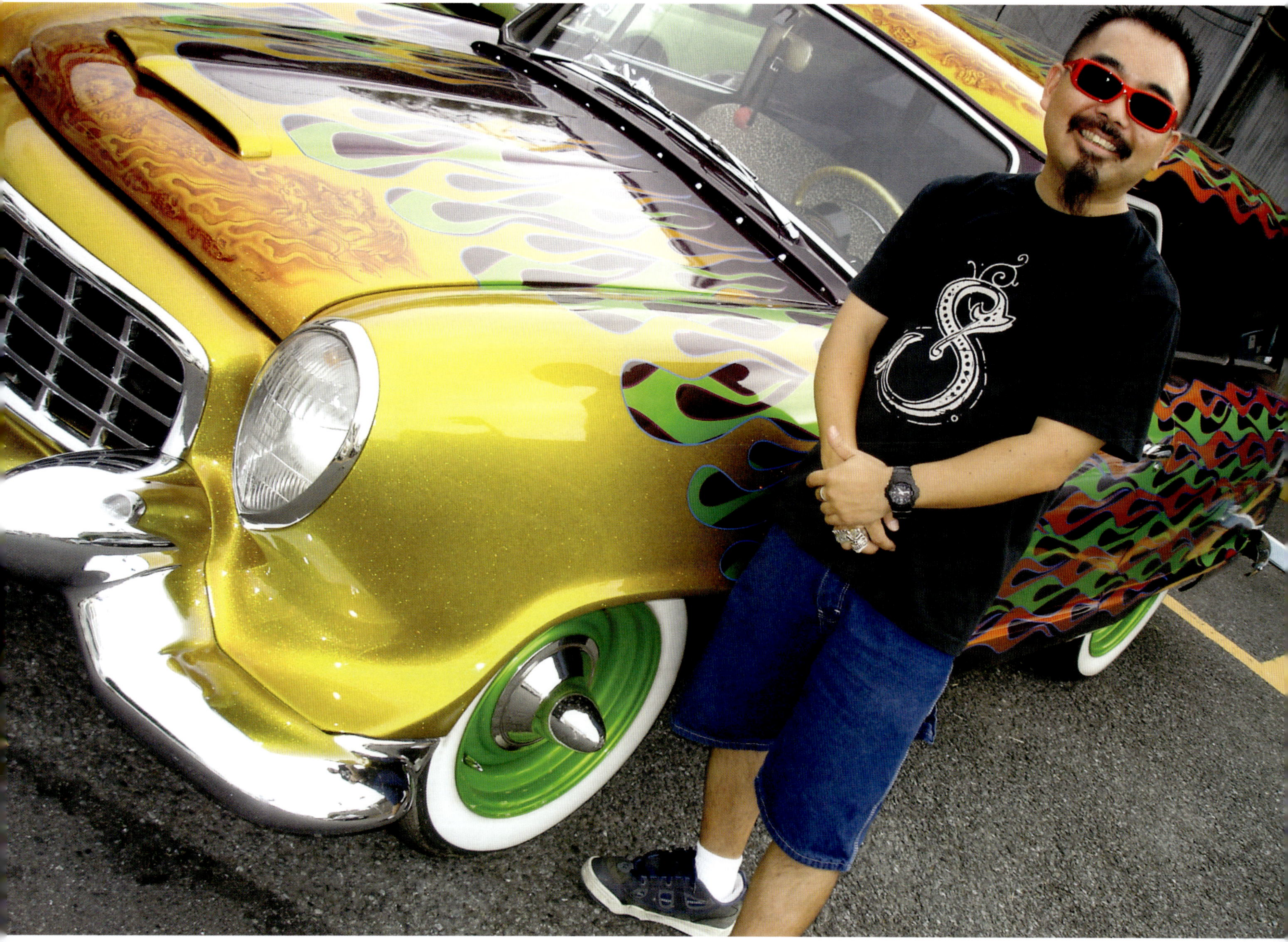

skateboard or pinstriping, hot rods and '50s fashion; but it hasn't really been brought together. Our Rock of Ages show is the first time in Japan to try to bring this all together. Kustom Kulture unites it all so everybody at INKRAT and others thought it was important to do such a show that had different references. I wanted to have it during the day so people could see each other and talk and share ideas and learn."

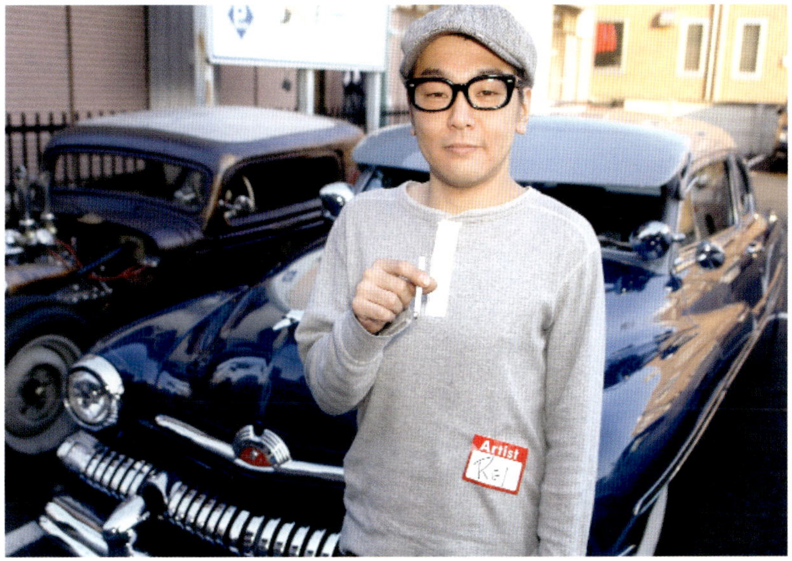

Above: Rei Mizushima

Left: Nash Yoshii and Pussy Wagon

"Japanese people do not know real Kustom Kulture. What we promote in the Rock of Ages show is what has become Kustom Kulture—pinstriping, hot rods, music, skateboard, all kinds of things. We tried to have a lot of ways for people to be interested. If a person is interested in hot rods they can do that, if a person wants to know about hot rod music and tattoo they can do that, because all this culture is connected! We think this is interesting and important."

Kustom Kulture enthusiast, writer, photographer, Editor-in-Chief of *Burnout Magazine (For Koolest Car People)*, owner of the store Detroit Junk and 2005 winner of Best Custom trophy at the Hot Rod Custom Show for his Pussy Wagon, Nash Yoshii was an important contributor to the show. He has a comprehensive understanding of the growing fascination in Japan about this phenomenon and the history behind it.

Nash said, "Kustom car Kulture first started 20 years ago in Japan with Shige at Moon Eyes in Yokohama in 1985. In 1986 he started the first American style car show in all Japan, in Tokyo, called 'Street Car Nationals.' Then after two years, in 1989, he introduced pinstriping to Japanese customers. They had no idea what this all meant. Shige had a connection to Ed 'Big Daddy' Roth who showed him about pinstriping. This 1989 show introduced pinstriping and Roth to Japan."

で、INKRATのスタッフも他の人も、色々な関連するものが見られるカスタム・カルチャー・ショーをやることが大切だという意見で一致しました。そしてショーは昼間にやりたかったのです。他の人に会えて、話ができて、アイデアを分かち合えて、勉強できますから。」

「日本人は本当のカスタム・カルチャーを知りません。ロック・オブ・エイジズ・ショーでやろうとしていることは本物のカスタム・カルチャー、つまりピンストライプ、ホットロッド、音楽、スケートボードなど、あらゆるカスタム・カルチャーを見せる事です。色々な方法で人々に興味を持ってもらうよう努力しました。ホットロッドに興味がある人にも、ホットロッド・ミュージックやタトゥーについて興味がある人にも楽しんでいただけるショー。こういうカルチャーはみんなつながっているからです。こういうことが面白いし、また大切だと思うのです。」

カスタム・カルチャー愛好家、作家、写真家、『Burnout Magazine (For Koolest Car People) (車が好きなカッコいい人たちのためのバーンアウト誌)』編集長、Detroit Junk オーナー、そして所有のプッシーワゴンでホットロッド・カスタム・ショーの2005年最優秀カスタム賞を獲得したNash吉井は、ショーの重要な貢献者だった。彼は日本で急増するカスタム・カルチャーに対する興味と、その背後にある歴史を包括的に理解している。

「日本でのカスタム・カルチャーは20年前に始まりました。1985年に横浜のMoon Eyes (ムーンアイズ) のシゲさんが始めたのです」とNashは言う。「1985年、シゲさんは東京でストリート・カー・ナショナルズという初のアメリカ式のカー・ショーを開始しました。これが全国でも初めてのショーでした。それから3年経った1989年、彼は日本のカスタマーにピンストライピングを紹介しました。カスタマーの方は、それがどういう意味を持つのかさっぱり分かっていませんでした。シゲさんは、エド"ビッグダディ"ロス氏と知り合いでしたから、彼にピンストライピングを実演してもらったのです。1989年のショーでは、ピンストライピングとロス氏本人を日本に紹介しました。」

「それから1989年にはヒロという名前の人がMoon Eyesで働き始めました」とNashは続ける。「彼はピンストライピングを始め、それを日本の車関係の雑誌に紹介しました。それ以降、すべてが変わってしまいました。その時点でカスタム・カルチャーには、ピンストライピング、カスタムペイント、ドラッグレース、モンスターなどが含まれていました。それから1992年、著名なピンストライパーだったヴォンダッチが亡くなり、1993年、ロバート・ウィリアムス、エド"ビッグダディ"ロス、『Juxtapoz』誌のクレイグ・ステシックがオレンジ郡にあるラグーナ美術館に、このようなヴォンダッチ・カルチャーを紹介しましたのです。これにより1993年7月、大規模なショーがあり、書籍が出版され、カスタム・カルチャーという名前が世界的に知られるようになったのです。」

「1993年に出版された書籍、『Kustom Kulture』は非常に重要でした」とNashは続ける。「あの本がすべてを正式なものにしました。色々な話題になり、すべてを結びつける一部になりました。あの本を最初に手に入れたのは1994年でした。私は1994年にNashの車を購入し、COOPという人が描いた葉巻を吸う悪魔の絵の面白いステッカーを見つけました。でも、それがどういう意味なのかさっぱり知りませんでした。まるで別の惑星から来たようなものでした…。そして、ロサンゼルスのLa Luz de Jesusギャラリーで開催されたWacko Art展で、とうとうこのCOOPという人に会うことができました。COOPはそこで展覧会を催し、私は初めて彼の作品を目にしました。」

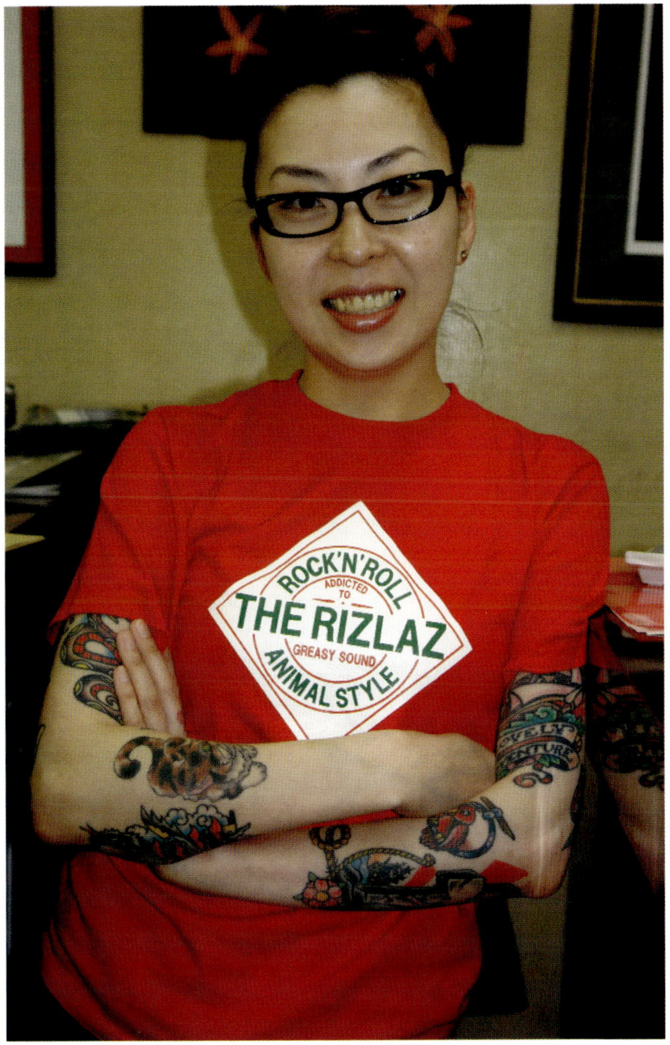

Satsuki
Scratch Addiction, Tokyo

"That same year a guy named Hiro started working at Moon Eyes. He started pinstriping and introduced it to Japanese car magazines. Everything changed after this happened. At that point Kustom Kulture included pinstriping, custom paint, drag racing and monster art. Then in 1992, famous pinstriper Von Dutch died and in 1993 Robert Williams, Ed 'Big Daddy' Roth and Craig Stecyk from *Juxtapoz* magazine introduced this culture to the Orange County Laguna Art Museum in July, 1993, with a big art show and book titled *Kustom Kulture*. All this made the phrase a part of world knowledge."

"That book was very important. It formalized everything and started discussion. It began putting the whole thing together. I first got the book in 1994. I bought my Nash car in 1994 and I saw a funny looking sticker of a devil smoking a cigar painted by somebody named COOP. But I had no idea what this all meant. It was like from a different planet. I finally met COOP at the Wacko Art show at the La Luz de Jesus Gallery in LA. COOP had a show there, and I saw his work for the first time."

"I had always wanted to open a store full of car stuff. Models, t-shirts, Hot Wheels toys, antiques, but always American pre-1970s cars. These are what I like. For me, cars after 1970 are 'going to be ugly.' American cars went to compact sizes due to the gas crisis. I especially love 1950s cars. Japan believes 1950s cars are very special."

"Japan imposes a special tax on 1950s American cars—$1000 U.S. every year for the big engine cars. Sometimes having old American cars had a stigma attached to it in Japan, and this still exists. Most car status in Japan is associated with European cars. People in Japan still are not interested in an aesthetic that involves older American cars. For many, these old cars bring up difficult things."

「車関係のものでいっぱいの店をずっと開きたいと思っていました」と彼は続ける。「モデル、Tシャツ、ホットホイールの玩具、アンティークなど。それも、全部アメリカの、それも1970年以前のもので…。1970年以前の車が気に入っているのです。私にとって1970年以降の車は見苦しいという感じですね。オイルショックがあったためにアメリカ車はコンパクトになりました。私は特に1950年代の車が大好きです。日本では1950年代の車は特別なものだと思われています。」

「日本は1950年代のアメリカ車に特別税を課しています。大型エンジンの車には毎年1000ドルの税金がかかります。古いアメリカ車を持つことは、日本では不名誉だと思われた時代がありました。今でもそう思われることもあります。日本では、ステータスのある車といえばほとんどヨーロッパ車を連想させます。日本では、古いアメ車のデザインは今でも気に入られていません。こういう古い車を見ると、社会的な問題を思い出す人がたくさんいるのです…。」

Nashには、カスタム・カルチャーに対し明確な愛着がある。本人もうまく説明できないが、アメリカ車鑑賞を取り巻く物質的そして文化的魅力の決定的な虜になっている。彼は、その愛着は昔の物質的な生活に対するノスタルジックな衝動や美化された概念につながっていることを認める。

「私は1967年に生まれました」と彼は語る。「私のNash車は1955年に製造されました。この車を運転するとタイムマシンを運転しているような気がします。雨が降っているときはワイパーがフロントガラスを往復しますが、新車のワイパーとは動きが違います。中央から始まってフロントガラスの左右の端へと動くのです。その動きを見ていると自分が別の場所にいる気がして…。別世界ですね。なぜそういう場所に行きたいのか分かりませんが、ワイパーの違う動きを見ながら、自分が1950年代に生きていて、Nash車の窓から外を眺めながら道路をクルーズする様子を想像するのです。」

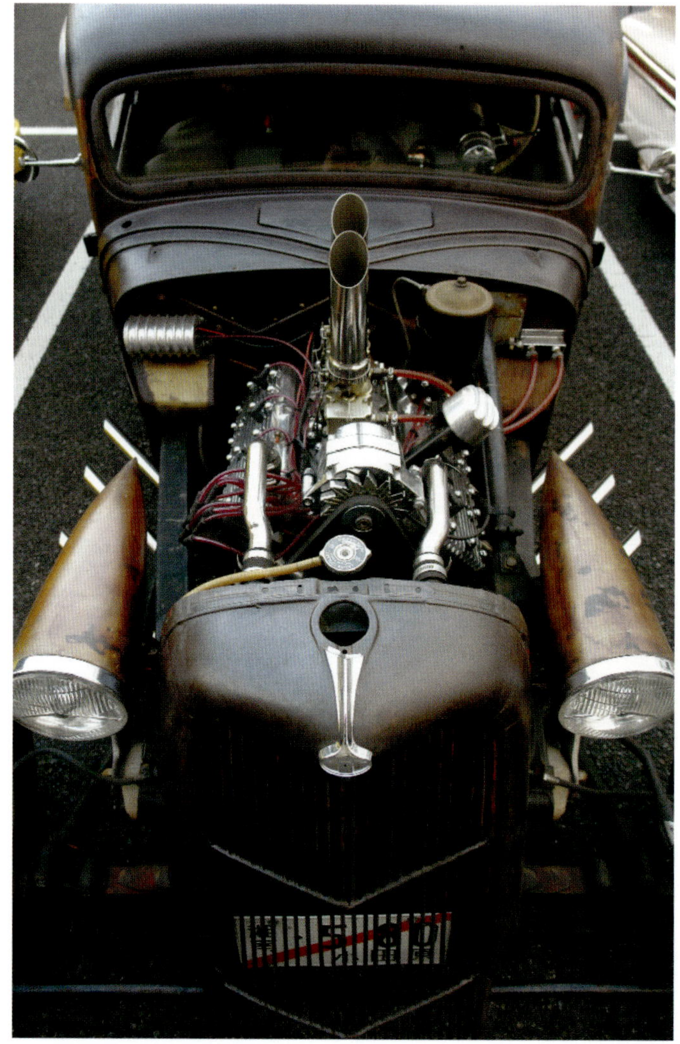

Nash's attachment to Kustom Kulture is emotional. For reasons that he cannot fully explain, he feels a sense of total commitment to his attraction to the material and culture surrounding American car appreciation. He admits that his attachment has something to do with an abstract intersection of nostalgic impulses and romanticized notions about older material life.

"I was born in 1967," Nash said. "My Nash car was built in 1955. When I drive in my car I feel like I am driving in a time machine. If it is raining, I watch my windshield wipers go back and forth; but they do not move like new cars. They go from center out to the left and right edges of my windshield. I see them moving differently and this brings me to a different place, a different world. I don't know why I want to go there but I look at the wipers moving so differently and imagine I am a person in the 1950s looking out the Nash window cruising down a street."

"In Japan, there was no cruising culture. It did not exist but is a dream for me. You cannot cruise in Japan; the streets are no good for cruising. In 1997 I wrote a magazine column called Artist and Hot Rod. I interviewed Robert Williams and talked about all this, the American cruising lifestyle, this dream lifestyle. I introduced some of this to Japan. American dream, 1950s, Kustom Kulture roots, dreaming about a lifestyle of consumer bliss."

"Hip Japanese people developed an interest in this American style of life—the American Dream of life as something to look at and think about. For these people, the whole thing was like a dream, a new Floating World of images and ideas. People in Japan became very interested in my magazine column about all this."

"I traveled back and forth to America five times a year buying things for my Detroit Junk store. I saw American artists living this dream life. Japanese kids had no information about Kustom Kulture but

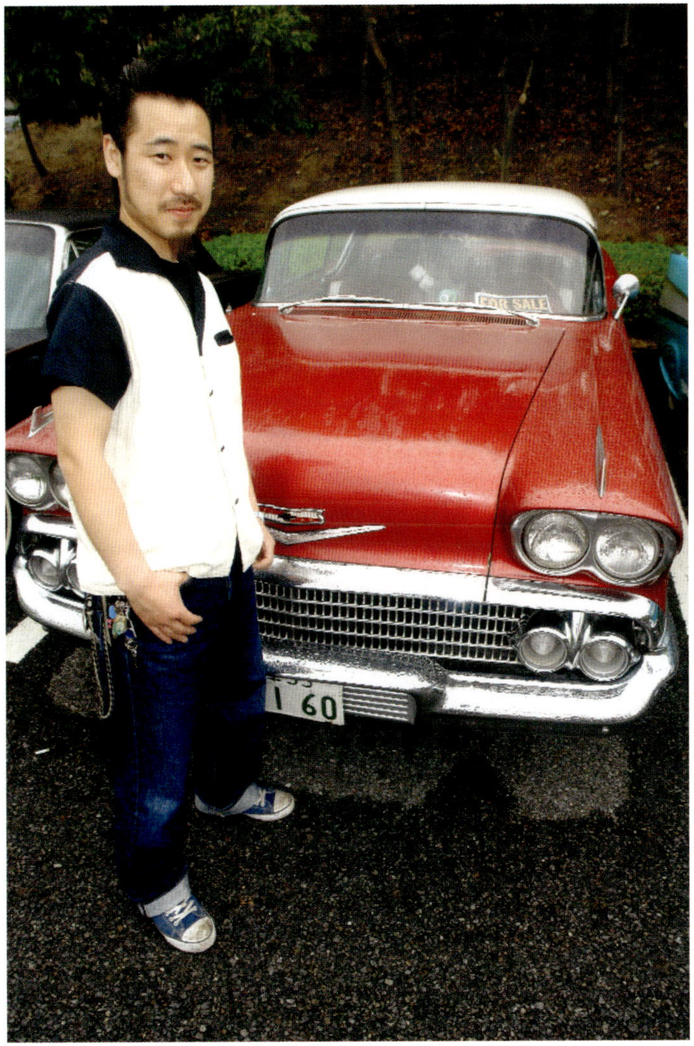

Above: Kazunori Tange
1958 Chevy 350 V8

Left: '35 Ford Pick up
Owner: Shorty, Pumpkin Sally

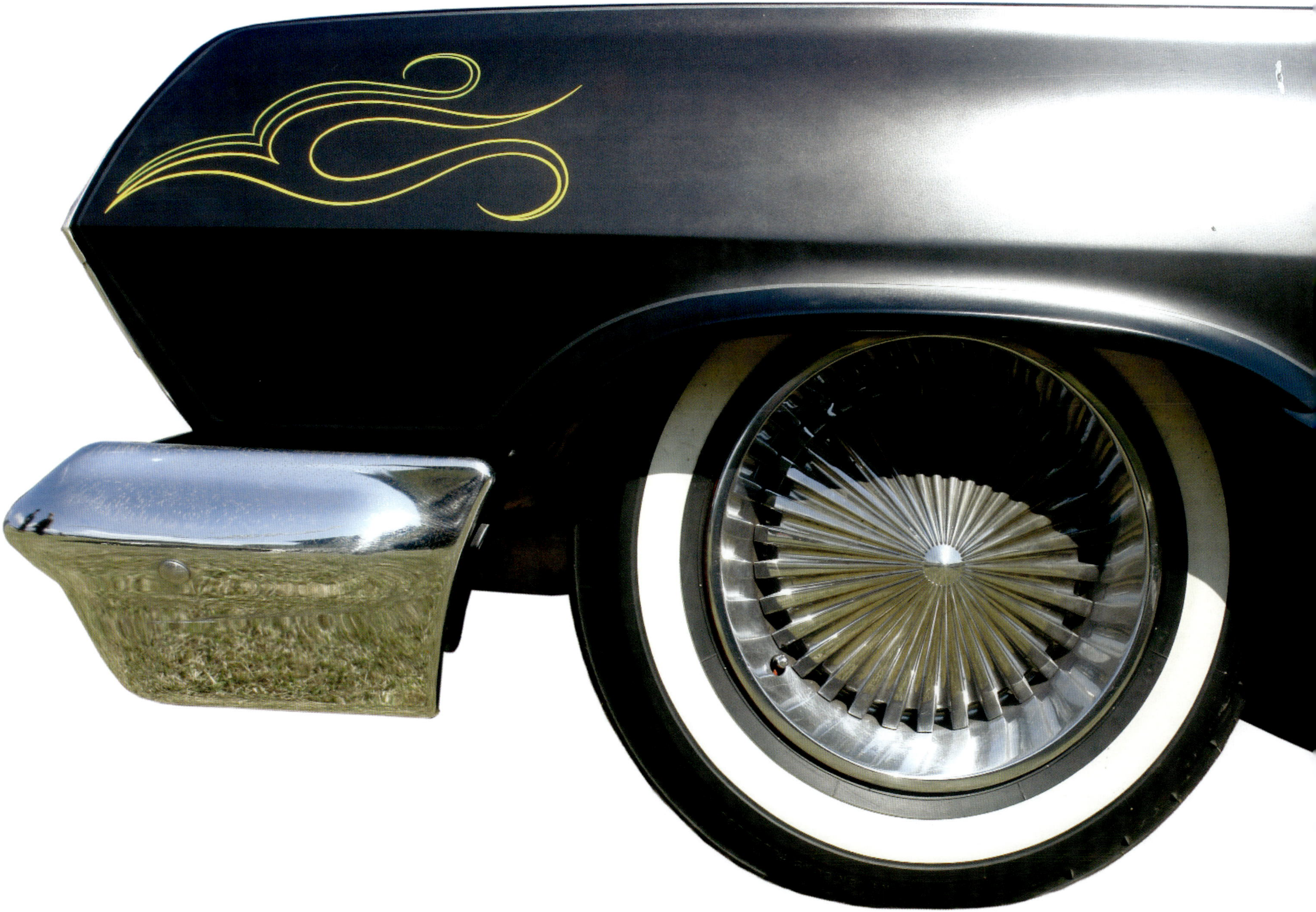

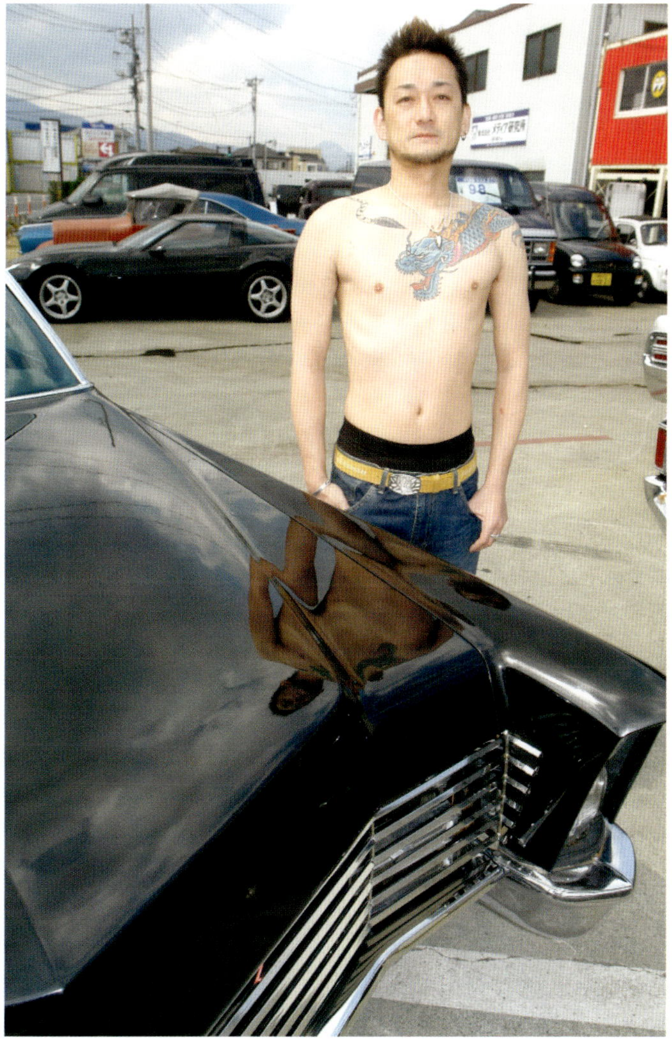

'68 Cadillac
Owner: Tokorozawa

my column introduced the whole thing all over Japan. In 1999 I started *Burnout* but I still wrote for the other car magazine. I talked about 'burning rubber' as a metaphor for male power. 'Burning rubber' became a lifestyle reference in Japan. It meant hyperactivity, an endless energy to create."

"In 2000 I had a Kustom Kulture gallery show and invited many American and Japanese artists to participate. I did this as a way to connect people. Because of the differences of language and culture I felt that people had a hard time connecting, so I put together the Tokyo Groovy show in 2000. I did it three times. 300 people came in 2000, 500 came in 2001 and 700 came for the last show in 2002. I met Rei and Izumi of INKRAT at the 2002 show through a tattooer friend named Sid who is from Orange County in Southern California. He had a hot rod and always drove them."

"Rei at INKRAT wondered about combining the Kustom Kulture with tattooing. Normally, Kustom Kulture did not include music, skateboarding and tattooing. It had a lot to do with the California lifestyle. But we were always talking about real California culture. We made the June 25th Rock Of Ages show as a way to combine the real aspects of this movement for Japanese people to see. For me, the reason to combine all this in a show is to create some passion for people. In 2002-2003 Sid started his Rock of Ages show in California. He combined cars, tattoos, music and pinstriping. Rei and I were influenced by Sid's show, but Rei wanted to introduce this type of show to Japan."

"I thought that the show was important because I could do it with them. Together we combined tattooing, surfing, skateboarding and Kustom Kulture. I believe that Kustom Kulture creates excitement in all different kinds of people. It cuts across gender and class. People find Kustom Kulture interesting because it is not regular life, not a usual thing. It is a different arrangement of reality that acts as a

「日本にクルージング・カルチャーはありません。存在しませんが私にとっての夢です…。日本でクルーズはできません。道路がクルージングに向いていないからです。1997年、「アーティストとホットロッド」と題したコラムを雑誌に書きました。ロバート・ウィリアムスをインタビューし、このアメリカン・クルージング・ライフスタイルというか、夢のライフスタイルについて話をしました。私はある程度この夢を日本に紹介しました。アメリカン・ドリーム、1950年代、カスタム・カルチャーのルーツ…。消費者天国のライフスタイルについての夢です。」

「ヒップな日本人はこのアメリカン・スタイルの生活に対する興味を示しました。生活上のアメリカン・ドリームとは鑑賞と考慮に値すべきものであるということです…。新しい浮世のイメージとアイデアと言いますか、彼らにとっては全部が夢のようなものだったのです。日本に住む人は、こういったことに言及した私の雑誌のコラムにすごく興味を示すようになりました。」

「私はDetroit Junk店の商品を購入するため、年に5回、アメリカへ行き来するようになりました。そこでこの夢の生活を送っているアメリカ人のアーティスト達に出会いました。日本の若い子たちはカスタム・カルチャーについて何も知りませんでしたが、私がコラムでこれについて日本中に紹介しました。1999年、『Burnout Magazine (For Koolest Car People)』を発刊しましたが、同時に他のカー・マガジンにも執筆していました。そこで男性のパワーの表象としての"バーニング・ラバー(車を急発進させてタイヤを焦がすこと)"について話しました。バーニング・ラバーは、日本でのライフスタイルの参照事項となりました。これは極度に活発なこと、ものを創作する終わりのないエネルギーを意味しました。」

「2000年にはカスタム・カルチャーのギャラリー展を開催し、アメリカと日本からの多数のアーティストを招待しました。展覧会は人々を結びつける手段でした。言葉や文化の壁が、この障害となったと感じました。そこで2000年にTokyo Groovy Showを企画し、3回開催しました。2000年には300人、2001年には500人、最終回の2002年には700人が来場しました。2002年の展覧会ではINKRATのレイとイズミと知り合いました。南カリフォルニアのオレンジ郡から来たシドという名前のタトゥー作家の友達の紹介でした。彼はホットロッドを持っていて、いつもホットロッドを運転していましたね。」

「INKRATのレイは、カスタム・カルチャーとタトゥーを組み合わせることについて考えていました。カスタム・カルチャーは通常、音楽やスケートボード、タトゥーなどは含みませんでした。それはカリフォルニアのライフスタイルでした。でも、私たちはいつも"本物"のカルチャー、つまりカリフォルニアの文化について語り合っていました。私たちは6月25日のロック・オブ・エイジズ・ショーを、この運動の本物の側面を組み合わせて日本の人たちに紹介する手段にしました。私にとって、1つのショーにこれら全部を盛り込んだのは、人々の情熱を生み出したかったからなのです。2002年から2003年には、シドがカリフォルニアでロック・オブ・エイジズ・ショーを始めました。彼は、車、タトゥー、音楽、ピンストライピングを組み合わせました。レイと私はシドのショーに影響を受けました。レイはこういうタイプのショーを日本に紹介したい、こういうショーがやりたかったのだと思いました。」

「このショーをINKRATのレイとイズミと一緒にできることが、大切だと思いました」とNashは回顧する。「私たちは一緒になってタトゥー、サーフィン、スケートボーディング、

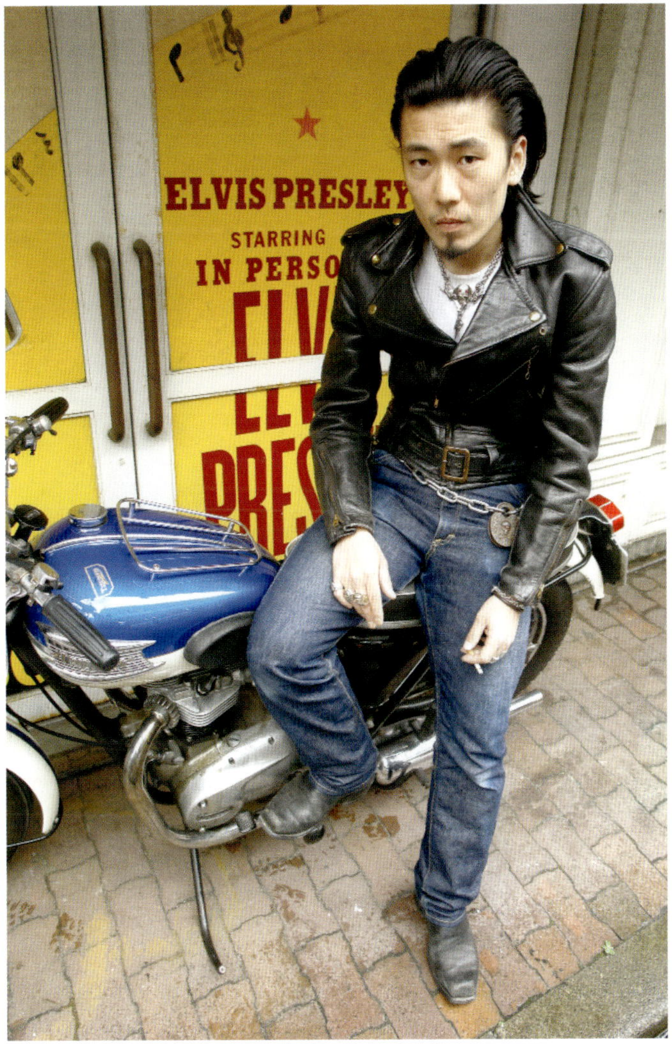

Sawada Issey
Harajuku, Tokyo

catalyst to bring people someplace different. They can travel in time if they want or not. It's up to them where they want to go."

"There is a California connection beneath Kustom Kulture—the Pacific and a notion of the exotic world beyond. I feel that the common interest in Kustom Kulture can combine people from different places. In Japan we combine things together and have always been doing this. A kind of America was superimposed onto life in postwar Japan. The history between these places affected life here permanently, and it will continue. Kustom Kulture people are all interested in the same thing. This is an important process and I want to bring it everywhere."

The mythos of this imposed Americanism is complicated but not all that necessary for young Japanese to fully understand. Ultimately, they are experimenting and flirting with new notions of an expanding "self" in their increasingly global lives. The symbols that surround Kustom Kulture reveal universal issues of youthful validation and rebellion against orthodox authority. These ideas then turn into redefined ways of living. The assortment of behaviors and symbols surrounding custom American automobiles opened a psychological gulf for young, mid-20th century American teens. A sense of newness, freedom and raw power developed; and this novel theme has come to influence a growing number of young people in Japan who are infatuated, like young people everywhere, with the process of transformation.

In its purest form, Kustom Kulture continues to embody a passion for making things, for altering, redesigning and reinventing objects outside the norm. Young people in Japan are reframing this process in their tattoos, clothing, body language and attitudes. They are exploring a pre-existing curiosity and using it as a motivating power to help them remake themselves and figure out who they are.

そしてカスタム・カルチャーを合体させたのです。カスタム・カルチャーは、性別や社会的階級を超越し、色々な人に刺激を与えることになると信じています。人はカスタム・カルチャーが普通の生活ではない、一般的なものでないから興味を示すのです。これらは現実を異なる形に整理にし、人生の違う場所に人を集める触媒として機能するのです。望むなら時間をさかのぼれる…。どこに行きたいかは本人次第なのです。」

「カスタム・カルチャーのもとに、カリフォルニア・コネクションがあります。太平洋と、そこをまたいだ異国の世界…。カスタム・カルチャーへの共通の興味はさまざまな場所からの人々を結びつけることができると感じています」とNashは結論づける。「日本では、ものごとを組み合わせます。これまでずっとそうしてきました。戦後の日本はアメリカ的なものを生活に重ね合わせました。これらの場所の間で、日本の生活は永久的に影響され、これからも変わり続けていくでしょう。カスタム・カルチャーの愛好家たちは皆その部分に興味があるのです。これは重要なプロセスであり、私はこれを広めていきたいのです。」

この重ね合わされたアメリカ的気質は複雑だが、日本の若者にとってそれをすべて理解することはそれほど必要ではない。究極的には、若い日本人は、ますますグローバルになる人生で自分自身を広げていくという新しい概念を試している。カスタム・カルチャーを取り囲むシンボルは、若さの正当性、伝統的権力に対する反抗という世界共通の問題を明らかにし、そしてこうしたアイデアは人生を問い直す手段となった。カスタムのアメリカ車を取り囲むさまざまな行動やシンボルは、20世紀中期のアメリカン・ティーンの精神的な裂け目を開いた。そしてそれは新しさ、自由、粗野な力といった若者特有の感性を発展させていった。この新しいテーマは、世界中のあらゆる若者と同様、変貌のプロセスに夢中になる多くの日本の若者にも影響を与えるようになった。

その最も純粋な形において、カスタム・カルチャーは物を作ること、通常の様相を超えたものへと改造、再設計、再発明することに対す

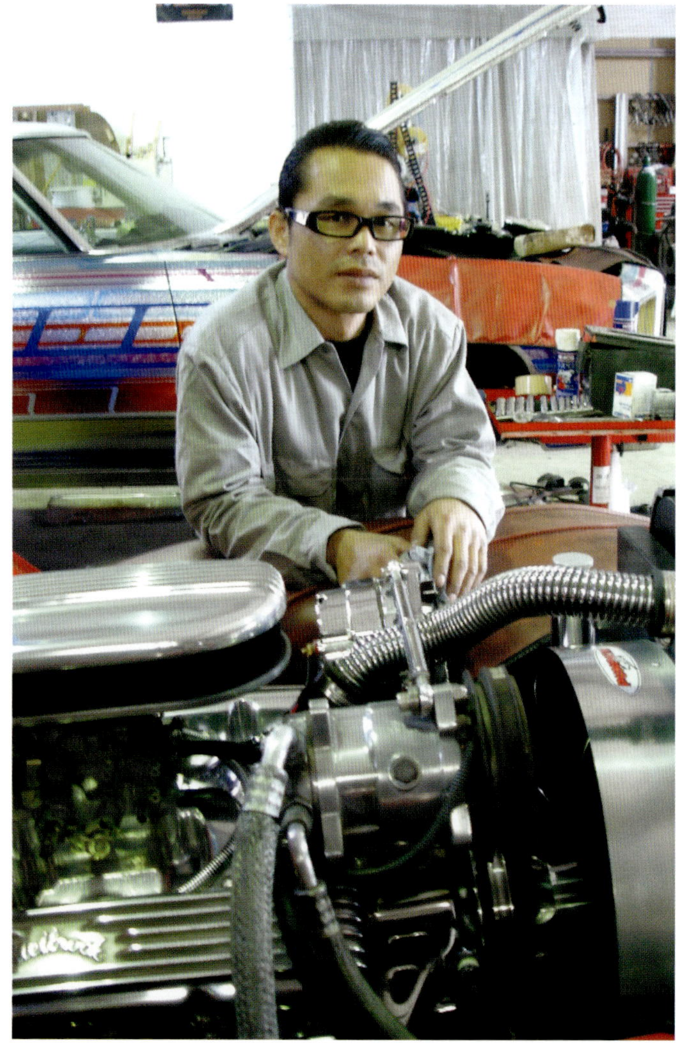

Above: Shorty, Pumpkin Sally

page 39: Hirofume Hosono and son Kousei
1936 Dodge sedan, chopped roof, full hydraulics

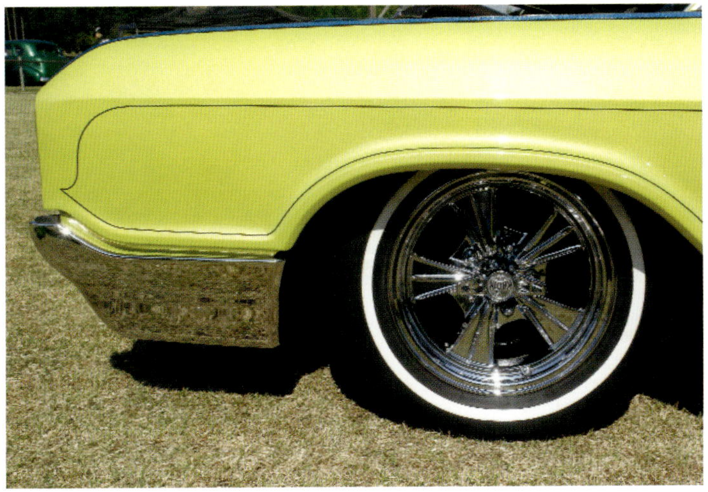

The Tokyo Kustom Kulture t-shirt slogans are probably very mysterious for young Japanese outside that lifestyle. It is not necessary for everyone to understand the particulars of the messages; the words trigger a romantic and nostalgic fascination with a distant time, place and concept that developed in America between the 1930s and 1960s. The image of a hot rod obviously represents more than just a preoccupation with nuts and bolts. It is a re-energized symbol of American iconic power connected deeply to the ascendancy of a nuanced youth identity in the U.S. and, now, urban Japan.

Enthusiasts don't have to know what it all means. In the current world, wearing clothing with some reference to it is enough. Innovations created by the original inspirational visionaries Von Dutch and "Big Daddy" Ed Roth or builders George and Sam Barris, Joe Bailon, Bill Cushenberry, Dean "Kid Jeff" Jeffries and Gene Winfield were referential to a specific time and place. THE LAKES were the dry lakebeds outside L.A. that were turned into hot rod proving grounds; Dean MOON developed the fuel block system that delivered equal fuel pressure to a multi carburetor, Ford FLATHEAD 8 big block V8. Esoteric differences between Ford 94 and Stromberg 97 carburetors are argued by connoisseurs. Knowing that Cadillac was the first in 1951 to develop the overhead valve push-rod motor and that Chrysler's hemi-headed engine pushed the 170mph nine-second quarter-mile speeds of the early 1950s into the seven-second 180-190mph speeds of the late 1950s and the four-second 200-300mph speeds of the 1960s and '70s are a part of what really happened. But this original process of artistic freedom, custom redesign and expression is very complicated and far too specialized for general understanding. It has now coalesced into an aesthetic sensibility and mystique and acts as inspiration for others.

る情熱を具体化し続ける。日本の若者はこのプロセスをタトゥー、服装、ボディランゲージ、態度の中に再構成している。彼らはすでに持ち合わせている好奇心を模索し、それを動機付けの力として利用して自分自身を作り変え、自分とは一体誰なのかを解明しようしている。

東京のカスタム・カルチャー・Tシャツに書かれたスローガンは、日本の若者が見たり着用するには非常に不可解なものだろう。だが全員がメッセージの詳細を理解する必要はない。書かれている言葉は、1930年代から1960年代のアメリカを形作る場所、コンセプト等、遠く離れた昔に対するロマンチックかつノスタルジックな興味を反映している。当然のことながら、ホットロッドのイメージは「ボルトやナット」などの機械的詳細に夢中になる以上のことを表している。それはアイコン的なアメリカン・パワーの再活性化のシンボルであり、アメリカの、そして今日では日本の若者の微妙なアイデンティティの台頭に深く関連している。

これがすべてどういう意味をなすのか日本の若者は知る必要はない。私たちの新しい世界で、それにつながりのある服装をしているというだけで十分なのだ。ヴォンダッチやエド"ビッグダディ"ロスのようなインスピレーションを生み出すビジョナリー、あるいはビルダーのジョージとサム・バリス、ジョー・ベイロン、ビル・クッシェンベリー、ディーン"キッドジェフ"ジェフリーズ、ジーン・ウィンフィールドの背後には、時間と場所が停止した過去に対するクリエイティブな決断と解釈があった。ホットロッドの性能試験場だったLA郊外にある水が枯れた湖底「ザ・レイクス」。マルチキャブレターに同等の燃料圧を送り込む燃料ブロック・システム、大型ブロックのフォード・フラットヘッド8Vエンジンを開発したディーン・ムーン。フォード94とストロンバーグ97のキャブレターの微妙な違いについて論争する人たち。オーバーヘッド・バルブ・プッシュロッド・モーターを1951年に最初に開発したキャデラック。1950年代初期の9秒で4分の1マイル走るスピード（時速170マイル）を1950年代後期の7秒（時速180～190マイル）、さらに1960年代と70年代の4秒（時速200～300マイル）に押し上げたクライスラーのへミヘッド・エンジン…。これらはこの停止した時間と場所で起きた実際の出来事の一例である。しかし、このオリジナルな芸術的自由のプロセス、カスタムの再設計と表現は、非常に複雑であり、大半の人々にとって捉えにくいものだ。これが今、美的感性と神秘性に融合し、人々のインスピレーションとなっているのである。

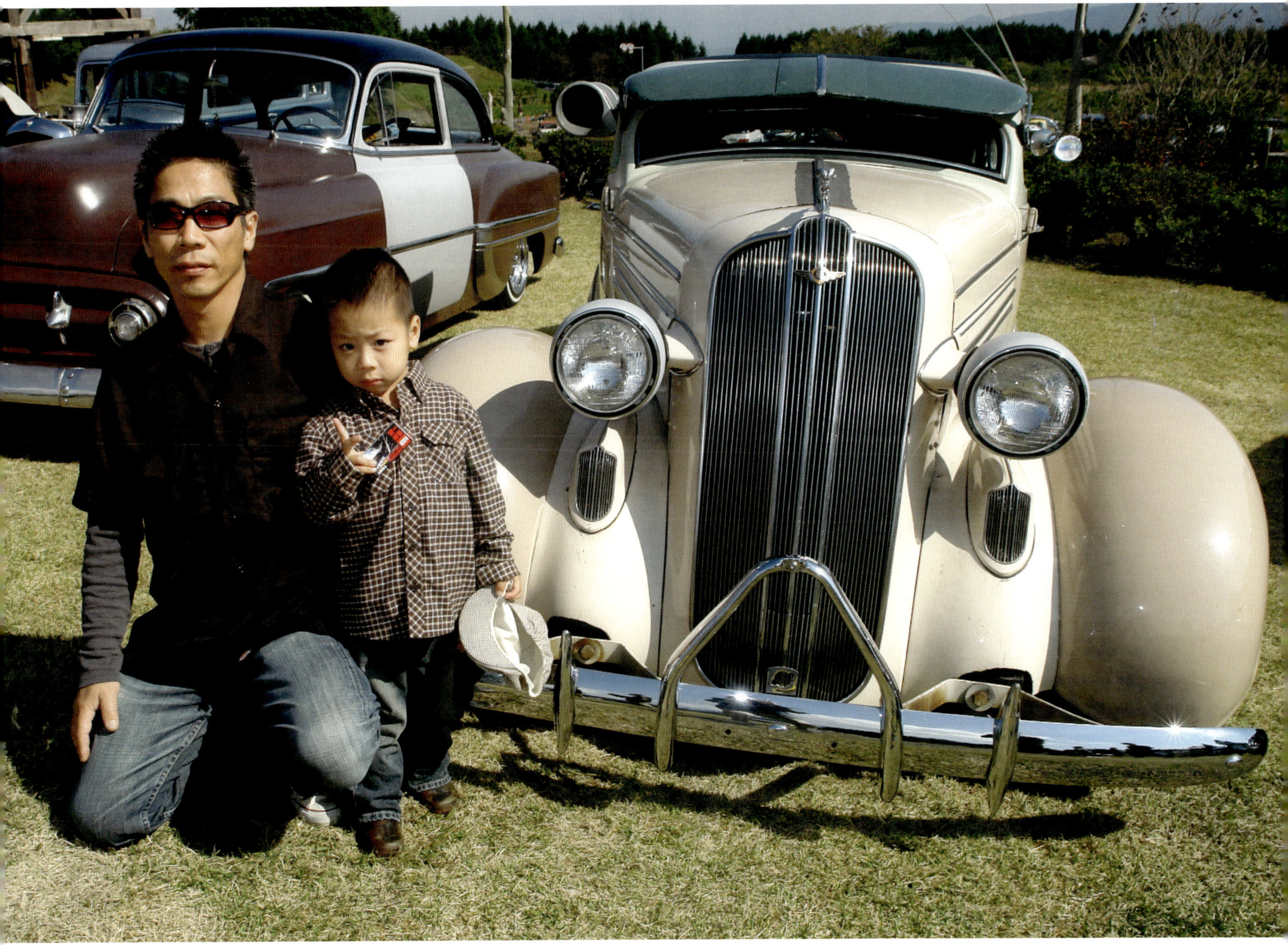

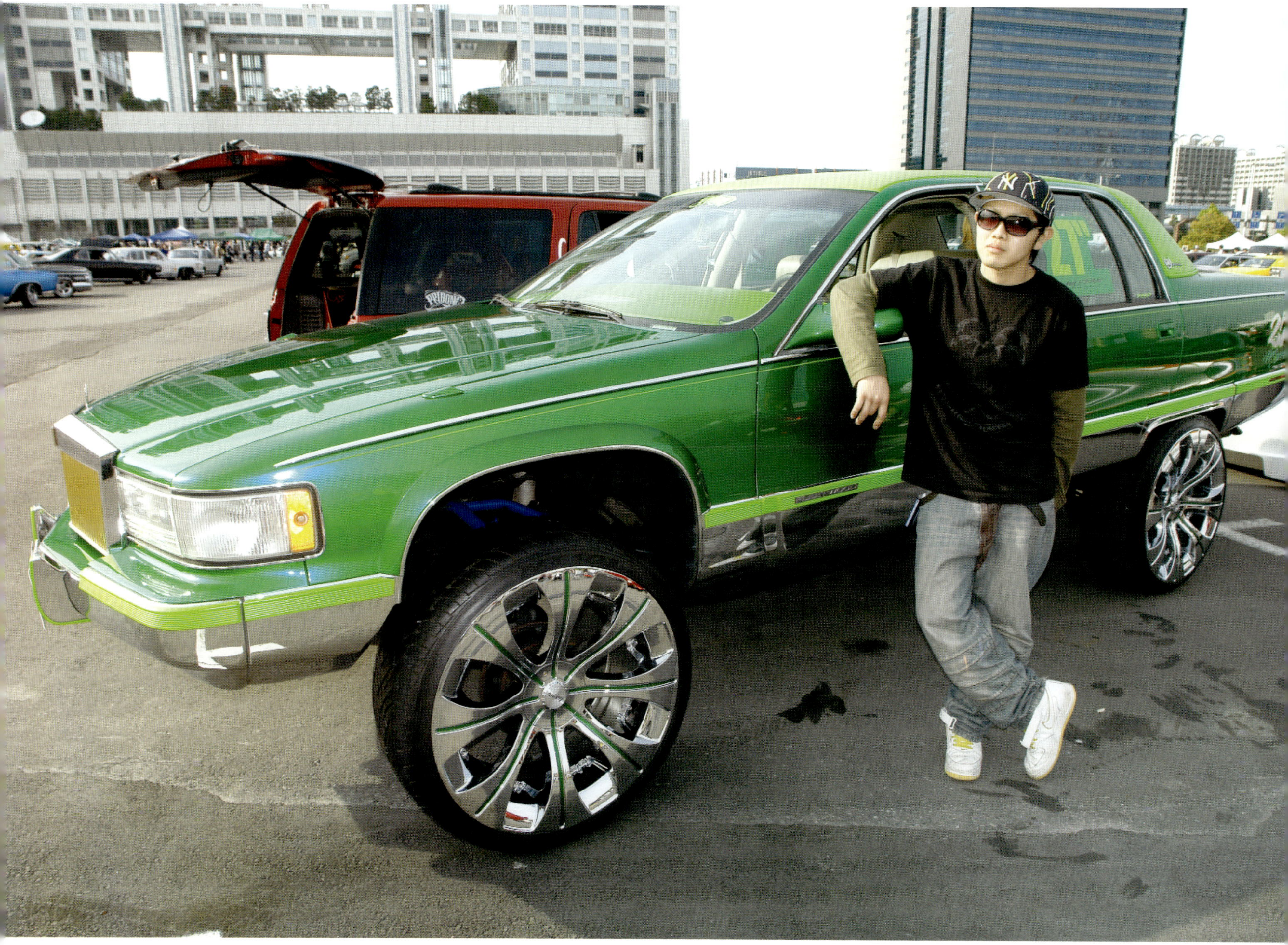

Chapter Two:
Mooneyes - The 21st Tokyo Street Car Nationals

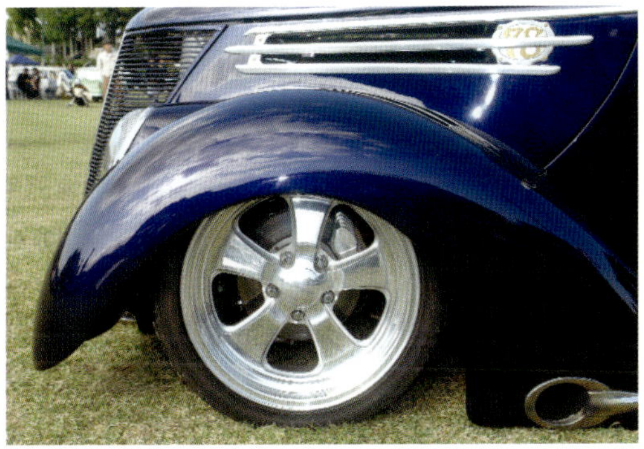

Left: Tokyo Street Car Nationals
Boosted Caddy

There are over seven hundred cars parked next to Tokyo harbor in a simply paved lot at Odaiba, Rainbow Town. Most of the auto subculture styles are gathered together under the sun for the Twenty-First Mooneyes Street Car Nationals event. Domestic stock subcompacts mingle with domestic customized subcompacts. Preserved and customized WWII era cars boasting nuanced multi-tone pinstripe paint and gold plated "face jobs" sit next to early 1950s classic American Chevy muscle cars. A bright lime green, late model Cadillac standing very high on oversized chromed wheels and super-skinny tires shimmers in the sun. Its owner pauses nearby, wearing a New York Yankees baseball hat pitched slightly to the right like the front-end hydraulics of his car. The presentations at the show are relaxed but also deliberate and aesthetic. Hoods are open to show off an impressive engine box and wing doors are up to display plush leather interiors. The statements are quiet, but the owners are definitely saying something with their machines.

The people gathered at the Mooneyes event are part of a growing group in Japan that has latched onto a mysterious and powerful automotive sensibility. They are intrigued about a complicated collage of time, images, objects and ideas that were first popularized around cars in post WWII America. Their interests are diverse and connected with an assortment of automotive subcultures and sensibilities that range widely. Vintage, classic, Kustom, stock, modified. Domestic or imported, phantom or real, every devoted group has a car, a period, a body style, an engine package, suspension choice, tire stance and choice of paint and painting technique. The culture of cars is thick with options of sensibilities and aesthetics. The decisions are deeply personal and reveal a complex history and a confusion of emotions.

These vehicles are loaded mixtures of mechanics, language and

ムーンアイズ — 第21回ストリート・カー・ナショナルズin東京

東京湾近郊、お台場レインボータウン。何の変哲もないアスファルトの駐車場に700台以上もの車が停まっている。ありとあらゆるカー・サブカルチャーの感性が、第21回ムーンアイズ・ストリート・カー・ナショナルズのイベントに向けて青空の下に集合した。国産サブコンパクト市販車が、カスタマイズされた国産サブコンパクト車と肩を並べて停まっている。第二次大戦時代から保存され、カスタマイズされた車は、多彩なピンストライプ・ペイントや金メッキの装飾を誇り、1950年代の代表的アメリカ車シェビー・マッスルのとなりに停車する。明るいライムグリーンの新型キャデラックは、クロムめっきを施した細いタイヤの上に非常に高く乗ったボディを備え、日の光にきらめく。車のオーナーは、ハイドロで押し上げられた車前部のように、ニューヨーク・ヤンキースの野球帽を少し斜めにかぶっている。会場はなごやかな雰囲気ながら、念入りに計画され、美的感覚にあふれていた。ボンネットを開き、ウィングドアを上げて、印象的なエンジンボックスや豪華な革製インテリアを誇示する。控えめながらも、オーナーは車で何かを表現していることは明らかだ。

ムーンアイズのイベントに集まった人々は、神秘的でパワフルな車の感性を手に入れようとする、急増する日本の人口の一部だ。彼らは、第二次大戦後のアメリカで最初に広まったイメージ、オブジェ、アイデア、時代など、車をめぐる入り組んだコラージュに強く引き付けられている。彼らの興味の対象はさまざまで、各種の車に関連する幅広いサブカルチャーと感性につながっている。ヴィンテージ、クラシック、カスタム、市販車、改造車。国産車か輸入車か。幻影か本物か。ありとあらゆる好みのグループには、特定の車、時代、ボディ・スタイル、エンジン・パッケージ、サスペンションの選択、タイヤ・スタンス、そしてペイントや描画技法の選択肢がある。カー・カルチャーでは感性と美的感覚の選択を存分に楽しめる。その決定はあくまでも個人的なものであり、複雑な歴史と感情の混乱状態を示している。

各自の車の横に立つ日本の若者たちは、車を機械学、言語、ファッションのすべてを取り込んだものとして体験する。これらは彼らにとってノスタルジックで美化されたシンボルの、本物の、そして同時に空想上の景観を示している。彼らコレクターにとって、そのつながりは、最初に『アメリカン・グラフィティ』などのアメリカのフィクション映画や、彼らが生まれる前あるいは幼いころの音楽から、そして社会と文化の違う状況下で生まれた表現をスタイル化したものを基盤としている。このような感情とイメージは、日本における異国のレトロ空間に、これらの愛好家がかなりの時間とお金をつぎ込んで再現され、普及してきた。これは車とそれが走る道路のユニークな神話から生まれた自由と変貌というアメリカ独特のコンセプトを取り込み、模索しているのだ。

横浜のシゲ菅沼は、1992年、著名なアメリカの自動車アクセサリーとカスタマイズの会社「Moon Eyes（ムーンアイズ）」を、その創設者であるディーン・ムーンの家族から買い取った。ムーンは、もともと1950年代に革新的燃料ブロックシステムの開発で知られた人だ。このシステムは、マルチキャブレターの改造型フォード・フラットヘッドV8エンジンで、さらに多くの燃料を使用することによって馬力を向上するものだった。ムーンアイズ社は後にホットロッドとカスタム・カー・カルチャーの象徴の1つとなった。

近年、菅沼は日本で急成長するカスタム・カルチャーの重要な原動力として活躍してきた。彼は横浜のムーンアイズ店をこの運動に関連する情報や製品の拠点に仕立て上げた。カスタム・カーのイベントは年間を通して予定が組まれている。

fashion that are a simultaneously real and fantasized mindscape of nostalgic and romanticized symbols. Most of the associations are grounded in stylized representations generated first by American fictional films like *American Graffiti* or music sources from before they were born or too young to notice. The emotions and images have been recreated and filled out by these devotees at considerable expenditure of time and money.

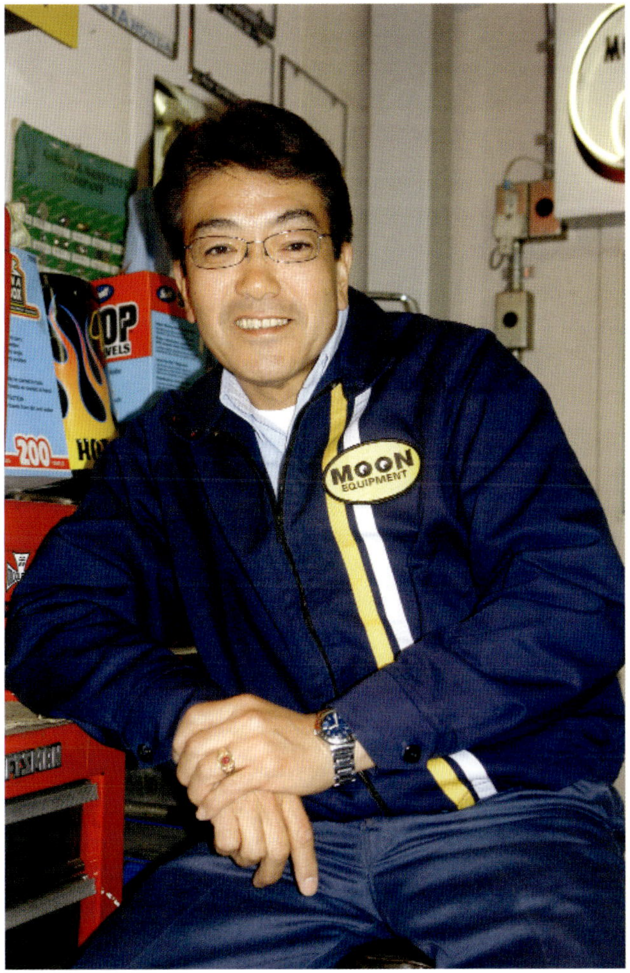

Shige Suganuma
Mooneyes owner

Shige Suganuma of Yokohama, Japan, bought the famed American MOONEYES auto accessories and customizing company in 1992 from the family of company founder Dean Moon. Originally in the 1950s, Moon was known for his innovative fuel-block system that provided altered, multi-carburetor Ford Flat-Head V8 engines with more fuel and, therefore, more horsepower. The Mooneyes Company became one of the iconic symbols of hot rod and custom car culture.

In recent years Suganuma has been an important motivating force in the growing Kustom Kulture movement in Japan. He has crafted his Yokohama Mooneyes store into an important center of information and products associated with the movement. There is a year-round schedule of custom car events that include swap meets, car shows and the Shifters car club, which was founded in 1998. Suganuma was born in postwar Japan in the early 1950s, and personally experienced a nascent pro-American cultural shift that evolved at that time.

"This growth of interest in Kustom Kulture has been an interesting thing to watch," Shige said. "Japan is an interesting place in terms of how it processes cultural information from the outside world. This is a theme that has always existed here. I was born at a time in Japan after the War when American culture was influential in good and bad ways. This process of exchange between America and Japan is mysterious for me. I have been intrigued by it since I was a kid."

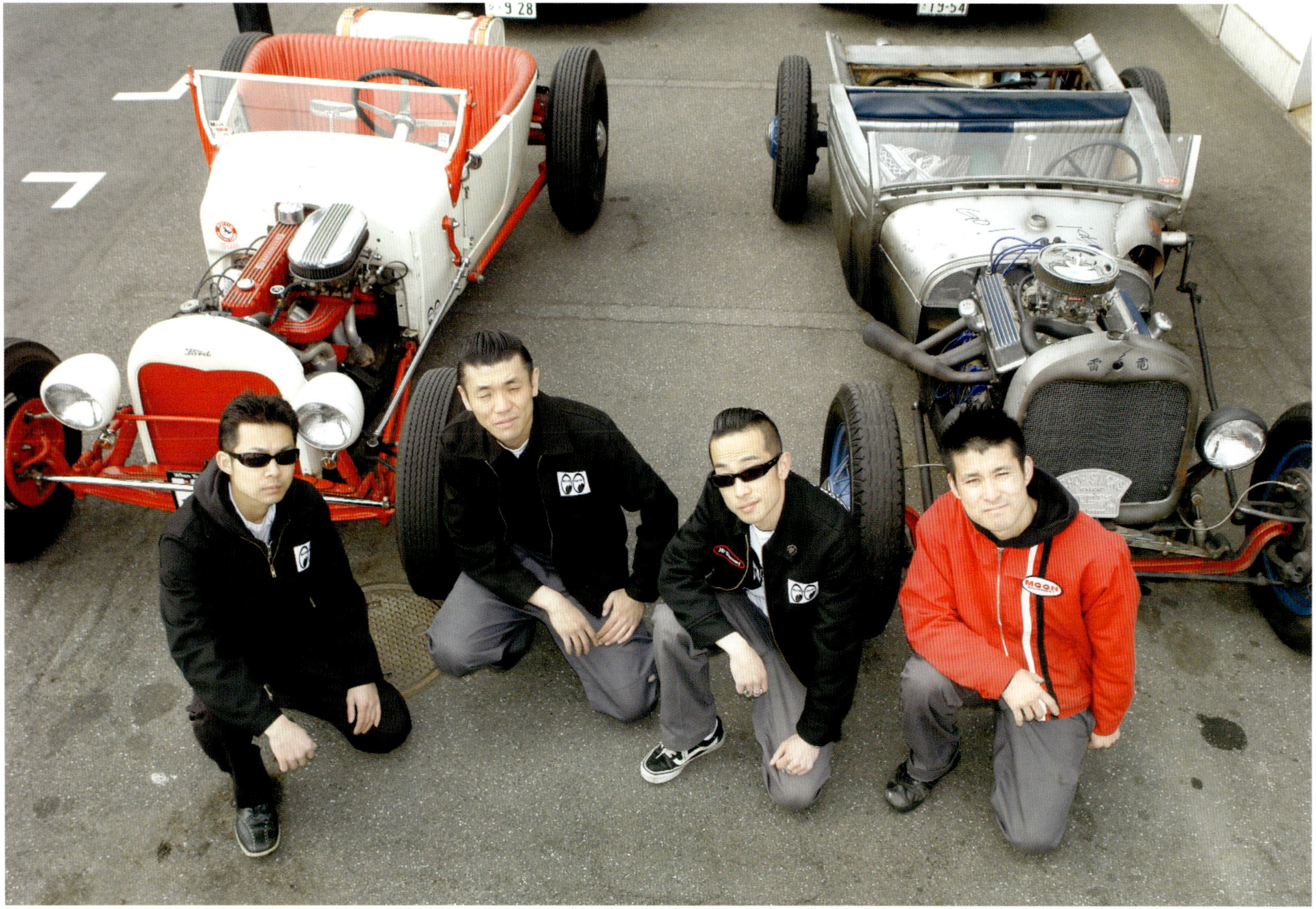
MOON

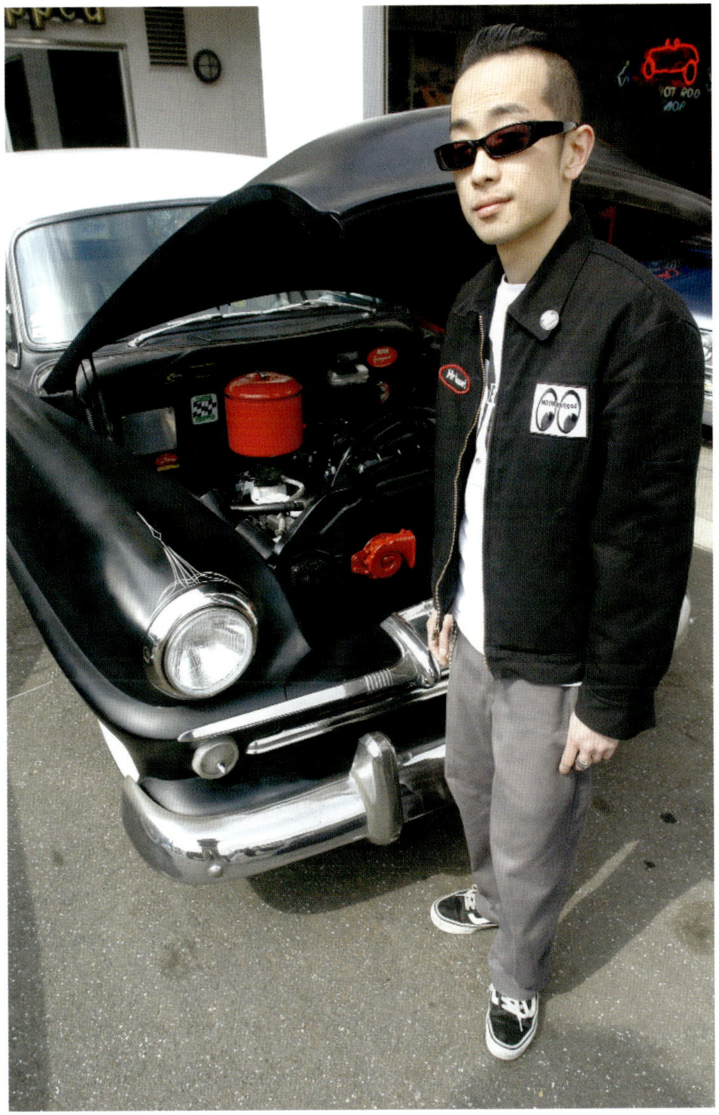

Above: Toshi Endo
1954 Plymouth Plaza Suburban
Straight six 230, stock package
Pinstriping: Hoo Doo Man, Yokohama

Left: Mooneyes Crew
L-R: Koji Sato, Takefumi Sakue, Toshi Endo, Sohei Murakami

"In Japan, there has been this unique relationship with America among many young people. This myth of space and freedom and driving that is seen as an act of transformation has always fascinated me. Japan is a small place and the culture has strictness to it. Young people in Japan see America as this place that is big—big, powerful cool looking cars; long highways that go across huge expanses of space like Route 66 through the desert. The whole thing is a dream to Japanese young people. I was born during a period in Japanese history when all these ideas were so alien and unthinkable, so forbidden in many ways. Young people now live this dream by coming to my store, attending car shows, wearing some of the symbols that represent this Kustom Kulture. Mooneyes is a part of this."

At the Mooneyes event, many car owners and their families are dressed in clothing and hairstyles from the periods their cars were manufactured. Others are dressed in trendy hybrid fashions that maintain some kind of synchronicity with their vehicles. The towering green Cadillac owner is all hip-hop, the Chevy muscle owners are tasteful Grease, and the domestic subcompact owners could be in a mall parking lot in New Jersey. Ages split high and low depending on the car style. Some of the spectators who have come to have a look and appreciate are also a part of the overall theater-like mood. Men slick back their hair and wear period shirts, sweaters, belts, shoes and sunglasses. Some women wear period lipstick colors, jewelry and puffed up hairstyles. A few couples have dressed their children period style too. Like in America where the romanticized images of the 1950s tend to dominate car events, many of the re-creators at this event are also playing the '50s part with one important difference—there are no Americans at the event, and everyone, without exception, is speaking Japanese. Car owners ceremoniously bob and bow greetings to one another among their pristine historic American cars. The intersection of culture and time is blurry.

スワップ・ミート、カー・ショー、そして1988年に設立されたシフターズ・カー・クラブなどがある。彼は戦後、1950年代初期に生まれ、そのころ日本の都会で展開した親米的な文化転換の発生期を身を持って体験した。

「カスタム・カルチャーに対する興味が増えていることを目撃するのは面白いですね」とシゲは言う。「日本は海外からの文化的情報をどのように処理するかという点で非常に面白い国だと言えます。これは日本にずっと存在してきたテーマです。私が生まれたのは戦後の日本で、アメリカ文化がその良し悪しにかかわらず影響力を持っていました。このアメリカと日本の交流は私にとって謎めいたものです。子供のころからずっと興味を抱いてきました。」

「カスタム・カルチャーは、1993年、カリフォルニア州ラグーナビーチで開催された“Kustom Kulture”という名前のショーをきっかけに、後に広く知られるようになりました。このショーはたくさんの情報を初めて集結させたものでした。ヴォンダッチ、エド“ビッグダディ”ロス、ラット・フィンク、ロバート・ウィリアムスらと彼らが描いたものが、もっと多くの人々に知られるようになりました。その焦点は一般的な制度にとらわれないクリエイティブな変貌についての神話的なアメリカ気質でした。アメリカでのカスタム・カルチャーは、車と運転に関する人の考え方を変えることで始まりました。」

「日本でも、多くの若者の間でこのアメリカ気質との同様な関係が築かれてきました。空間と自由と運転の神話は、変貌の行為と見られてきました。私はこれに対してずっと興味を持っていました。日本は狭い国で、その文化は厳格です。日本の若者はアメリカを大きな国だと思っています。広大でパワフルで、カッコいい車とか、途方もなく広がる大地に延びる長いハイウェイ — 砂漠を横断するルート66など、日本の

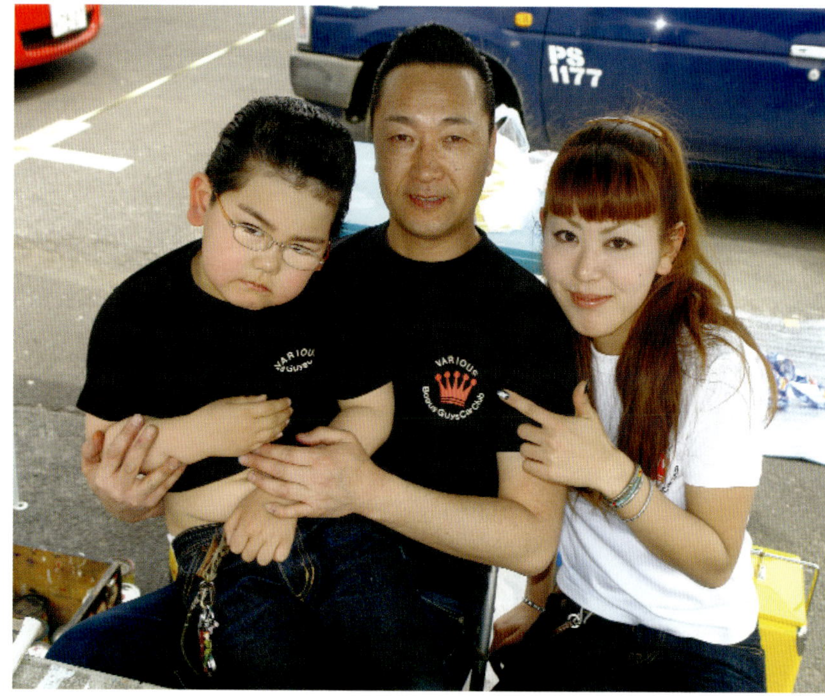

Above: Yasushi Tanaka and family

Right top: Southern California, Compton Style

Right bottom: Masuo Hara
1968 Buick Electra 225

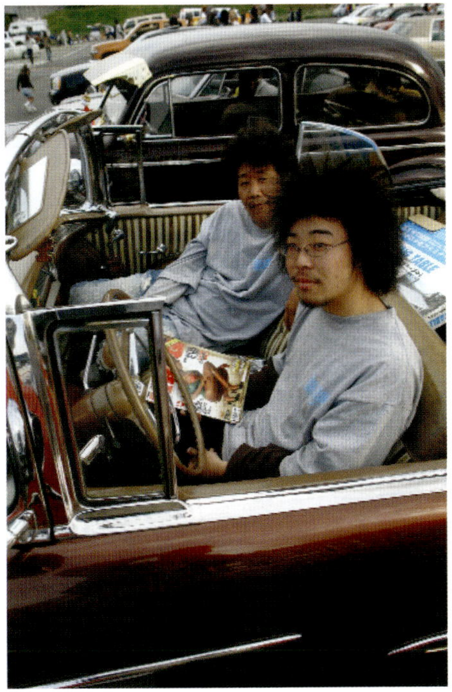

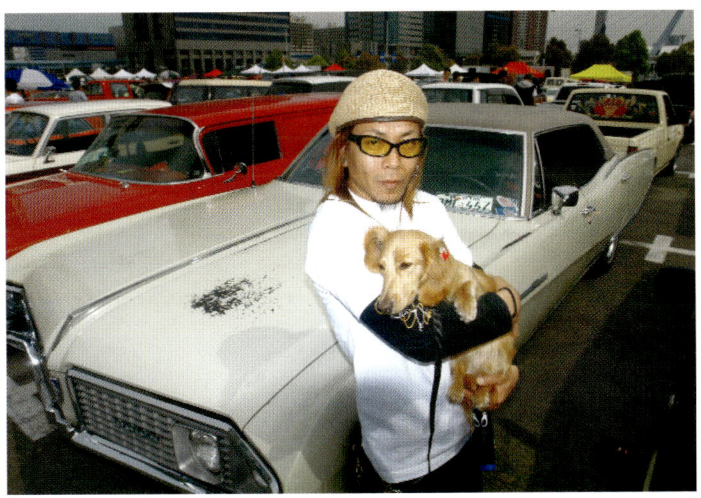

Some car owners have crossed lines of appearance relating to race and ethnicity. There are California-style lowriders with drivers skilled in the cholo cultural visual codes. Two young men with high afro-style hair sit in a chocolate brown mid-'50s SoCal style Chevy convertible with the top dropped to accommodate their big hair. The visual package they project is supported by a carefully selected sound track of esoteric '70s and '80s soul music, played at a tasteful level from their car's expensive sound system. The driver has a pair of gold-rimmed shades resting perfectly on his nose bridge and a skillfully positioned afro-pick jutting sideways out of his 'do. The presentation is seamless.

Nothing seems out of place or fabricated among the car owners. It is all very convincing. In some ways the chocolate Chevy, green Cadillac or '50s muscle car owners might be strangers involved in a guessing game; but any spectator would be hard pressed to see cracks in their presentations or where they have missed their cues. One club calling itself "Various-Bogus Guys Car Club—Since 2007" seems to have a different take. The members sit in folding deck chairs drinking beer next to an assortment of cars that do not look dedicated to any one sensibility. Masuo Hara stands at his cream colored 1968 Buick Electra 225 holding a small lap dog in his arms. He wears his club's t-shirt but nothing else that speaks of fanatical attachment to car culture. His car's wheel wells exhibit considerable signs of rust and rot, and the hood has a large rusted area where the paint has long been baked away by engine heat. He bought the car in California in 2006 because he liked its size and condition. He was impressed that it was really used and looked like it had been driven a lot on American roads. He has yet to change the tires.

Masuo opens his hood, pauses over the huge V8 and pulls at the oil dipstick. It drips black with oil that is badly in need of a change. "This oil is old," he says. "I kept it. All the way from America." The interior of the car smells like used bubble gum. There are a half

若者にとってすべてが夢のような話です。私はこれにとても興味があります。こういうアイデアがかつての日本ではまったく異質であり、考えられなかった時代 — 多くの意味で禁断であった時代に私は生まれました。若い人たちは、私の店にやってきたり、カー・ショーに参加したり、カスタム・カルチャーを表すシンボルの服を着るなどして、今この夢を実現させています。ムーンアイズは、その一部なのです。」

ムーンアイズのイベントには、多数の車のオーナーとその家族がやってくる。それぞれの車が製造された時代の服やヘアスタイルを取り入れて。オーナーの中には、その車との共時性を保つトレンディなハイブリッド・ファッションを採用している者もいる。そびえたつようなグリーン・キャデラックのオーナーはすべてがヒップホップ、シェビー・マッスルのオーナーは趣味のいいグリース、そして国産のサブコンパクト車のオーナーはニュージャージーのショッピングモールの駐車場にいるような雰囲気を出している。年齢は車のスタイルに応じて高齢と若年に分かれている。これを楽しむために来た観衆の中には、全般的な劇場ムードに溶け込んでいる人もいる。男性はオイルで髪をテカテカにし、その時代のシャツやセーター、ベルト、靴、サングラスを着用している。女性はその時代の色の口紅や宝石類をつけ、膨れ上がったヘアスタイルにしている。数組のカップルは、その子供も含め、時代に沿ったスタイルで参加している。アメリカと同様、カー・イベントでは1950年代の美化されたイメージが支配的となる傾向があるが、このイベントでも多くが50年代を再現している。ただ、1つだけ大きな違いがある。イベントにアメリカ人は見えず、参加者は例外なく日本語を話している点だ。車のオーナーは、ピカピカの歴史的なアメリカ車の間で、お互いに礼儀正しくおじぎをしている。文化と時間の交差点は曖昧だ。

車のオーナーの中には、人種と民族性の一線を越えた者もいる。カリフォルニア・スタイルのローライダーに乗っているドライバーはメキシコ系アメリカ人の文化的外観の基準に精通しているようだ。また大きなアフロヘアスタイルの2人の若者は、50年代中期の南カリフォルニア・スタイルのチョコレート色のシェビー・コンバーチブルに乗っている。屋根を開けて、大きな髪型の邪魔にならないようにして。彼らが醸し出す視覚的イメージを、車の高級サウンド・システムから上品な音量で流れ出る厳選された70年代・80年代のソウル・ミュージックが補っている。ドライバーは金縁のサングラスを鼻にかけ、アフロヘアにアフロピックを横向きに巧みに配置させている。そのプレゼンテーションには非の打ちどころがない。

車のオーナーの中には、場違いであったり、でっち上げのようなものは見当たらない。すべて非常に説得力があるのだ。ある意味では、チョコレート色のシェビーやグリーンのキャデラック、50年代のマッスルカーのオーナーは、推測ゲームに興じる他人同士かもしれないが、観衆がそのプレゼンテーションにおける失敗やディテールの間違いを見つけるのは容易ではない。これに対して「Various-Bogus Guys Car Club—Since2007（色々ないんちき野郎のカークラブSince 2007）」という名前のクラブは違ったアプローチをとっているようだ。メンバーは、いずれの感性にも関連しないような種々雑多な車の横で折りたたみのデッキチェアに腰掛け、ビールを飲んでいる。クリーム色の1968年ビュイック・エレクトラの横に立つ原マスオは、腕に小さな飼い犬を抱いている。クラブのTシャツを着てはいるが、それ以外、カー・カルチャーへの熱狂的な執着は見られない。車のホイールウェルにかなりの錆や腐食が見られ、ボンネットの一部はエンジンの熱でペイントが焦げて錆びている。彼はこの車を2006年にカリフォルニアで購入した。そのサイズと状態が

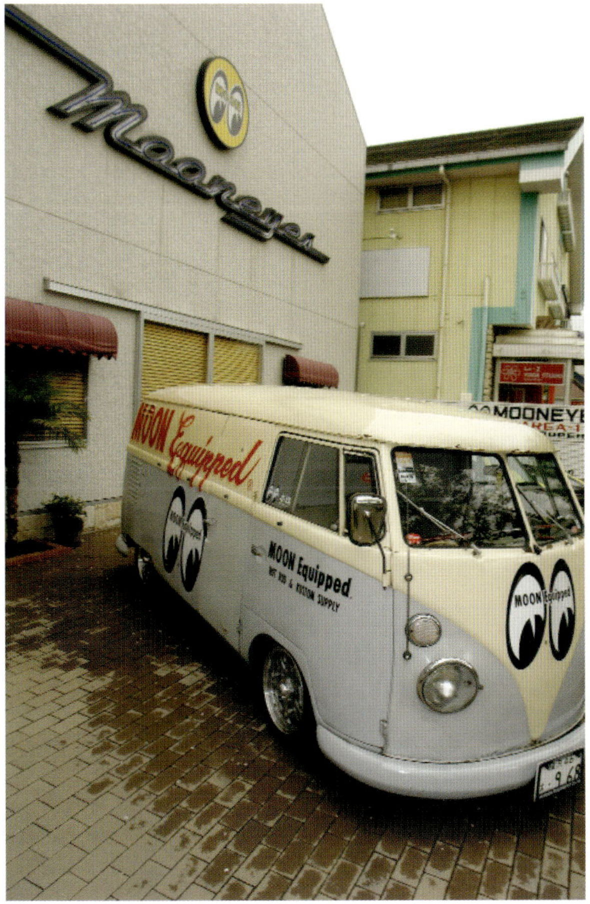

Mooneyes VW

dozen sun faded Christmas tree shaped air fresheners hanging off the rear view mirror with corny American highway vernacular expressions like “Keep On Truckin’,” “If This Van’s A Rockin’ Don’t Try Knockin’.” In the back, the floor is littered with a few crumpled American brand beer cans and an assortment of Taco Bell takeout food wrappers. “I kept these too,” he says. “I brought them from America.” Masuo’s car is an intentional cultural artifact of American auto usage behavior. He is the proud curator of this authentic presentation.

“In Japan, in places like Tokyo and Osaka, many middle aged men are fascinated with the 1950s in America,” Shige continues. “They have a deep connection to this period. During the 1960s it was difficult for younger Japanese people to understand what was going on in the U.S., but they wanted to know. So whatever information got through had an exotic strangeness to it. Younger guys today in Japan might have different feelings about America. It’s hard to tell. Many of these tastes can be very personal and private. I first went to the U.S. in 1977. When I was twenty-one, I got a 1960 T-Bird. I needed parts, and I had seen a book with some information about parts available between Chicago and California.”

“I got my driver’s license when I was eighteen. My first car was a VW van. I wanted to make it a surfer van. During the 1970s surfing culture was very popular in Japan. People thought buying the van was odd—that it must be for work. Then in 1976 I bought the T-Bird, and in 1977 I bought a 1971 Plymouth Satellite. In 1978 I bought a 1968 El Camino. It was not a popular thing for older people to do, younger people all wanted one.”

“1978 was an important year for the exchange of automotive culture. This is when the car sensibility was internationalized. European carmakers impressed and entered the American car market. European and Asian economies had been rebuilding during the

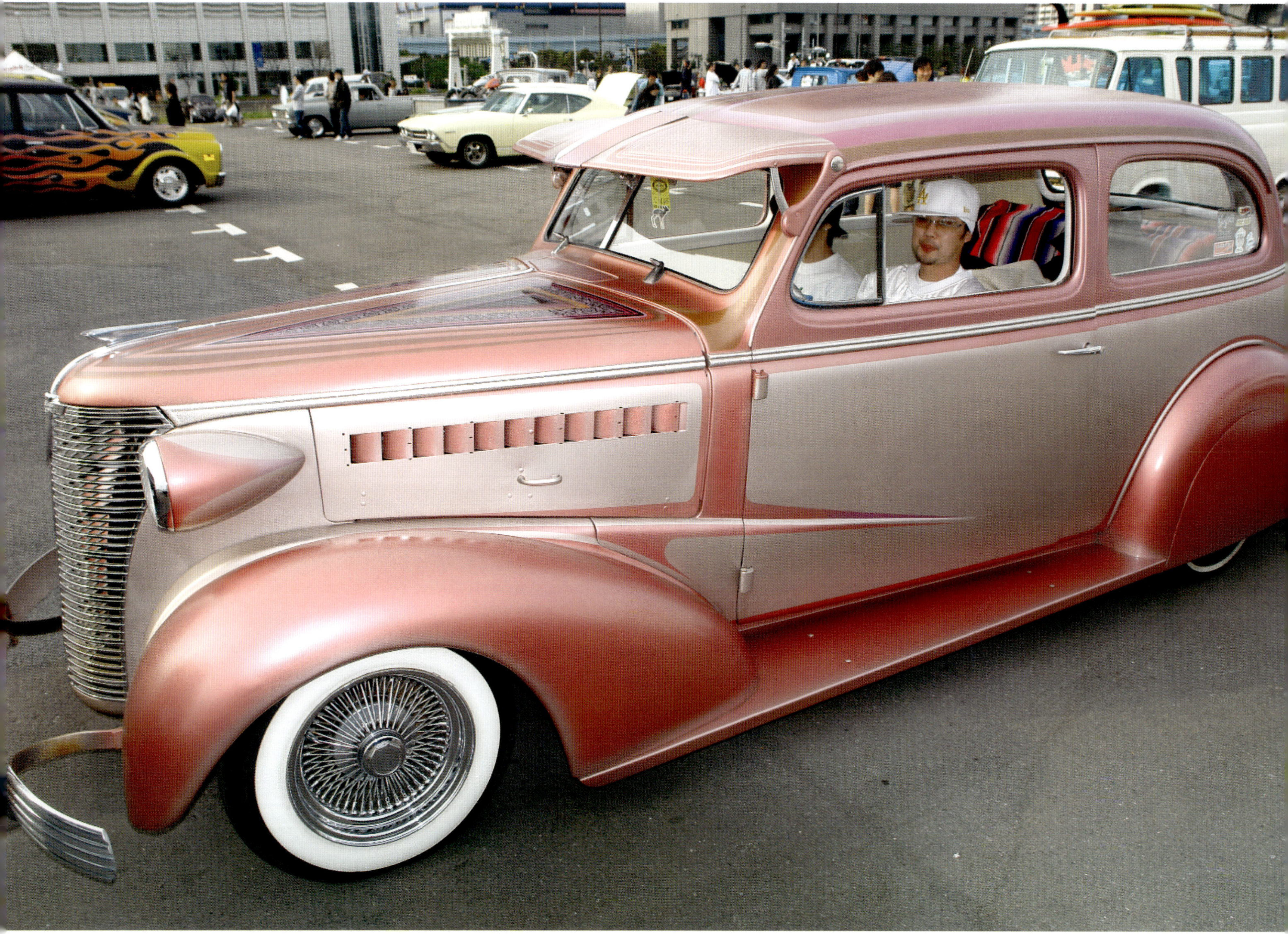

1950s and '60s, when economic power was limited to other parts of the world. The U.S. was really powerful in the postwar climate. In contrast, my parents were limited by the postwar situation in Japan. Then in the 1970s things changed."

"During the 1950s there was no TV in Japan, no refrigerators. Japan existed in a different realm. America had come through the postwar expansion with industrial strength and a powerful culture during the '50s and '60s that accompanied this expansion. Then there were the gas shortages of the 1970s, which was a turning point for car quality in Japan and Europe. American car culture changed forever."

"In 1987 the first Tokyo Street Car Nationals was the first Japanese event for American style cars. 80% of the two hundred cars were customs. At this first show, there was no information about what to do to a car. Many owners managed somehow to find magazines with ideas about what could be done to a car. I was very surprised to see so many people come to the show. For the first show, cars came from as far away as Osaka to the south and Aomori to the north. This was a big thing. This year we had 750 cars and 100 swap meet booths."

"I felt it was important to enjoy this culture. I wanted to do it out of a sense of personal interest and ambition. I had the show as a way to develop an interest and was impressed to see the enthusiasm. In 1987 car culture was about cars and people working on their cars, pinstriping and clothes. It was a pioneer show and I think it influenced people. Things have changed so much. During this period, I had a 1969 Camaro that I wanted to sell. I painted my phone number on the rear quarter window with the words 'For Sale.' Some Japanese newspaper took a photo of my car with the painted sign and published it. People saw this and then all these people painted their rear quarter windows with 'For Sale' signs and their phone numbers. This became a fad. Japan is a funny place."

Left: Postwar Occupation period car

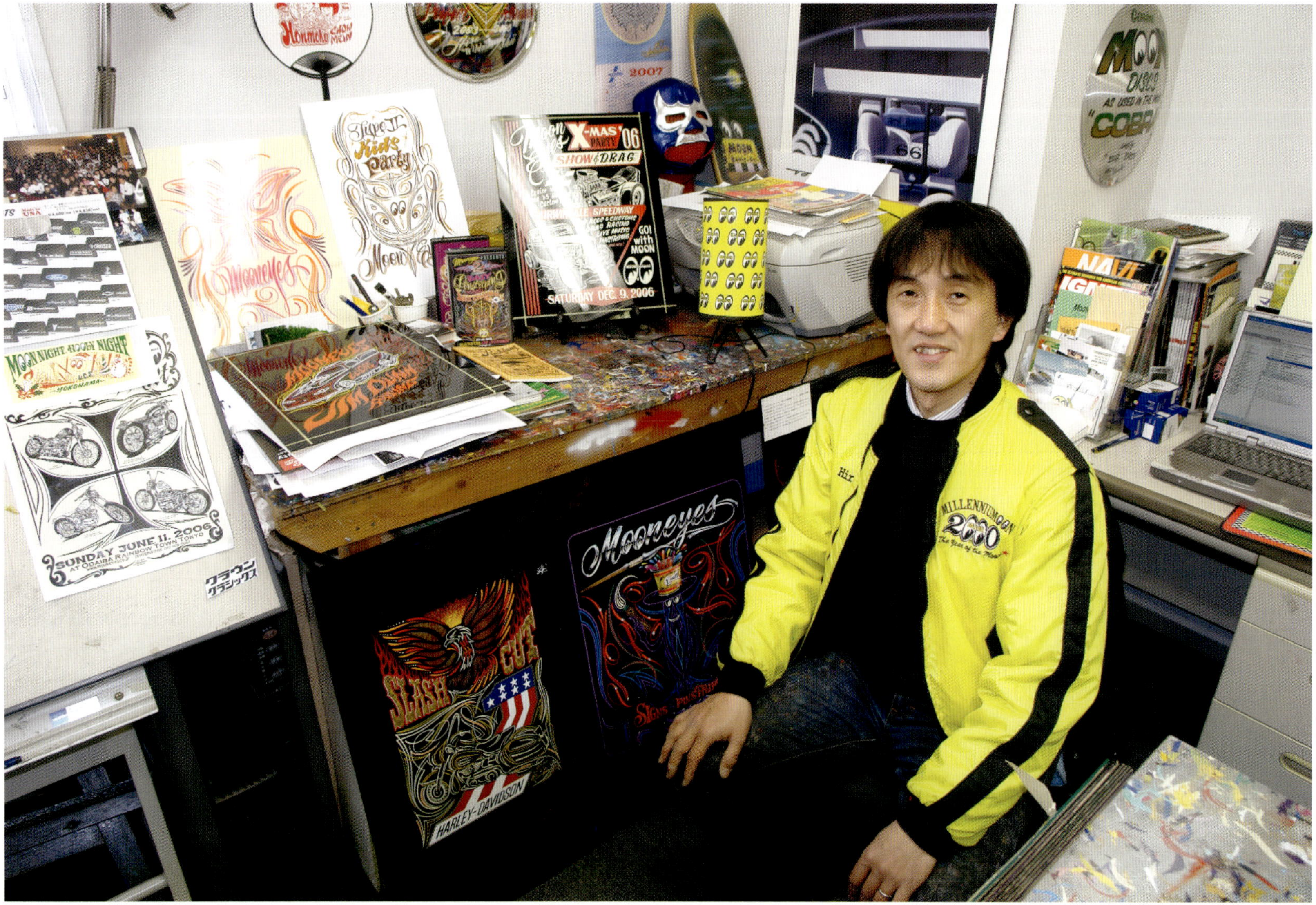
X-MAS PARTY '06
SHOW & DRAG
SATURDAY DEC. 9, 2006
GO! with MOON
Mooneyes
MOON NIGHT MOON NIGHT
SUNDAY JUNE 11, 2006
AT ODAIBA RAINBOW TOWN TOKYO
クラウン
クラシックス
Mooneyes
SLASH CUT
HARLEY-DAVIDSON
MILLENNIUMOON
2000
DISCS
"COBRA"
2007
NAVI

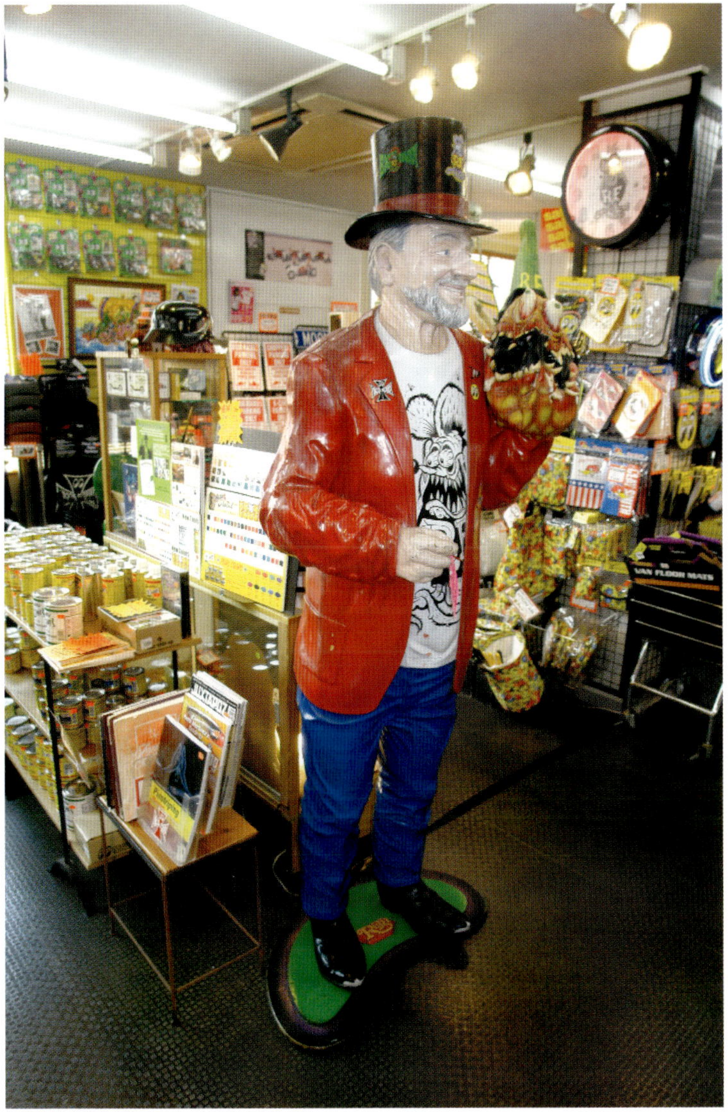

Above: Ed "Big Daddy" Roth
Mooneyes store, Yokohama

Left: Wildman in his Mooneyes studio

The presence of Mooneyes in Yokohama has introduced a large measure of authenticity to American classic, custom, hot rod and muscle car appreciation in Japan. The mystique associated with the Moon name runs deeply into car culture in America, and Shige has been responsible for introducing and contextualizing this in Japan. In 1990, he invited Kustom Kulture icon Ed "Big Daddy" Roth to attend the Street Car Nationals show. Roth brought his dagger brushes and One Shot paint, and for an entire day pinstriped cars and objects at the show in front of a mesmerized group of car enthusiasts. It was the first time the painting technique had been demonstrated to a Japanese audience, and it opened a large door of curiosity.

"I always liked pinstriping," Shige says. "But it is a very difficult technique. I tried, but it was too much. I knew a young sign painter named Hiro Ishii, who had a very good hand at painting. I had first met him as one of my customers. I bought him some dagger brushes just to see what he thought. He had never seen a brush like it, but he had heard of the style. At the 1990 show he watched Roth paint all day and thought about the new painting style. I think if I hadn't brought Roth over to that show, people would not have seen pinstriping and the appreciation about it, and Kustom Kulture in Japan, might be different. Later, Hiro started working at Moon and I sent him to Los Angeles to meet with Roth. Then they both drove to Roth's home in Utah. During the visit, Roth gave Hiro a new artist name, 'Wildman'."

There is an impressive second floor painting studio in the Mooneyes main building where Wildman works. Clusters of recent paintings are grouped together on small tables and the floor. Many are original art used to print the event posters Mooneyes is famous for. A cluster of cleaned dagger brushes rests next to cardboard painting palettes colorful with dried paint. The room smells slightly of One Shot. Wildman navigates around his paintings and reaches for a particular

気に入ったからだと言う。車が実際に使用され、アメリカの道路を相当走ったように見える所に感銘を受けたのだ。彼はタイヤをいまだに変えていないと言う。

マスオはボンネットを開き、巨大なV8エンジンを上から見てオイル・レベルゲージを引っ張り出す。真っ黒なオイルが滴り、オイル交換が絶対必要なことが分かる。「このオイルは古いんです」と彼は言う。「でもこのままにしておきます。すべてのマイルがアメリカから来たんですから…。」車のインテリアは、噛み捨てられたバブルガムの臭いがし、バックミラーには日光で色褪せたクリスマスツリーの形のエア・フレッシュナーが５～６個つるされている。それにはハイウェイ特有のダサい決まり文句が書かれている。"Keep On Truckin' (進み続けようぜ)"、"If This Vans A-Rockin' Don't Try Knockin'(このバンが揺れ動いているなら邪魔しないでくれよ)" などだ。後部座席には、つぶれたアメリカ製ビールの缶や、タコ・ベルのテイクアウト・フード用の包装紙などが色々と散らかっている。「これも、このままにしておきます」と彼は言う。「私がアメリカから持ってきたものなので。」マスオの車は、アメリカ人が車を使用する行為を示した意図的な文化遺物と言える。彼はその博物館学芸員であり、本物のプレゼンテーションを誇りに思っている。

「日本では、東京や大阪のような場所では、多くの中年男性が1950年代のアメリカにすごく興味を持っています」とシゲは続ける。「あの時代に非常に深いつながりを感じています。1960年代では、日本の若い人たちにとってアメリカで何が起こっているのか理解するのが困難でしたが、知りたいのも事実でした。ですからこちらに到達した情報はどんなものでも異国の雰囲気がありました。今日の日本の若者は、アメリカに対して違った感覚を抱いているかもしれません。その辺はちょっと分かりませんが。こういう趣味の多くは個人的でプライベートなものなのです。私が初めて渡米したのは1977年でした。21歳のときに1960年のＴバードを手に入れました。その部品が必要で、シカゴとカリフォルニアの間でそういう部品を売っている店があることを本で見たのです。

「私は18歳のときに運転免許を取りました。最初の車はVWのバンでした。これをサーファー・バンにしたかったのです。1970年代にはサーフィン・カルチャーは日本で非常に人気がありました。バンは仕事用だからって、そんなものを買うのは変だと思われました。それから1976年、Ｔバードを買い、1977年には1971年プリマス・サテライトを購入しました。さらに1978年には、1968年エルカミノを買いました。年配の人には人気がありませんでしたが、若い人はみんな欲しがっていました。」

「1978年はカー・カルチャーの交流にとって非常に重要な年でした」とシゲは続ける。「それは車の感性が国際化した年でした。ヨーロッパの自動車メーカーはアメリカの自動車市場に強い印象を与え、これに参入しました。1950年代と60年代はヨーロッパとアジアの国々の経済は再建中で、経済的繁栄は他の地域に限定されていましたからね。戦後の環境ではアメリカは非常にパワフルでした。たとえば、私の両親は日本の戦後の状況に制限を受けていました。ところが1970年代になって変化が起こりました。」

「1950年代の日本にはテレビも冷蔵庫も存在しませんでした。日本は別の世界にあったと言えます。戦後に進出してきたアメリカは、50年代と60年代にその産業力やパワフルな文化を伝えました。それから1970年代にはガソリン不足が発生しました。あれは日本とヨーロッパの車の品質における転換期でした。あのときにアメリカのカー・カルチャーは永遠に変わってしまったのです。」

「21年前の1987年、アメリカン・スタイルの車を集めた第１回ストリート・カー・ナショナルズは、日本で初めてのイベントでした」とシゲは説明する。「200台の車のうち80%

dagger brush. He explains that it was given to him by Ed "Big Daddy" Roth.

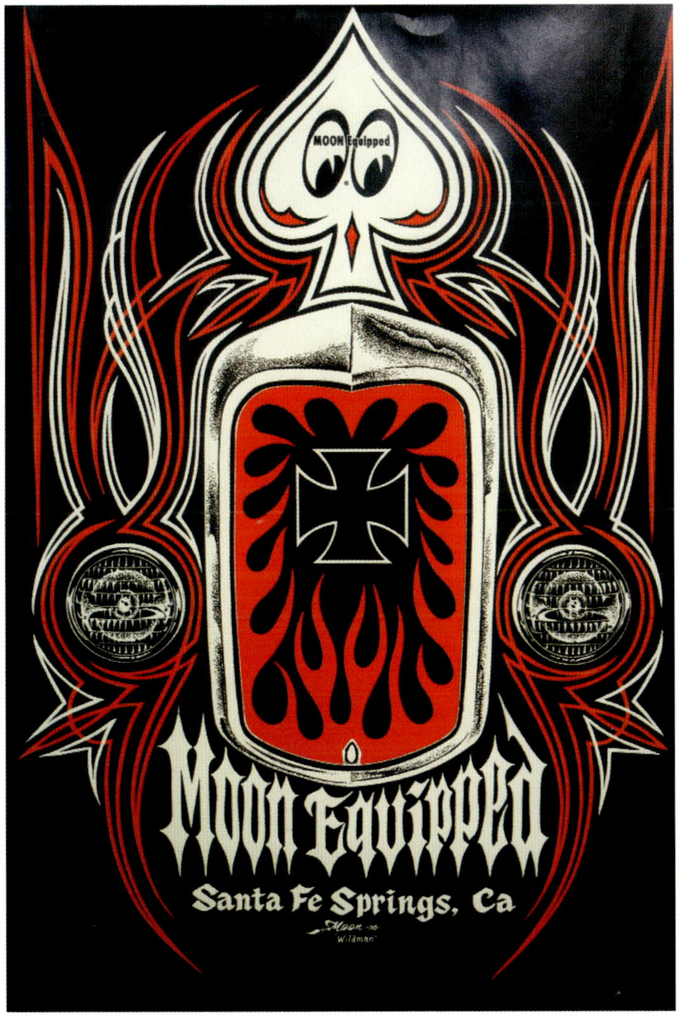

Wildman artwork

"The first time I saw Roth pinstriping," Wildman said, "I watched and wondered about it. Roth sat with me and showed me about the brush. He showed me about pinstriping and how to use the different brushes and paint."

"During Spring 1989, I was still working as a sign painter. Then I moved to Mooneyes and became the first pro pinstriper in Japan. In 1990, I flew to LA to see some art shows. I met with Roth, and we went to Utah together. I stayed for a very intense week with Roth at his farm. It was my first trip to America. I knew very little about it. I did not speak English. Roth made me drive from L.A. to Utah. He pointed in one direction and told me to keep driving. I had no idea what he meant. He fell asleep in the front seat next to me. I had no idea where we were going, and I couldn't read any of the signs. I kept driving and driving. The land was amazing; there was all this space. It was like watching a movie. I was very nervous because I had never seen anything like it. It was very big. Then there was a large dead deer on the road. There were dead animals all over the road. I had never seen anything like this. The land was so vast, so open; it was like a different planet. I had no idea about the route number signs, town names. Roth was lying there snoring, and I became very scared. I had no idea where I was going."

"Finally I became scared because we had been driving for a very long time. It was now dark. I pulled over and woke Roth up. He started laughing; he couldn't believe it. He thought the whole thing was hysterical. He said, 'You are amazing, this is your first time in America, you don't understand English, you can't read English, but you've been driving for hours through the desert, lost. You finally wake me up. You are a wildman!'"

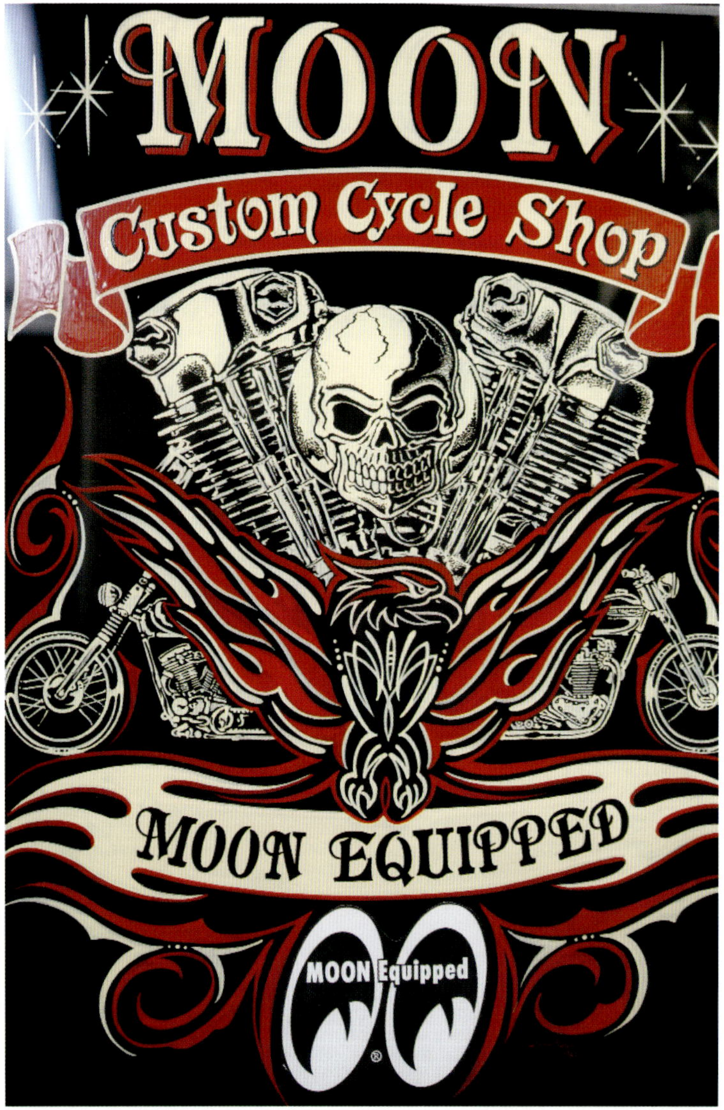
MOON
Custom Cycle Shop
MOON EQUIPPED
MOON Equipped

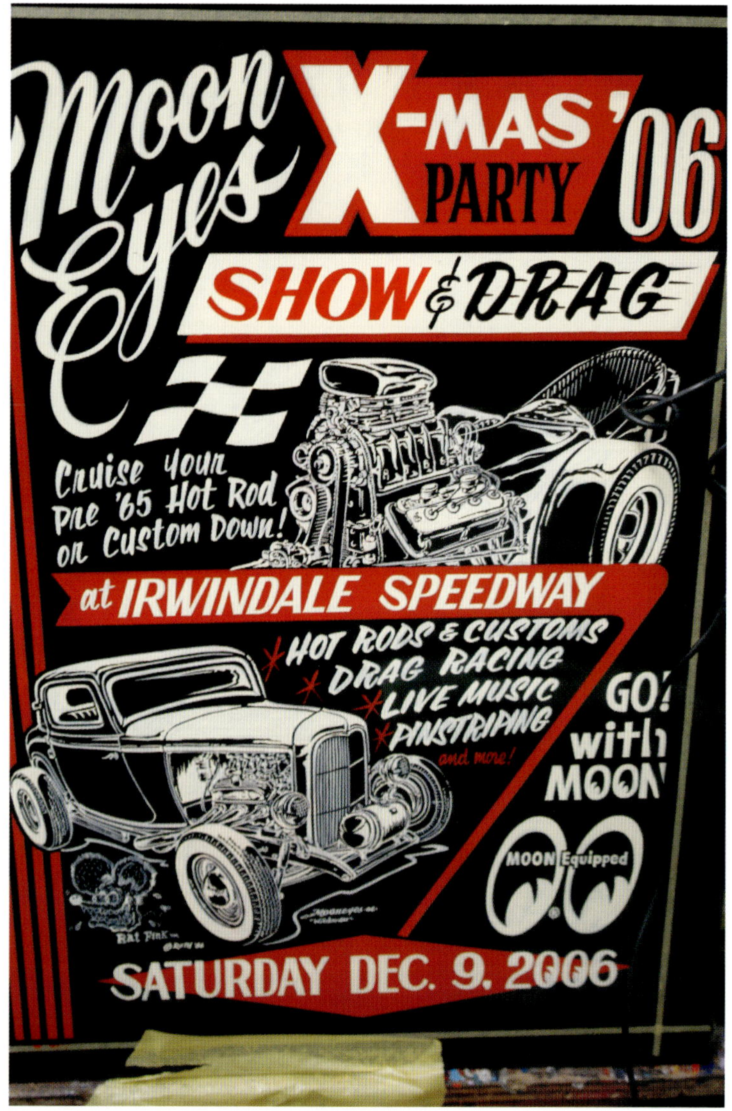
Moon Eyes
X-MAS PARTY '06
SHOW & DRAG
Cruise your Pre '65 Hot Rod or Custom Down!
at IRWINDALE SPEEDWAY
HOT RODS & CUSTOMS
DRAG RACING
LIVE MUSIC
PINSTRIPING
and more!
GO
with
MOON
MOON Equipped
SATURDAY DEC. 9. 2006

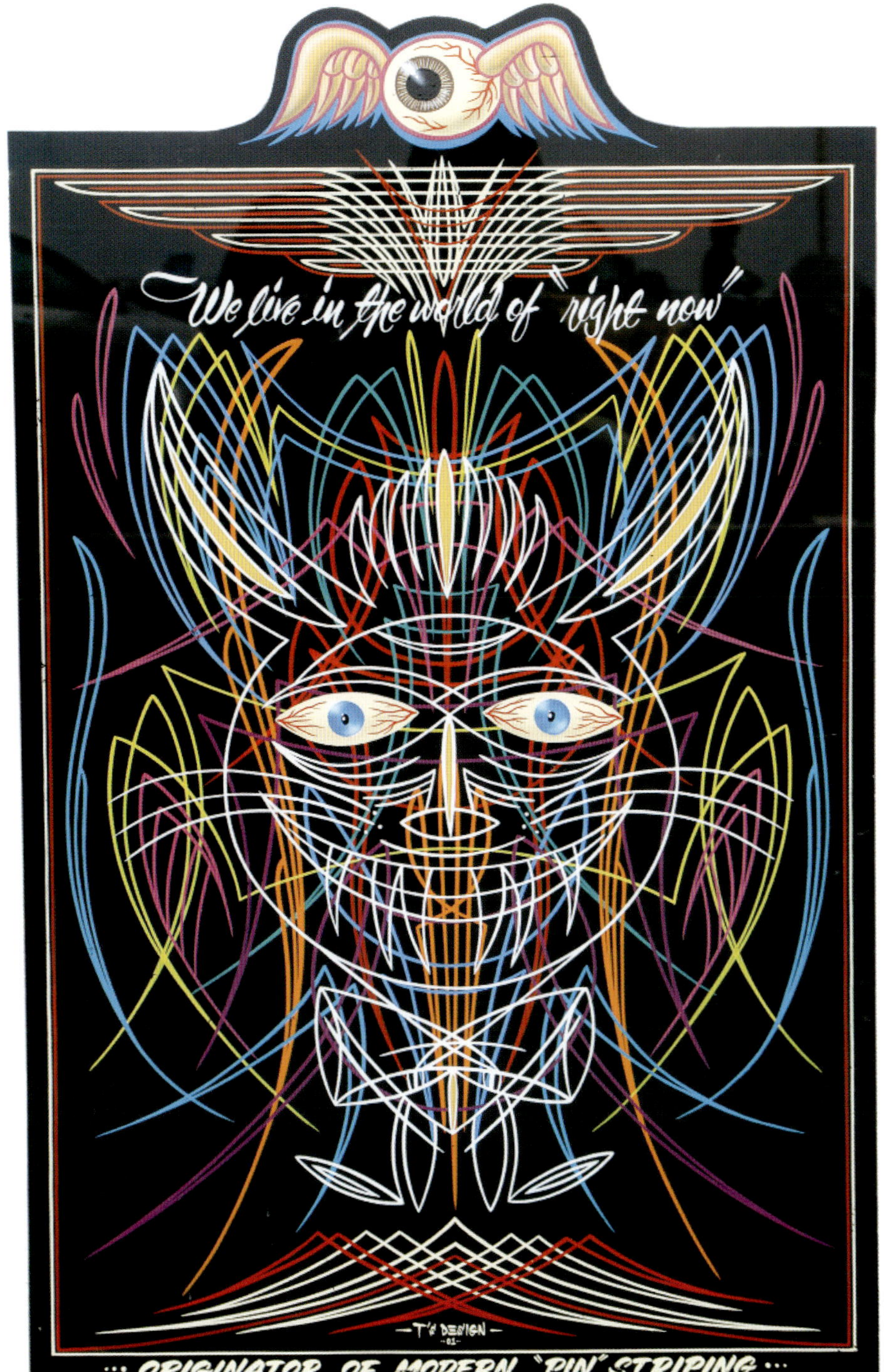

Left: Wildman artwork

Right: Pinstriping by Yasushi Tanaka
Homage to Von Dutch

はカスタムでした。最初のショーでは、車に何をするかについての情報はまったくありませんでした。多くの車オーナーは雑誌などから車に対してできることのアイデアを見つけ出してきました。本当にたくさんの人が来場したのを見て驚きました。最初のショーには南は大阪、北は青森から人が集まりました。これは大きな出来事でしたね。今年は750台の車と100店のスワップ・ミート・ブースが出ました。その後、ショーの内容が拡大して、ミニトラック、フォルクスワーゲン、ローライダー、ストリートロッド、カスタム、マッスル・カー、ピンストライパー、ファッション・アクセサリーも含めるようになりました。」

「カスタム・カー・カルチャーは楽しむことが大切だと感じました。個人的な趣味と大望をもってやりたいと…。1986年には横浜にムーンアイズ店舗を開店しました。ショーはみんなに興味を持ってもらうためにやったのですが、参加者の情熱には驚きました。1987年では、カー・カルチャーは、車とそれに取り組む人たち、ピンストライピング、衣料が対象になりました。カー・カルチャーの草分け的ショーで、人々に影響を与えたと思います。本当に色々なことが変わりました…。1969年カマロを持っていたときでの話です。その車を売りたかったので、リア・クォーター・ウィンドウに自分の電話番号とともに“For Sale”とペイントで書いたんです…。ある日本の新聞が、そのサインの付いた私の車の写真を撮って掲載しました。たくさんの人がこの記事を見たようで、それからみんながリア・クォーター・ウィンドウに“For Sale”のサインと自分の電話番号をペイントで書くようになりました。これが流行になったんです。日本というのは変な国ですよね。」

横浜のムーンアイズの存在は、日本におけるアメリカのクラシック・カー、カスタム・カー、ホットロッド、マッスル・カーに対する本物の認識を紹介するうえで大きな役割を果たした。ムーンの名前で連想する神秘的雰囲気はアメリカのカー・カルチャーに深く浸透しているが、シゲはこれを日本に紹介し、状況を説明した本人である。1990年、彼はカスタム・カルチャーの象徴、エド“ビッグダディ”ロスを招き、ストリート・カー・ナショナルズに参加してもらった。ロスはダガー・ブラシとワンショット・ペイントを持参し、1日中会場で車やオブジェにピンストライプを施し、多くの車ファンを魅了した。日本の観衆の前でこのようなペインティング技術が実演されたのは初めてで、これが好奇心のドアを大きく開くことになった。

「私はこれまでずっとピンストライピングが気に入っていました」とシゲは言う。「でも、あれは本当に難しいテクニックです。自分でやってみましたが無理でした。ペインティングがすごくうまい石井ヒロという若いサイン・ペインターを知っていました。彼とは最初、私のお客として知り合いました。彼のためにダガー・ブラシを購入して、彼がどう思うか聞いてみました。彼はその種の筆は見たことがなかったのですが、そういうスタイルがあることを話には聞いていたようです。1990年のストリート・カー・ナショナルズ・ショーで、彼はロスが1日中ペインティングを続ける様子を見て、新しいペインティングのスタイルについて考えました。もし私がロスを連れてこなくて、ピンストライピングを誰も見たことがなく、そういう認識が生まれなかったとしたら、日本のカスタム・カルチャーは違ったものになっていたかもしれません。その後、ヒロはムーンで仕事を始め、私が彼をロサンゼルスに送ってロスと会わせました。そこから2人はユタ州にあるロスの家まで運転しました。訪問している間にロスはヒロに“ワイルドマン”というアーティスト名をつけました。」

ワイルドマンが仕事をするムーンアイズ本館2階には印象的なペインティング工房がある。最近のペインティングが小さなテーブルや床に重なっている。多くはオリジナル・アートであり、ムーンアイズの有名なイベント・ポスターの印刷に

"We came to a café next to the highway. There were all these lowriders parked at the café. So Roth says, 'Slow down,' and starts yelling out the window at the lowrider guys. I had no idea what he was yelling, so I got frightened. I was convinced these guys were going to beat the hell out of us. Of course they knew Roth, and it was just for fun."

"We finally made it to Roth's farm. It was the first house I had stayed in in America. The house was crazy. It was all surrounded by signs, cars, fiberglass concept bodies and a mountain of paint cans. I was shocked and amazed. Roth made us dinner, and I wondered where was his wife? All Roth could cook was eggs with not too much meat and nothing else. He had donuts too. So we ate eggs and donuts three times a day for a week."

"I think about this now and know how special it was to be with Roth and to learn from him. At the time, it was all very strange and I didn't realize the significance. What I really learned from Roth was about the soul and emotion of Kustom Kulture. He was a positive thinker and he passed this theme on to me. He taught me to paint things that made positive and strong and amazing statements. Roth really felt that the purpose of his art was to make people happy. He taught me about this."

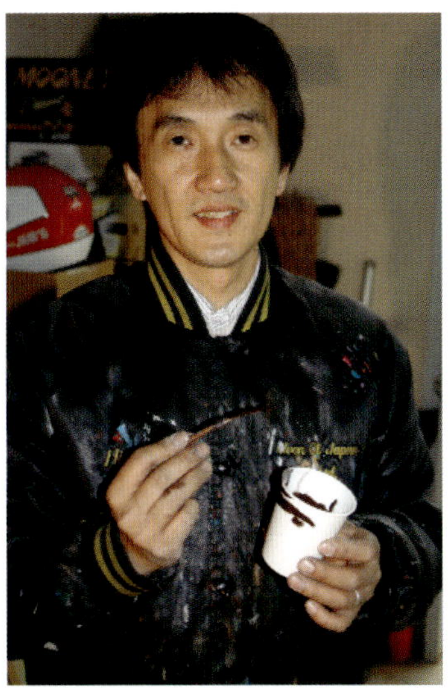

Wildman painting with Roth dagger brush

"He showed me that he always could see people looking at his Rat Fink and feeling good. This was very important to him. He came over every year for car shows. He brought over Beatnik Bandit II to the shows. The positive vibe around people looking at his cars was very important to him. I learned about this from Roth."

"There is a sense of communication with the brush and learning about the brush. About emotion and communicating emotions through the mind to the hand to the brush to the paper. We learn about this process in Japan from when we are young. We learn

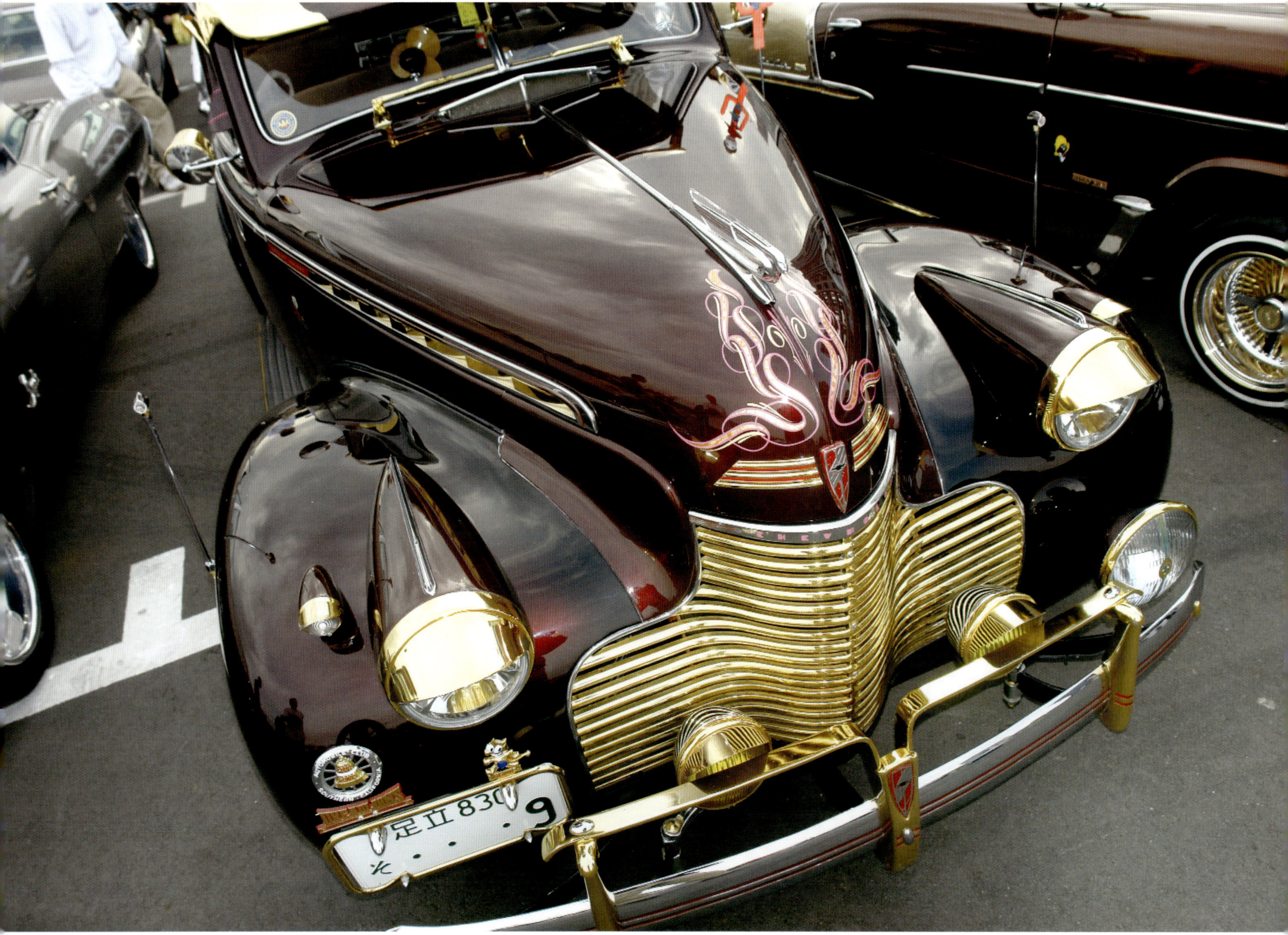
足立830
9

"Modern automobiles need some human elements on them. Without it they look as though they have been ground out by a mechanical monster."

Von Dutch – *Car Craft*, 1956

War period car – 1940 Chevrolet Master DX
Gold plated face

about a sense of connection and the communication of very complex ideas and emotions through the hand and brush. As a pinstriper in Japan, I might have a different idea about the painting process. Other Japanese pinstripers might, too."

"When I started pinstriping, I was amazed at how different it is. I was amazed at how different the stroke and flow is. It is a totally different way to use the brush. When I started I did not speak English. I was asked to pinstripe and paint lettering on people's cars. The English letters meant nothing to me. I saw them only as designs, like a Western person sees *kanji*. I had to get used to the new brush and style. The whole thing of pinstriping was very abstract to me."

"Von Dutch is the soul of Kustom Kulture. His painting is not just lines. Roth and Von Dutch brought soul to the paint. Roth always told me that Dutch's work was legendary. It was always clear to me that Roth really respected Dutch, not just for his painting but for what he had done to the whole art of cars and the culture of it. Like Roth, I also feel that if Dutch had not existed and painted cars, there would be a completely different feeling about the whole Kustom Kulture thing."

"The first time I saw anything about Von Dutch was more than 25 years ago in a book. There were a few photos and some history. When I saw this, I could begin to understand that this art and culture had a depth. A history and certain personalities had created art. They were artists and innovators. At that time years ago, I was fascinated with the process that Roth and Von Dutch had created in their art. I never thought there would be so many pinstripers in Japan. I am amazed by the interest it has generated. It had never been seen before in Japan, and no one had any idea what it was."

"There are different styles. Von Dutch and Tommy the Greek were

使用されたものだ。乾燥したカラフルなペイントが残るダンボールのパレットの横には、きれいに洗われたダガー・ブラシがたくさん並んでいる。部屋はわずかにワンショットの臭いがする。ワイルドマンはペインティングの周りを通り抜けてある1本のダガー・ブラシを手に取った。それはエド“ビッグダディ”ロスが彼にくれたものだという。

「ロスがピンストライピングをやるのを初めて見たのは1990年のストリート・カー・ナショナルズ・ショーでした」とワイルドマンは言う。「それを見て、色々思いを巡らせました。ロスは私と一緒にすわって筆について教えてくれました。ピンストライピングのやり方や、異なる筆やペイントの使い方を見せてくれました。」

「1989年の春、私はまだ看板制作の仕事をしていました。89年の8月、私はムーンアイズに転職し、日本初のプロのピンストライパーになりました。1990年、アート展を見るためにLAに飛びました。そこでロスと再会して、一緒にユタ州に行きました。私は彼の農園に滞在し、非常に集中した1週間を過ごしました。私にとって初めての渡米で、アメリカについてほとんど何も知りませんでした。英語も話せませんでしたしね。ロスは、LAからユタまで私に運転させました。彼は一方向を指差して、その方向に運転を続けるよう言いました。それがどういう意味なのかよく分かりませんでしたが、彼は助手席で居眠りを始めました。私はどこに向かっているかも分からず、道路の標識を読むこともできませんでした。ただ延々と運転を続けました。大地は広くて、それはもうすごかったですね。まるで映画を見ているようでした。そういう場所は見たことがなかったので非常に緊張しました。すごく広大なのです。それに道路には死んだ大きな鹿がいました。死んだ動物が道路のあちこちに転がっていました。ああいうものは見たことがなかったですね。」

「大地は広くてオープンで、まるで他の惑星にでもいるようでした。道路の番号の標識や街の名前などはぜんぜん分かりませんでした。ロスは寝転んでいびきをかいていて、私はだんだん怖くなってきました。いったいどこに向かっているのは検討もつきませんでした。」

「ずいぶん長い間運転して、とうとう怖くなりました。もう暗くなっていました。道路わきに車をとめてロスを起こすと、彼は笑い出し、信じられないといった様子でした。彼にはその状況がおかしくてたまらないようでした。彼はこう言いました。『君はすごいね。アメリカへ来たのは初めてで、英語は分からないし、読むこともできない。それでも砂漠をわたって何時間も運転を続け、道に迷ってしまった。それで、ようやく僕を起こしたわけだ…。君はワイルドマンだ！』」

「それからハイウェイのそばにあるカフェにとまりました。カフェの駐車場にはたくさんのローライダーがいました。そこでロスは『スピードを落としてくれ』と言い、窓ごしにローライダーの連中に対して大声を上げました。彼がなぜその連中に怒鳴っているのか分からず怖い思いをしました。絶対あいつらに殴り倒されるんだと思いましたね。もちろんロスは彼らと知り合いで、ふざけていただけでした。」

「ようやくロスの農園に着きました。私がアメリカで滞在した初めての家でした。それは無茶苦茶でしたね。周りには標識や車、ファイバーグラスのコンセプト・ボディなどがいっぱいでした。ペイント缶が山のように積み上げられていました。ただショックと驚きでしたね。ロスがディナーを作ってくれましたが、奥さんはどこにいるのだろうと不思議に思いました。彼が作ってくれたのは卵と少しの肉だけで、他には何もありませんでした。ドーナツもありました。というわけで、私たちはそれからの1週間、卵とドーナツを1日3回食べました。」

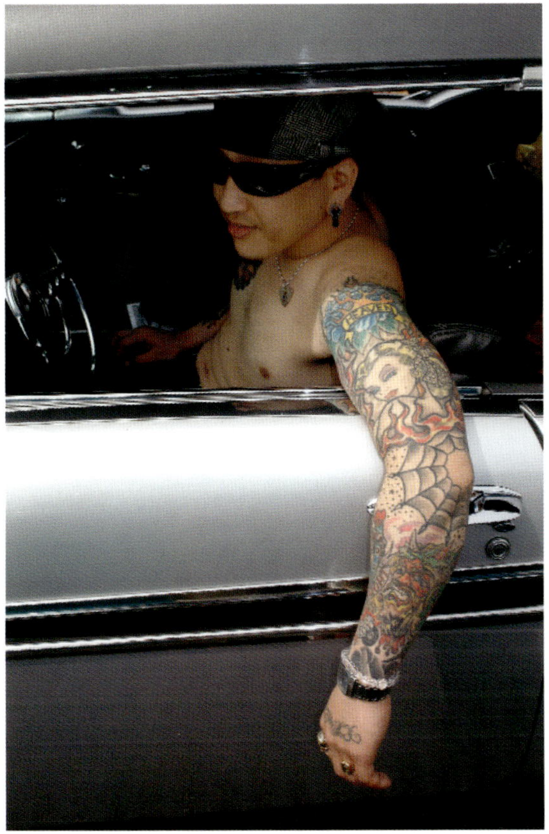

Above: Mazin
Tri-Chevy
Dream Machine Chevy Club
Slow Rollers Car Shop, Shiga

Right: Goshu Okita
Mooneyes

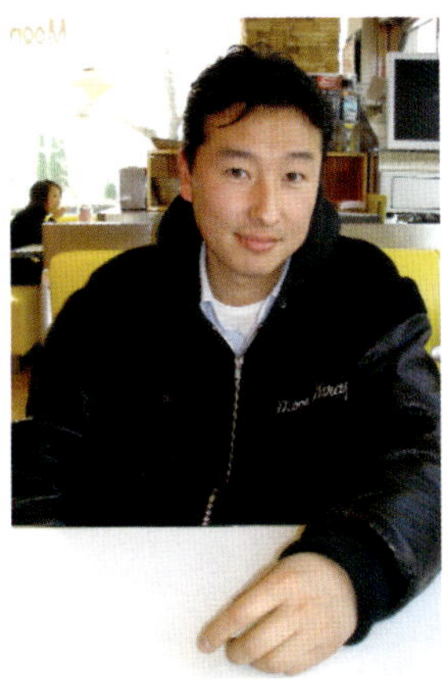

special innovators. My style is different. Maybe it is more detailed and sensitive, being more sensitive and precise, with a Japanese perspective. Maybe there is a different connection with this and the emotions and a deep understanding of communicating with a brush? I always saw Roth's work as combining these elements, and was always impressed with his original work. I always remember seeing this connection in his work and I try to bring it to every piece I do. I have my own perspective, but I always return to a person like Roth for inspiration. This is very important to me. I try to bring it to a different place but I always pay respect to these deep roots."

Goshu Okita is thirty-six years old and has worked at Mooneyes for several years. He was born in Japan but as a teenager lived in Manhattan, New York City and attended high school there. He later retuned to Japan to attend college. He has always been involved in car culture in Japan and has experienced the growing interest in Kustom Kulture.

"During 1985-86 things began to change in Japanese car culture," Goshu said. "Especially in a place like Yokohama. There were many people out in their cars. There is a bridge, the Bay Bridge, between Yokohama and Tokyo. There was always a big cruise weekend meeting on the bridge. All different types of cars. I'd always see the big Mooneyes wall. Important car builders would come to Mooneyes: Roth, Boyd Coddington, David Featherston, Billy Gibbons. I would be the interpreter. It was difficult to explain the whole hot rod thing to my parents. My family has been in the textile industry for three generations. My father thought my interest in cars was strange but trusted that I was getting into something creative. He did not understand but thought I was getting involved in a cultural thing with its own sense of beauty. I would show photos of Kustom Kars to my Dad, and rather than seeing the world of Kustoms as strange, he could see the aesthetics of it—the designs and the traditions, a way of doing something."

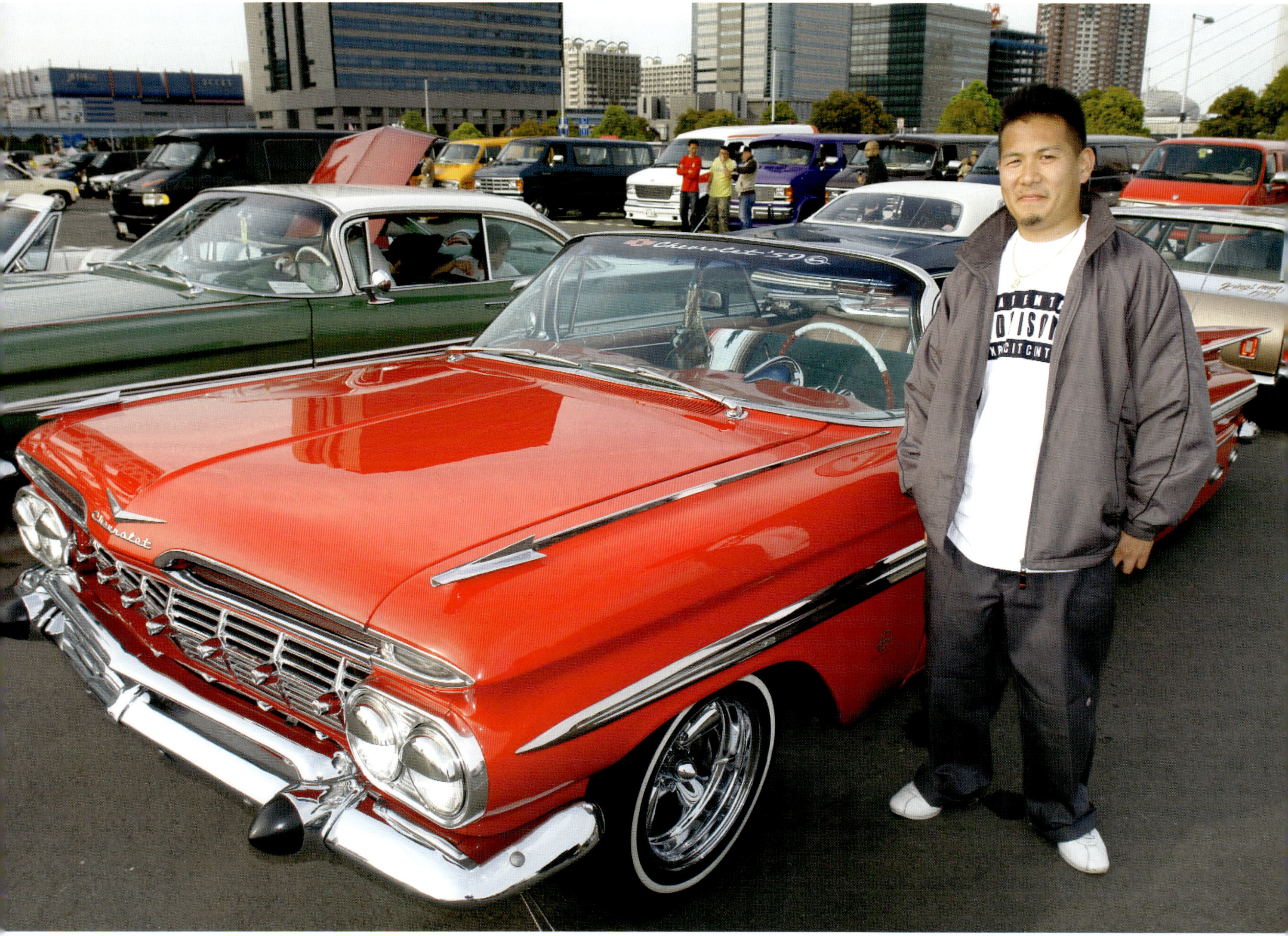
Chevrolet

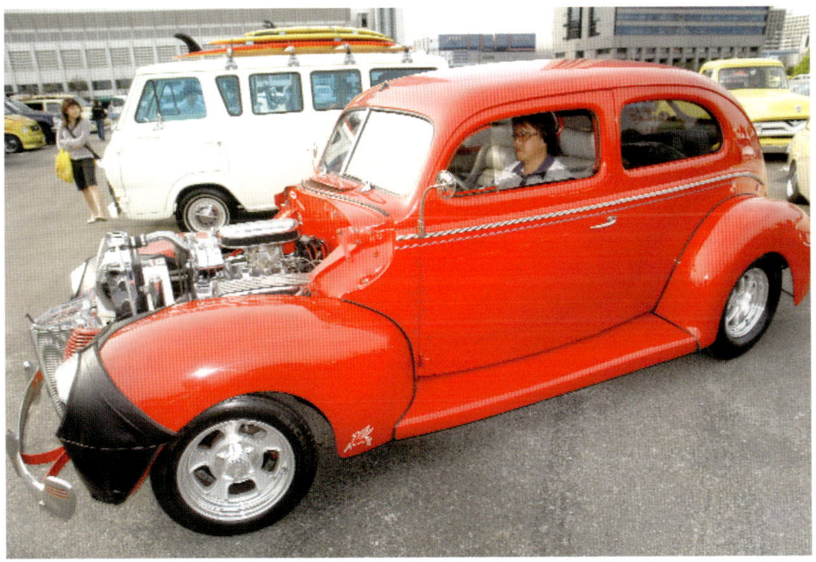

Above: 1940 Ford, 350 V8
Built by Shorty, Pumpkin Sally

Left: 1959 Chevy Impala and owner
"Beauty on a budget"

"My first car was a black, 1969 square box style, full-sized car. It was a gangster car and my friends were amazed. I bought and sold cars for a while. Maybe in one year I would have 200 cars, buying and selling. I was working at Mooneyes trying out as many cars as possible, meeting people. There was a big cruise culture that developed in Yokohama. We'd cruise down to the water. At one time there would be hundreds of cars cruising from the harbor to the Bay Bridge. Then the police started to notice. They had no idea what was going on. What were all these cars and people doing? The whole thing was very strange for them. They started blocking off the streets where people cruised and very quickly this really stopped the cruise culture in Yokohama. There was no place left to go."

"Cruise culture in Yokohama was just about moving around. The whole street would be blocked off with cars. It was spontaneous. You might know the people or maybe not. Yokohama developed a cruise culture, and people would come in from other cities. These days are now remembered nostalgically by car people in Yokohama. Now, every two months, forty to fifty cars come to Mooneyes and then they cruise Yokohama. Some people travel 5 or 6 hours to be a part of this cruise scene. It is becoming more heavily attended. Domestic car cruises are well attended. All the cars have been customized to some degree."

"Car culture has changed in Japan because of the Internet. Before, information flowed differently. There was less information and it was impossible to get updates on what was going on. Now creativity is being shared between East and West. Now, many people come from the West to see the customizing in Japan. There is an openness now and more expression in terms of customizing. There is so much I see in the West and so much I see in Japan. It is shared more easily. This openness is all new and is working to strengthen the whole movement."

「今、こうやって考えてみると、ロスと一緒に時間を過ごして、彼から学ぶことができたのは本当に特別なことだったと思います。そのときはすべてが奇妙でその重要性に気づきませんでしたが…。ロスから学んだ本当に大切なことは、カスタム・カルチャーの魂と感情でした。彼はものごとを前向きに考える人で、その考えを私に譲ってくれました。前向きで力強く、驚くべきメッセージのあるものを描くようにと教えてくれたのです。ロスは、彼のアートの目的は人を幸せにすることだと心から感じていました。彼はそれを教えてくれたんです。」

「ロスは人々が彼のラット・フィンクを見て楽しく思っているのが分かることを示してくれました。これはロスにとって非常に大切なことでした。彼は毎年、カー・ショーにやってきました。ビートニック・バンディットIIをショーに持ってきました。彼の車を見に来る人たちの明るい雰囲気が彼にとって非常に重要でした。私はこれをロスから学んだんです。」

「筆とコミュニケーションをしている感覚、その筆について何か学んでいるような感覚があるのです」とワイルドマンは言う。「それは感情です。感情の伝達は心から手へ、手から筆へと伝わります。日本ではこのプロセスを子供のころから学びます。手と筆を通して、つながりの感覚、そして非常に複雑な観念や感情のコミュニケーションをはかることを学ぶのです。日本のストライパーとして、ペインティングのプロセスについては違った考え方をしているかもしれません。他の日本のストライパーもそうかもしれませんね。」

「ピンストライピングを始めたとき、まず、ずいぶん違うものであることに驚きました。ストロークや流れの違うことに…。まったく異なる筆の使い方です。これを始めたころ、私は英語が話せませんでした。人の車にピンストライプを施したり、文字をペイントするよう頼まれましたが、英語の文字は私にとって何の意味もなしませんでした。ただデザインとして見ていただけです。ちょうど西洋人が漢字を見るようなものです。そして新しい筆とスタイルに慣れなければなりませんでした。ピンストライピングは私にとってすべて非常に抽象的なものでした。」

「ヴォンダッチはカスタム・カルチャーの魂でしょうね…。彼のペインティングは単なる線ではありません。ロスとヴォンダッチはペイントに魂をもたらしました。ロスは私にダッチの作品は伝説的だといつも言っていました。ロスが本当にダッチを尊敬していたのがよく分かりました。ペインティングだけではなくて、車のアートとそのカルチャー全体に対して彼が行ったことに対してです。もしダッチがいなくて車にペインティングをやらなかったとしたら、カスタム・カルチャーに対する感覚はまったく違ったものになっていたと、ロス同様、私も感じています。」

「ヴォンダッチについては25年以上も前に本で初めて見ました。それには数枚の写真と歴史について書かれていました。これを見てこのアートとカルチャーには深さがあることが分かってきました。歴史とある特定の人々の個性がアートを創ってきたのです。彼らはアーティストであり、イノベーターでした。何年も前のあのころ、私はロスとヴォンダッチが彼らのアートのために創り出したプロセスに強く惹かれました。でも日本でこんなにたくさんのピンストライパーが生まれるとは思いもしませんでした。多くの人々にこんなに興味を持ってもらっていることに驚いています。それまで日本では見られないものでしたし、誰もそれが何か知りませんでしたからね。」

「スタイルには色々あります。ヴォンダッチとトミー・ザ・グリークは特別なイノベーターでした。私のスタイルは違います。もっとディテールがあって繊細な感じでしょうか。日本的観点があって、より精密です。精度と感情のつながりに何か違いがあるのでしょうか？ 筆とのコミュニケーションへの

"To me, a Japanese artist like Wildman is part of this continuum of heart of Kustom Kulture. Mooneyes and the cruise nights and swap meets and the Tokyo Street Car Nationals are a big part of this too. These connections from Von Dutch to Roth to an artist like Wildman say so much about our world today. A sharing of ideas and styles and tastes."

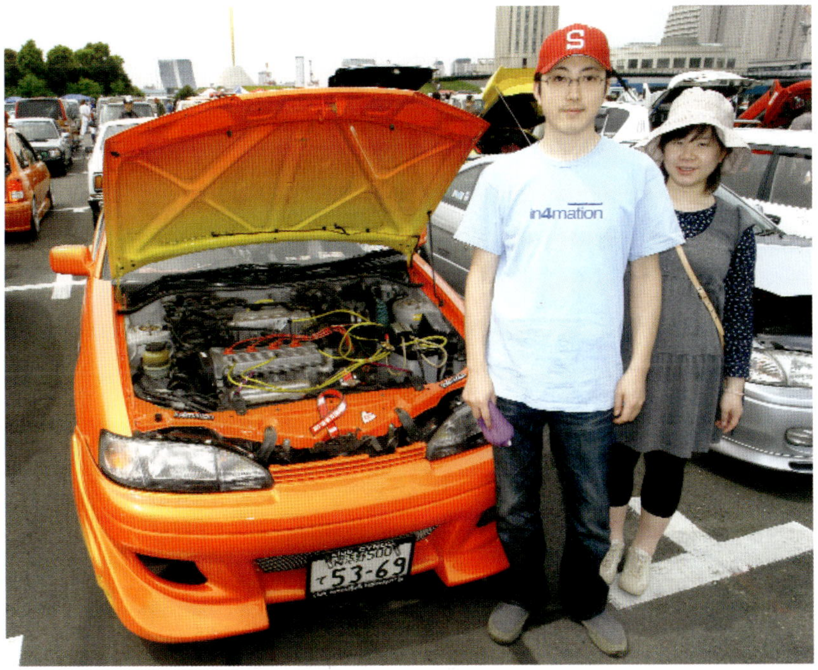

Toshihiko Endo and wife Junko
1995 Toyota Cynos
Engine stock Japan, re-wired Delco

The Mooneyes Tokyo Street Car Nationals event has brought together an assortment of people who feel the urge to go public with their car enthusiasm. Parked in orderly rows of taped off car-sized rectangles, owners are relaxed and open to the possibility of sharing their unique stories. Toshihiko Endo and his wife Junko stand quietly next to their custom painted, orange glitter-flake 1995 Toyota Cynos. They have driven to the show from the Gyotoku area in Chiba Prefecture, and Toshi is quick to mention that their Cynos was also sold in America, where it is called the Paseo. They go to swap meets once a month within a two-hour radius of the Tokyo-Yokohama area to visit with friends old and new and to talk about cars.

Inside the couple's car, across the dash top, is an assortment of shiny level gauges tilted towards the driver's position: vacuum pressure, oil pressure, water and oil temperature. Toshi explains that he occasionally adds a new gauge as a cosmetic and fashion statement. He would buy new wheels if he could and has his eye on a set of four TSW Rocket wheels that are made in the U.S. If he lived in America he would add these wheels and, therefore, would like to add them here in Japan. This association and blending with the United States is important to him.

"I like to compare the USDM (United States Domestic Market) with the JDM (Japanese Domestic Market)," Toshi says. "My friends and I spend a lot of time comparing and analyzing the differences between the specifics of each market, and many Japanese domestic car people we know intentionally change parts in their cars from

深い理解でしょうか？ 精度と感情の組み合わせは自然なものです。ロスの作品にも常にこれらの要素が組み合わされていることを知っていましたし、ロスのオリジナルの作品にはいつも感銘を受けていました。ロスの作品にこのつながりがあることをいつも思い出し、それを自分の全作品にも活かそうとしています。私には私自身の観点がありますが、いつもロスのような人の所に戻り、インスピレーションを得るのです。これは私にとって非常に大切なことです。異なる場所に行こうともしますが、いつもこれらの深い根源に対して敬意を持っているのです。」

Goshu 大喜多は 36 歳。ムーンアイズで何年も働いてきた。日本生まれだが、10 代のころニューヨーク市のマンハッタンに住み、ハイスクールに通学。その後、帰国して日本の大学に在籍した。これまで常に日本のカー・カルチャーに携わってきた彼は、カスタム・カルチャーに対する興味が膨らんでいくのを目の当たりにしてきた。

1985 年から 86 年の間に、日本のカー・カルチャーに変化が起こり出しました」と Goshu は語る。「横浜のような場所ではこれは特に顕著でした。自分の車で出かける人がたくさんいましたから。横浜と東京の間にベイブリッジという橋があります。週末には橋の上で大きなクルーズ・ミーティングがありました。いろんなタイプの車でね。いつもムーンアイズの大きな壁が見えました。重要なカー・ビルダーはみんなムーンアイズを訪問します。ロス、ボイド・コディントン、デイビッド・フェザーストン、ビリー・ギボンズ。そういうときには私が通訳をやります。でもこういうホットロッドのことを自分の親に説明するのはむずかしいですね。私の家族は 3 世代にわたって織物の産業に携わってきました。父の目には変なものに映ったようでしたが、何かクリエイティブなことに関わっているのだと私を信頼してくれました。彼には理解できませんでしたが、私が何か独特の美的センスのある文化的なものに関与しているのだと思ってくれたのです。父にカスタム・カーの写真を見せると、カスタムの世界が変なものと思うのではなく、その美的感覚の方を見てくれます。デザインや伝統、そのやり方ですね。」

「私の最初の車は、四角いスタイルの 1969 年の黒い大型車でした。暴力団風の車で、友達を驚かせたものです。しばらくの間、車の売買をやっていました。ある年には 200 台持っていたこともあります。私はムーンアイズで働きながら、できる限りたくさんの車を試し、色々な人に会いました。そして横浜では大きなクルーズ・カルチャーが生まれました。みんなで水辺まで運転していくのです。ときには何百台もの車が港からベイブリッジまでクルーズしていることもありました。しばらくすると警察がこれに気づきましたが、いったい何か起こっているのか検討がつかないようでした…。こんなにたくさんの車と人がいったい何をやっているのか？ 警察にとってはすべてが奇異に見えたはずです。やがて警察がクルーズする道路を封鎖し始め、これで横浜でのクルーズ・カルチャーはあっという間に終わってしまいました。他に行き場はありませんでした。」

「横浜のクルーズ・カルチャーは、ただ動き回るだけでした。道路全体が車で埋まり、動けなくなりました。まったくの自然発生です。顔見知りの人ばかりだったり、まったくの初対面の人ばかりだったりということもありました。横浜で生まれたクルーズ・カルチャーには、他の街からも人がやってきました。横浜の車ファンは、今、あのときのことを懐かしく思い出します。現在は、2 ヵ月おきに 40 台から 50 台の車がムーンアイズにやってきて、それから横浜をクルーズします。ムーンアイズは朝に 40 〜 50 台の国産車でクルーズをやっています。このクルーズ・シーンに参加するために 5 〜 6 時間運転して来る人もいます。参加者の数はすごく多くなってきました。国産車のクルーズにはたくさんの方が参加しています。車はなんらかの形でカスタマイズされたものばかりです。」

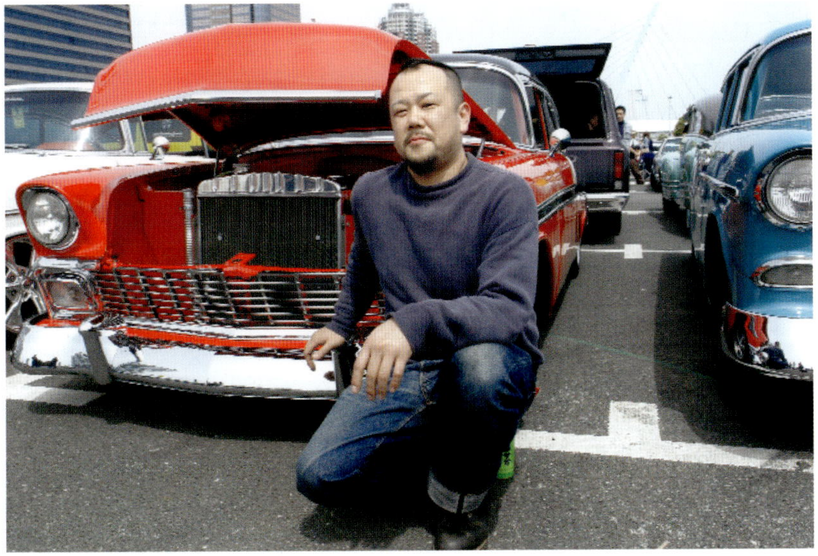

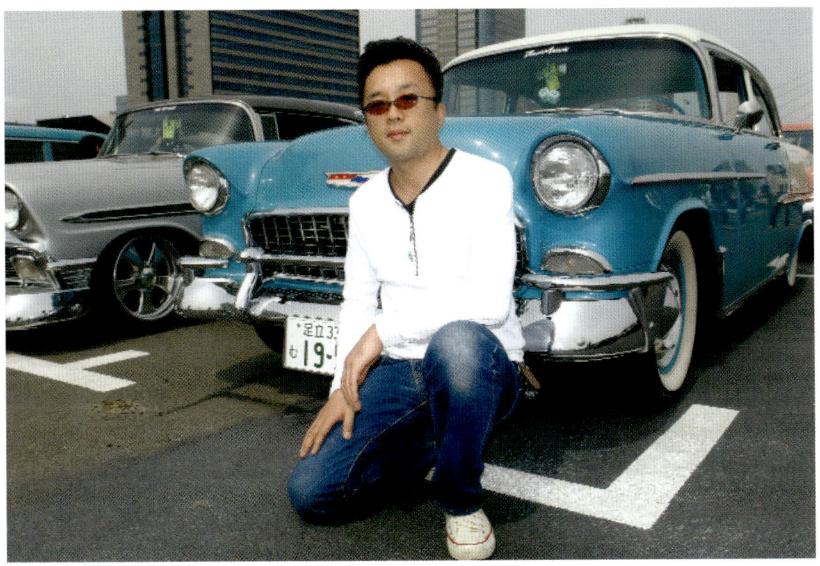

Top: Yoshinori Yokoto
1956 Tri-Chevy 350 ZZ4 engine
Dream Machine Chevy Club
Slow Rollers Car Shop, Shiga

Bottom: Yoshiki Kudo
1955 Tri-Chevy, Stock 350 V8
Dream Machine Chevy Club
Slow Rollers Car Shop, Shiga

Japanese to American. They rework, rewire or replace their stock Japanese engine component packages, adding American parts because of the cultural associations. They are attracted to this replacement of parts because they feel the addition of 'American made' on a Japanese car looks good. It is like wearing some fashion clothing made in America. We feel it is important to interact with this type of American culture."

"The engine is the heart of the car. We do not change our engines but keep them original. They are just like our hearts, Japanese. The wiring is like the nervous system of the car. We change these systems to American made to be just as we feel our minds have been changed by American influences. I have many friends that have done this to their cars. It can get deep."

Yoshinori Yokota stands quietly next to his 1956 Chevy Bel Air that is painted a rich blood red with a black top. He points at the paint and holds his left index finger and thumb a couple inches apart in a gesture of thickness saying the word "Thick." He pops the hood and reveals the classic street rod 350 ZZ4 Chevy small lock engine inside. The engine and everything around it look like a museum presentation. It represents an esoteric rebalancing of Chevy engineering strategies and innovation that included new cylinder, piston, lifter and camshaft designs producing an impressive 355 horsepower. "This is a very special engine," Yoshi says. "It is very important for me to put this classic engine into my car. The old rule said one cubic inch to one horsepower. In 1955, Chevy changed this rule with this new small block V8 engine. This engine was a new system from the old Chevy in-line 6 'Blue Flame' that produced only 123 horsepower. The 1955, '56, '57 Bel Air 'Shoe Box Trio' is called Tri-Chevy. I have always wanted to own this car."

There are a half dozen classic '50s Tri-Chevys parked together near Yoshi's car. The owners are all members of the Dream Machine

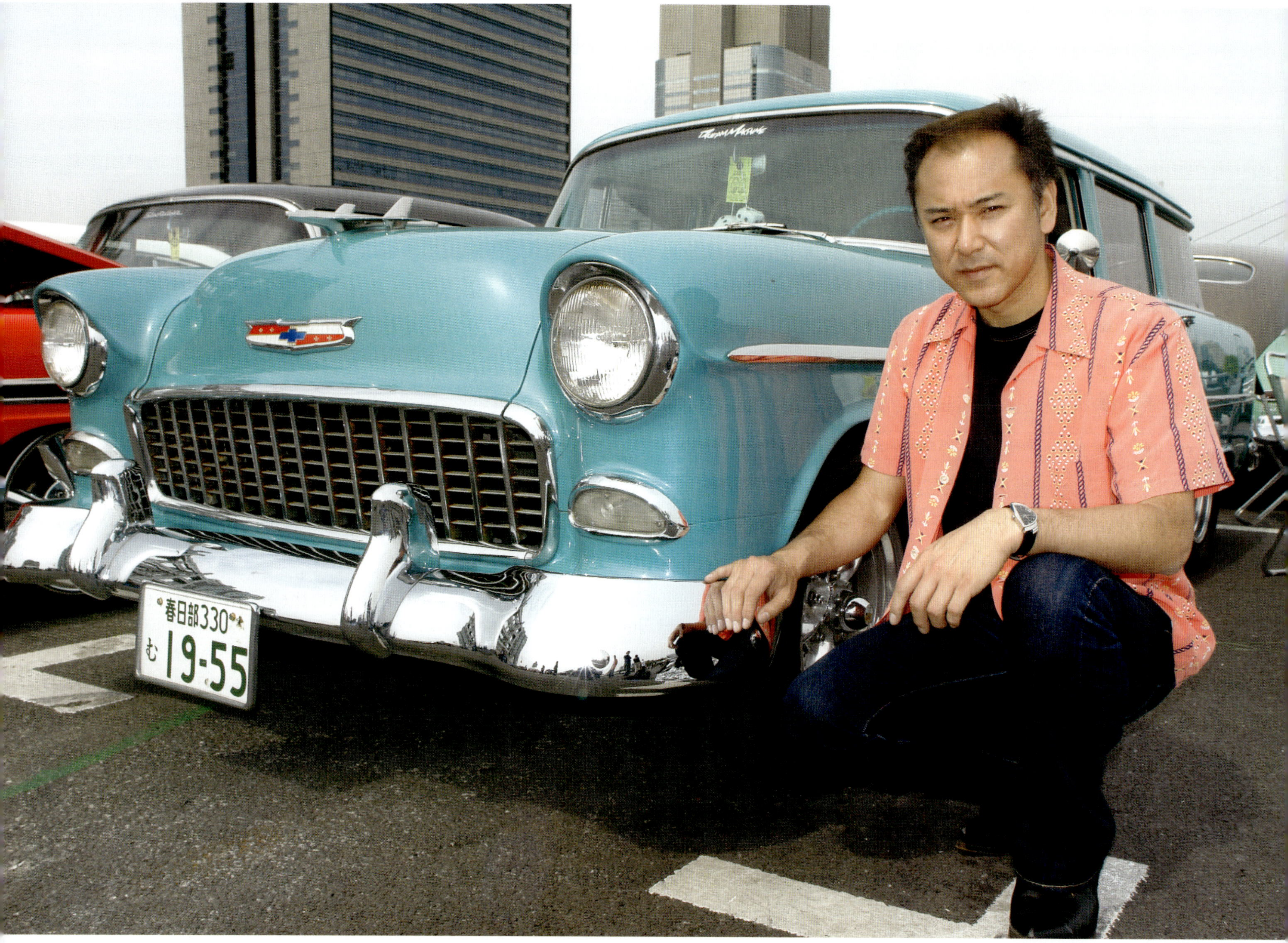
春日部330
む 19-55

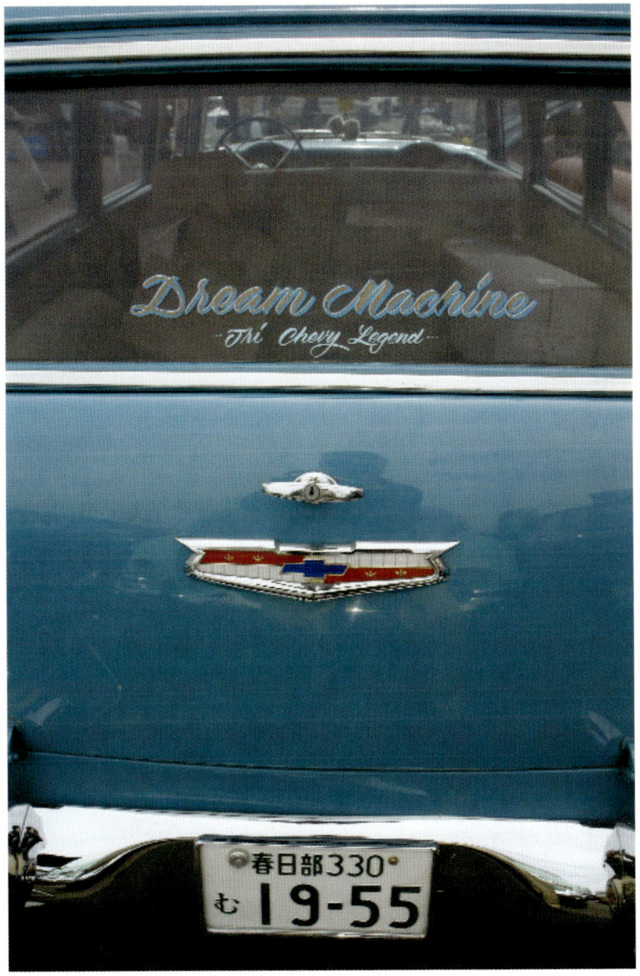

Above: Kazutoshi Yamada's rear window lettering

Left: Kazutoshi Yamada
1955 Tri-Chevy wagon, 350 V8, special package
Club King, Dream Machine Chevy Club

Chevy Club and many have their club name painted on rear windows in stylized letters. They are associated with the Slow Rollers Car Shop located near Kyoto in the city of Shiga. The club king Kazutoshi Yamada stands next to his turquoise blue 1955 Chevy Bel Air wagon talking with his club members. "This car has a 350 V8 with a special package," he says. "I have owned it for two years. When I bought it, the car needed a lot of work. I worked on it every day for two years. I liked the design, and I liked the car. That's why I bought it. '55 was an interesting year for these cars. Chevy changed the style of things. When you look at 1954 Chevy and 1955 Chevy they look so different. This design has something I cannot describe. It just has this something that is special. It looks like history. I live in Saitama. I feel very smooth and very fast when I drive this car. I work on this car, and I know this car. I drive it to four car shows every year with my club. It is very important for me to drive my car. We have had our club for ten years and we all feel the same. We need to drive our cars."

Yoshiki Kudo lives in Tokyo and has owned his 1955 Tri-Chevy for a year. "Some Japanese people see me drive my car and ask why?" He says."I like American culture. When I was sixteen, I saw the movie *American Graffiti.* I had this feeling about the movie and the cars and the culture. I don't know why but I felt this connection. This car is a Tri-Chevy Bel Air classic American muscle car. It is sharper and lower. It has the 'egg crate' grill. I bought this car in Japan. I drive around Tokyo and feel such satisfaction. It is a very simple feeling of happiness. The most impressive culture I know is 1950s American culture. It feels very shiny to me. This period is very strong and very impressive. I drive through the streets of Tokyo and feel complete. I feel like I am driving in the 1950s, but I was born in 1962. My Mom and Dad met in the 1950s and I think this period is in my blood. It is a part of me. I feel very smooth and fast when I drive the car. I drive my car every day. It is important to drive my car."

「日本のカー・カルチャーはインターネットによって変化しました。昔は情報は違った形で流れていました。情報量も少なく、何が起こっているかを知ることは不可能でした。今では西洋と東洋でクリエイティビティを共有しています。西洋から多数の人が日本のカスタマイズを見に来ます。今はオープンで、カスタマイズの表現がもっと多様になっています。西洋にも日本にも見るものがたくさんあります。共有することがより簡単になりました。こういうオープンさは最近のことで、運動全体を強化するために機能しています。」

「私にとって、日本のような場所では、ワイルドマンのようなアーティストはカスタム・カルチャー中核の流れの一部です。ムーンアイズ、クルーズ・ナイト、スワップ・ミート、そしてストリート・カー・ナショナルズも、その大きな一部をなしています。ヴォンダッチからロス、そしてワイルドマンのようなアーティスト。これらのつながりは今日の世界を明確に表しています。アイデアやスタイルや趣味の共有ですね。」

ムーンアイズのストリート・カー・ナショナルズ in 東京は、車に対する情熱をみんなに知らせたいという強い気持ちを抱くさまざまな人々を呼び集めた。車のサイズに合わせてテープで区切られた場所にきちんと駐車し、オーナーはくつろいだ様子で、各自のユニークな話を分かち合おうとする。遠藤俊彦と妻のジュンコはオレンジ色のグリター・フレークをカスタム塗装した 1995 年トヨタ・サイノスの横に静かに立っている。2 人は千葉県行徳地区から運転してショーにやって来た。トシはサイノスがアメリカでも販売されていること、アメリカではパセオと呼ばれていることを間髪入れずに教えてくれた。彼らは東京・横浜地域の車で 2 時間の範囲のスワップ・ミートへ毎月 1 回行き、昔からの友達や新しい人たちに会い、車について話をすると言う。

このカップルの車の中を見ると、ダッシュボードの上に色々な光沢のあるレベル・ゲージがドライバー席に向けて備え付けられている。真空圧力、ハイドロ、水温、油温などの計測器だ。トシは新しいゲージを装飾やファッションの目的でときどき付け加えるのだと説明する。できれば新しいホイールも購入したくて、4 本 1 組の米国製 TSW ロケット・ホイールに目をつけている。仮にアメリカに住んでいたとしたらこのホイールを付けるだろうから、ここ日本でも取り付けたいのだそうだ。このアメリカとのつながりや融合が彼にとって重要だと言う。

「USDM（米国国産市場）と JDM（日本国国産市場）を比べるのが好きですね」とトシは言う。「私は友達とそれぞれの市場の仕様の違いを比較分析することに長い時間を費やし、日本国産車を持つ多くの知り合いは自分の車の部品を意図的に日本のものからアメリカのものに変えたりします。市販の日本製エンジン部品セットを再加工・再配線・交換などし、文化的な関連性を求めてアメリカの部品を加えます。彼らはこのような部品の交換に魅力を感じているのです。日本車にアメリカ製のものを加えるのはカッコいいものです。ちょうどアメリカ製のファッション衣料を着ているようなものです。このようなタイプのアメリカ文化との交流が大切だと感じています。」

「エンジンは車の心臓部なので変えずに元のままにしておきます。ちょうど私たちの心臓と同じで、日本人のままです。配線は車の神経系のようなものです。このシステムをアメリカ製のものに取り換えます。まるで私たちの心がアメリカの影響を受けて変わったような感じがします。私の友達でこれをやった人がたくさんいます。奥は深いのです。」

横田ヨシノリは、リッチなボディを濃い赤、屋根を黒く塗装した 1956 年シェビー・ベルエアの横に言葉少なに佇んでいる。彼はペイントを指差し、左手の人差し指と親指を 5 cm ほどの間隔に開くジェスチャーで、「Thick（分厚い）」と伝える。ボンネットを開いて、その中にあるクラシックなストリートロッド 350 ZZ4 シェビー小型ロックエンジンを見せて

Towards the end of the afternoon, people begin to tidy the aprons around their cars. As if a silent alarm has sounded, lawn chairs are folded, sun umbrellas retracted and coolers stowed. Two young men parked next to each other, in Fords that have come to symbolize the decade they were produced in America, seem to be in no rush to leave. They pause at the impressive reverberation of the hundreds of cars that are simultaneously turning the starter keys, but make no move to call it a day.

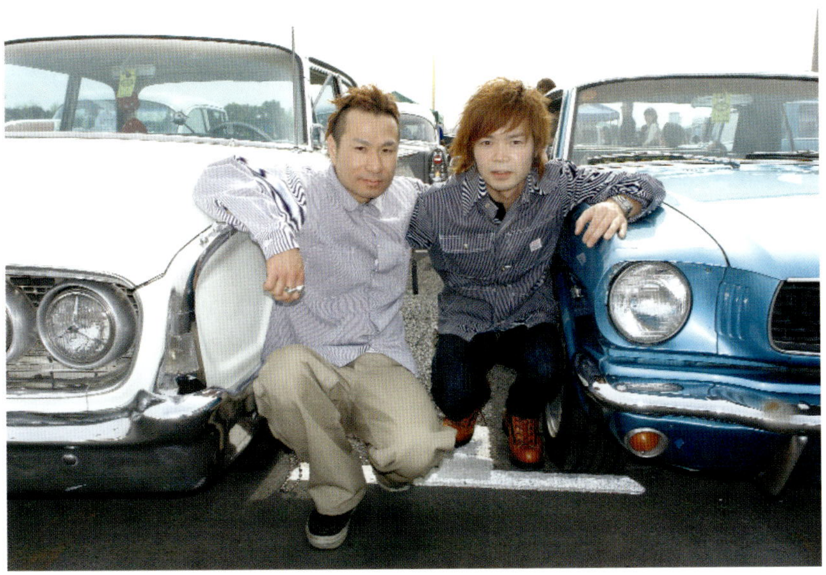

L-R: Mitsuru Baba, 1960 Ford Fairlane, 352 V8
Murone Yoshihiro, 1966 Ford Mustang, 289 V8

One, Murone Yoshihiro, is twenty-eight years old with wispy hair that is tinted blondish and falls across his forehead L.A. beach-boy style. He kneels at the grill of his crystal blue '66 Mustang hard top polishing the iconic Mustang horse ornament. Mitsuru Baba is about the same age and stands next to his cream colored 1960 Fairlane two-door listening to the rumble of engines that surround them. "I'm in service; he's in sales—look at his hair," Mitsuru says with a chuckle. "We both work at the same Ford dealership here in Tokyo. My car has a 352 V8. I bought it four years ago. I like this tail-fin style. It is very special. 1960 was the last with this look. This is important to me. I love Fords, and my life is about working on them. I went to Ford school for 2 years, and I studied. Now I am Ford. Fords are different cars: they look different and move different and sound different."

Murone points behind the Mustang horse grill and describes his engine. "This car has a classic Ford 289 V8 stock engine package. I have owned this car for three years. I bought it in Yokohama. I always like Ford Mustangs. I sell Fords because I like Fords. This galloping horse is a special car idea. I look at my grill horse, and I think about freedom. When I drive my car I like to think about this horse running. I think about where this horse has run. I have never seen America, but I want to drive to these places where this horse has run."

くれた。エンジンとその周りにあるすべては、まるで博物館の展示のようだ。シェビーのエンジニアリング戦略と革新の再バランスを試み、新しいシリンダー、ピストン、リフター、カムシャフトの設計などで、力強い355馬力を出す。「これは非常に特殊なエンジンです」とヨシは言う。「このクラシックなエンジンを自分の車に入れることが私にとっては非常に大切です。古いルールでは1馬力に対して1立方インチと言っていました。1955年、新しい小型ブロックV8エンジンでシェビーはこのルールを変えました。このエンジンは、123馬力しか出ない古いシェビーのインライン6"ブルーフレーム"からの新しいシステムです。トライシェビーと呼ばれる1955年、56年、57年のベルエア"シューボックス・トリオ"。私はずっとこの車が欲しかったんです。」

ヨシの車の近くには6台の50年代クラシック・トライシェビーが駐車している。オーナーは全員がドリーム・マシーン・シェビー・クラブのメンバーで、その多くにはクラブの名前が後部の窓に図案化した文字で書かれている。彼らは滋賀県にあるスローローラーズ・カー・ショップと親交がある。クラブのリーダー、山田和利は、ターコイズ・ブルーの1955年シェビー・ベルエア・ワゴンの横に立ち、クラブ・メンバーと話をしている。「この車は特殊なパッケージの350 V8を備えています」と彼は言う。「2年間所有しています。買ったときには手入れが色々と必要で、2年にわたって毎日修理しました。このデザインが好きで、この車が気に入って買いました。こういう車にとって55年は面白い年でした。シェビーはスタイルを変えたのです。1954年のシェビーと1955年のシェビーは、すごく見た感じが変わりました。このデザインは口では言い表せない何かがあります。特別な何かです。歴史とでもいいましょうか。私は埼玉に住んでいます。この車を運転すると非常にスムーズで非常に速いですね。私は自分でこの車を修理して、この車について隅々まで知っています。クラブの連中と毎年4つのカー・ショーにこの車を運転して行きます。自分の車を運転することは私にとってとても大切なことです。クラブは創設以来もう10年になりますが、みんな同じように感じています。私たちは自分の車を運転する必要があるのです。」

東京在住の工藤ヨシキは、1955年トライシェビーを所有して1年になる。「私が自分の車を運転していると、なぜそんな車を運転しているのか聞く日本人がいます」と彼は言う。「私はアメリカ文化が気に入っています。16歳のとき、映画『アメリカン・グラフィティ』を見ました。あの映画と車と文化に感じるところがありました。なぜそんなつながりを感じたのかよく分かりません。この車はトライシェビー・ベルエア。クラシックなアメリカのマッスル・カーです。車体がもっとシャープで低くなっています。"エッグクレート・グリル"が付いているんですよ。この車は日本で買いました。東京の街中をドライブしますが本当に満足感があります。シンプルな幸せっていう感じですね。」

「最も印象的だと思う文化は1950年代のアメリカ文化です。それは私にとって本当に輝いているような気がします。この時代は非常に強くて印象的だと思いますね。東京の道路を運転していると、自分が完璧な気がします。1950年代に運転しているような気分になります。でも私が生まれたのは1962年です。両親が出会ったのが1950年代でしたから、あの時代の血が私の中で流れているのでしょうか。まるで体の一部なんです。この車は毎日運転しています。運転していると自分が非常にスムーズで速いと感じます。この車を運転することは大切なのです。」

午後も終わりに近づくころ、参加者は各自の車の周りを片付け始めた。まるで音の聞こえない警報がなったかのように、ローン・チェアや日よけのパラソルがたたまれ、アイスボックスがしまい込まれる。だがアメリカで製造された年代を代表するようになったフォードを隣同士で停めている若い2人には、急いで帰ろうとする気配はない。何百台の車が同時にイグニッション・キーを回す印象的な残響に一瞬沈黙するが、切り上げようとするそぶりを見せない。

室根由寛は28歳。ブロンドがかった色に染めた細長い髪はLAのビーチボーイ風に額に垂れている。彼はクリスタルブルーの66年マスタング・ハードトップのグリルの前にひざまずき、マスタングを象徴する馬のオーナメントを磨いている。馬場ミツルも同じくらいの年齢で、クリーム・カラーの1960年フェアレーン2ドアの横に立ち、周りのエンジンの轟音に耳を澄ましている。「私は修理で、彼は販売をやっています。あの髪の毛を見てやって！」とミツルはクスクス笑いながら言う。「2人とも東京の同じフォード特約店で働いています。私の車は352 V8搭載で、4年前に買いました。テールフィンが気に入っています。すごく独特のものです。こういう外観は1960年が最後でした。これが私にとって大切なのです。フォードが大好きで、フォードで作業をすることが自分の生き甲斐です。フォードの学校に2年通って勉強しました。今は自分がフォードです。フォードは一味違う車です。見た感じも運転した感じも、音も違います。」

室根はマスタング・ホースのグリルの後ろを指差し、エンジンについて説明する。「この車は代表的なフォード289　V8市販エンジン・パッケージを搭載しています」と彼は言う。「この車は3年所有しています。横浜で買いました。ずっとフォード・マスタングが気に入っていました。フォードが好きだから売っているのです。このギャロップしている馬に特別な意味があります。このグリルの馬を見ると自由について考えるのです。この車を運転するとき、馬が走っていること、そしてその場所を想像します。実際にアメリカを見たことはありませんが、この馬が走ったような場所を運転してみたいですね。」

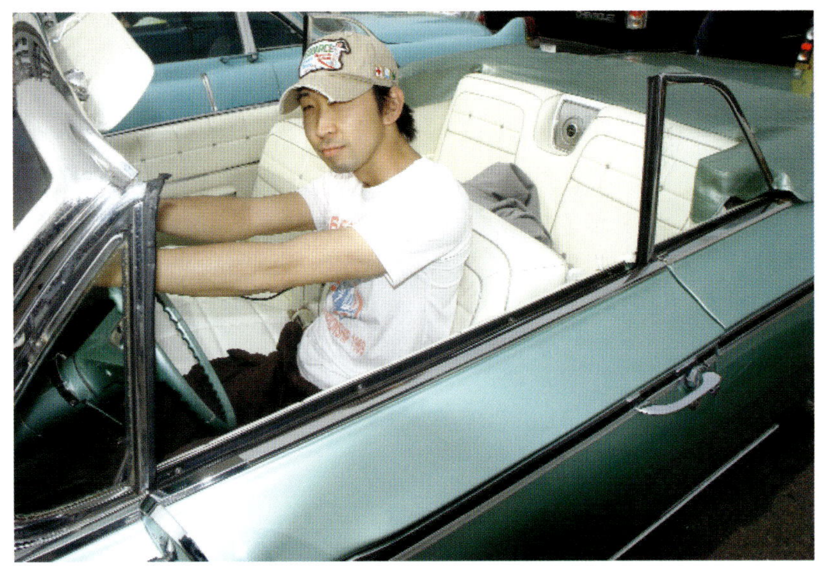

Chevy Impala

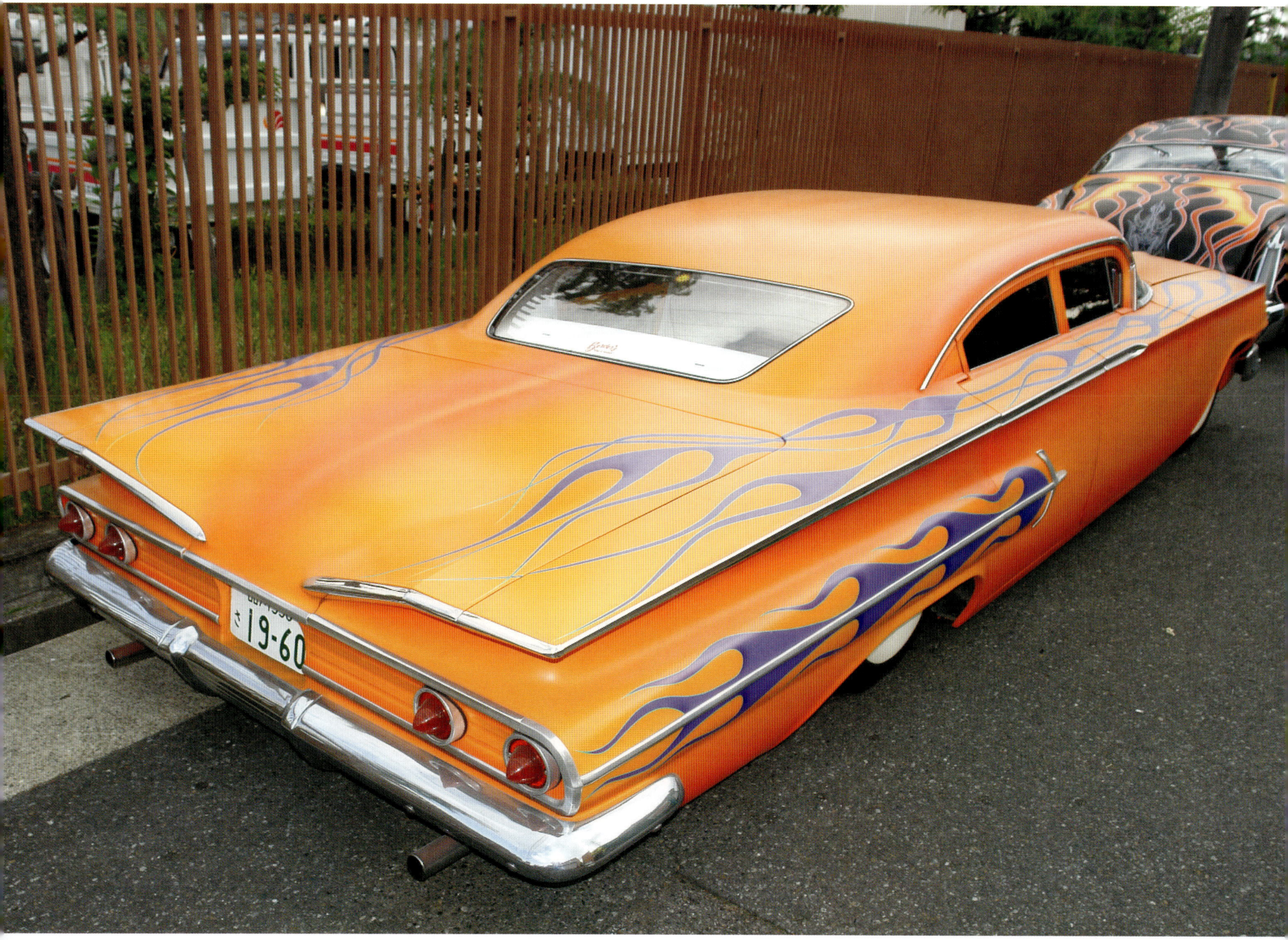
さ 19-60

Chapter Three:
Kustom Kar Builders

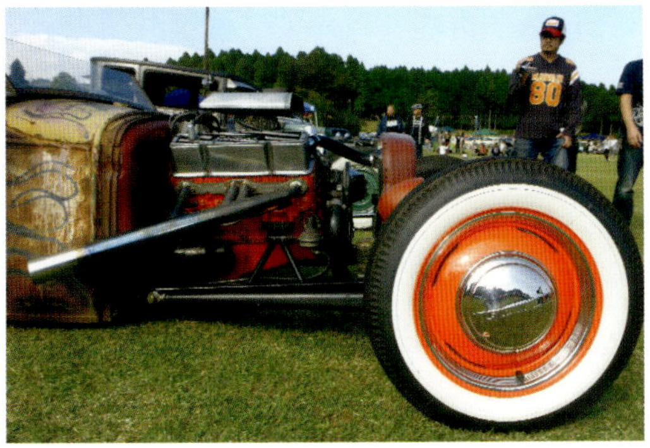

Left: 1960 Bel Air Chevy
Built by Border's Nagoya

There are custom car builders and customizers throughout Japan who have cultivated noteworthy reputations working on automobiles. Some geographical areas focus on specific looks, car makes and models or styles associated with nostalgic periods of time. Most, if not all, of the cars that are worked on and modified are American in origin. Some of the Japanese builders shadow styles and decision-making rationales standardized over the years in American custom car culture, while others integrate new concepts that reflect uniquely Japanese-inspired innovations. custom car customers everywhere seek out both standardized and novel artistic sensibilities and the builders who can produce them. There are lineages of innovation, style and ability traced to historic builders like George and Sam Barris, Joe Bailon, the Ayala Brothers, Gene Winfield, Bill Cushenberry, Darryl Starbird, Ed Roth and Von Dutch or, to more recent innovators, Chip Foose, Larry Ericson and Thom Taylor.

Because of distance, language difficulty and an inability to access information, builders in Japan may be unaware of historical connections to individual kustom innovators in America. This sense of isolation has been minimized recently due to the Internet, but it still exists. Among many builders and collectors, artistic sensibilities have been formed through a different dynamic of information exchange. Rather than experiencing a satisfying or defining nostalgic association based on knowledge about legendary American car builders or deeply esthetic appreciations about Chevy or Ford engine efficiency and power, Japanese kustom builders and their customers might trace their likes or dislikes of car makes or models, engine packages or customizing techniques to an image of a car they saw as kids in movies like *Two Lane Black Top*, *Grease*, *American Graffiti* or the popular American 1970s TV show *Happy Days*.

The power of a nostalgic statement, whether a hair or clothing style,

カスタム・カー・ビルダー

今日、日本中に車への仕事ぶりで大きな評判を得ているカスタム・カー・ビルダーやカスタマイザーがいる。地域によってはある特定の時代のノスタルジックな外観や型式、モデル、スタイルを専門にしているところもある。手を加えたり改造する基になる車は、ほぼすべてアメリカ製だ。日本のビルダーには、アメリカで年月を経て標準化されたカスタム・カー・カルチャーの様式や意思決定の論理的根拠に忠実な者もいれば、日本独自の着想による革新を反映させた新しいコンセプトを取り入れる者もいる。各地のカスタム・カーの顧客は、それぞれの嗜好を反映したスタイルを求め、そしてそれを作り出せるビルダーを求めている。日本のビルダーには、ジョージとサム・バリス、ジョー・ベイロン、アヤラ・ブラザーズ、ジーン・ウィンフィールド、ビル・クッシェンベリー、ダリル・スターバード、エド・ロス、ヴォンダッチのような歴史的ビルダー、またもっと最近のイノベーターとしてチップ・フース、ラリー・エリクソン、トム・テイラーらに連なる改革、様式、能力の系譜がある。

地理的距離、言葉の壁、情報入手の困難さなどの問題によって、日本のビルダーはアメリカの個々のカスタム・イノベーターとの歴史的な関連性を知らないことが多い。このような知識の孤立は、インターネットの発展により近年ずいぶん少なくなったが、未だ存在している。多くのビルダーとコレクターの芸術的感性は、異なる情報入手手段を介して形成されてきた。つまり、日本のカスタム・ビルダーとその顧客は、アメリカの伝説のカー・ビルダーについてや、シェビーやフォード・エンジンの効率や馬力に対する深い美的評価について懐かしむ体験からではなく、子供のころに見た『トゥー・レーン・ブラックトップ』、『グリース』、『アメリカン・グラフィティ』などの映画、あるいは1970年代に人気があったアメリカのテレビ番組『ハッピー・デイズ』などの車のイメージから、型式やモデル、エンジン・パッケージ、カスタマイズ・テクニックの好き嫌いを決めている可能性がある。

ノスタルジックな表現の力は、それが髪型や服装のスタイル、歌、車のモデルなどのいずれであっても、歴史との神秘的かつ熟考された対話を形作っている。今日の私たちの世界は、過去からのわかりやすいリファレンスや力強い連想を再編集した、流動的なコラージュのようなものである。クラシック・カー、カスタム・カー、ホットロッドを中心に展開するパフォーマンスと観衆の感覚は、ノスタルジックな表現を活性化させ、新しい形の視覚的威厳を生み出す。しかし、日本のカー・ビルダーは、取り入れれば効果的な車のデザインを作り出せるはずの歴史的リファレンスの認識は曖昧だ。彼らはそれよりも想像と現実の両面から風変わりな様式的表現を試し、独自の認識プロセスを基にした美を主張しているのだ。

日本のカー・ビルダーと車の愛好家は、この特殊な認識プロセスを介し、影響を受けたさまざまな名称やイメージの組み合わせを選ぶことによって、自分が誰であるかを明確にしようとする。車に対する美的感覚は、マスコミが伝えるスタイルやテーマ、あるいはアメリカのさまざまな地域で人種、民族、社会的階級からもたらされる広範な問題と、そこから発生したスタイルによって今も形成されている。静岡のBat Mobileなど、日本のビルダーのなかにも、カー・カルチャーの持つ伝統的および民族的なつながりに重点を置く者もいる。Bat Mobileとは、1966年のテレビ番組『バットマン』で使用された、あこがれのカスタム・デザイナー、ジョージ・バリスが設計した車だ。ショップの名刺と雑誌広告には"Complimento en Vivo! Kustoms and Low lows"と書かれており、南カリフォルニアのメキシカン・ローライダー・スタイルに敬意を表している。そのグラフィックには、ソンブ

a song or a car model, forms a mysterious, but deliberate, dialogue with history. Today our world represents a fluid, re-edited collage of recognizable historical references and statements with powerful associations. A sense of performance and audience revolves around classic, custom and hot rod cars that energizes this history and creates a new form of visual prestige. Car builders in Japan have a mixed awareness about the historical references that combine to create an effective car design. They are experimenting with an exotic stylistic language that is both imagined and real, and they create statements of beauty based on their unique process of recognition.

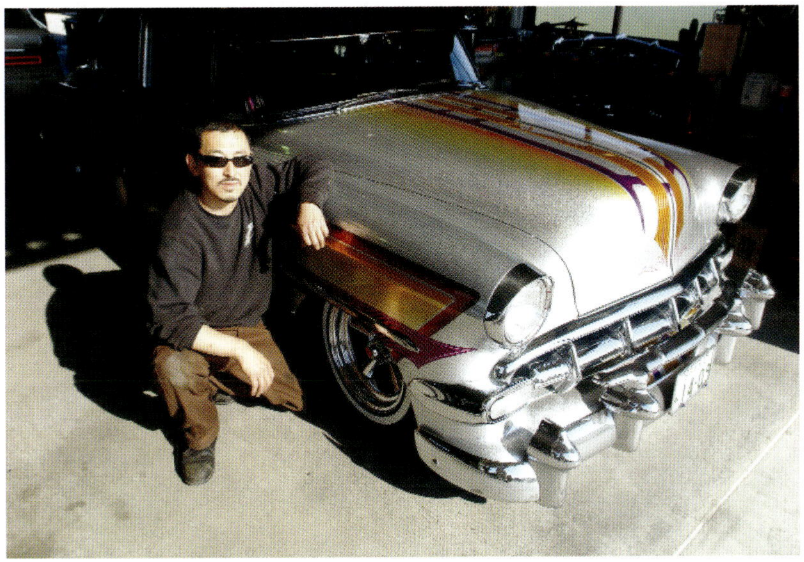

Hisashi Ushida, Cholo's Custom, Nagoya
1954 Chevy 210, 235 straight six, three speed
Dual exhaust, front hydraulics, rear air shocks

Japanese car builders and enthusiasts identify themselves by choosing a mixture of names and images that are informed through this special process of recognition. A sense of car aesthetics continues to take shape that emphasizes connections between car styles and themes from the media or broader issues of race, ethnicity and class that have evolved around cars in different regions of America. Some Japanese builders, like Bat Mobile of Shizuoka emphasize both historical and ethnic car culture connections. The Batmobile car used in the 1966 television show *Batman* was designed by kustom designer icon George Barris. The shop's calling cards and magazine ads read "Complimento en Vivo! Kustoms and Low lows" and pay tribute to Southern California Mexican lowrider styles. The graphics combine images of buxom Hispanic women with sombreros as well as mustache and sunglass-wearing Hispanic men, a style formalized in Chicano culture since the 1940s.

In Nagoya, car builders Paradise Road, Border's, Cholo's, Good Fellas and R&B borrow from a mixture of car taste, movie and musical references that cut across a mixture of American cultural themes. Shoe Box of Yokkaichi City borrows its name from American muscle car insider vocabulary that refers to legendary Chevrolet designer Harley Earl-styled Tri-Five Chevies of 1955, '56, and '57 as Shoe Boxes. Nine Lives of Gifu uses classic 1950s

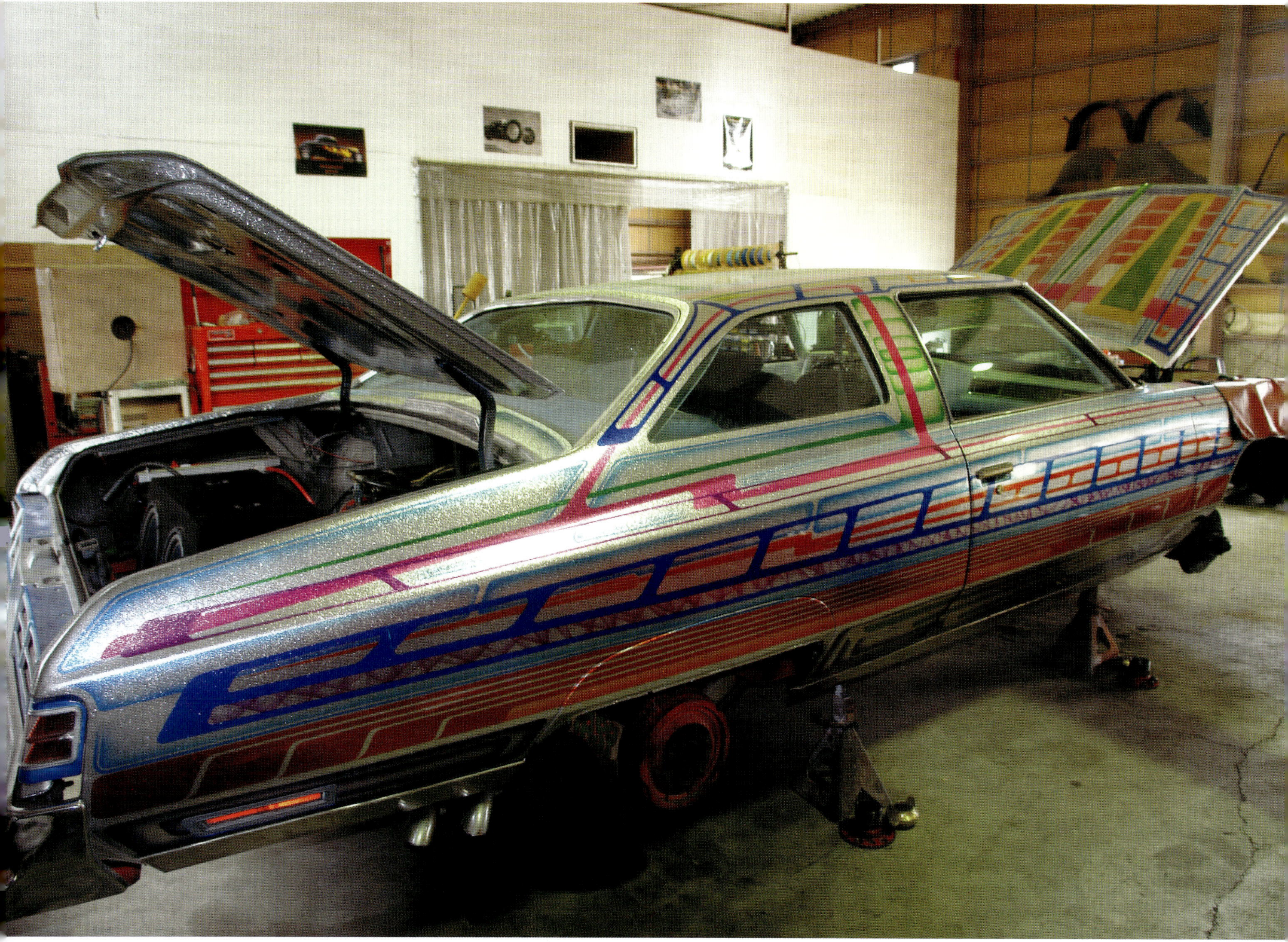

American tattoo iconography of a black cat and checkered finish flag.

Originally during the 1950s, American hot rod and custom builders deconstructed the cultural forms that had been created in Detroit and reassigned them with new countercultural significance. Today in Japan, custom car and rod builders and their customers have made conscious creative decisions to open a new dialogue with the information that has accumulated around these specialized historical sensibilities.

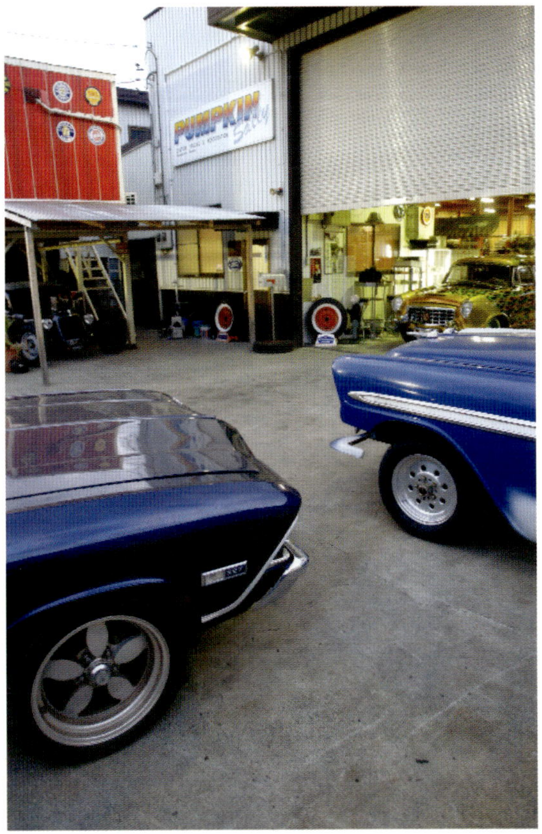

Above: Pumpkin Sally driveway

Left: Garage bay, Pumpkin Sally

In the coastal city of Odawara, in the central Kanagawa Prefecture region of Honshu, Tsuyoshi "Shorty" Sato is known for his mechanical finesse and design knowledge. He sees cars as objects of beauty but ultimately believes that they are machines meant to be driven, not just sit in a showroom. Every day he builds and fixes cars to make them drive well and thinks that this is his calling. In his early years, he worked as a mechanic in several garages and dealerships, and in 1997 opened his own garage he called Pumpkin Sally.

Shorty liked the lyrics, beat and melody of the Wilson Pickett song classic *Mustang Sally*. During the late 1980s and early '90s he and several of his friends drove Ford F-100 and 150 pickups and they formed a club. Among car culture people, the Ford F-100 and 150 truck is nicknamed the Pumpkin because of its odd, overly round hood shape. Shorty was looking for a shop name and ran the words Mustang Sally through his electronic dictionary. The definition that came up for "sally" referred to the old English term of an attack against an enemy. There was no reference to a woman's name. He decided this was too aggressive, and added the Ford F-100 nickname Pumpkin as a way to soften things. He drives a 1935 Ford pickup that he has thoroughly altered to create a neo-classic Hot Rod.

レロをかぶった胸の豊かなラテンアメリカ系女性と、ひげを生やしてサングラスをかけたラテンアメリカ系男性のイメージを組み合わせいる。これらは1940年代から南カリフォルニアのチカーノ・カルチャーで形式化されたスタイルである。

名古屋では、Paradise Road、Border's、Cholo's、Good Fellas、R&Bなどのカー・ビルダーが、アメリカ文化にまたがるさまざまな車の嗜好や映画、音楽などからテーマを借りている。四日市市のShoe Boxは、伝説的なシボレー・デザイナー、ハーレー・アール設計による1955年、56年、57年のトライ・ファイブ・シェビーを「シューボックス(靴の箱)」と呼ぶアメリカン・マッスルカー仲間のスラングにちなんで名付けられている。また、岐阜のNine Livesは黒猫とチェッカーパターンのフィニッシュフラッグという1950年代の代表的なアメリカン・タトゥーのデザインを利用している。

1950年代、もともとアメリカのホットロッドとカスタムのビルダーは、デトロイトで生産された文化的形態を分解して組み直し、新たなカウンター・カルチャー的意味を持たせた。今日の日本では、カスタム・カーやロッドのビルダーとその顧客は、意識的にクリエイティブな決定を行い、これらの専門的で歴史的な感性の周りに蓄積された情報との新しい対話を始めた。

神奈川県の中央にある海岸沿いの街、小田原市の佐藤剛(通称"ショーティ")は機械に対する手腕と設計知識で知られている。彼は車を美しいオブジェとしても見るが、究極的には運転するための機械であり、ショールームに陳列するだけのものではないと思っている。そしてこれが彼の使命だと考えて、より良

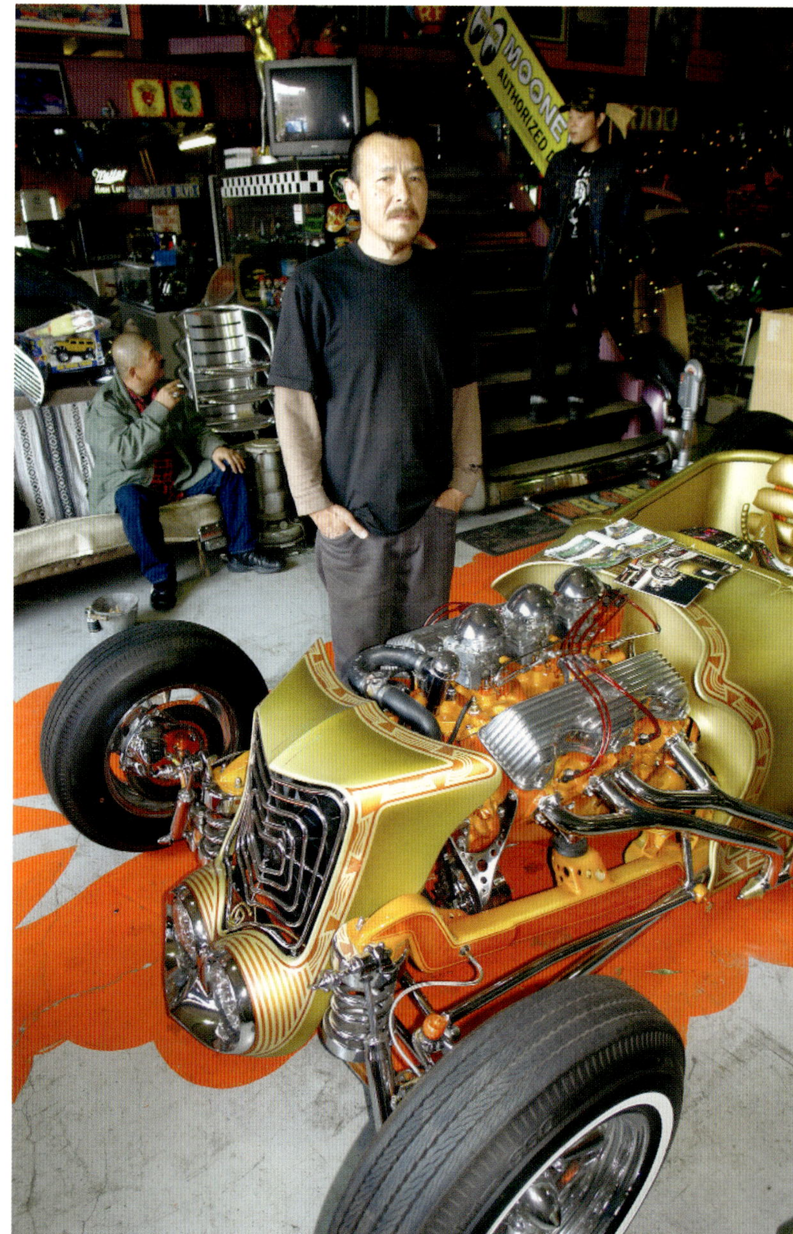

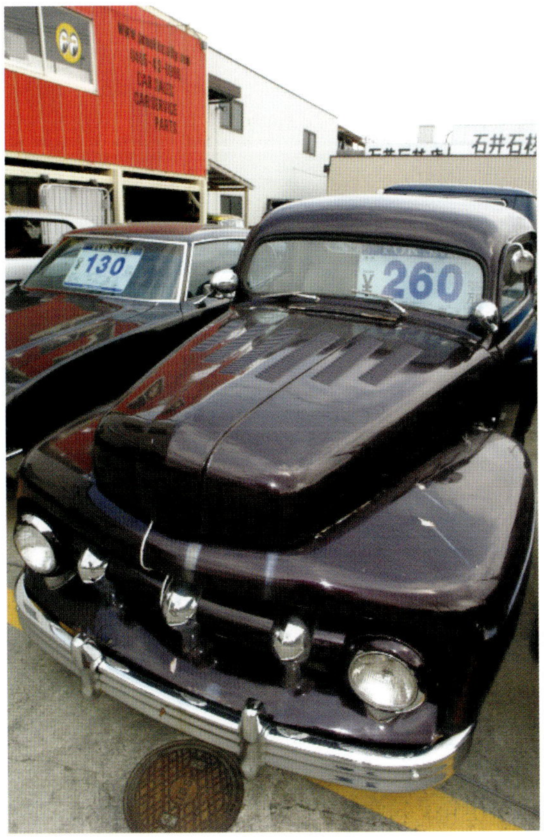

Above: 1951 Ford F-1 Pick-up, 327 V8
Re-built by Shorty

Left: Junichi Shimodaira, owner-builder Paradise Road, Nagoya with Galaxian 1927 Ford T Roadster. Model A frame rails, 1959 Chevy 348 V8, tri carburetors. 1970 Corvette, three speed transmission. Body and front mask mostly hand made.

Born in Odawara in 1967, Shorty considers himself to be a local guy. Because of auto driving license restrictions in Japan, he started working on and customizing motorcycles at age 16; and then, at 18, when he received his car license, began working on automobiles. He attended mechanic school for two years and was then hired by a major Japanese car company to work in the mechanical repairs department. In 1996 he opened his first small shop, then graduated to a second shop and has been at his current location since 2005. He's well-known in Odawara and his reputation now extends as far away as Kyushu, Akita, Fukushima and the U.S.

"Some mechanics know cars and some don't," Shorty says. "Some develop reputations because their work is reliable. I have a reputation because of my work. I have always seen cars as something to work on. I started at 16 as a motorcycle customizer. Then at 18 I started working on cars. I went to mechanic school for two years. I worked at a 4WD Jeep customizing shop and learned a lot about the customizing process. I had a Ford F-100 pick-up and always did my own work."

"I started a Ford F-100 Pumpkin car club in 1989. All the members wanted me to specialize in trucks but I have a bigger interest in mechanics. I have experience with Fords but as a young mechanic I saw other engines like Chrysler and Chevy. I saw these new systems as a challenge. I feel pretty confident in my basic engine knowledge—Ford, Chrysler, Chevy, Oldsmobile. Flathead 8s, Straight 6s, whatever. I think it is important to think about the total balance of a car. A car is not just about the engine. A car is the engine, front end, rear end combination."

"I devote all my time to building cars. Now that I have had the time to build my own car, I feel it is important to drive it. I think people who own hot rods and kustoms but don't drive them because of distance or fear of accidents are not really experiencing them. It is

く走れるよう車の組み立てや修理に日々携わっている。下積み時代には、あちこちのガレージや販売特約店でメカニックとして勤務し、1997年、「パンプキン・サリー」という名前の自分のガレージを開業した。

ショーティは、ウィルソン・ピケットの名曲『マスタング・サリー』の歌詞、ビート、メロディが気に入っている。1980年代後期と90年代初期、彼は何人かの友人とフォードF-100および150のピックアップ・トラックを運転し、クラブを設立した。カー・カルチャーの愛好家は、ボンネットの形が非常に丸く奇妙なフォードF-100と150トラックに「パンプキン」というニックネームを付けた。ショーティは店の名前を検討中で、電子辞書で「マスタング・サリー」という言葉を探してみた。「サリー」という言葉で見つかったのは古典英語に由来する「敵に対する何らかの攻撃」という定義であったが、女性の名前については何も言及されていなかったと言う。この名前では強すぎるので、もう少し柔らかくする意味でフォードF-100のニックネームである「パンプキン」を付け加えることにした。彼は自分で全面的にネオクラシックなホットロッドに改造した1935年フォード・ピックアップを運転している。

1967年に小田原で生まれたショーティは、自分を地元に根ざした人間だと言う。日本の免許証取得の年齢規制のため、まず16歳でバイクのカスタマイズを始め、その後18歳で自動車免許を取ってからは車のカスタマイズを開始した。自動車整備学校に2年間通ったのち、日本の大手企業の機械修理部で働いた。1996年、小さな最初のショップを開店し、2つ目のショップを経て、2005年より現在の場所で営業している。彼は小田原では有名で、その評判は、九州、秋田、福島、そしてアメリカまでも届いている。

「メカニックの中には車をよく知る人と知らない人がいます」とショーティは語る。「信頼できる仕事をすれば評判が得られます。私の評判は仕事に基づいたものです。車とは打ち込んで取り組める対象だとこれまでずっと考えてきました。16歳でバイクのカスタマイザーとして仕事を始め、18歳で車の仕事を始めました。自動車整備学校に2年間通い、その後、四輪駆動ジープのカスタマイズ・ショップで働いたときは、カスタマイズ・プロセスについてずいぶん勉強になりました。フォードF-100ピックアップを当時持っていましたが、整備はいつも自分でやっていました。」

フォードF-100パンプキン・カー・クラブは1989年に始めました。メンバーは全員、私にトラックを専門にやって欲しがっていましたが、私は機械的なこと全般にもっと大きな興味がありました。フォードでの経験がありますが、若いメカニックとしてクライスラーやシェビーなど他のエンジンにも携わることがありました。そのときこのような新しいシステムをチャレンジとして受け止めました。私はエンジンについての基本的知識にはかなり自信があります。フォード、クライスラー、シェビー、オールズモビル、フラットヘッド8、ストレート6など何でも。車を考えるとき、総合的なバランスとして考えることが大切だと思います。車はエンジンだけではありません。車は、エンジン、前部、後部の組み合わせなのです。」

「私は自分のすべての時間を車の組み立てに投入しています。今は自分のための車を組み立てる時間がありますし、その車を運転することの大切さも感じています。せっかくホットロッドやカスタムを持っているのに距離や事故を恐れて運転しない人は、その車を十分体験しているとは言えません。自分の車が動いているところを見ること、そしてその車が走るのを人が見られるようにすることが大切です。アメリカまで行き、大規模なカー・ショーに参加したことがあります。そこでたくさんの車を見て、エンジンの音を聞き、人がイベントに殺到している様子はいつも衝撃的です。車は動いているところを見せるのが大切です。なぜならホットロッドの良さ

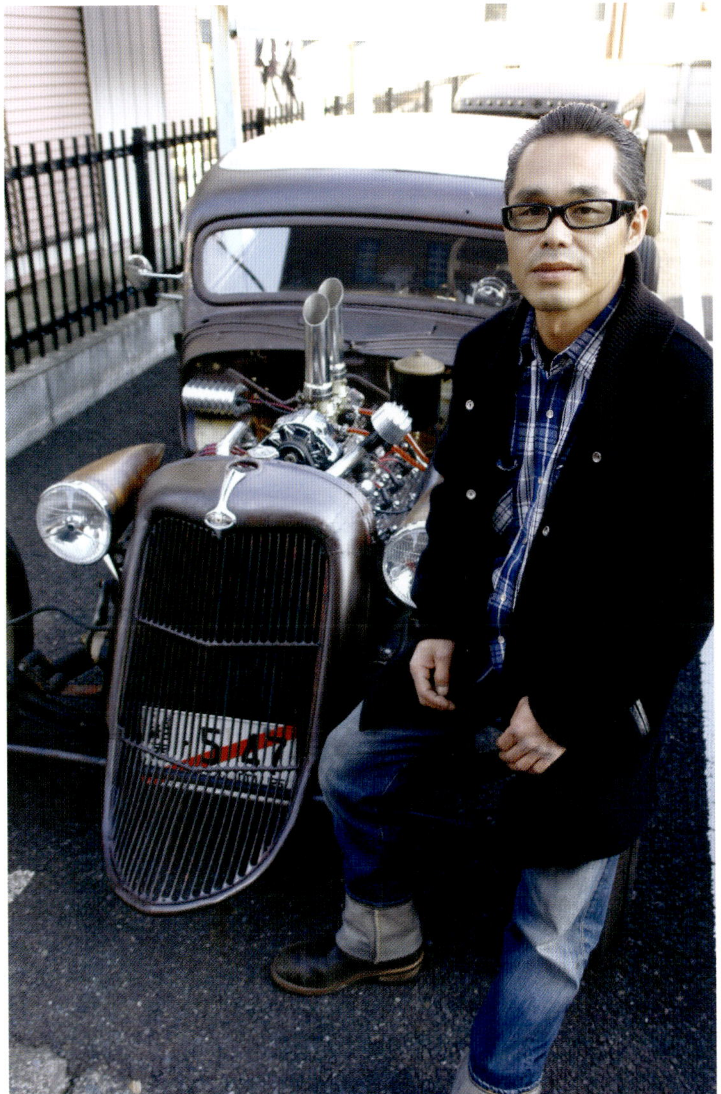

Shorty with his 1935 Ford Pick-up.

important to see the car in motion. I have traveled to the States and attended big car shows. It is always shocking to me to see the number of cars, to hear the engines and see people rushing to the event. It is important to show the cars in motion for all the people who still don't know the truth about hot rods, to prove these cars can actually be driven."

"People need to see these cars with their own eyes and feel the vibration and the smells. The excitement can only be felt by people who actually experience it. There are some things that cannot be communicated by words and images. This is something that is difficult to describe about my hot rod addict, mechanic addict life."

"I know my 60-plus-year-old car inside and out. All the information that is packed inside my car is revealed by the smooth sound and vibration. When I step on the gas and shoot through a corner, the excitement rushes through my body. I want more people to know this excitement. That is why I drive my car and participate in events all over Japan. I drive my 'Old American' around so people can see it. Cars are beautiful, cool, superior machines. And because it is a machine, you can do anything as long as the logic is there."

"When you drive an old car, it is difficult not to wonder about the time when the car was actually made. When I build a car, I look at the parts and think about the structures from the time they were made. I step closer to the hearts of the original designers and engineers who created the car. This is a very important thing for me and it has a big effect on the cars I build. I compare the conditions that existed when the car was originally designed in the past to the conditions today. The purpose and requirements for a car greatly influence the parts and structure of the car."

"Recently, I was working on a Ford F-100 pickup. I had to put myself into the past of this truck. I wondered about what it had carried.

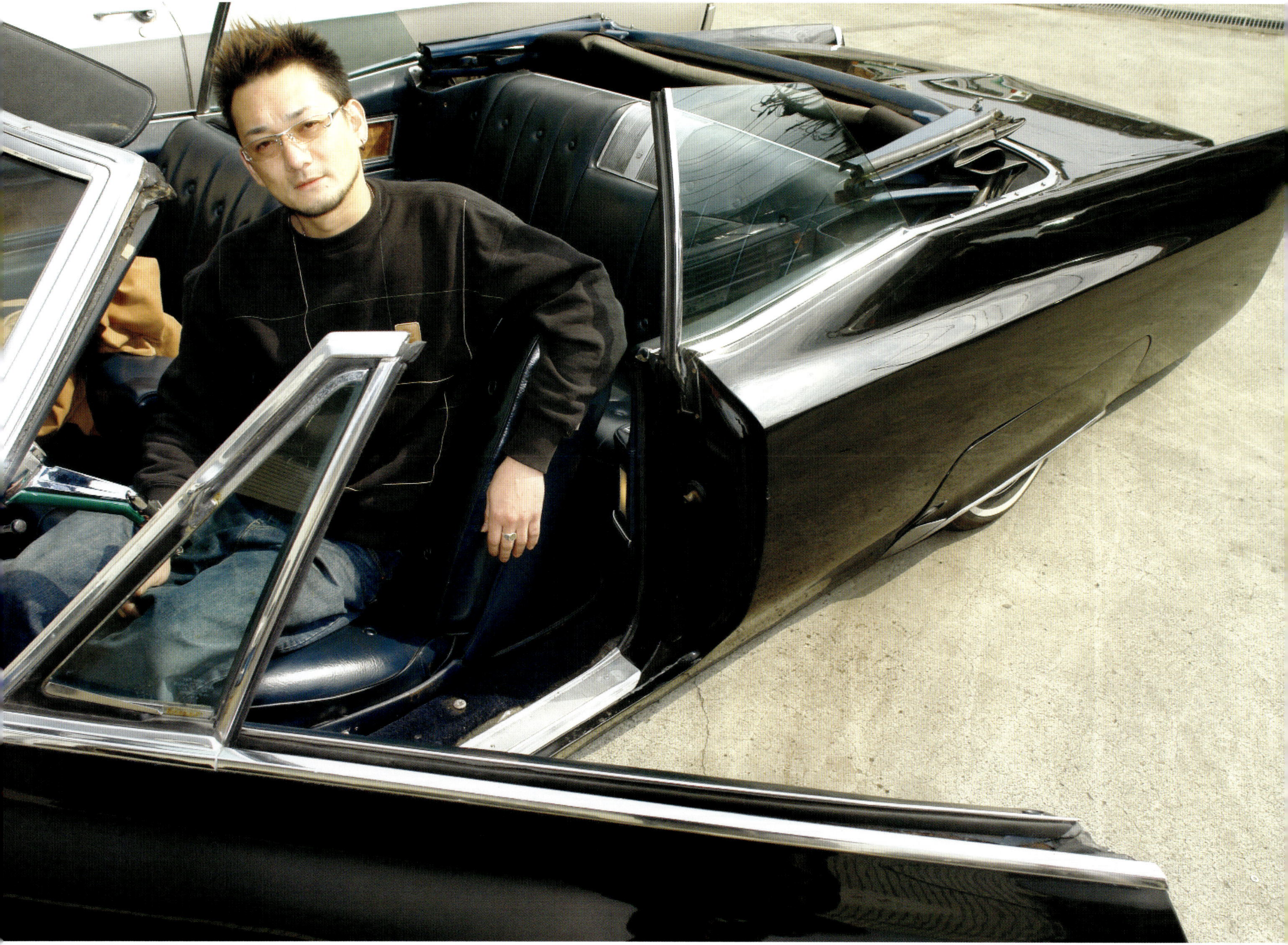

The suspension was built to endure weight. Rivets were used in the frame in order to supplement its loads. The truck was built to drive on dirt roads. The cab and the bed are separate. I compared this to an El Camino or Ranchero sedan truck. These are built to be driven on paved roads. They use sedan suspension in order to take the strain off the driver. Here, the first priority is about ease of driving."

"When I build a Kustom car, I always consider the roads that it will be driven on—the purposes it will be used for. First, the car must fulfill certain requirements, and the engine must run smoothly. I always think about the frame strength, where the maximum strength can be created. The car is then styled and finished. When I see a car driving down the street, I try to think about the basic structure. I try to imagine what the original design team thought. How and why certain parts and engineering were used, where certain things were placed and why. This is the excitement I feel when I look at a car."

The garage bays at Pumpkin Sally are swept clean and tidy. Shorty looks into the 350 V8 of a 1940 Ford as if he is reading a book. Outside in the lot there are a primer red '27 Ford Model T, a navy blue '51 Ford F-100 pickup with a classic 327 V8, a powder blue '56 Chevy and a black '68 El Camino. A customer, Tokorozawa, sits in his black '68 Cadillac convertible and waits for Shorty's attention. The massive car takes up a quarter of the lot. He fiddles with the hydraulics knob panel below the dash and gently adjusts the car's stance to a lower position. The rear pipes now sit an inch off the pavement. Cars fly past on the busy secondary road at the front of the parking lot as two schoolgirls wearing pleated skirt uniforms walk past. They sneak peeks into the parking lot, pause and look quizzically at the strangely low Cadillac. Shorty appears holding a windshield wiper blade like a lecturer's baton. He walks to the front of the Cadillac, bends under the open hood and taps gently at the air cleaner with the wiper as he explains the details of his diagnosis to Tokorozawa.

1968 Cadillac; Owner: Tokorozawa

が分からない人がまだたくさんいますからね。こういう車は実際に走れるんだということを証明するのです。」

「みんな、ホットロッドを自分の目で見て、振動を感じて、あふれる匂いを嗅ぐ必要があります。言葉や写真では伝わらない、それを実際に体験しなければ分からない感動です。それが私のホットロッド中毒、メカ中毒の生活を説明するのを難しくしています。」

「私は生産されてから60年以上経った愛車の内側も外側も知り尽くしています。車の中に詰まっている情報は、音のスムーズさや振動から分かります。アクセルを踏み、曲がり角をすばやく通り抜けるとき、感動が体を駆け巡ります。この感動をもっと多くの人に知って欲しいから、車を運転し、日本各地のイベントに参加するのです。この“オールド・アメリカン”を人に見てもらうために運転します。車は美しく、クールで、卓越したマシンです。しかしマシンですから、論理に従っている限り、自由に手がかけられます。」

「古い車を運転するとき、その車が実際に製造されたころについて思いを巡らさないわけにはいきません。車を組み立てるとき、部品を見て、それが製造されたときの構造について考えます。そこからもう一歩踏み込み、その車を作った元の設計者やエンジニアの心に迫ります。これが私にとって非常に大切で、作る車に大きな影響を与えます。車の目的と要件は、その部品や構造に多大な影響を及ぼすので、その車が過去の元々設計された時代に存在した状態を、現在の状態と比較します。」

「つい最近、フォードF-100ピックアップに手を加えました。そのとき、このトラックの過去について、それが何を運んだかなどに思いを巡らせました。サスペンションは重さに耐えられるよう作られており、運搬する荷重を支えるため、フレームにはリベットが使用されていました。そのトラックは、泥道を走るように作られており、キャブとベッドは別々になっています。これをエルカミノやランチェロのセダン・トラックと比較しました。これらは舗装道路を運転するために作られているので、セダンのサスペンションを利用して、ドライバーの負担を軽減します。ここで最優先事項は運転の容易さであることが分かります。いつも思うことですが、車の目的と要件が、その車の部品や構造に大きな影響を与えます。」

「カスタム・カーを作るとき、それが走る道路のことをいつも検討します。それが使用される目的です。まず、車は一定の条件を満たし、エンジンがスムーズに稼動しなければなりません。また、フレームの強度を最大にできるかも考えます。それからスタイルを決め、仕上げとなります。車が道路を走っているのを見かけたとき、基本的な構造について考えるよう努めています。オリジナルの設計チームはどう考えていたかを想像し、どのように、そしてなぜ特定の部品や技術が使用されたか、なぜそこに配置されたかなどを。私が車を見るときは、こういうことに興奮を覚えます。」

パンプキン・サリーのガレージ屋内は、きれいに掃かれ整頓されている。ショーティは、まるで本でも読むかのように1940年フォードの350 V8エンジンを覗き込む。屋外の駐車用地にはプライマーレッドの27年T型フォード、クラシック327 V8エンジンを搭載したネイビーブルーの51年フォードF-100ピックアップ、パウダーブルーの56年シェビー、そして黒の68年エルカミノが置いてある。顧客の所沢氏は愛車の黒の68年キャデラック・コンバーチブルに座り、ショーティを待っている。この巨大な車は用地の4分の1を占めている。彼はダッシュボードの下にあるハイドロのノブ・パネルをいじり、静かに車のスタンスを調整して低めにする。これで後部のパイプは路面からわずか1インチの位置まで下がった。駐車用地の前の車通りの多い道路に、プリーツスカートの制服を来た女学生2人が通りかかる。駐車用地をちらりと覗き、奇妙に車体の低いキャデラックを立ち止まっていぶかしげに見ている。そこへフロントガラスのワイパー・ブレードを指示棒のように持ったショーティが現れる。彼はキャデラック前部に近づき、開いたボンネットの下にかがみこんで、そのワイパーでエアクリーナーを軽くたたきながら彼の診断内容を所沢氏に詳しく説明する。

閑静な名古屋市中区大須にある宮川佳巳の衣料品店「ViSE」の前には、ハーレーダビッドソン・ショベルヘッド・ネオチョッパー・ラットバイクが５～６台停まっている。若い男性たちが各自のマシンの近くの歩道に座り、話をしたりタバコを吸ったりしている。ペースの速い大阪や東京とくらべると、中部地方での生活は穏やかで少し違う実直な雰囲気がある。佳巳の店の周辺は古い伝統とトレンディな新しいスタイルが静かに入り混じっている。彼の友人らは各自のバイクにもたれ掛かり、1930 年代、40 年代のアメリカのバイカーが着ていたチェックのウール・シャツと分厚いデニム・ジーンズを身に着けている。50 年代や 60 年代など、のちに人気となったレザーのスタイルではない。このような名古屋の若者たちによるスタイルを通した表現は、特定で独特なものだが、同時に非常に説得力があり、自然に見える。

名古屋市は、日本および世界中のカー・カルチャー愛好家の間で、カスタム・シティとして知られている。この街のもう１つの顔は、ハイオク・ガソリンの燃焼、カスタム高速アメリカ車、ホットロッド、ヴィンテージ・バイク、そしてそれを取り巻くカスタム・カルチャー・ライフすべてである。佳巳の ViSE 衣料品店と彼のラットバイク、ラットロッドの仲間たちは、日本の若者の間で増えている、アメリカのスピードマシンの神話とライフスタイルをブレンドした魅惑の体現者だ。彼らは 1950 年代のアメリカのホットロッダーのように、速さ、危険性、反抗を美とする神話のとりこになっている。

もともと 1949 年代後期から 50 年代初期、カリフォルニアやその他の地域のホットロッダーは、市販のアメリカ車とバイクを再設計し、個人輸送についての現状を再定義するスピードマシンに仕立て上げた。そして今日の日本では、車やバイクに対する新種の賞賛が、アメリカのノスタルジックな象徴であるタトゥー、服装、音楽、スタイリッシュなスピードマシンなどと、膨張しつつある日本の自己意識を融合させ、発展させる対話を始めた。

佳巳の店の前の静かな道は、このような新しくスタイリッシュな生活を模索する名古屋の若者が多く集まる場所になっている。彼はこう説明する。「もともと日本は伝統に則った生活を送っていました。しかし日本文化とこの古い生活は内面的でプライベートなもので、人生の一部を他の人たちと共有することなどありませんでした。ところが 1970 年代になって、生活は変わり始め、少し打ち解け始めるようになりました。それが 1980 年代になると、若い人たちは自分自身を探求し始め、自分が誰でどうやって今の自分があるのかに思いを巡らせました。これは大きなことでした。そして 1990 年代、古い文化と新しい文化の間に感覚の差が生まれました。若い日本人はファッションを好むようになり、服装や音楽、タトゥーは自己表現の新しい手段になりました。こういった新しい概念のほとんどはアメリカから来たものです。何を着るか、見た目をどうするか、どんな音楽を聴くか、そして何を運転するか。こういう表現の動きが徐々に起こり、今、さらに大きくなろうとしています。若者たちは、違う手段を用いて自分自身について考え、学んでいるのです。」

佳巳のショップの前に、ヤスヒロという若い男性が静かに駐車している。名古屋にある Marvelous Japan Car Club（マーベラス・ジャパン・カークラブ）のメンバーで、名古屋の Cholo's Kustom Kar（チョロス・カスタム・カー）によるピンストライピングで装飾した新型キャデラックを運転している。名古屋のアーティスト、彫ぎんによる伝統的な日本のタトゥーが、彼のシャツの袖から覗き出る。大きなアメリカ車の横にしゃがんだヤスヒロは、過去と現在からの感性の明確

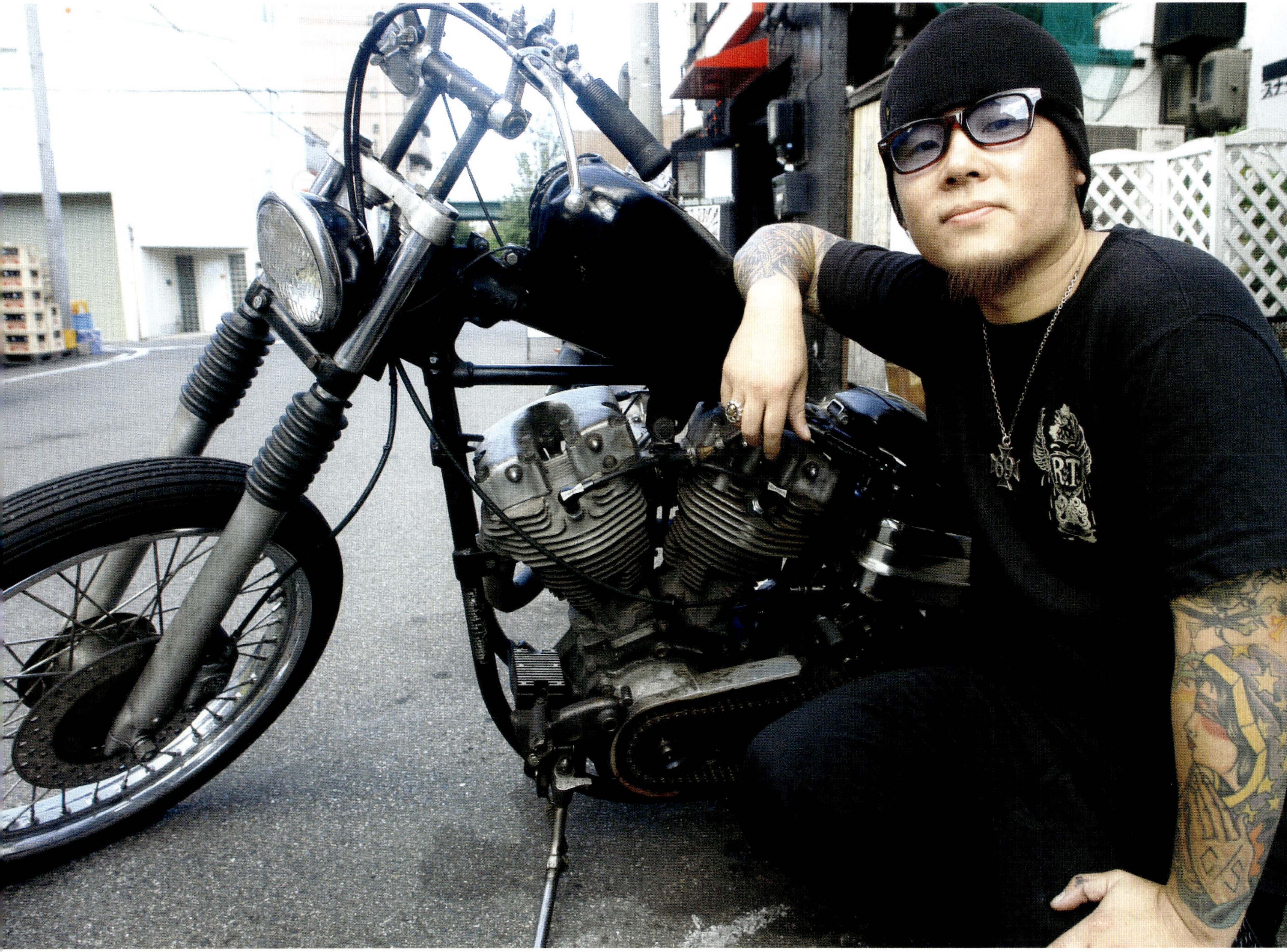

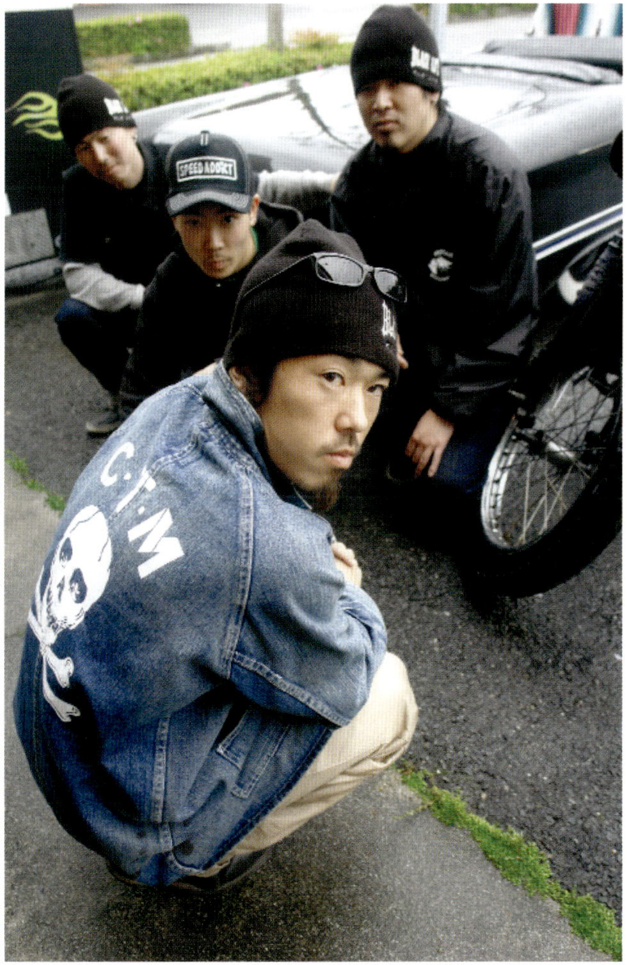

Above: Nagoya bikers

Left: Yoshiki Miyagawa with his Shovel Head, ViSE Clothing

A half-dozen Harley Davidson Shovelhead Neo-Chopper rat bikes are parked in front of Yoshiki Miyagawa's ViSE Clothing shop located in the quiet Osu Naka-Ku neighborhood of Nagoya. Young men sit calmly on the pavement near their machines chatting and smoking. Life in central Japan is slow and takes on a different down-to-earth quality compared to the fast-paced cities of Osaka and Tokyo. Yoshiki's neighborhood is a quiet blend of older history and trendy new styles. His friends lean against their bikes casually, wearing the woolen checked shirts and thick denim jeans of 1930s and '40s American bikers, not the leather of the later '50s and '60s. The style statements among these young Nagoya people are studied and specific but look very natural.

The city of Nagoya is known among car culture people throughout Japan, and the world, as Kustom City. This alter ego identity is all about burning high-octane gas, fast customized American cars, hot rods, vintage motorcycles and the Kustom Kulture life that surrounds it all. Yoshiki's ViSE clothing and his rat bike and rat rod friends are a part of a growing fascination among young people in Japan that blends the mystique of the American speed machine with a life style. Like the American hot-rodders of the 1950s, they are gripped by a mystique that recognizes velocity, danger and rebellion as beauty.

Originally in the United States during the late 1940s and early '50s, hot-rodders in California and elsewhere redesigned stock American cars and motorcycles into fast machines that redefined status quo ideas about personal transportation. Today in Japan, a new breed of car and bike appreciation has opened a dialogue that mixes American nostalgic symbols including tattoos, clothing, music and fast stylish machines with an expanding Japanese sense of self.

The quiet street in front of Yoshiki's shop is a meeting place for many Nagoya young people who are exploring this new stylish life.

な交差点を体現している。彼の感性は２つの異なる文化的方向にまたがっている。彼の横には、チョップされた1920年代のフォード・ラットロッドが何台か停まっている。トシという男性は500ciキャデラック・エンジンを搭載した26年T型フォードを、ジョージはシェビー327ci搭載の29年フォード・ピックアップを、ケイは350ciフラットヘッド８搭載の23年フォードを、そしてマサトはトヨタ４気筒エンジン搭載の23年フォード・Tバケットを運転する。皆若い男性だ。マサトのトヨタのマニホルド・ロゴからはＯとＡの文字が削り取られ、"TOY T" になっている。

愛知県内が春めき暖かくなるころの週末には、カスタムのバイクや車のイベントがいくつもあり、何百人ものファンを引き付ける。佳巳と彼の仲間らは、まずBreezy Biker Camp（ブリージー・バイカー・キャンプ）イベントに参加し、それから岡崎市中央総合公園で開催される「デッドヒイト三河」のイベントに向かう。

トシのチョップド26年T型フォードは、ミニマルなクラシックロッドだ。インテリアからはすべてが取り除かれ、余分なものは何もない。ドア内部の機械構造がむき出しになり、シートは床板の上をすべるように動き回る２枚のウレタンフォームだけ。ハンドルはシンプルで小型、パッドを付けてドライバーの手が振動でしびれないようにしてある。シフトレバーの握り部分はピンの付いた本物の手榴弾で、切迫する死をユーモラスに表している。

トシのような車では、ホットロッディングの身体的特徴は一目瞭然だ。TH 400トランスミッション搭載の500ciキャデラックV8から分厚い金属製ヘッドカバー・プレートを取り外してあるので、深いエンジンノイズを発する。スタイルを重視するためにすべての快適性は犠牲にされている。チョップされた狭いフロントガラスの前には大きなエンジンが設置されているため、外を見るのは難しく、トシは絶え間なく体を曲げて視界を確保しなければならない。信号で停まると、車体は極端に低く、これに対して信号は高い場所にあり、また屋根も非常に低く切られているため、トシは体を曲げて前傾姿勢で適当な角度を見つけ、肩越しに信号を見るしかない。追い越していく他の運転手らはこの車を見て信じられないか、面白がっているかで、年齢によってその反応が違う。彼は礼儀正しく手を振り、手榴弾のピンに手を伸ばして、ふざけてテロの真似をして見せた。

ホットロッディングは、スピードの身体的体験を模索する繊細な美的思想だ。様式化された高速マシンと人間との交点によって築き上げられた感性である。エンジンの馬力と乗り心地の組み合わせの観点からすると、技術的には難解な変数が生じるが、その基本は動きに対する様式化された身体的感覚に他ならない。ホットロッドに乗るのは苦痛だ。エンジンノイズで耳が、そして体を曲げたおかしな座り方で背中が痛くなる。フロアボードに座るとお尻は痛く、噴出するエンジンの熱にも当てられる。これら体験のすべてが身体的だ。トシの手はグリースにまみれ、指の爪深くにまで入っている。全部きれいに洗い取るのは難しいが、そんなことはどうでもいい。彼は洗い取るつもりなどまったくない。これがグリース・カルチャーだ。

手榴弾のピンは巨大なエンジンのリズムに合わせて飛び回っている。ホットロッドの感性のすべてに、起こりうる危険の感覚がある。トシの仲間らがカスタム・ハーレー・ラットバイクに乗って追い越していく。彼らはシートに低く座り、タバコか通行料のお金を探すかのようにデニム・ジャケットの胸のポケットに手を入れる。勢いよく飛び出るかと思えば後退する — 驚くべき馬力で危険なバレエを踊っているかのように。あるライダーは時速80マイル以上でかすめるように追い抜いていく。静かに左手の人差し指を上に突き立て、そのあと前方向を指差す。「向こうで会おうぜ」とでも言うように。そして彼はフットペグから足をはずし、非常に小さなシート

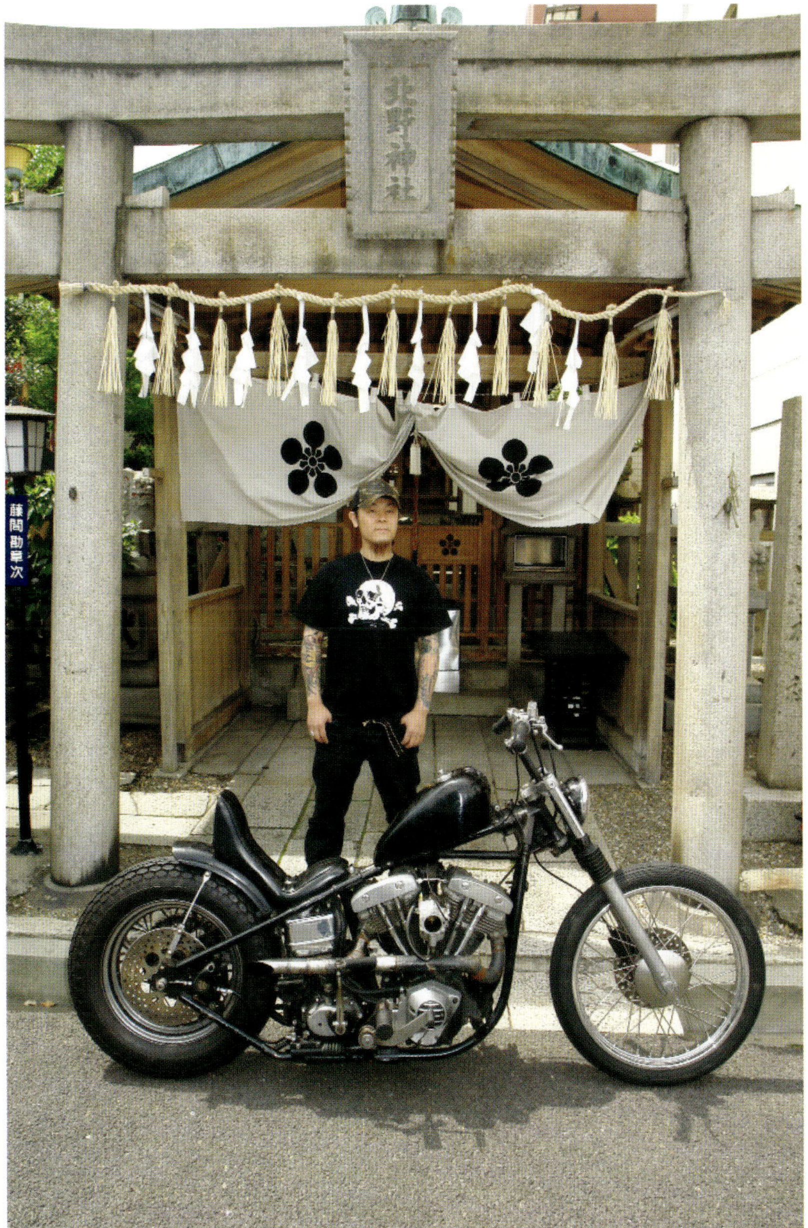

Yoshiki Miyagawa

He explains, "Originally in Japan things were traditional. The old lifestyle was an internalized, private thing. Sharing any part of your life was not done. During the 1970s, life started to change, open up a little. Then in the 1980s, young people started to look inside themselves. They wondered what had made them who they are. This was a big thing. By the 1990s a sense of difference happened between old and new culture. Young Japanese started to explore different fashions. Clothing, music and tattoos became a way to express yourself. Most of these new ideas came from America. What to wear, how to look, what music to listen to and what to drive. This has been happening for a while now and is building on itself. Young people here use these different ways to see themselves and learn about themselves."

A young man named Yasuhiro is parked quietly in front of Yoshiki's shop. He is a member of the Marvelous Japan Car Club of Nagoya and drives a dressed-up late model Cadillac with pin striping by the Cholo's Kustom Kar shop in Nagoya. He has traditional Japanese style tattoos by Nagoya artist Hori Gyn that sneak out from under his shirtsleeves. Squatting next to his large American car, Yasuhiro represents an eye-catching intersection of sensibilities from the past and present. He is straddling two different cultural orientations. Parked next to him are several chopped-up Ford rat rods from the 1920s. A young man named Toshi drives a '26 Ford T with a 500ci Cadillac engine; another named Joji drives a '29 Ford Pick-up with a Chevy 327ci; Kei drives a '23 Ford with a 350ci Flathead 8 and finally, Masato drives a '23 Ford T-Bucket with a Toyota 4 cylinder engine. The "O" and "A" letters have been ground off the Toyota manifold logo to leave TOY T.

As the spring weather warms in Aichi prefecture, there are several weekend custom bike and car events that attract hundreds of people. Yoshiki and his friends will ride or drive first to the Breezy Biker Camp event and then to the Dead Heat Mikawa event, which

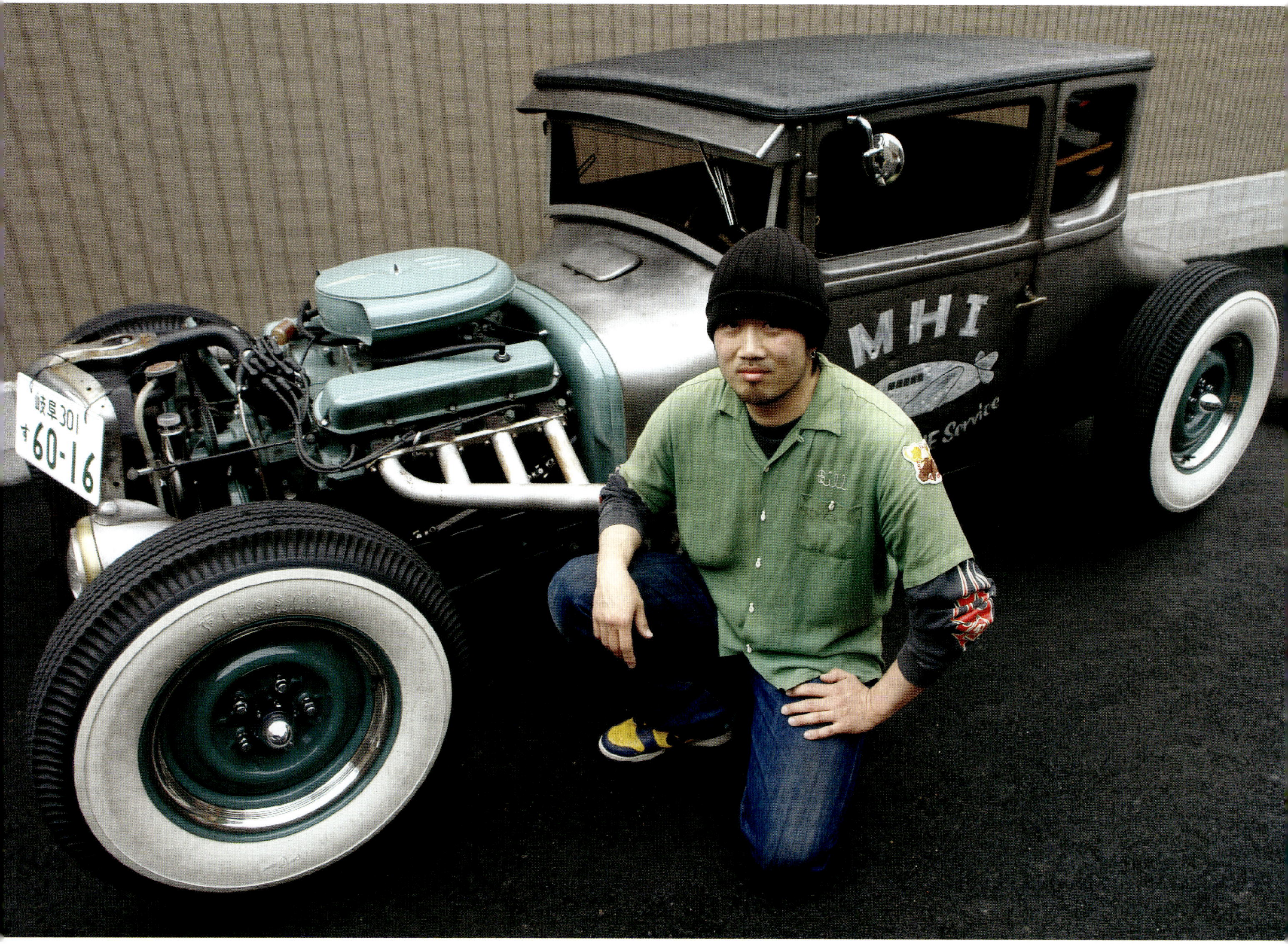
岐阜301
す60-16
MHI
Service
Firestone
Bill

is held at the Okazaki-shi Central Park.

The ride in Toshi's chopped '26 Ford T is classic minimal rod. Everything has been removed from the interior of the car, and there are no frills. The guts of the door mechanisms are exposed, the seats are two pieces of foam that slide around the floor boards to the rhythm of acceleration and the steering wheel is simple, undersized and padded to prevent the driver's hands from going numb from the vibrations. The gearshift knob is an authentic hand grenade with pin that contributes a humorous visual of impending death.

The physicality of hot-rodding is obvious in a car like Toshi's. He has unbolted the thick metal header cover plates off the 500ci Cadillac V8 with a TH 400 transmission, and the engine noise is profound. All comfort has been sacrificed for style. It is difficult to see out the chopped, narrow windshield over the big engine, and Toshi must constantly twist and turn for optimal visibility. Stopped at a traffic light, the car is too low and the light is too high. The roof is chopped so low that he cannot see. He must bend around and scrunch forward to find the right angle to see over his shoulder at the light. Passing motorists look at his car either in disbelief or excitement, depending on their age. He waves politely and reaches for the grenade pin in a gesture of mock terror.

Hot-rodding is a nuanced esthetic that explores the physical experience of speed. It is a sensibility that has developed as human beings intersect with fast, stylized machines. There are technically esoteric variables in terms of combining engine power with ride but the basic essence is about the stylized physicality of motion. Riding in a hot rod is an extreme sensation. Your ears hurt from the engine noise; your back hurts from being bent into an unnatural seated position, your ass hurts from sitting on the floorboards. It's hot from the cranked-out engine temperature. The whole experience is about physicality. Toshi has grease all over his hands and deep under his

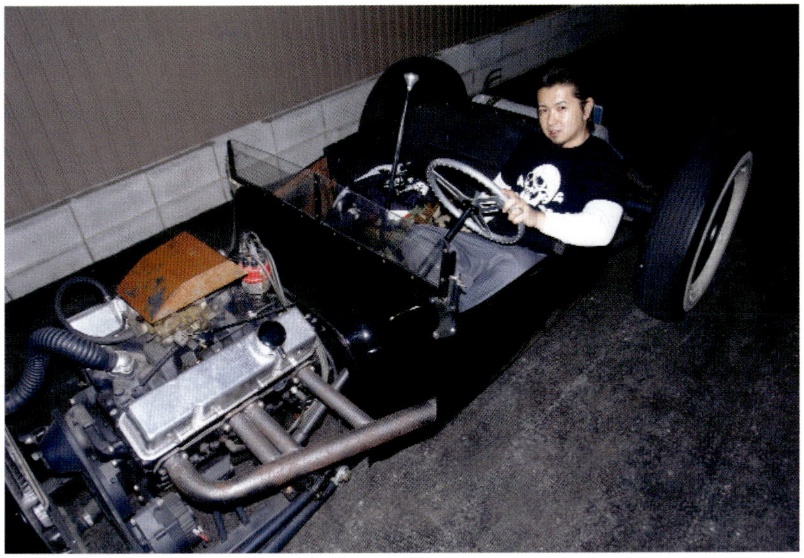

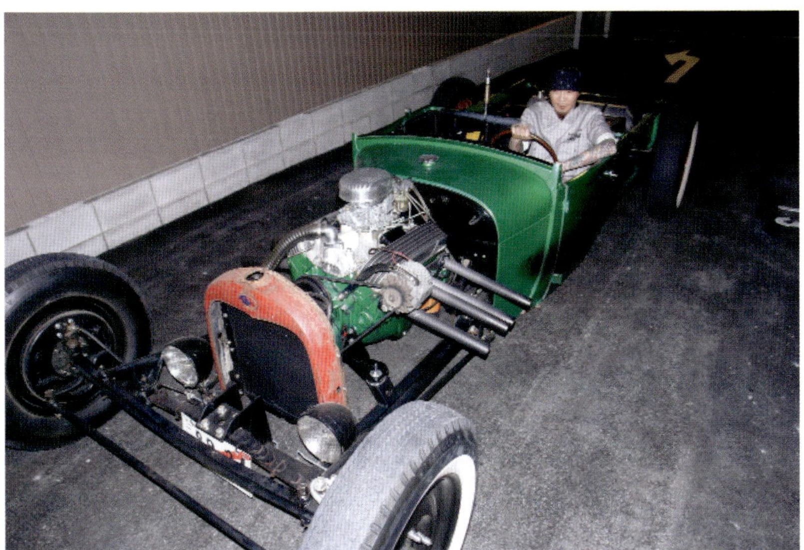

Above top: Kei with 1923 Ford, 350ci

Above bottom: Joji with 1929 Ford Pick-up, Chevy 327 V8

Left: Toshi with 1926 Ford T, Cadillac 500ci

によじ登る。ハンドルバーをしっかりと握り締め、ふざけた表情で飛び跳ねている。トシはそれを認めるかのようにかすかな笑みを浮かべた。

トシの車の中は禁煙だ。座席の後ろにあるタンクで満杯のハイオクが揺れ動き、キャブ内はそのリッチで魅惑的な匂いで満たされている。間違って火花でも起これば、シフトレバーの手榴弾のごとく爆発するだろう。ダッシュボードにあるハイドロ、温度、速度のシンプルな計測器は相当上がっている。それと歩調を合わせていないのはガソリン・メーターだけで、こちらはずいぶん下がっている。トシとその仲間らにとって、パワフルな機械の表象を自分が生まれ育った土地で運転することは、そこから脱出するような、そして再びつながるような感覚なのだろう。稀少で貴重なアメリカン・マシンに乗って全速力で走ると、そこには不可解ながら途方もなくエキサイティングなスリルがある。強烈なノイズ、塵埃、速度、服装。これらは、まず最初にどこで始まったかという前後関係がなければ何の意味もなさないが、トシと彼のホットロッドの仲間、若いラットバイカーたちは、歴史を再び想像することによって、彼らにとって元のものよりリアルな世界を作り出している。

藤井龍也は、故障したショベルヘッドのクラッチをパーキングエリアの舗道上で巧みに分解し、その部品をより分けて調べている。ライダーたちが携帯電話で状況を説明すると、その仲間は巣に舞い戻る蜂のように駐車場に次々入ってくる。若いバイカーたちは龍也を取り囲む。彼らはやっかいなエンジンのいい部品と悪い部品をすばやく選定する彼を眺めている。龍也は若いが、カスタム・バイク・ビルダーとして名古屋近郊では有名で高く評価されている。15分も経たない内に、クラッチとプライマリーベルトは再び組み立てられ、配置された。特殊なツールはなく、あるのは普通のレンチと蓄積されたエンジンについての感性だけだ。全員がタバコをもみ消すと、彼はバイクにまたがり、クランクを回して圧力を上げ、大きな弾ける音と同時にエンジンが始動する。歩道の縁石に停まった30台以上のバイクがその合図にしたがってエンジンを勢いよく始動すると、Breezy Biker Campカスタム・イベントに向かって走り出した。

龍也の「Duas Caras Cycles（デュアスカラスサイクルス）」のロゴは悲劇・喜劇の２つの仮面だが、これは南カリフォルニアのメキシコ系アメリカ人の刑務所の文化を示唆している。彼は31歳。10年以上にわたってバイクの組み立てに携わってきたが、今、その興味はユニークなカスタム・バイクを作ることへと移っている。幅の広い黒のハンカチを、ほとんど目を覆うくらい低くギャングスタイルで頭に巻きつけている。それには、金と欲と破壊を訴えるラップソングの歌詞が印刷されている。

スタイル的には、龍也は伝統的なバイカーのイメージから離れ、ディテールにこだわるさらに芸術的なマシン製作へと向かっている。かつてはディガーとボバーのネオチョッパーを製作していたが、彼の新しいバイクは極端に伸びたフレームと高く取り付けられたタンクを特徴とする新世代のデザインを模索している。カスタム・バイク組み立て、塗装などの全工程には３ヵ月以上を要する。エンジンを再構築した後、フレーム、タンク、排気システムの設計・組み立てを行う。部品はインターネットで探したり、アメリカへも定期的に出かける。彼のバイクは日本のハーレー・ダビッドソン誌の表紙を飾ったこともある。

彼のDuas Carasガレージには、５～６台の分解されたハーレーとインディアンがあり、その周りにはそれらの部品が秩序正しく配置されている。壁に沿って４台の仕上がったバイクも並んでいる。長くて低い黄色と黒の1970年代イーストベイ・スタイルのディガー、銀と青のネオチョッパー、そしてタンクが高く取り付けられた２台のボバーだ。これらのマシンとその極端なスタイル化は衝撃的であると同時に見慣れた感覚をも生み出している。龍也の作品はステータスと歴史が存在し、彼が独自に組み合わせた要素にはプレスティージがある。アメリカ文化の力と創意は、マシン自体、および車輪駆動技術への誘惑の形態の普及とアクセスに見られる社会的プロセスに示されている。龍也と彼の顧客は、この歴史とそのスタイル化は美的感覚を再定義するインスピレーションであると認識しており、この認識の一部を担うため、彼はカスタム・バイク・ビルダーとして、形態、機能、色、テクスチャーなど過去から学んだ例と、高度に巧みで独創的な意思決定プロセスを組み合わせている。

何百人ものバイク愛好家たちが、Breezy Biker Camp フェスティバルで、駐車したバイクやテントの間を動き回っている。屋台では焼き餃子や、タコやイカの串焼きを売っている。集まったマシンのほとんどはアメリカ製だ。カスタムや市販のハーレー、それにヴィンテージのインディアンも何台かある。長く引き伸ばしたネオチョッパーに乗る若くてスタイリッシュな女性も何人かおり、可愛いピンクやシルバーに塗装されたタンクが女性っぽい雰囲気を出している。その女性たちはお揃いのピンク色のヘルメットをかぶり、長袖にフリンジが付いた、体にぴったり沿ったスエードのジャケットを着て、その襟にはカウボーイ・パターンのピンクのバンダナをアクセントにしている。中には金色のアンクル・バックルが付いたピンクのバイクブーツを履いている女性もいる。

数人の長髪の男性たちはアメリカ・インディアンをテーマにしたバックスキンのファッションを身にまとい、スクワッシュブロッサム（カボチャの花）のパターンの銀やターコイズ、またはベアクロー（熊のつめ）をモチーフにした、大きく見ごたえがあるアリゾナ風のネックレスを着けている。彼らは、古代英文字と頭蓋骨モチーフを組み合わせたカー・クラブのエンブレムやパッチ付きの黒の革ジャケットを着たバイカーの中に入り交じっている。参加者の多くは、羽をつけたアメリカ・インディアンのテーマがなぜか圧倒的に多いアメリカのバイカー・イベントを真似ている。ここでは、かつて大陸が陸続きで人種につながりがあった可能性を示すかのように、彼らの外観には十分説得力がある。性別によってカウボーイとインディアンがはっきり分かれているのも面白い。若い女性は鳥の羽のバンドが付いたカウボーイハット、若い男性はターコイズを着用している。このイベントはアメリカ南西部のバイカー・ジャンボリーを連想させるが、そういうイベントでは、上品に焼いたシーフードとは対照的に、空気がローストしたビーフの脂っぽい匂いでいっぱいになるものだ。人々は覆いの下に座って静かにビールを飲み、バーベキューグリルの番をしている。フェラチオのようにホットドッグを食べるバイク・レーサーや、バストを見せびらかす太ったギャルなどはどこにもおらず、レーナード・スキナードの歌「フリー・バード」のクラシックなアメリカのギター・ソロが風に流れている。

名古屋には、地域の神話創出に貢献した有名なカスタム・カー・ビルダーが何人かいる。それぞれのショップは、車をどう改造すべきかという点で異なるセンスを持っているが、スタイルの選択肢と嗜好は、アメリカ、特にカスタム・スタイルの起源であるカリフォルニアとつながりがある。これらのガレージの前に停められた高度に様式化された車は、そのガレージ独自の美的感覚に沿った外観やスタンスを保っている。車はランダムな選択の副産物ではなく、ボディライン、形態、色の組み合わせ、スタンス、エンジン・パッケージとマフラーの震動ノイズなど、決定につぐ決定の連なりが組み合わさり生まれる。特定のカスタム形態に対するこだわりは、不思議な慣例主義と、美と調和に対する私的な賞賛を表している。

Paradise Road は名古屋市名東区にある。このガレージは下平淳一が所有・経営し、1987 年からローライダーやカスタム・カーを組み立ててきた。彼は一般的にカスタマイズされないようなアメリカ車のブランドや型を選ぶことで知られて

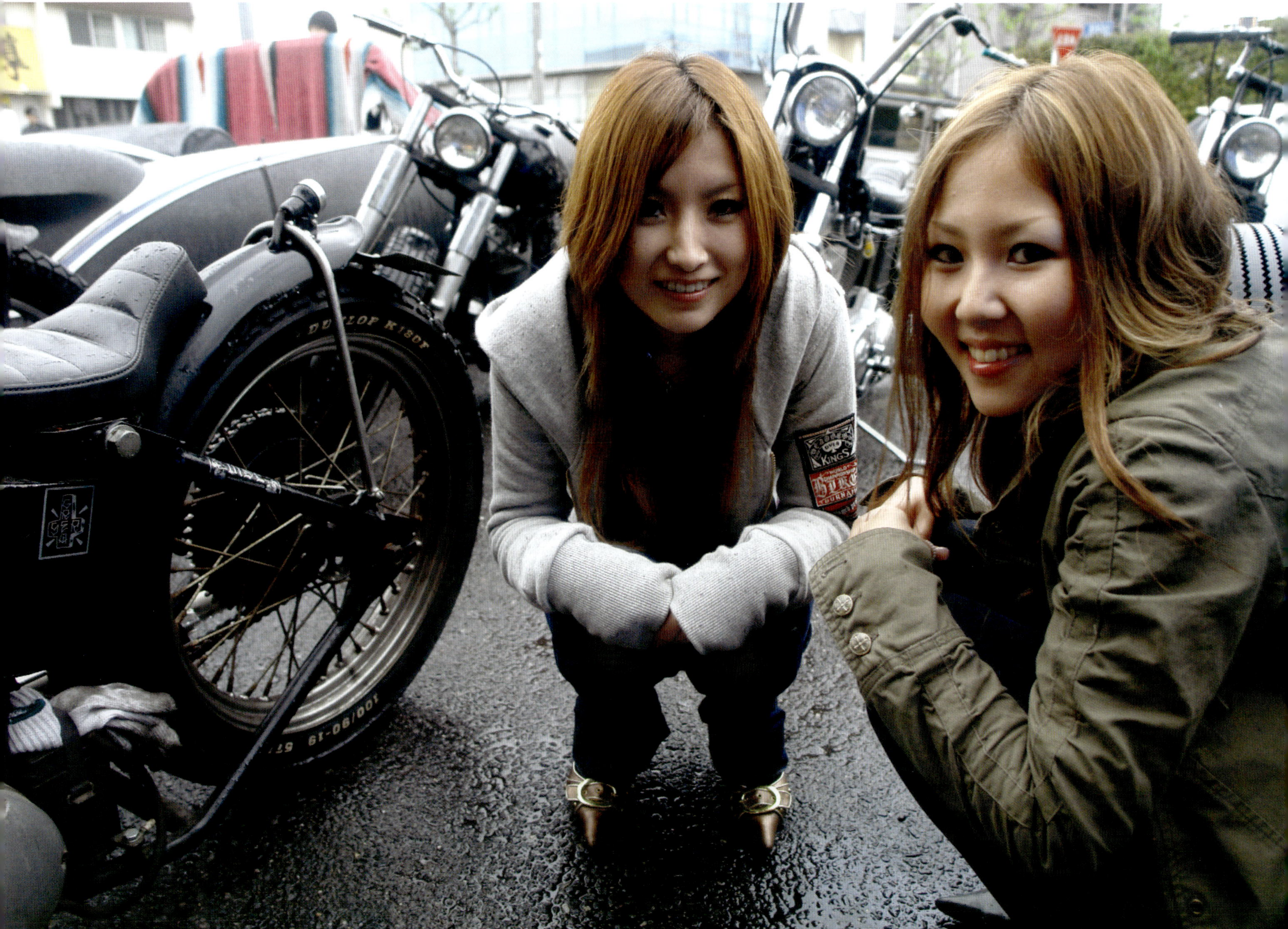
DUNLOP K180F
KINGS

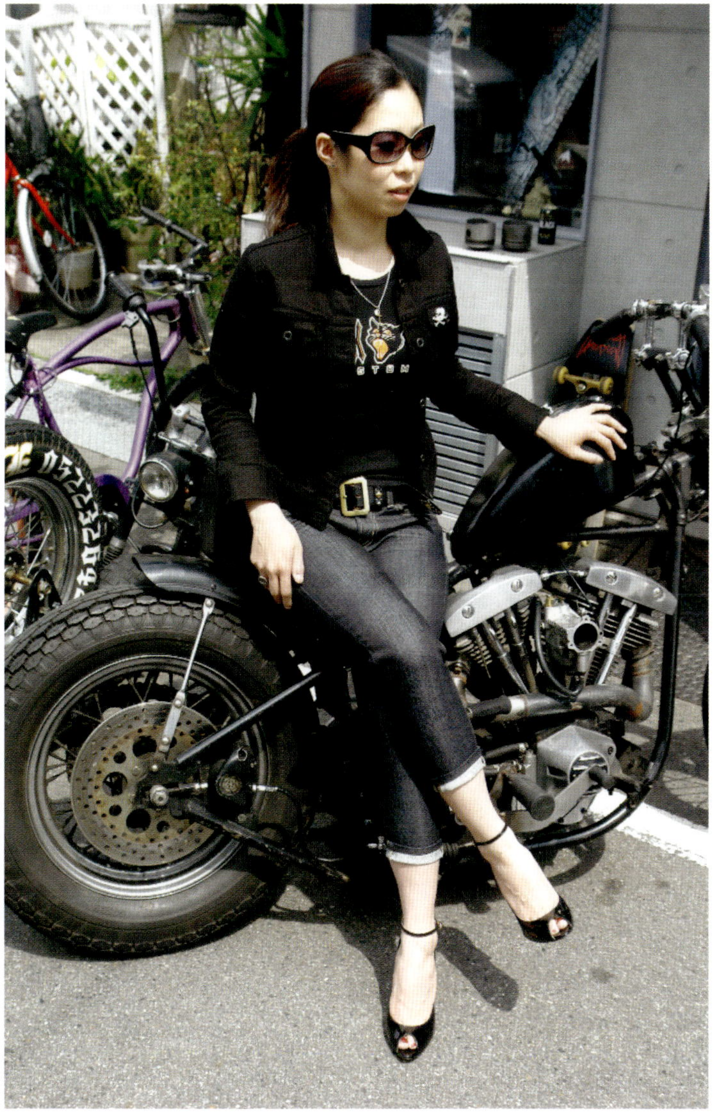

Above: Rei of ViSE Clothing

Left: Nagoya Biker girls

fingernails. It will not be cleaned out easily but that doesn't matter. He has no intension of cleaning it; this is a grease culture.

The pin on the hand grenade jumps around to the rhythm of the huge engine. This sense of ensuing danger runs through the hot rod sensibility. Toshi's friends fly past on their Kustom Harley rat bikes. They sit low on their seats and reach into the chest pockets of their denim jackets looking for cigarettes or toll money. They burst ahead and then fall back in a dangerous but incredible ballet of horsepower. One rider blurs past at more than 80mph. He gestures calmly with his left hand, index finger pointed up and then forward as if to say, "See you there..." He then climbs off of his foot pegs up on to his small (very small) seat. Holding firm to the handlebars, he jumps up and down with a giddy expression on his face. Toshi lets out a faint smile of approval.

There is no smoking in Toshi's car. The cab smells of the rich, seductive, high-octane gas slopping around in the topped off tank behind the seat backs. One wrong spark and the car would indeed go off like the shifter hand grenade. The simple gauges across the dash for oil pressure, temperature, and speed are wound pretty tight. The gas gauge needle answers to a different drummer and moves noticeably downward. For Toshi and his friends there must be something dislocating and then reconnecting about interacting with their powerful mechanical signifiers on native turf. To race through their landscape with rare and highly prized American machines, the thrill is mysterious but also incredibly exciting. The extreme noise, the grit, the velocity, the clothes—none of it has any meaning without the context from where it all began. Without the history it is reduced to nothing; but Toshi, his hot rod friends and the young rat bikers have re-imagined history into something that for them is more real than the original.

Tatsuya Fujii sifts through the broken Shovelhead clutch pieces

いる。彼は異なるラインを持つ変わったボディスタイルで実験することを楽しんでいるのだ。最近、淳一は、アメリカに住む顧客のために、ロドリゲスと呼ばれるユニークなショー・カーを製作した。高度にスタイル化された1930年フォード・セダンで、ローチェスター製の高性能バックドラフト・キャブレターを持つがっしりしたオールズモビル・エンジンを搭載している。車のラインは、革新的なグリル、フェンダー、ラニングボードで徹底的に改造されている。Paradise Road は今年創立20周年で、現在の場所に移ってから5年になる。エド"ビッグ・ダディ"ロスは2001年12月にこのショップを訪問している。

「名古屋のショップはみんなお互いにフレンドリーですね」と淳一は言う。「色々なガレージからの色々な車が一緒になって、クルーズ・ナイトをいつもやっています。ここのカー・カルチャーは東京のような場所とは少し違います。ああいう場所ではお互いに分かち合うとか、オープンな雰囲気がありません。東京と大阪は大都会ですが、名古屋はもう少し小さくて、人々の姿勢が違います。ここにはトヨタや、ヤマハ、ホンダがあり、それがまたカー・カルチャーの雰囲気を増しています。」

「日本のローライダー・カルチャーは名古屋で最初に始まりました。ここの車愛好家たちはそれを自負しています。名古屋の人は特別ですね。田舎の人のようにオープンです。名古屋はロサンゼルスの兄弟都市、メキシコ・シティの姉妹都市です。それがここに住む人の文化的興味に大きな影響を与えています。メキシカン・カー・カルチャーについての大きな関心と、ローライダー・シーンに対する興味には明確なつながりがあります。日本のこの地域は、港や海へのアクセスがあるため、ベイエリアと呼ばれており、名古屋ではこの輸送手段を基盤に、製造業が盛んになりました。」

「日本でのローライダーに対する興味は1980年代に始まりました」と淳一は続ける。「そのころ、ほとんどのカスタム・カー愛好家は暴走族でしたね。(「暴走族」とはバイクと車のクラブやギャングで、1950年代に始まった。騒音の非常に大きい改造車を無謀に運転することと反社会的な活動が特徴。一般的に新人ヤクザを募集する温床と考えられている)あの連中は、まず車体のすごく低い車に興味を示しました。日本の若い車愛好家にとって低いスタンスが重要でした。まず、サスペンションをカスタマイズし、かなり下げます。それからエンジンを再調整し、新しいペイント・カラーを使います。」

「最初にカーマガジンを見たのは1981年、21歳のときでした。初めてローライダーとハイドロサスペンション・システムを見たのはそのときです。それがカリフォルニアのメキシコ人文化が基盤になっていることなど、まったく知りませんでした。ローライダーの外観が気に入ったので、それの文化についての情報を探し始め、写真を見たり、本を探したり、どんな部品が必要なのか人に聞いて回ったりしました。でも日本では、それについて知っている人は当時誰もいませんでした。すごく低くて、すごくクール。こんなクールな車は誰も見たことがありませんでした。」

「初めてLAに行ったのは27歳のときでした。4～5日滞在してローライダーを見て回ろうという計画でした。バンナイズ大通りを見つけて、すごい車をたくさん見ました。それはもう本当に信じられないほどでした…。日本に戻ってトラック運転の仕事を辞め、海外での免許を取得するために時間をかけました。最初の旅行のとき、ローライダー店の名刺をもらったので、それを保管しておきました。2回目の旅行は、友人と一緒に行って3週間滞在しました。英語はまったく話せませんでしたが、旅行ガイドブックを持っていて、それをレンタカー屋の人に見せて、カー・カルチャーを探していることを伝え、ローライダーについて聞いてみました。彼は私たちの頭がどうかしているんじゃないかと思ったみたいで、車を貸すのを心配しているようでした。ギャング・カルチャーにも興味があったので、コンプトンにも行きました。

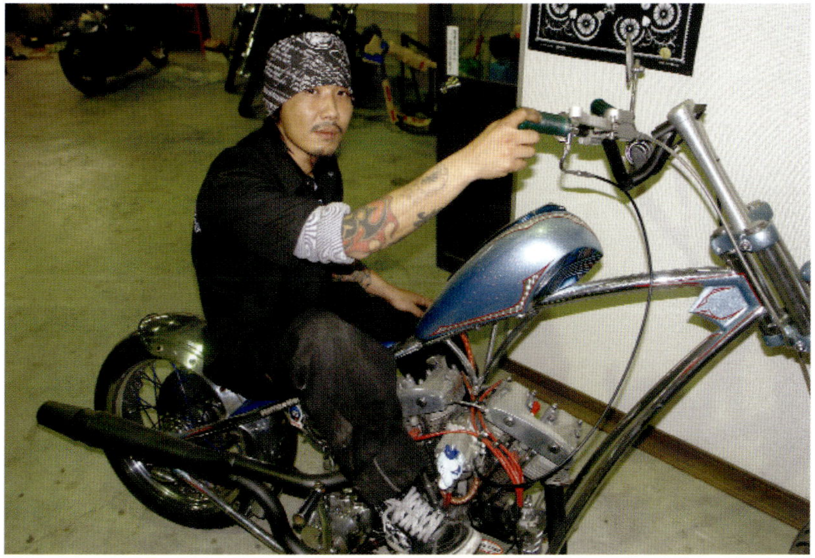

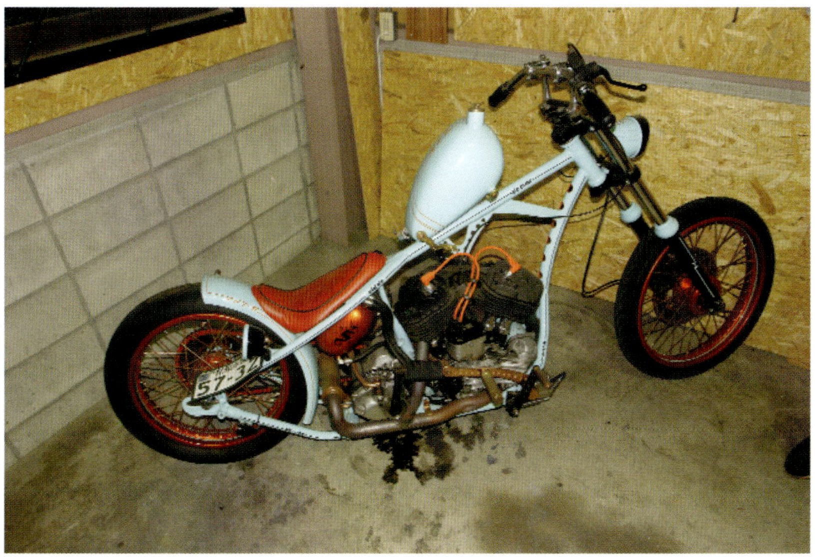

Top: Tatsuya Fujii - Duas Caras Cycles, Nagoya

Bottom: Duas Caras Cycles, design and built

he has skillfully disassembled onto the rest-stop driveway. Riders are talking on their cell phones, describing the situation to friends who stream into the parking lot like bees returning to the hive. He is surrounded with young bikers watching him quickly pick through the good and bad parts of the temperamental engine. Tatsuya is young, but his reputation as a kustom bike builder is much respected in the Nagoya area. In less than 15 minutes, the clutch and primary belt is reassembled and set. There are no special tools, just a couple of simple wrenches and his accumulated sensibility about engines. He climbs on the bike, cranks and loads the compression and then kicks it over with a loud pop as everyone grinds out their cigarettes. Thirty or more curbed bikes follow his cue, fire up and resume the race towards the Breezy Biker Camp custom event.

The tragedy and comedy masks logo of Tatsuya's Duas Caras Cycles hints a reference to SoCal cholo jailhouse culture. He is 31 years old and has been building motorcycles for more than ten years, but his attention is now turned to building very unique kustom bikes. A broad, black handkerchief wraps low around his head and almost covers his eyes gangster style. It is printed with words from a rap song that speak of cash and greed and ruin.

Stylistically, Tatsuya is moving away from the traditional biker identity towards machines that are more artistic, with more detail. In the past he built old style Diggers and Bobber Neo-Choppers, but his new bikes explore a new generation of design styles that feature radically stretched frames and high mounted tanks. It takes him more than three months to design, build and paint a kustom bike. He rebuilds the engine and then designs and fabricates the frame, tank and exhaust system. In search of parts he surfs the Internet and travels regularly to America. His bikes have been featured on the cover of Japan Harley Davidson magazine.

あのとき自分たちが何をやっているのか、さっぱり分かっていませんでした。あの人は私たちによく車を貸してくれたものだと驚いています。」

「ダウンタウンを運転していてペップボーイズの店を見つけました」と淳一は続ける。「この車用品の店については聞いたことがありました。店の近くにはすごく低い車体の車を運転する黒人たちがいました。車はどれも驚くようなワイヤーホイールが付いていて、塗装も非常に巧妙でした。それからローライダーがいっぱい並んだ店を見つけ、タイヤ、リム、スタンス、ペイントなどについて質問してみました。写真もたくさん撮りました。あの近所の人たちにとって、私たちの行動は変に見えたのでしょうね。驚いていたようでした。1人の女性が私たちを見て、何か尋ねました。彼女が何を言ったのかはさっぱり分かりませんでしたが、でも心配しているようでした。今考えてみると、危ないから気をつけろと言ってくれたのでしょう…。」

「日本に帰ってきてから、その写真を暴走族の連中に見せました。皆すごいショックを受けましたね。メキシカン・ローライダーの社会についてはまったく何も知りませんでしたから。彼らはあごに手をあてて写真に見入っていました。頭の中で色々考えているのが分かりました。」

淳一や暴走族らにとって、海外のマシンに見られる美的感覚は深遠なものだった。これは、流れると同時に取り残された時代から連想された不思議な感情とも言えた。写真に写ったカスタム・マシンは、遠いどこかから示された変化と決定の数ある項目から、視覚的調和を生み出す新しいプロセスを体現していた。この新しいカスタマイズ・プロセスは理性と非理性が巧みに組み合わされ、マシンによる強烈な感情的興味に満ちた因襲の再設計手段を表していた。

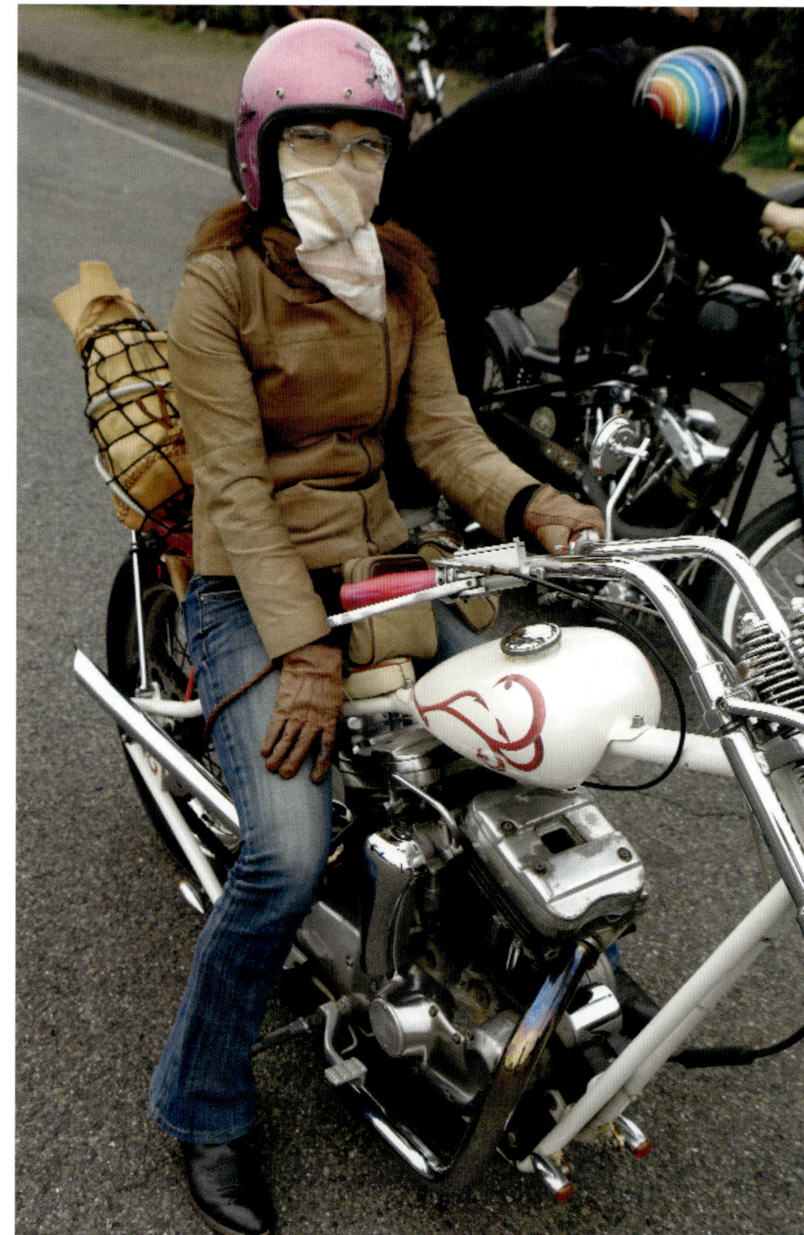

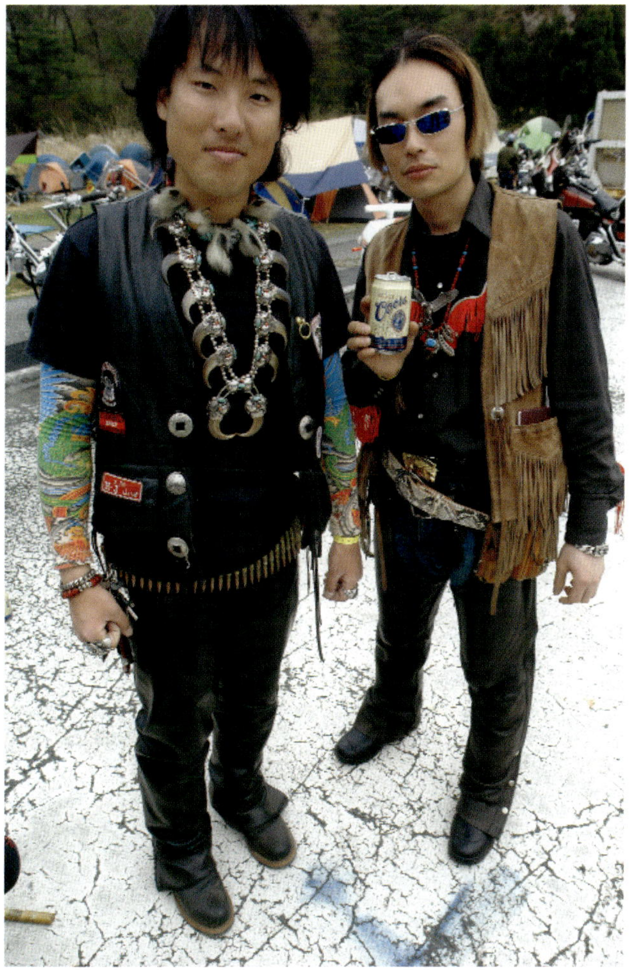

Above & Left: Breezy Biker Camp attendees

In his Duas Caras garage there are a half-dozen disassembled Harleys and Indians surrounded with organized collections of their parts. Against the wall are four finished bikes, a long and low yellow and black 1970s East Bay style Digger, a silver and blue Neo-chopper and two Bobbers with high mounted tanks. The machines and their extreme stylizations are both shocking and familiar. There is status and history associated with Tatsuya's work; a prestige of combined elements that he has personalized. Here, the power and ingenuity of American culture is represented by its machines and also the social process of popularization and access to seductive forms of wheeled technology. For Tatsuya and his customers there is awareness about this history and its stylizations as inspiration for a redefined sense of beauty. As a kustom bike builder he is a part of this process of recognition that combines historical examples of form, function, color and texture with a highly skilled and inventive decision-making process.

Several hundred biker enthusiasts mill around among the parked bikes and tents at the Breezy Biker Camp festival. Food stalls sell grilled gyoza dumplings and skewers of BBQ octopus and squid. Most of the machines are American in origin, custom and stock Harleys and a few vintage Indians. There are several younger stylish women riding stretched Neo-shoppers that have been feminized with tanks painted in pinks or silvers. The women wear matching pink helmets and form-fitting suede leather jackets with long sleeve fringe accented at the collar with pink cowboy-patterned bandanas. Some of the women have pink motorcycle boots with gold ankle buckles.

A few long-haired men wear Native American Indian-themed fashions that feature buckskins and large impressive (really impressive) Arizona-style squash-blossom silver and turquoise or bear-claw necklaces. They mingle with more typical black leather jackets sporting an assortment of club rockers and patches that combine skull motifs with Old English-type fonts. Many attendees mimic

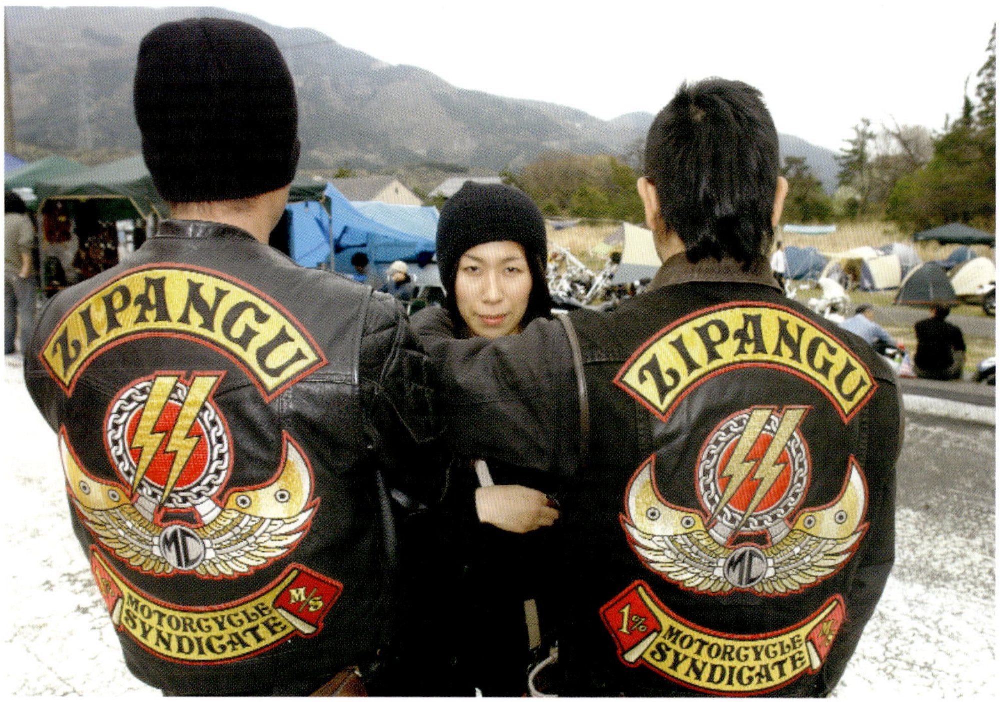
ZIPANGU
MOTORCYCLE SYNDICATE
ZIPANGU
1%
MOTORCYCLE SYNDICATE

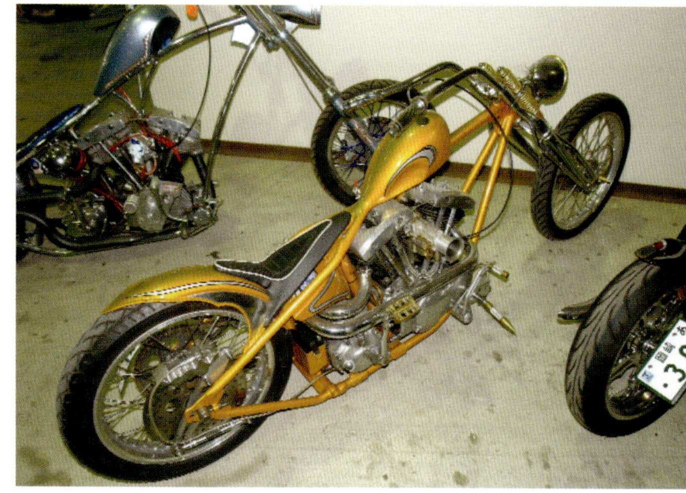

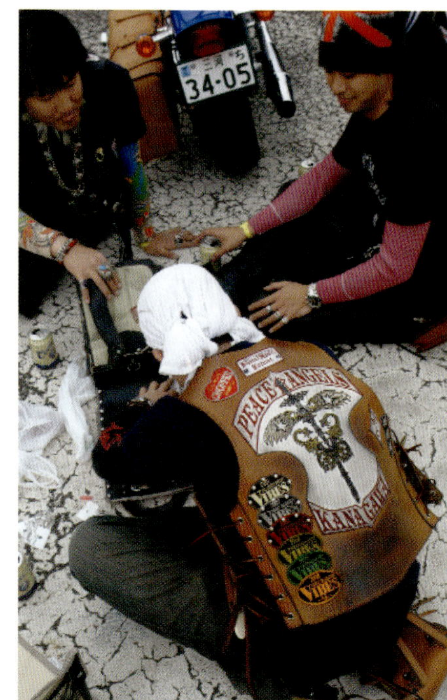
34-05
PEACE ANGELS

American biker events where, for some reason, feathered Native American Indian themes dominate. Here, possible land bridge racial connections make the visuals more convincing. Genders split between cowboys and Indians—young women wear the cowboy hats with bird feather bands and the young men wear the turquoise. It is all reminiscent of an American Southwest biker jamboree where the air would be thick with roasted fatty beef instead of delicately grilled marine life. Groups of people sit under their tarps quietly drinking beer and tending to their smoking hibachis. There are no fellatio-like hot dog-grabbing bike races and no fat chicks showing off their tits but the classic American guitar solo from Lynyrd Skynyrd's song, "Free Bird," is on the wind.

Far left: Zipangu club rockers

Left top: Duas Caras Cycles, design and built

Left bottom: Peace Angels

Below: Paradise Road, 1938 Dodge

Following pages: 1951 Mercury - Syu Merk, work by Border's Owner: Syu Chan

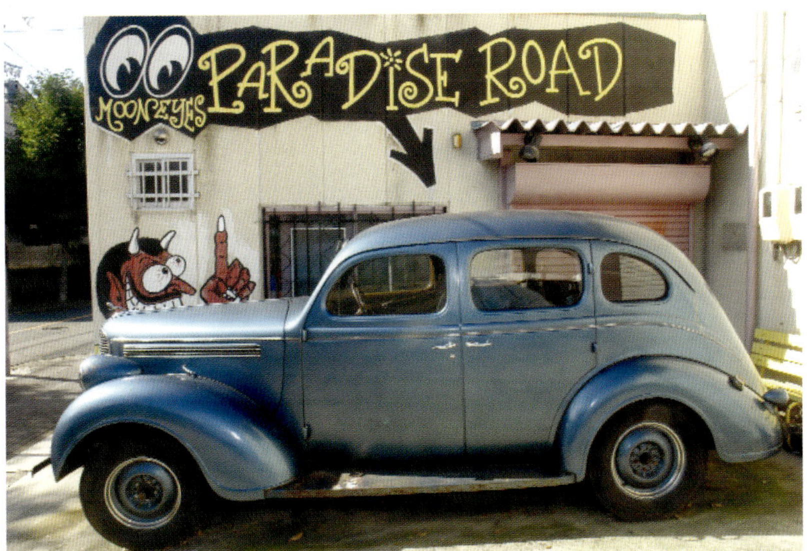

There are several kustom car builders in Nagoya with notable reputations that have contributed to the area's mystique. Each shop has a different sensibility about how a car should be modified. Choices and tastes in stylization are connected to root sources in America and particularly California where kustom style first originated. Highly stylized cars sit in the driveways of garages with looks and stances connected to the specific esthetics of the garage. The cars are not the byproduct of random choices. Bodylines, forms, color combinations, stances, engine packages and muffler percussion noise represent lineages of the decisions that combine to create a car. The perseverance of some kustom forms over others reflects a mysterious conventionalism and a privately appreciated sense of harmony and beauty.

Paradise Road is located in the Meitou-ku section of Nagoya. The garage is owned and operated by Junichi Shimodaira, who has been building lowrider and kustom cars since 1987. He is known for choosing American car brands and styles that are not usually customized. He enjoys experimenting with unusual body styles with different lines. Recently, Junichi created a unique show car called Rodriguez for a customer in America. It is a highly stylized 1930

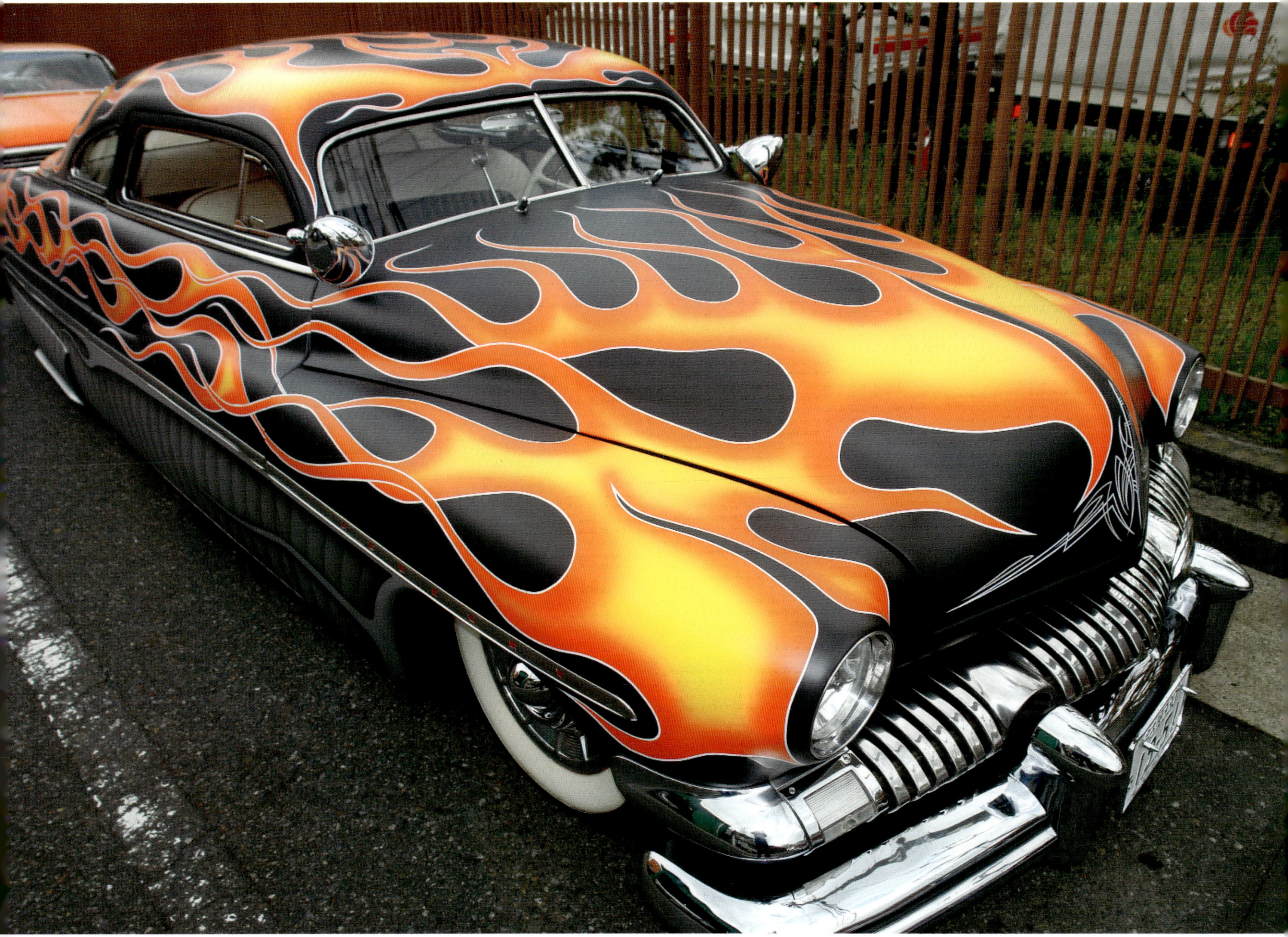

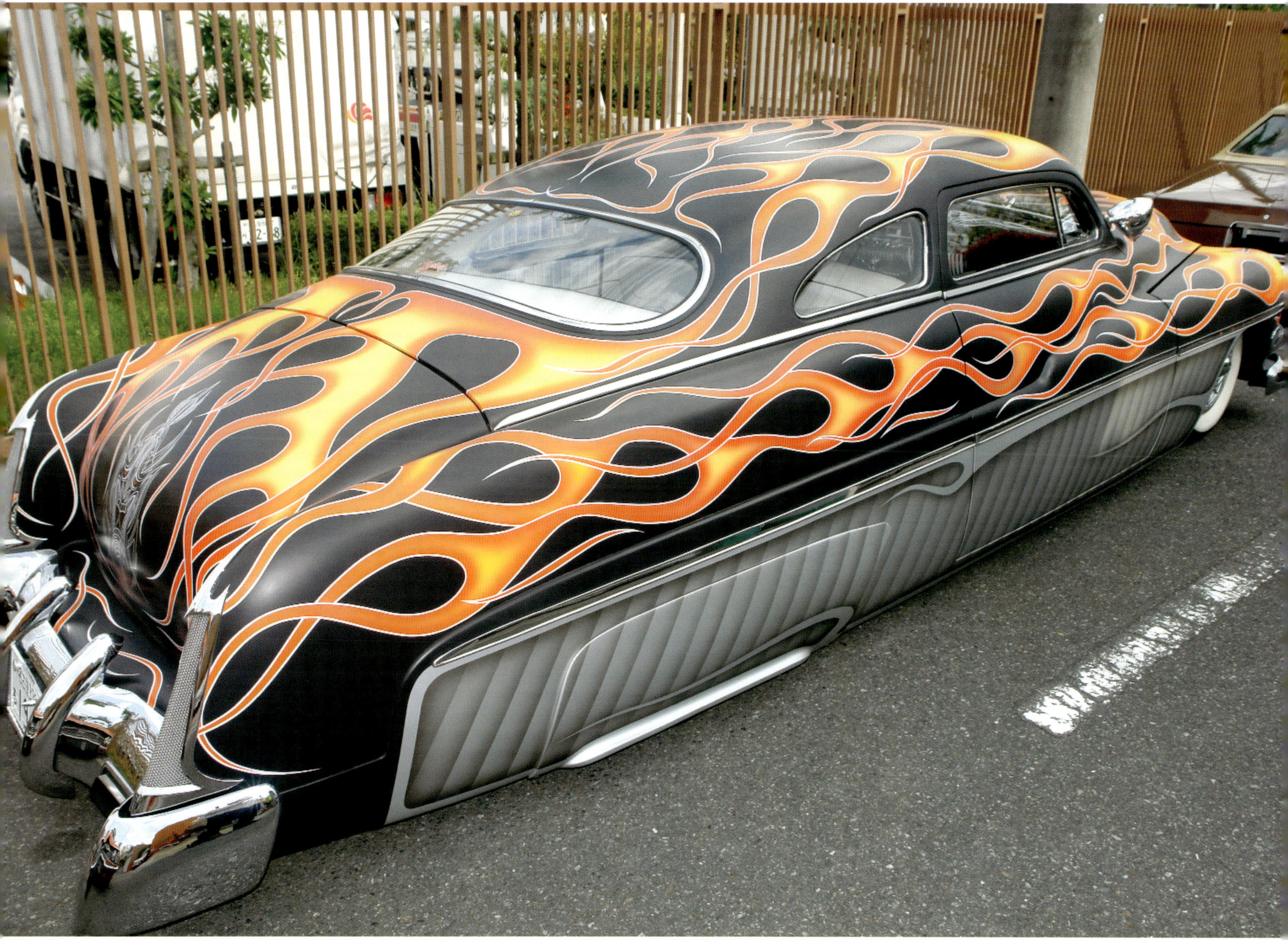

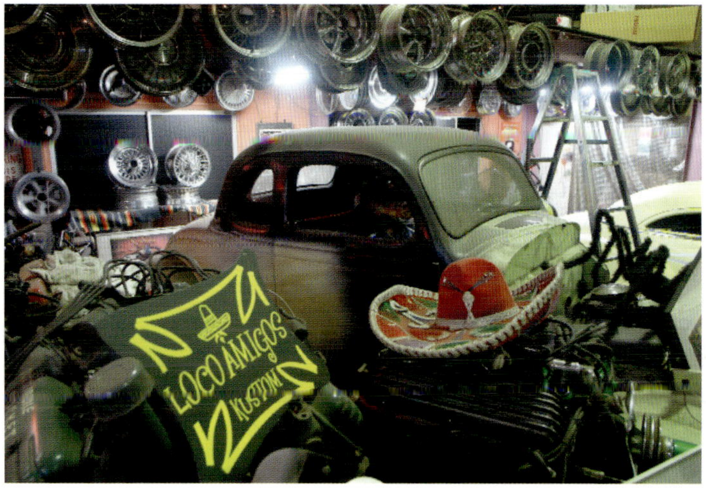
LOCO AMIGOS
KUSTOM

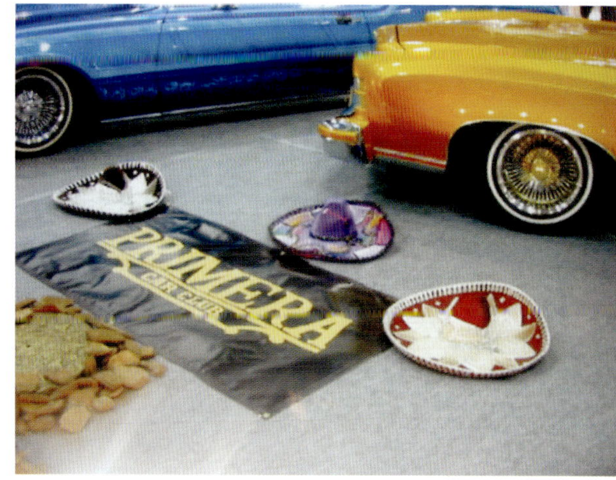
PRIMERA
CAR CLUB

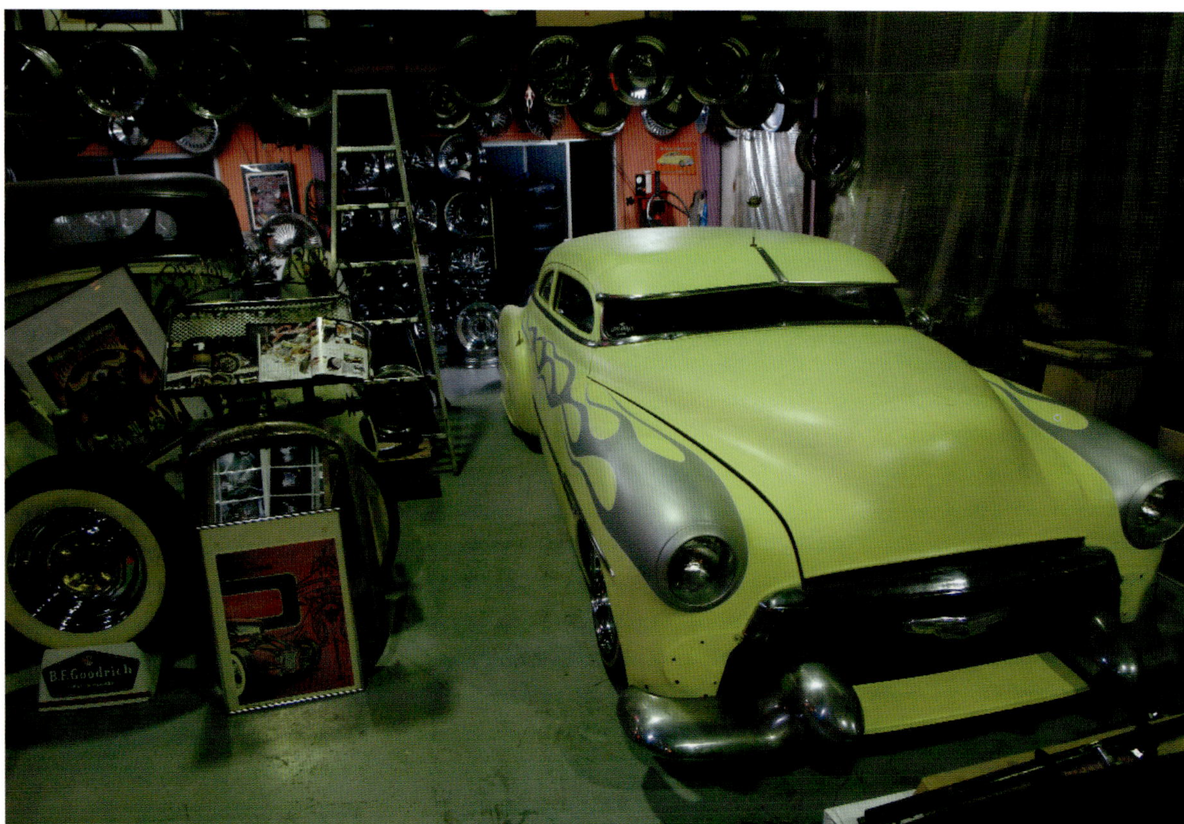
B.F.Goodrich

Ford sedan with a beefy Oldsmobile engine, which has a high performance back draft Rochester carburetor. The lines of the car have been radically modified with innovative grill, fender and running board shapes. This is the twentieth anniversary of Paradise Road, and he has been at his current location for five years. Ed “Big Daddy” Roth visited the shop in December 2001.

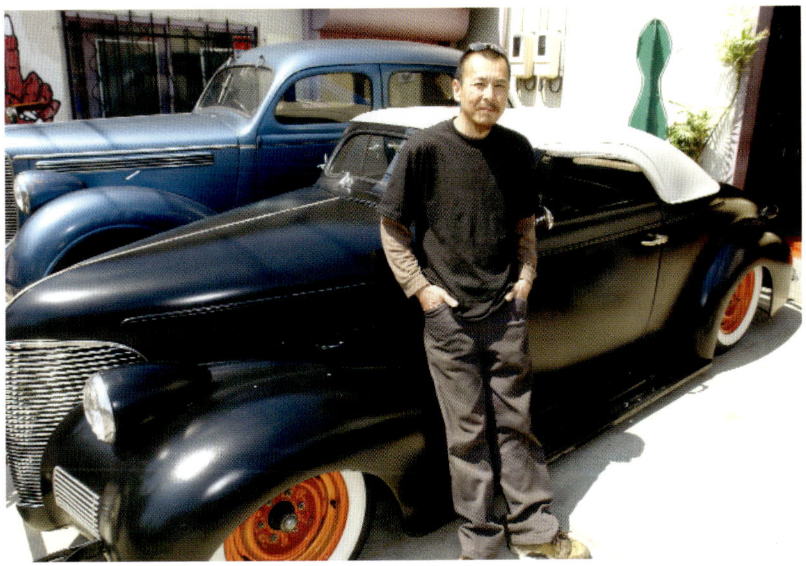

Above: Junichi Shimodaira
Leaning against 1939 Chevy chop

Far left top: Loco Amigos Kustom

Left top: Primera Car Club presentation with Mexican motif.

Left bottom: 1951 Chevy Styleline 2-door sedan “El Pacifista”
Hydraulics, custom rear frame work, 1970 Corvette
S/B 350 V8 w/TH 350 auto trans to 10 bolt Chevy rear end

“All of the shops in the Nagoya area are friendly with each other,” Junichi says. “We often have cruise nights together with many different cars from different garages. The car culture here is different from places like Tokyo. They don’t share too much there, it isn’t an open kind of feeling. Tokyo and Osaka are big cities; Nagoya is smaller and people here have different attitudes. The Toyota, Yamaha and Honda companies are here, and this adds to the car culture feeling.”

“Japan lowrider culture first started in Nagoya, and car people here are proud of this fact. Nagoya people are special; it is a country kind of place where the people are open. Nagoya is the brother city of Los Angeles and sister of Mexico City. This has had a big influence on the cultural interest of the car people here. There is a lot of excitement about Mexican car culture and our interest in the lowrider scene is definitely connected to that. This part of Japan is referred to as the Bay Area because of the harbor and access to the ocean. Nagoya has always been a heavy manufacturing area because of the shipping.”

“Interest in lowriders started in Japan during the 1980s,” Junichi continues. “At that time most custom car guys were *bosozoku.*” (Editor’s note: These bike and car clubs and gangs originating in the 1950s were often recruiting grounds for the *yakuza* and were known for antisocial behavior, recklessly driving very loud, modified vehicles.) “These guys were the first to get interested in the low-low look of cars. The low stance was important for young car guys in

「私は17歳で高校を中退しました」と淳一は続ける。「バイクでひどい交通事故を起こしました。その後ガソリンスタンドで働き、メカニックの仕事を見て覚えました。6ヵ月後に自動車修理工場に転職し、そこで2〜3年働きました。1980年にそれを辞めて、しばらくアルバイトをやり、その後、また違うガソリンスタンドで働き始めました。そこでも車を扱う人がいましたが、今までとちょっと違うタイプの人でした。その人から新しい技術をたくさん学びました。そのころはシェビー・カマロを持っていたので、アメリカ製V8 350ciを修理する方法を勉強しました。その職場でアメリカ製V8を初めて見て、取り組んだことを憶えています。シェビーV8の改造は簡単で、修理も調整も楽。馬力を上げるのも容易でした。そこで2年働いてから、名古屋でトラックの運転手になりました。当時は運転しながら、いつもローライダーのことを考えていました。」

「ある夜、仕事が終わった後でチーチ・アンド・チョンの映画を見に行きました。ハイドロが付いた車を見たのはそのときが初めてで、ますますローライダーに興味を持つようになりました。車があんなことをやるのを見てショックでしたよ。どうやって、ああいうふうにジャンプできるのか分かりませんでした。まったく驚きでした。」

「トラック運転手の同僚何人かとカー・クラブをつくりました。アメリカン・グラフィティのカー・クラブと同じように"ファラオス"という名前をつけ、そこで偽物のローライダーや偽物のカスタムを作りました。アメリカの車を買えなかったので、古い日本車を使って、ローライダーやホットロッドを真似したんです。ときどき他の日本のカー・クラブと会ったりして、アメリカのカー・クラブについての情報を得ました。そのころの名古屋は孤立していました。」

「1987年、トラック運転の仕事を辞めてLAに行きました」と彼は語る。「帰国してから、アメリカのアンティーク・カーの玩具や看板を扱うショップを開業することに決めました。そのときに、LAでは日本と比べて車の部品が安いことにも気づきました。私の最初のショップは、アメリカのアンティーク・カーの玩具や、こっそり持ち込まれた車の部品などを売る小さい店でしたが、友達がたくさんできました。車の愛好家たちがたむろしたり、たまに何かを買うような場所でした。日本ではそのころ、徐々に多くの人がローライダーに興味を示すようになり、1987年、第1回東京ストリート・カー・ナショナルズが催されました。いいタイミングでしたね。ムーンアイズのシゲさんが初めてたくさんの車愛好家を結集させました。これをきっかけにして、すべてが急発進しました。」

「最初のショーではハイドロの付いた車が1台だけありました。みんな口をぽかんと開けたまま立ち尽くしていました…。車から逃げていく人もいました。どうやってあんなジャンプができるのか、みんなまったく分からなかったようです。オーナーは東京の人で、ジャンクヤードを持っていました。1960年代のフォード・カントリー・スクワイア・ステーションワゴンで、これを飛び回らせていました。みんなかなりショックを受けていましたよ。私はあの車を見て、これがやりたいと思いましたね。」

「LAからの名刺を保管していたので、その名刺にあった住所にハイドロ機器を注文しました。そしてモンテカルロを持っていた友達に、この機器を取り付けてもいいか聞いてみました。彼は私を見て『ぼくの車をジャンプさせたいわけ？』って聞きかえしました。そしてそのキットをモンテカルロの後部に取りつけさせてくれましたが、彼はまだどうも心配な様子でした。あんなことをやらせてくれたのが今でも驚きです。彼はあれでもうモンテカルロは終わりだと確信していたようです。そして道路でその車を飛び回らせてみたら、車が幽霊にでも取り憑かれたかのように、みんな逃げ出しましたね。この車が私のすべてを変えてしまいました。」

Japan. First they customized the suspensions to drop it way down. They re-tuned the engines and used new paint colors."

"I first saw car magazines back in 1981 when I was 21 years old. That's when I first saw lowriders. I had no idea they were based in California Mexican culture. I liked the look of those low cars, so I started digging around for more information about the culture of it. I would see a photo and I'd looked for books and talked with people about what kind of parts you would need. Nobody in Japan knew anything about it. Very low and very cool, nobody ever saw cool cars like this."

"I went to L.A. for the first time in 1987 when I was 27 years old. My plan was to stay four or five days looking around for lowriders. I found the Van Nuys Boulevard cruise scene and saw all the amazing cars. It was incredible. I went back to Japan and quit my truck-driving job, and spent time getting an international license. That first trip I had found a business card from a lowrider shop and saved it. The second trip I went back with some friends for three weeks. We didn't speak any English but we had this tour book we showed the car rental guy. We told him we were looking for car culture and asked about lowriders. He thought we were crazy and worried about renting us a car. We were interested to find the gangster culture so we went to Compton. We had no idea what we were doing. I am amazed that guy rented us a car."

"We were driving around downtown and saw a Pep Boys shop. I had heard of these car accessory shops. There were black people driving around in very low cars near the shop. They all had amazing wire wheels and very slick paint jobs. Then we saw a shop full of lowriders. We tried to ask about the tires and the rims and the stance and the paint. We were taking many photos. This must have looked very funny to people in this neighborhood. I think they were amazed. I remember one lady looked at us and asked us something.

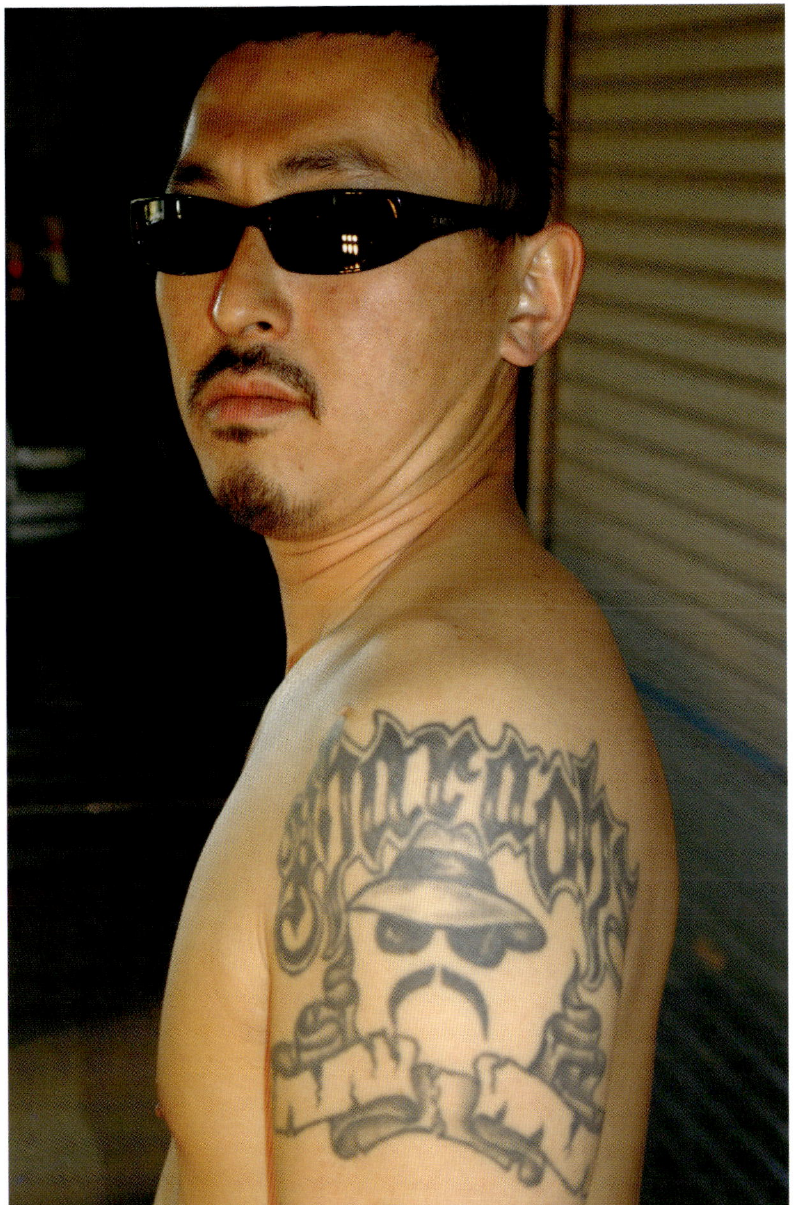

Above: Hisashi Ushida, Cholo's Custom

Following pages: In progress vintage Chevy rebuild
1947 Chevy Fleetline

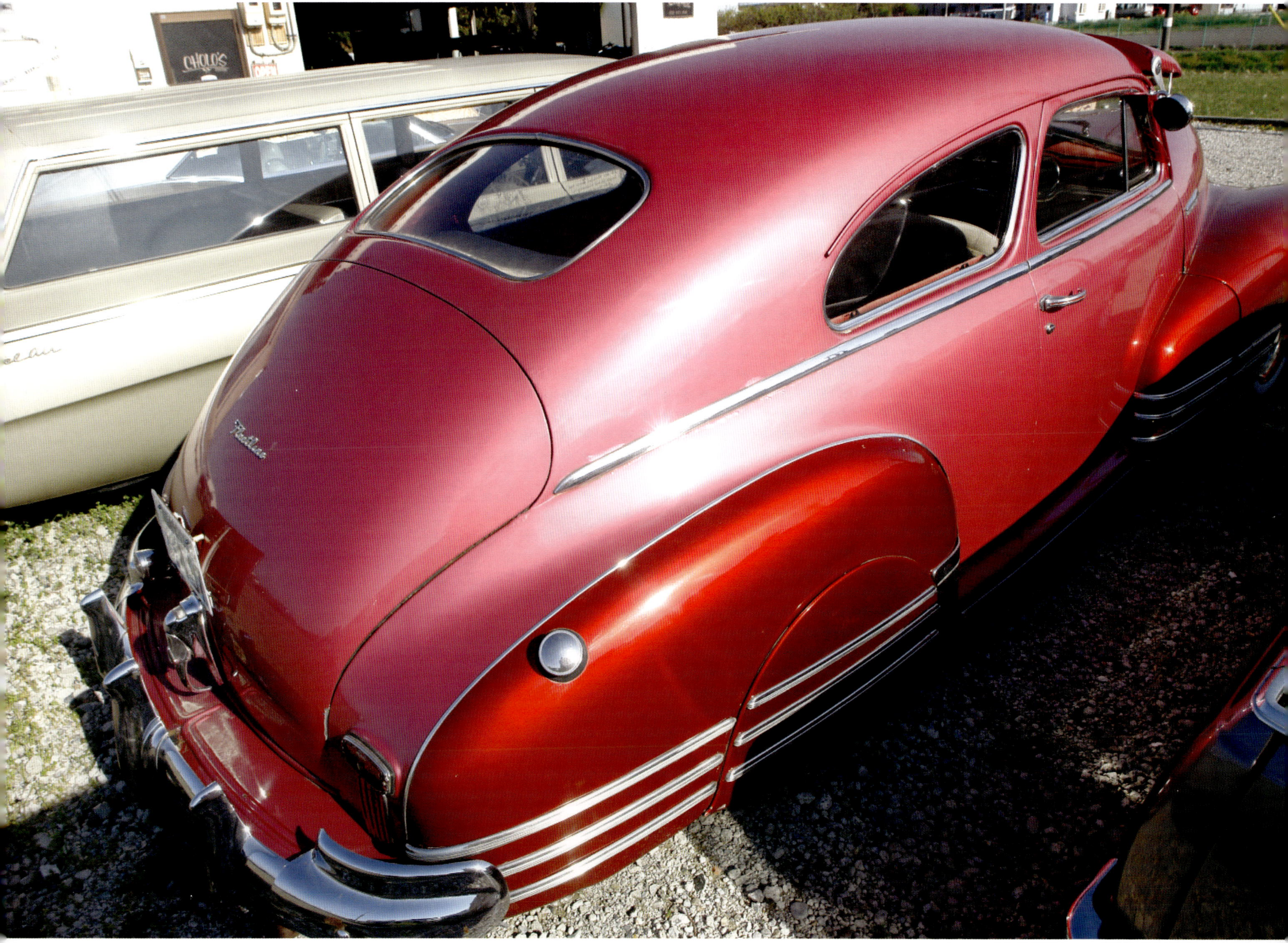
CHOLO'S

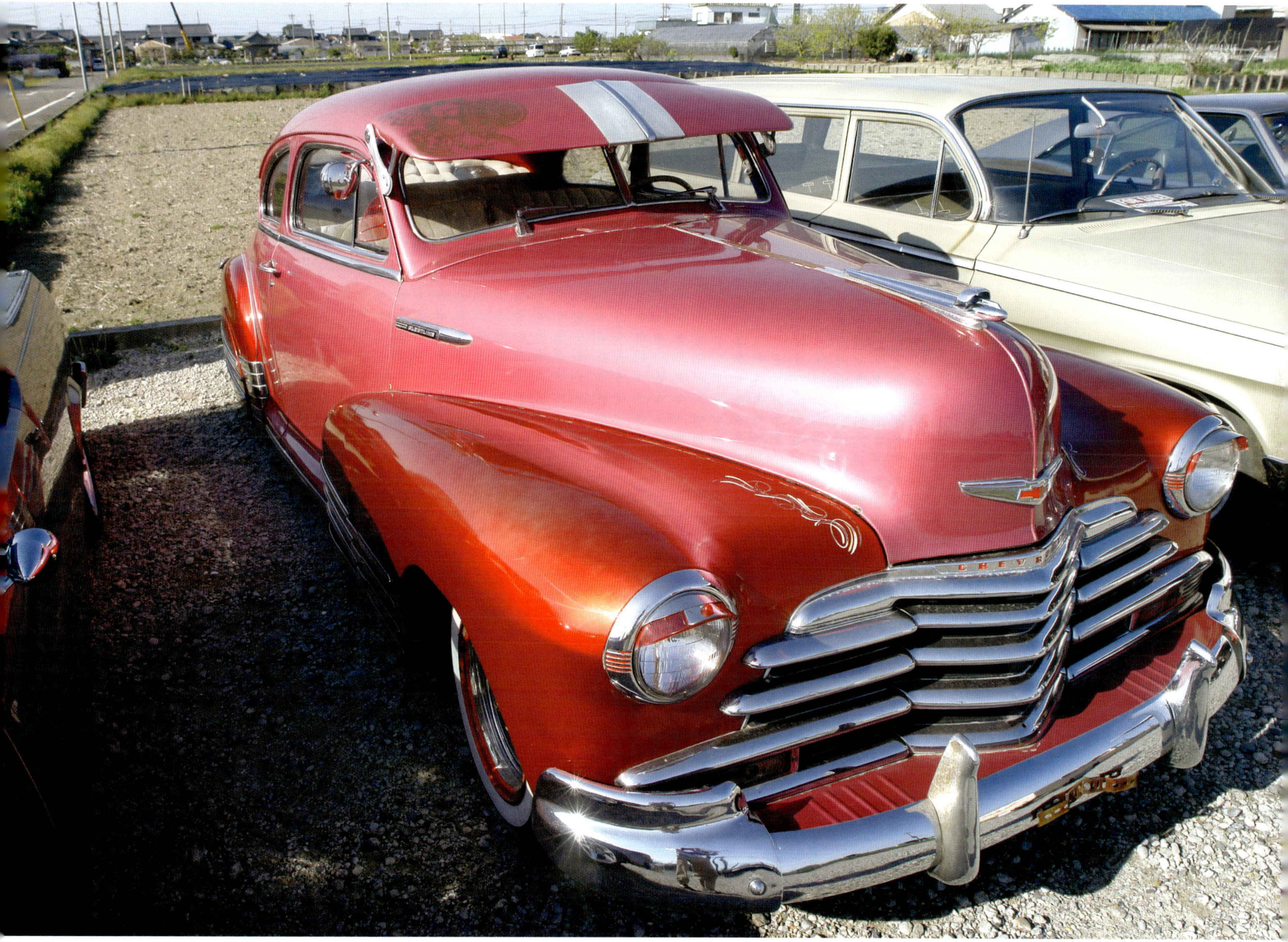

「このショップでもう5年になります」と淳一は結ぶ。「車の仕事は全部自分でやり、友達がボディ塗装を担当しています。名古屋のショップはフレンドリーですよ。ここのカー・カルチャーはすごくクールです。」

Border's (ボーダーズ) のオーナー、加藤秀樹は、ガレージの前の木製ベンチに腰掛け、静かにタバコを吸っている。ガレージ前の狭い道には見事なカスタム・カーが2台停まっている。強烈なブルーの炎が描かれた鮮やかなオレンジ色の1960年ベルエア、そしてシューちゃんという名前の若い男性が所有する黒の51年マーキュリーだ。この車は「Syu Merk」として知られている。車はどちらも光沢仕上げではなく、タフな雰囲気を生み出すつや消しで塗装されている。ベルエアのルーフはかなりチョップされ、非常に軽やかな感じになり、速い印象を醸し出している。マーキュリーの大きなボンネットには、力強くクラシックな炎が描かれ、濃いオレンジから明るい黄色へのグラデーションになっている。ノーズとテール部分には愛知県岡崎市に住むアーティストのマコトがストライプを加えた。

ガレージとその舗道には作業中の車が停められている。ターコイズ・ブルーの29年A型フォード・レトロロッド、48年ビュイック・スペシャル、代表的マッスル・スタンスのフォームグリーン67年シェベル・ワゴン、そしてバラバラになったマーキュリーがいくつか置かれている。バックにはボブ・マーリーのレゲエ音楽が流れている。秀樹は自分の車を眺めて微笑んだ。彼のもとにある車は歴史への認識だけではなく、同時に改造されうる可能性も認識させる。極端にチョップされたオレンジのベルエアは、クールさとクレイジーさが同時に見られ、鮮やかなオレンジに重なった力強いブルーの炎という深いコントラストは刺激的だ。これらの色が見慣れた感覚と未知の感覚の間で緊張感を生み出し、ドライバーと鑑賞者双方にとっての車の意味を変える。これらは現実と想像の両方の世界にまたがっている。夢の中の恐ろしいイメージでありながら、単なる車でもある。この奇妙さは少しシュールだが、これこそが視覚的パワーの根源なのである。

これらの車は、まるで造形コレクションのようにガレージ前の舗道に停まっている。アメリカ人にとって、これらの形状は目覚めることを待っている眠った記憶と漠然とした連想として共鳴し、互いや、社会の意識の中を通って循環する。だが、秀樹にとっては異なる共鳴のプロセスが広がる。多くの点で、彼は循環から抜け出た空白のページのようなものだ。彼は形状と造形の間のつながりと歴史を認識することを学びはしたが、それは実際に覚えておくようなものではない。まるでまったく何も起こらなかったかのようだ。彼にとってそれは単に認識としてのみ存在する。

ガレージの2階には、車の玩具で完全に埋め尽くされた、ガラスの飾り棚でいっぱいのショールームがある。この部屋は必ずしも子供のためのものではなく、車に夢中になっている大人のモデルカー・コレクターのためのものでもある。実際に何百台という数のホットウィールやレヴェルの模型セット、希少なコレクタブルから、ブリキやプラスチック製の縮尺モデルにいたるまで、すべてがきちんと並べて整理されている。この部屋は、今や玩具や模型の会社が製造するようになった、カスタマイジングのミニチュア例を展示する博物館だ。車の愛好家たちは、Hirohata Merc や CadZZilla のような伝説的な車のミニチュア版を所有することに大きな関心があり、重要な車はほとんどミニチュア化されてきた。

「Border'sでは、もう19年以上車を作ってきました」と秀樹は言う。「最初は隣がバーだったもっと小さい場所にいました。そこではアメリカで買い付けた中古のアメリカ車の販売を行っていました。最初はミニトラックに凝っていましたが、それからもっと大型のアメリカ車に興味が移り、今はカスタム・マーキュリーです。何年も前には国産中古車の販売業者をしていました。」

We had no idea what she was saying. She looked worried. I now know she was telling us to be careful."

"When we got back to Japan I showed these photos to some *bosozoku* guys. They were completely shocked. They had no idea about this Mexican lowrider scene. They had their hands on their chins looking at the photos. I could see their gears grinding."

For Junichi and the *bosozoku,* this sense of beauty from exotic machines was profound, a mysterious sentimentality connected to associations that were both fluid and frozen in time. The kustom machines in the photos represented a new process of creating visual harmony from a long list of variables and decisions from a far off place. This new customizing skillfully combined the rational with the irrational and the machines represented a paradigm of reinvention loaded with intense emotional interest.

"At seventeen I dropped out of high school," Junichi continues. "I had a bad motorcycle accident. I worked in a gas station, and watched and learned from the mechanics. Six months later I changed jobs to a repair garage and worked there for two or three years. I quit in 1980 and did part-time jobs. Then I worked at a different gas station. There was a car guy there, who had a different style. I learned a lot of new techniques from him. At the time I had a Chevy Camaro. I started to learn how to service an American V8 350ci. I remember the first time I saw and worked on an American V8. Modifying a Chevy V8 was easy, easy to fix and tune easy to increase horsepower. I worked there for two years and then quit and became a truck driver in Nagoya. I was driving and thinking about lowriders."

"One night after work I went to see a Cheech and Chong movie. It was the first time I saw a car with hydraulics and I became even more interested in the lowrider scene. I was shocked to see a car

Inoue, 1950 Chevy Fleetline four-door, 235 straight six, hydraulics, member Pharaohs Car Club

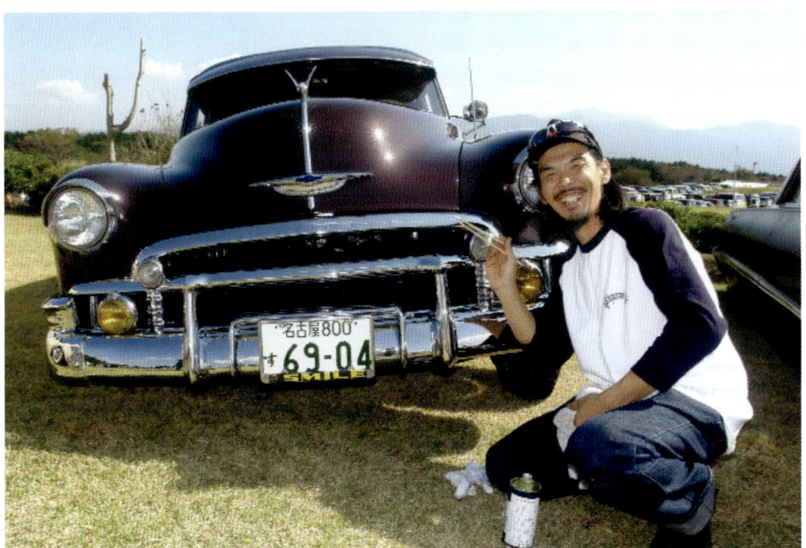

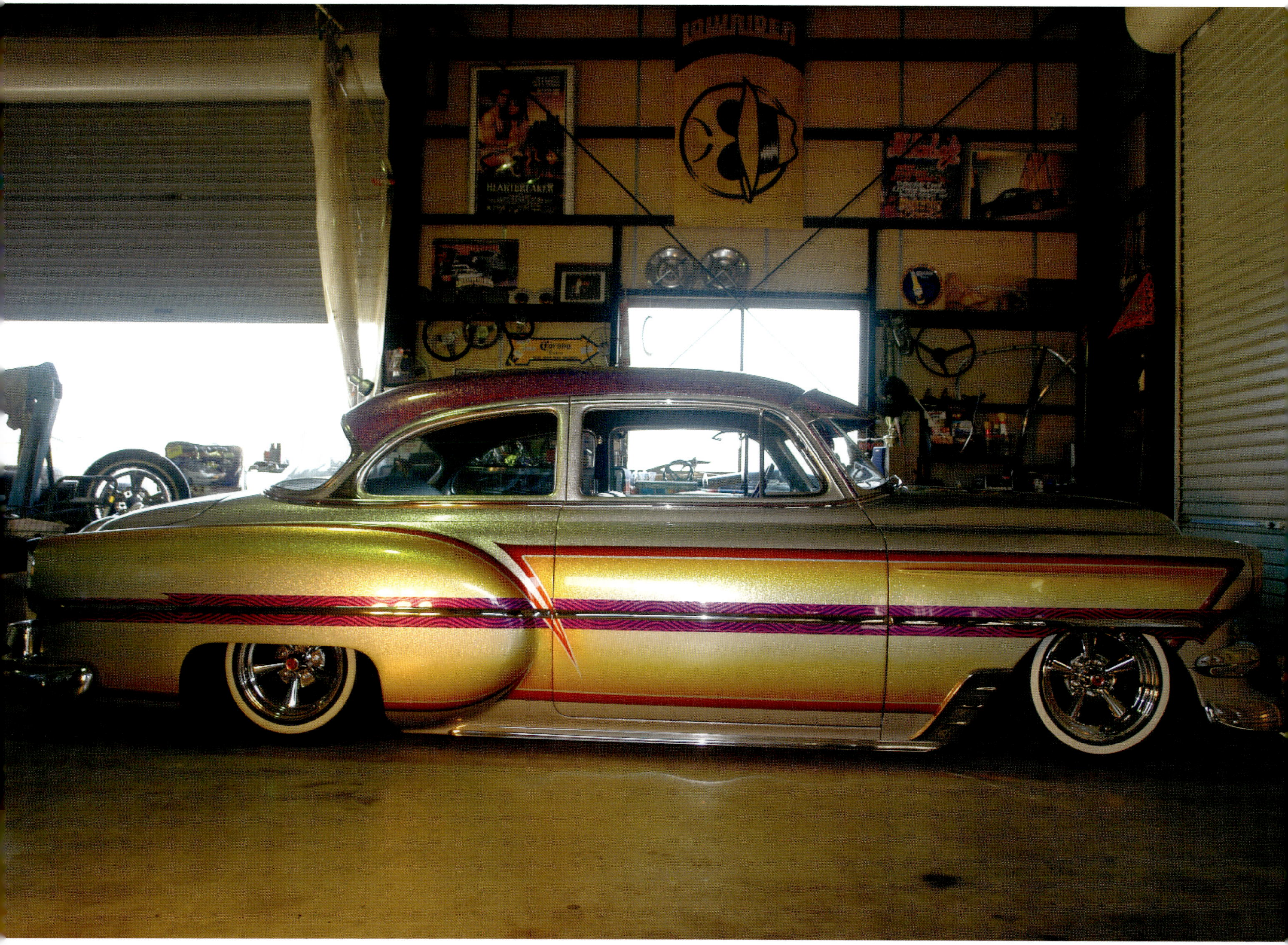
LOWRIDER
HEARTBREAKER
Corona

doing this. I didn't know how they made it jump like that. It was really amazing."

"Some of my truck driver co-workers and I formed a car club. We called it the Pharaohs, just like the car club in *American Graffiti.* We made fake lowriders and fake kustoms because we couldn't buy American cars. We used old Japanese cars to make facsimile lowriders and hot rods. Sometimes we would meet other Japanese car clubs, and we got information about U.S. car clubs. At that point Nagoya was isolated."

Left: Hisashi's Chevy 210

Below top: c.1980s; bouncing Monte Carlo and Volvo. First hydraulic cars in Nagoya.

Below bottom: c.1980s Domestic Japanese Kustom with flame paint job

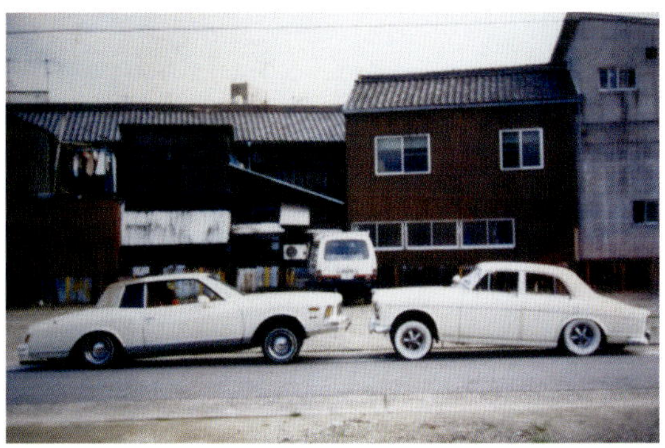

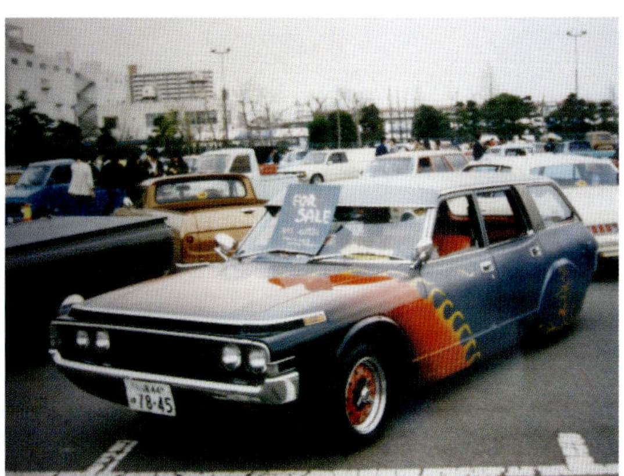

"In 1987 I quit my truck driving job and went to L.A.," he says. "When I came back I decided to open a shop. I liked American antique car toys and signs. In L.A., I noticed that car parts were cheap compared to Japan. My first shop was small, I sold American antique car toys and smuggled car parts. It was a small shop, but I made a lot of friends. It became a place for car people to hang out and maybe buy something. At the time more people in Japan were becoming interested in lowriders. The first Tokyo Street Car Nationals show was in 1987, which was good timing. Shige at Mooneyes brought together a lot of car guys for the first time. The whole thing took off after that first Street Car Nationals show."

"There was only one hydraulic car at that first show. Everybody stood around with their mouths open. Some people ran away from the car. They had no idea how it could do that jumping. The owner was a Tokyo guy who had a junkyard. He had a 1960s Ford Country Squire station wagon, and he made it jump around. People were completely shocked! I saw this car and thought, I want to do this."

"I had a business card from L.A., a company that sold hydraulic equipment so I placed an order with them. I had a friend with a Monte Carlo so I asked if I could install this equipment in his car. He looked at me and said 'What? You want to make my car jump?'

「ルーフをチョップして、スタンスを非常に低くした、カスタムのアメリカ車に興味を持つようになりました。この低さがカッコいいのです。うまく説明できませんが、とにかくすごくクールです。ルーフがチョップされていてもスタンスが低くないと駄目ですね。最低です。ローライダーのスタイルとか考え方とかファッションは、Paradise Road の淳一さんに影響されました。」

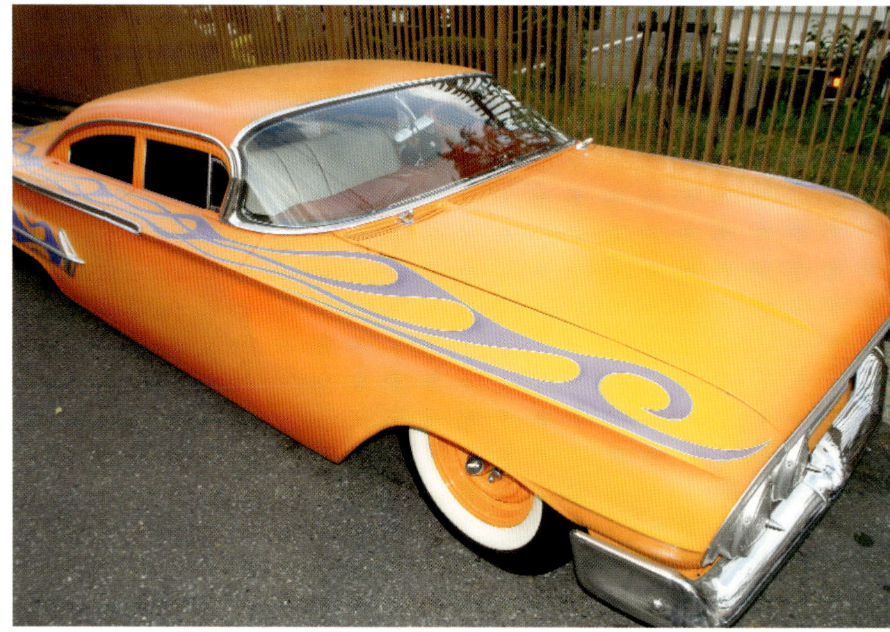

秀樹は続ける。「LA に引っ越した友達がいて、旅行で訪ねたとき、ローライダーに関する雑誌があることに気づきました。それに驚き、実際にローライダーを探し始めました。昔、『アメリカン・グラフィティ』という映画を見たことを憶えています。あれにずいぶん影響を受けました。デュース・クーペとかマーキュリーなどのローライダー。私はカスタム・スタイルがすごく好きですが、1970 年代のチョロ・スタイルでなくても構いません。私にとっては 49 年～ 51 年のマーキュリーが最高のスタイルですね。」

「最初はアメリカでカスタマイズされた車を買って、それを日本で売っていましたが、車に施された仕事の出来は良くありませんでした。そこで、市販のヴィンテージ・カーを購入し、日本に持ってきて、修理やカスタマイズを行えばもっといい出来になると思いついたのです。車をカスタマイズするには２年くらいはかかるでしょうが、それでも出来上がりはもっといいものになります。最近、このプロセスのために５台の車を仕入れました。車を修理するだけに１年、完全なカスタマイズと塗装を含めると計２年ほどかかるプロセスです。有能な日本のピンストライパー何人かと一緒に仕事をしたことがありますが、なかでもマコトは私のためにたくさんの仕事をしてくれました。彼は才能あるアーティストです。それから 1989 年に Mr. G が Border's で１年間働いていました。Border's が彼の最初の職場で、一緒にこの仕事を始めました。彼は働き者で勉強家、しっかりした能力があり、そしていつも熱心です。」

I put the kit in the rear end of his Monte Carlo. He was worried. I am still amazed he let me do it. He was convinced that was the end of his Monte Carlo. Then we made his car jump around in the street. People ran away like the car had ghosts. This car changed everything."

"I have been at this shop for five years now," Junichi concludes. "I do all the car work myself, and I have a friend who does all the painting. Nagoya shops are friendly. The car culture here is very cool."

Owner Hideki Kato relaxes on a wooden bench in front of his Border's garage calmly smoking a cigarette. There are two impressive kustoms parked out front in the narrow street, a bright orange 1960 Bel Air with intense blue flames and a black '51 Merc known as the Syu Merk that is owned by a young man named Syu Chan. Both cars are painted in a matte finish rather than high gloss which adds a tougher edge to their mood. The roofline of the Bel Air has been chopped considerably and the car has a very sleek weight to it. It looks fast. The huge hood of the Merc is shaped by bold, classic flames that fade from rich orange to bright yellow. The nose and tail have been striped by artist Makoto, who lives in Okazaki, Aichi.

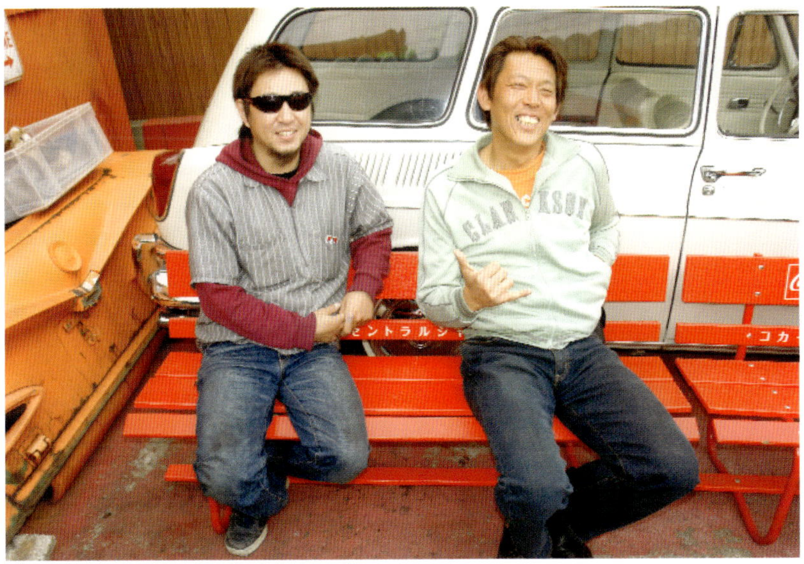

Above: Hideki Kato (right)
Border's "King of Kustom"

Left: 1960 Bel Air
Chopped, glass, dropped, rebuilt, paint by Border's

There are cars in progress parked along the driveway and inside the garage—a turquoise blue '29 Ford model A retro-rod, a '48 Buick Special, a foam green '67 Chevelle wagon with a classic muscle stance and a few other Mercs that lay in pieces. Reggae music by Bob Marley plays in the background. Hideki smiles as he overlooks his cars. There is an awareness of the history in his inventory but also an awareness of the possibility to modify it. The radically chopped orange Bel Air looks both cool and crazy. The deep contrast of the bold blue flames over the bright orange is provocative. The colors create tension between the familiar and the strange that changes the meaning of the car for both the driver and viewer. It is

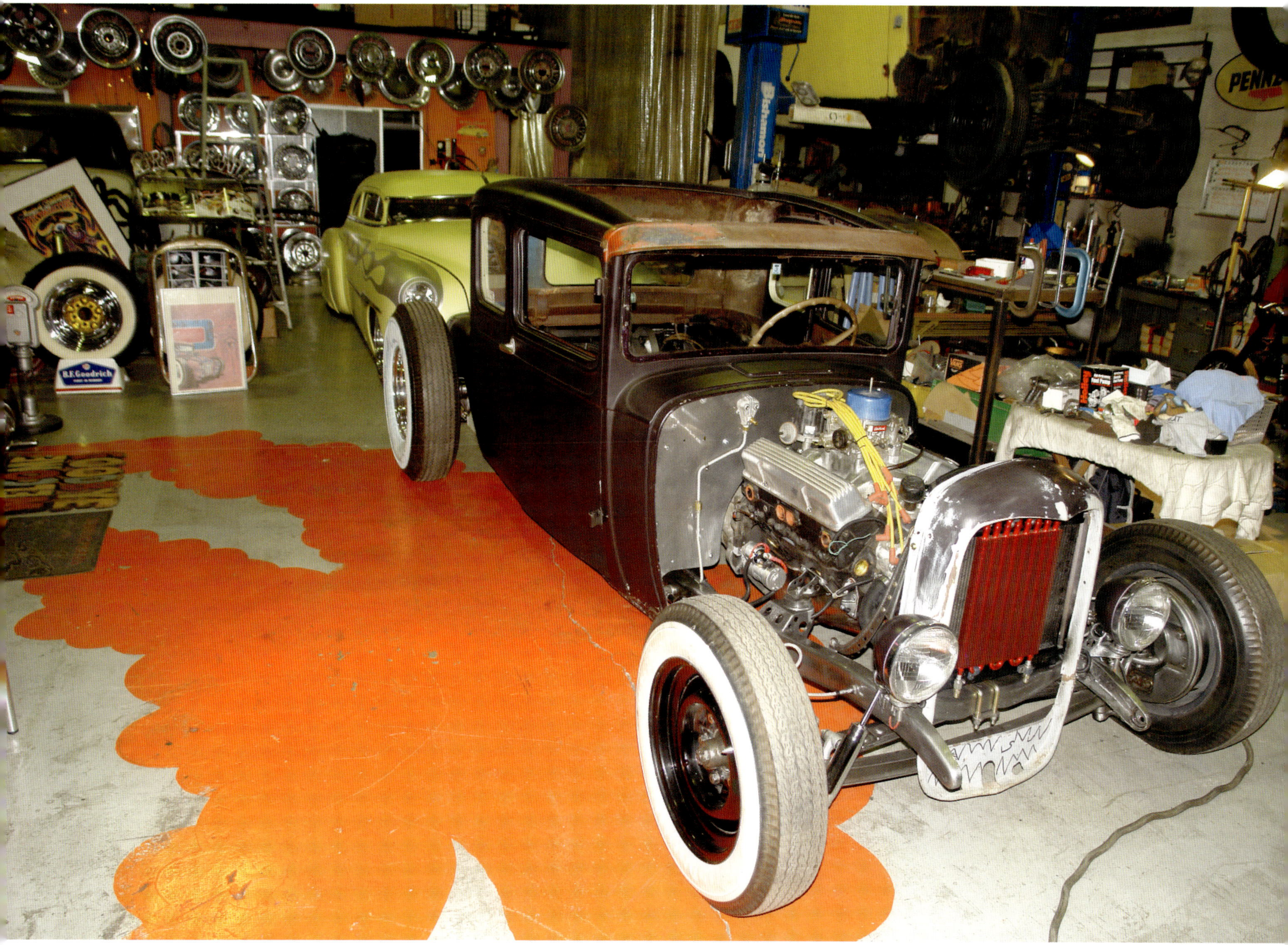
B.F.Goodrich

both real and imaginary; maybe a scary image in a dream, or is it just a car? The strangeness is a bit surreal, which is the root of its visual power.

These cars sit in the driveway as a collection of forms. For an American, these shapes resonate as dormant memories and vague associations waiting to be awakened. They loop through each other and the consciousness of the culture. For Hideki, a different process unfolds. In many respects he represents a blank page that is out of the loop. He has learned to recognize the connections between the shapes and the forms and the history, but it is not part of his cultural memory. His responses, and creations, are based on pure aesthetic recognition of these vehicles' potential as malleable, functioning sculptures.

Above the garage space there is a showroom with glass cabinets and shelving units completely overloaded with car toys. This room is not for youngsters but for adult model-car collectors who are infatuated with automobiles. Literally hundreds of Hot Wheels and Revelle model kits and rare, collectible to-scale tin or plastic cars are all organized in tidy rows. The room is a museum of miniature examples of customizing that are now manufactured by toy and model companies. Among car people there is a huge interest in owning a mini version of legendary cars like the Hirohata Merc or CadZZilla, and most important cars have been miniaturized.

"We have been creating cars at Border's for more than nineteen years," Hideki says. "I was first located in a smaller place that had a bar next door. I sold American used cars; I would buy them in America and bring them here. At first I was into Mini trucks; then I shifted my interest to larger American cars and now Kustom Mercurys. Years ago I was a used car dealer, selling Japanese cars."

"I became interested in Kustom American cars with chopped roofs

1929 Dodge, Ford Model A front end, Chevy 350. Extensive frame re-configuration by Junichi.

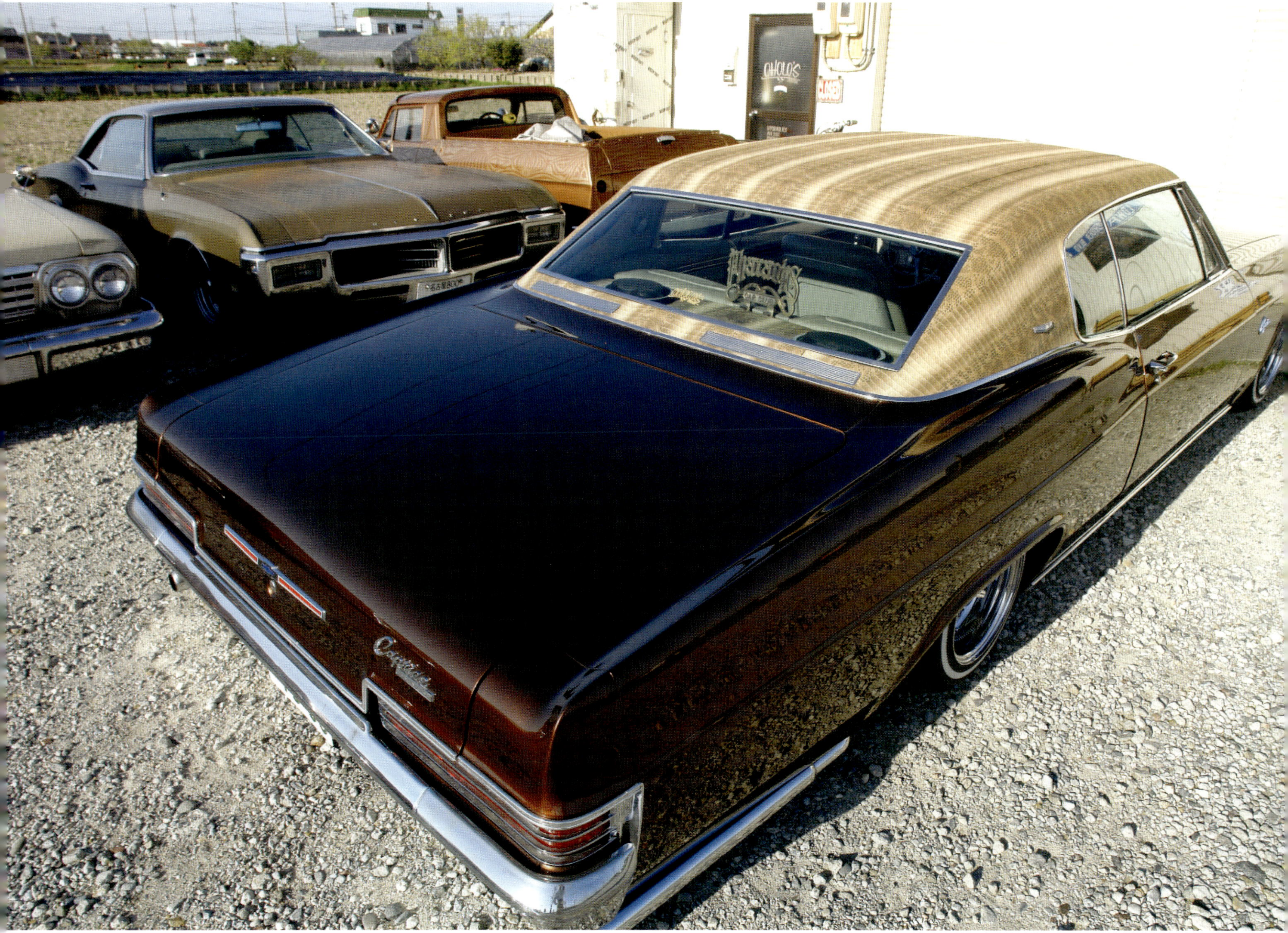
CHOLO'S

and a super low stance. This low thing is very *kakkoii* (cool). I can't explain it; the look is just very cool. A car with a chopped roof but without a low stance does not look good. It just sucks. Lowrider style, thinking and fashion have all been influenced by Junichi at Paradise Road."

"I had a friend who moved to L.A.," Hideki continues. "I would visit him, and on one trip I noticed a magazine about lowriders. I was amazed and started to look around for these guys. I remembered seeing the movie *American Graffiti*. It was very influential to me. The Deuce Coupes and the Mercurys, the lowriders. I love the Kustom styles but not necessarily the Cholo 1970s style. For me the classic '49-'51 Mercs are the look."

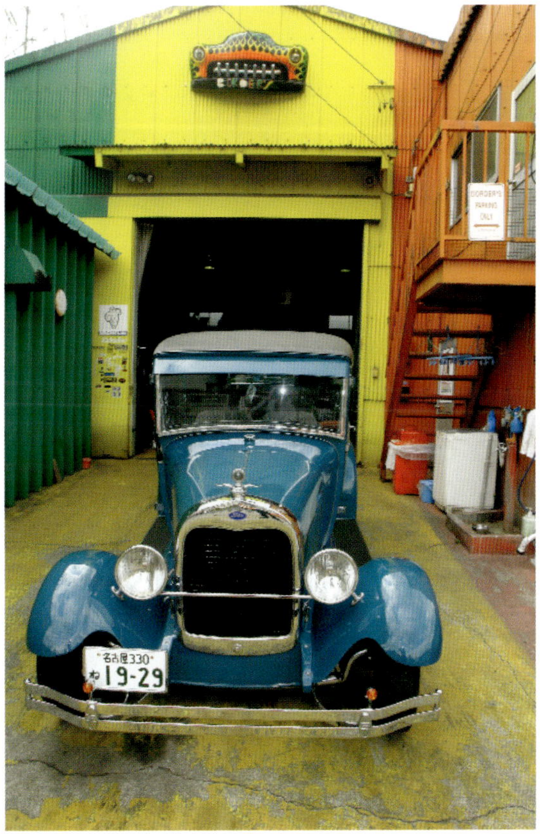

Above: 1929 Ford Retro-Rod

Left: Snake skin roof

"At first I bought customized cars in America and sold them in Japan but the work on the cars was bad. So I decided a better idea was to buy stock vintage cars and bring them to Japan and repair and customize them here for a better job. Maybe it would take me two years to customize the car, but the end result was better. I have brought five cars through this two year process. To fix a straight car is maybe one year; to fully kustomize and paint a car is two years. I have worked with a few talented Japanese pinstripers. Makoto has done a lot of work for me. He is a talented artist. Mr. G worked for a year at Border's in 1989. He and I started at Border's together. He is a hard worker and learns well. He has always had strong ability and dedication."

"When I chop a roof, I have to bend the glass and tilt the pillars. The process is very exact and complicated. My customers have no problem waiting two or three years for a car. They understand. Some like to come and look at what I am doing. Others just wait and look at the finished car. I talk a long time with my customers about the tolerances in the chop and drop. How it will affect the look of the car's stance. The whole thing is an ongoing process."

「ルーフをチョップすると、ガラスを曲げてピラーを傾ける必要があります。このプロセスは正確にやらないといけませんし、複雑です。私の顧客は車が出来上がるまで２年でも３年でも平気で待ってくれます。それがプロセスの一部だからです。何をやっているかちょくちょく見に来る人もいれば、仕上がるまでただ待つという人もいます。面白いですね。チョップとドロップを行った場合の車の耐性についてや、車のスタンスが外観にどのような影響を与えるかなど、顧客とは長い時間をかけて話します。全部がいつも進行中なのです。」

「車に対する愛着心が起こりますね」と彼は言う。「すごく離れたところに住んでいるオーナーに納車するときは、車が自分のもとから離れていくのが寂しいです。クルーズ・ナイトはそんな車と再会するチャンスで、自分の車と連絡を取り続ける手段としてクルーズを企画します。クルーズはオーナーたちがつながりを作り、車を名古屋に里帰りさせる手段です。名古屋のショップはお互いにフレンドリーで、助け合うなどのカー・カルチャーがあるため、愛知のカスタム・シティとして知られています。私達はこれを誇りに思っています。」

「状況は最近になってずいぶん発展しました。５年前は車の数もカスタム・カー・カルチャーに関係した人もすごく少なかった。特に空間に関しては、日本の生活はアメリカとはずいぶん違います。ここでは空間は深刻な問題です。どこに車を保管するかという問題ですね。駐車場での保管は高くつきます。しかし、バイクは保管が簡単ですから、その影響で日本におけるチョッパー・カルチャーはずいぶん成長しました。」

「サーフィンとカスタム・カルチャーが好きですね。こういうことに夢中になるのは建設的です。10年前、品行が悪く10回くらい刑務所に入れられました。それから人生を変えようと決心したのです。車とサーフィンによって、前向きに取り組む生き方に変わり、人生をきちんとさせることができました。親のいない子供たちのために時間を提供したのも自分にとって良かった事です。クリスマスにはサンタクロースの衣装を着て、小さな子供たちにプレゼントを配りました。車マニアの日本人がサンタの服を着ているなんて面白い光景ですよね。車によって私の人生は拓けたのです。」

「日本での車やショーに対する関心はずいぶん変わりました。1990年代にはカー・ショーが数回あっただけで、集まった車も100台くらいでした。ショーへの参加数は1998年がピークでしたね。数回の大きなショーにおそらく500台の参加があったと思います。今はショーの数が増えましたが、参加する車の数は今でも多いです。平均的なショーで300台は出ているでしょう。かなりの規模です。500台規模のショーになると事故が起こったりして危なくなります。なので多くのショーでは1970年以前の車、300台までなど制限をつけています。そのおかげで車の質がずいぶん高くなりました。カスタマイズの知識や技術が変化・向上しました。名古屋のカー・ショップ間の連係が状況を促進しましたね。雰囲気がいいです。」

「若い人たちが関わってくれています。彼らの観点はより純粋ですね。カスタム・カーを見て『わあ、いいな！』と言ってくれますが、年配の人はこういう車を見るとうるさいとか怖いとか考えます。『車体が低すぎる。なぜこんなことするのか？これ何だ』ってね…。近年、カスタム・カルチャーはもっと高いレベルへと成長しています。でも実際に車を所有する人の数は減っていると思います。ガソリン価格の上昇や古い車には特別税がかかる上、車をどこに保管するかという問題もあります。でも、興味の核心部はもっと強くなっています。全般的な興味は少なくなったかもしれませんが、中核をなす人の献身が大きく、人数は少なくなっても、純粋な関心が以前より高まっています。」

「アメリカではカー・カルチャーには男らしく強いというイメージがつきものですが、日本ではそうではありません。

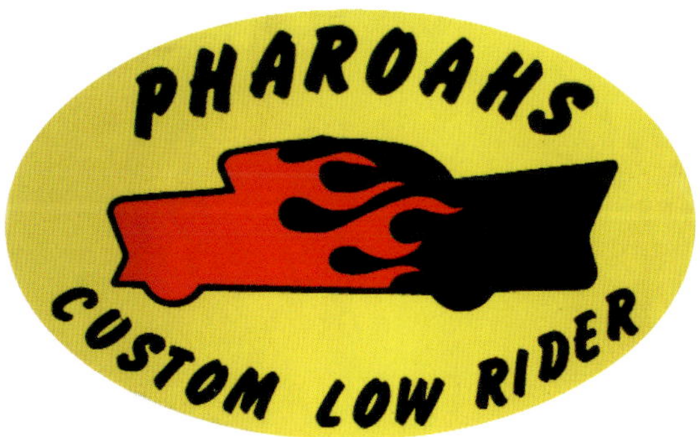

Pharoahs club sticker

"I get emotionally attached to the cars," he says. "When I sell a car to an owner who lives very far away, I am sad to see the car go. Cruise nights are a way for me to reunite with the cars; I organize the cruises as a way to keep in touch with my cars. These cruises are a way to make connections between owners and to bring the cars back to Nagoya. The shops in Nagoya are friendly with each other and we help each other."

"The scene has expanded a lot recently. Five years ago there were very few cars and people involved in kustom car culture. Life in Japan is different from a place like America in terms of space. Here, it is a very real issue. Where can you keep a car? The price of a garage, or space, is high. The chopper culture in Japan has grown a lot because the bikes are smaller, easier to keep."

"I like surfing and Kustom Kulture. These are positive things to get into. Ten years ago, I had some bad behavior and I went to jail maybe ten times. Then I decided to change my life. Cars and surfing became a positive thing to pursue so I changed my ways and cleaned up my life. I started donating time to orphan children. This has been very good for me. Cars have changed my life. At Christmas time, I wear a Santa Claus suit and give away gifts to little kids. A Japanese car guy in a Santa suit—this is interesting. Cars have brought me into a different life."

"The interest in cars and shows has changed a lot in Japan. Back in 1990 there were only a few car shows. Maybe 100 cars would show up. Show participation peaked in 1998 when maybe 500 cars would attend a few big shows. Now there are more shows and the number of cars is still high. Maybe 300 cars are involved in an average show. This is a good size. An event with 500 cars becomes dangerous because accidents happen. Many shows are limited to 300 cars, 1970 and older. Now the quality of the cars is much higher. The knowledge and skill of customizing has changed and improved. The relationship

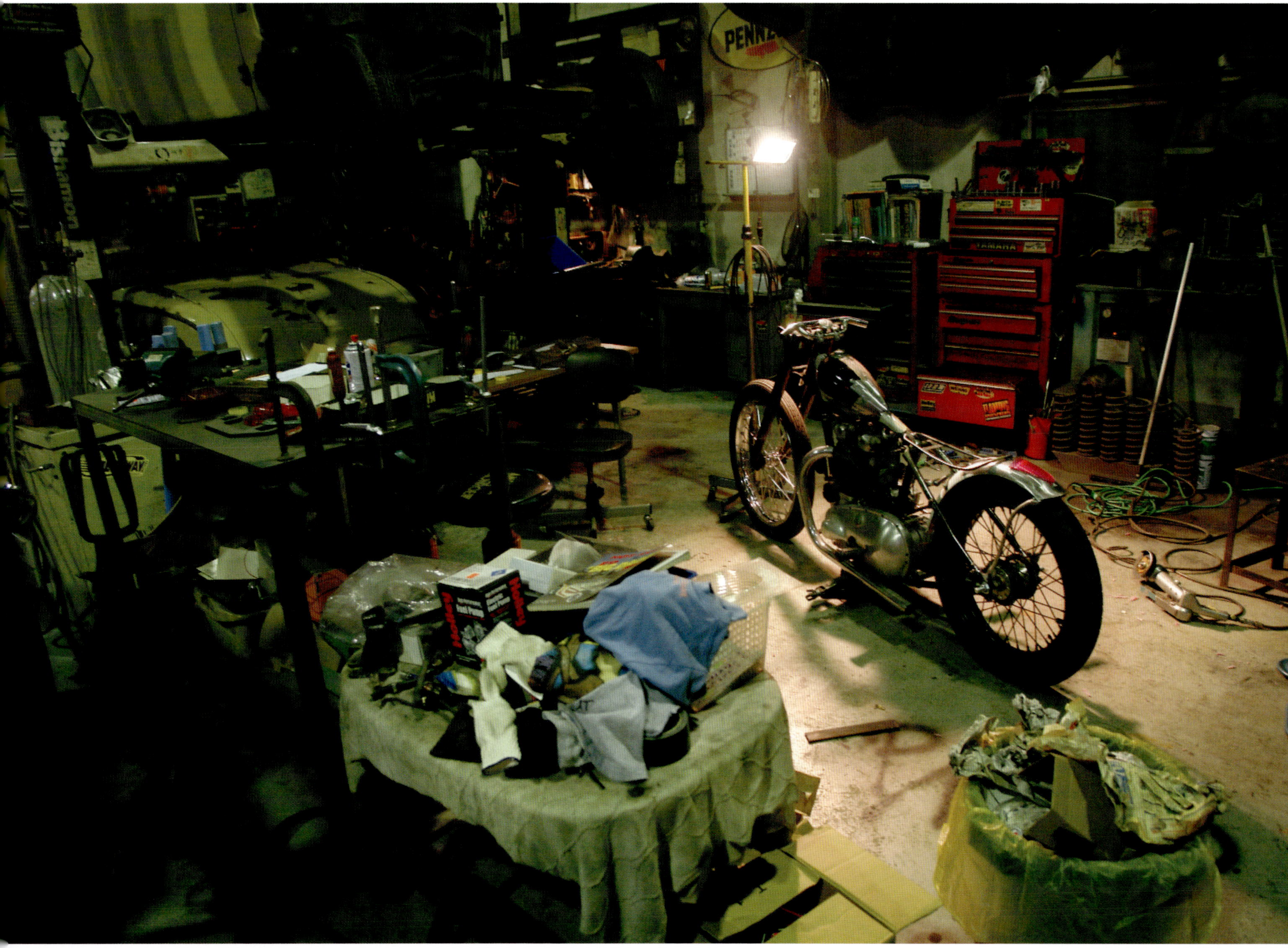
YAMAHA

among car shops in Nagoya has promoted the whole scene here. The vibe is good."

"Younger people are getting involved. Their views are more pure. They see kustom cars and say, 'Wow! So nice!' Older people see the cars and think 'This is too noisy, scary, the cars look scary. Too low. Why? What is this?' Kustom Kulture is growing to higher levels. But maybe the number of people actually owning the cars is dropping—gas prices. Older cars have a special tax, and there is the question of space and where to keep them. A stronger core of interest has developed. I think that there might be less general interest and more of a core dedication. So, there are fewer people but a stronger, more pure interest."

"In America there is a macho toughness associated with car culture. In Japan this isn't so. It is seen as more of an art form. A pureness of expression. This issue of toughness is not involved. In Japan it is an aesthetic appreciation. The beauty of the line, the design, the stance. I am aware of historical builders in America, but I really don't pay too much attention. I know what the classic guys have done, but I want to do my own thing."

Thirty minutes outside central Nagoya into the Ama-gun, Miwa-cho area the land opens up into small, 200 by 200-foot squared-off, undeveloped lots. The roads narrow and follow the border lines of each property. In the not-so-distant past this was agricultural land and there could have been soybean cultivation here. Some lots have nothing in them but low scrub; others have boxy, industrial, steel prefab buildings.

The driveway in front of Hisashi Ushida's Cholo's Custom garage has a '66 Chevy Caprice with a textured snake-lizard top and candy root beer paint. The car is dropped low, an inch off the gravel. There is no cover from the sun and the metal flake, high-gloss paint

Paradise Garage,
1950 Triumph Speed twin, 500cc

もっと芸術作品のように捉えられています。表現の純粋さですね。強いかどうかはあまり関係がありません。日本では線やデザイン、スタンスの美しさなどの美的価値の鑑賞です。アメリカの歴史的に有名なビルダーについては知っていますが、それほど気にしてはいません。代表的な人たちの仕事は知っていても、私は自分らしさを追求したいのです。」

名古屋から郊外へ30分。海部郡美和町には、200フィート四方の開発されていない敷地がある。道路は狭く、それぞれの土地の境界線に沿って続いている。さほど遠くない昔、ここはかつて農地で、大豆の栽培が行われていたそうだ。利用されていない敷地には低木が生えているだけだが、鉄の箱のような工業用プレハブ小屋の建つ敷地もある。

牛田尚志のCholo's Customのガレージ前の舗道には、スネーク・リザードのテクスチャーの付いた屋根とキャンディ・ルートビアのペイントで塗装した66年シェビー・カプリスがある。車体は低く、砂利の地面から1インチしか離れていない。太陽を遮るカバーはなく、金属フレークの高光沢塗料が光の中できらめく。尚志は静かな男性だ。車は代表的なシェビー327 V8、ハイドロ、手動3段変速ギアを搭載していると説明する。「この車は速くて低い」と言い、静かにクローム製のツインテールパイプを指差す。

日射を避けたガレージ内は涼しい。薄暗いガレージの隅にはシルバーのフレークペイントで塗装した1954年シェビー210の2ドアセダンが置かれている。そのシルバーと対照的に、赤、黄、オレンジ、青の直線的チョロ・スタイルのカラーデザインが際立っている。尚志はボンネットを指差し、その下に収まったパッケージを説明する。235ci直列6気筒エンジン、3段変速手動トランスミッション、デュアルエグゾースト、フロントハイドロ、リアエアなどだ。「この車は15年前に名古屋に来たんです」と彼は説明する。「この車には長い間、時間をかけて取り組んできました。」

「この新しいショップで仕事を始めて4年になります」と彼は言う。「かつてはParadise Roadで仕事をしていました。今、35歳です。チョロ・ローライダーの外観が好きです。輝きがあって、低くて、地面をこするような感じがいいです。ジャンピングカーの跳ね回るハイドロなどにはあまり興味がありません。純粋にローライダーの美観がいいのです。すごく低い、とことん低いのが大切です。」

「私は名古屋のPrimera(プリメーラ)カークラブのメンバーです。ここ名古屋に住む車愛好家の多くにはメキシカンの感性があると思います。メキシカンの感性が名古屋の感性だと言えます。私たちは車の表面、スタイル、スタンスをチョロに変えます。こういう非常に低い外観が気に入っています。これらの車はとても美しく、この種の美しさが好きなのです。うちではエンジンからボディ、塗装にいたるまで、あらゆる仕事をやります。時間のかかるゆっくりしたプロセスを経て、こういう車ができるのです。その際、解決しなければならない問題も出てきますが、そこから学ぶことも車を生み出すプロセスです。いい車を作るには時間がかかるものです。」

名古屋市のもう1つの地区、中川区で、今井義隆はGood Fellas(グッド・フェローズ)ガレージを所有・経営している。店名はマーティン・スコセッシ監督の現代ギャング映画にちなんで名づけられている。これは車とはまったく無関係の映画で、冷酷なアメリカの無法状態を神話化し、演出して見せたものだ。

紺色のファスナー式ジャンプスーツを着た義隆がガレージ内を歩く。混み合ったガレージ内には5～6台のヴィンテージ・アメリカ車がジグザグに置かれている。隅には49年キャデラック霊柩車が、48年ポンティアック、49年・51年マーキュリーと共に、作業の開始を待っている。彼は今43歳。13年間車の仕事に焦点を置いてやってきた。「カスタム・スタイルが好きです」と義隆は言う。「車の往年の外観、

shimmers in the brightness. Hisashi is a quiet man. He explains that the car has a classic Chevy 327 V8, hydraulics and a manual three speed. "This car is fast and low," he says, gesturing calmly to the twin chrome tail pipes.

It is cooler inside the garage away from the sun. In the corner a 1954 Chevy 210 two-door sedan with silver flake paint rests in the semi-darkness. The silver is highlighted with angular Cholo style color accents of red, yellow, orange and blue. Hisashi points at the hood and describes the package underneath that includes a 235ci straight six with a three-speed manual transmission, dual exhausts, front-end hydraulics and rear air. "This car first came to Nagoya fifteen years ago," he explains. "I have been working on it for a long time. I'm taking my time with this car."

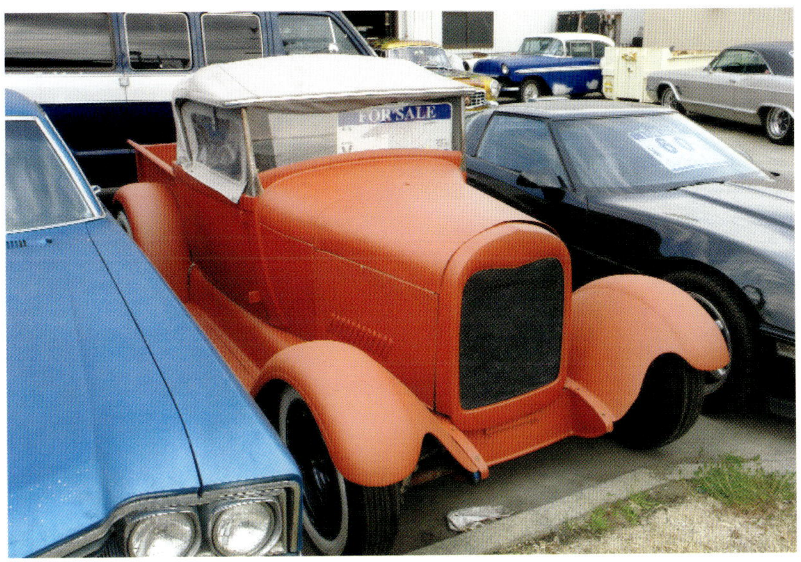

1927 Ford Model T

"I have been working at my new shop four years now," he says. "Before, I worked at Paradise Road. I am thirty-five years old. I like the Cholo Low Ride look. It is beautiful—shiny, low, scraping. I am not really interested in the hopping hydraulics of jumping cars. I just like the pure aesthetic of low cars. Very low—the lowest; this is important."

"I am a member of the Primera car club in Nagoya. There is a Mexican sensibility among many car people here in Nagoya. The Mexican sensibility is the Nagoya sensibility. We change the faces of our cars, the style and stance, to be Cholo. This is the look we like. These cars are very beautiful. I do all the work on these cars from engine to body to paint. It is a long and slow process to make a car like this. There are difficulties that must be solved but it is a learning to create a car. Good cars take time."

In a different Nagoya district called Nakagawa-ku, Yoshitaka Imai owns and operates Good Fellows Garage. He has named it after the Martin Scorsese contemporary gangster epic that has nothing to do

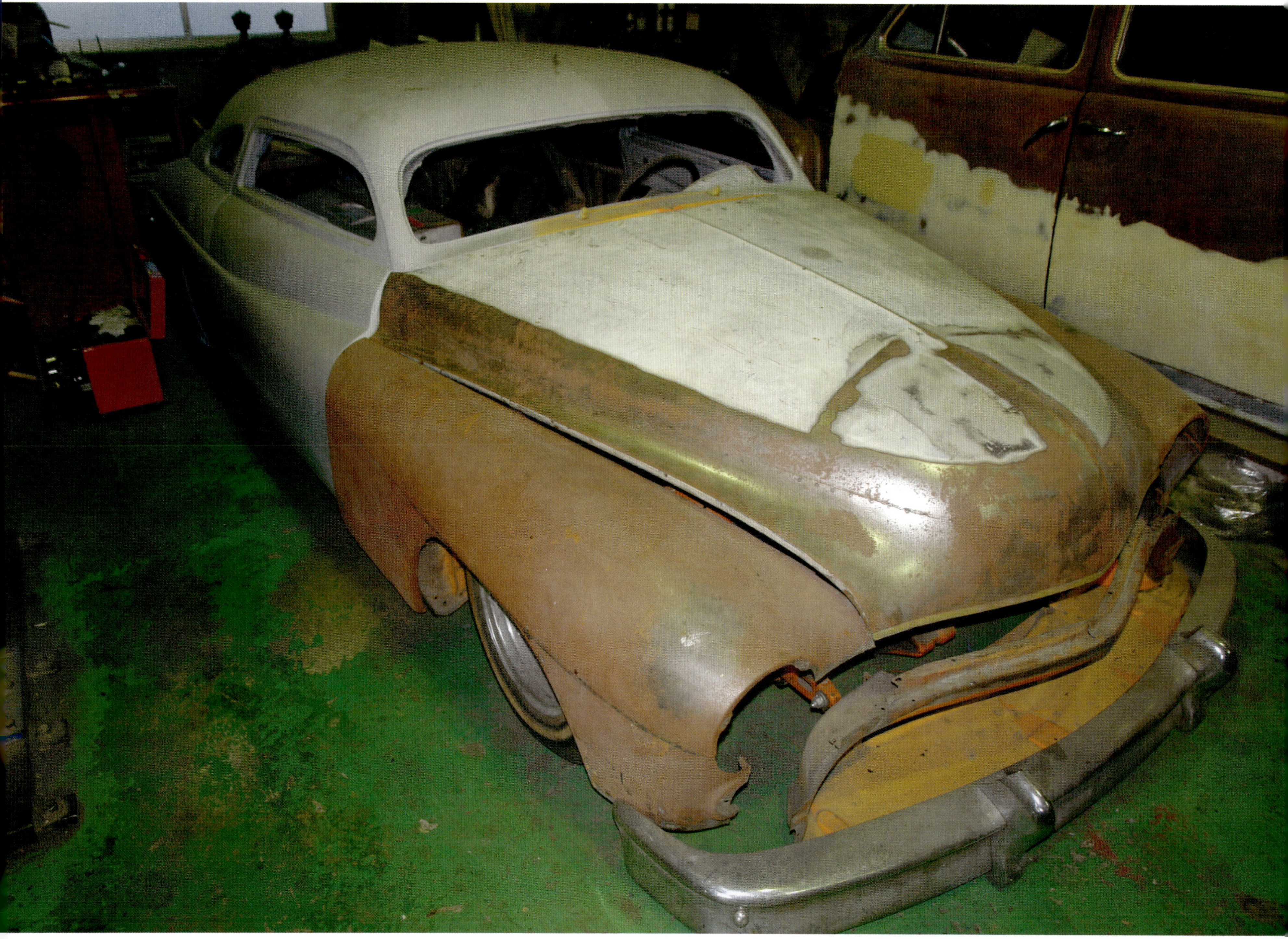

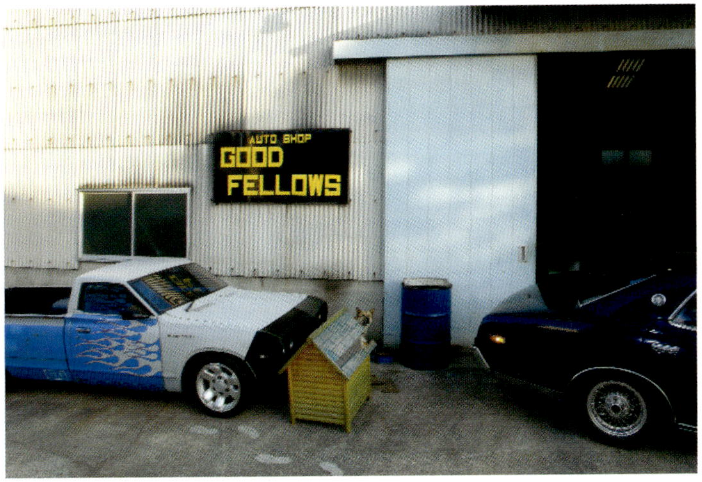

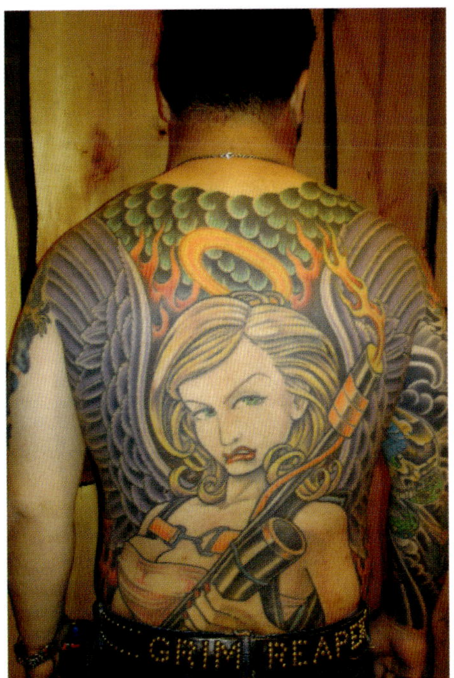

Above top: Good Fellows Garage

Above bottom: Gangster Girl tattoo on Daisuke Hamada by Horitomo-formerly Washo. Kustom Kulture Now event.

Left: Sleeping beauty

with cars and everything to do with a particular mythologized brand of ruthless American lawlessness.

Yoshitaka walks through his garage wearing a zip-up dark blue mechanic's jump suit. The space is crowded with a half dozen vintage American cars zigzag-parked closely together. In a distant corner a '49 Cadillac hearse awaits attention along with a '48 Pontiac and '49 and '51 Mercurys. He is 43 years old and has focused on car work for thirteen years. "I like the kustom style," Yoshitaka says. "I like the Old School look of cars, the hot rod look. I use the internet and also my customers' connections with their friends to locate cars in America. I have mostly found cars in Arizona and California, but I've found cars in all parts of America. I find them, buy them and bring them to Japan. Then I rebuild them."

"My favorite cars to work on are Pontiacs and Buicks. These are rare cars and not typical rebuild jobs. I have been working on a 1948 Pontiac that I found in Arizona. It has a big block Chevy 427 V8 engine big and powerful. In 2003 I found a 1949 Mercury in Oklahoma that was already chopped and sectioned. I have a friend in Arizona so I called him and told him I had found a very interesting car. My friend went to look at the car and brought it to Arizona by truck. Then I flew to Arizona to see the car. I bought it immediately and brought it to California and made arrangements to ship it to Japan. This is a long and involved process, but is what is important to me. These cars are important to me."

"When I was seven years old I started liking Japanese domestic cars," he continues. "When I turned ten my interest in U.S. cars began. Corvette, Trans-Am, Camaro—muscle cars. Then I shifted my interest to older and kustom cars from the 1940s-'50s. When I was a teenager I saw the movie *American Graffiti.* I liked 1950s culture, rock and roll and '50s cars. It was like a dream for me and my friends."

ホットロッドの見た感じが気に入っています。インターネットや顧客の友人とのコネを使って、アメリカにある車を見つけ出します。ほとんどはアリゾナかカリフォルニアからですが、アメリカ全土からも見つけています。見つけるのも、買い取るのも、日本に持ってくるのも仕事の一環です。それから私が組み立てます。」

「私が気に入ってよく手を加えている車はポンティアックとビュイックです。こういう車は稀少で、一般的な改造の仕事ではありません。今はアリゾナで見つけた1948年ポンティアックに取り組んでいます。すごく大きくてパワフルな、シェビー427　V8ビッグブロック・エンジンを搭載しています。2003年にはオクラホマで1949年マーキュリーを見つけました。すでにチョップド、セクションド済みでした。アリゾナに友達がいるので、彼に電話をかけ、面白い車を見つけたことを知らせました。友達はその車を見に行き、トラックでアリゾナに運び、それから私がアリゾナまで飛んで、その車を見に行きました。その場ですぐに買い取ってカリフォルニアまで持っていき、日本へ出荷する手配をしました。これは長くて複雑なプロセスですが、私にとっては重要なことです。こういった車が私にとって大切なのです。」

「7歳のころ、日本の国産車が好きになりました」と彼は続ける。「10歳になったときにアメリカの車に興味がわきました。

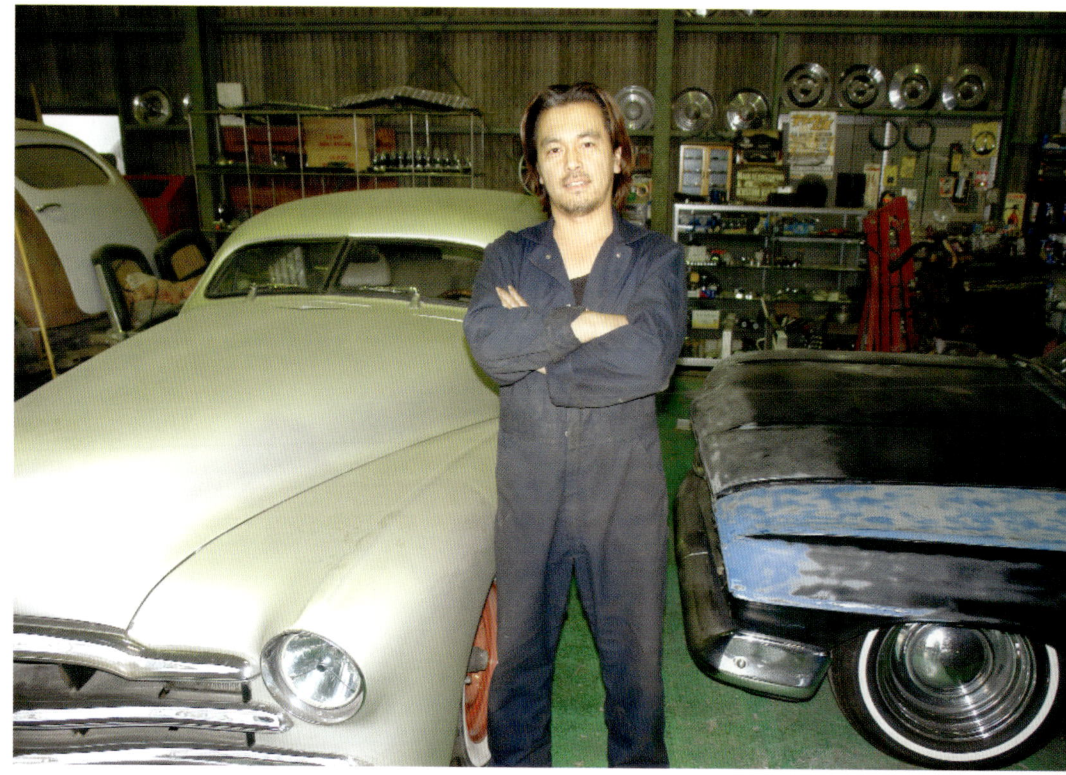

"That whole American lifestyle is a dream life. Like a floating world life. A dream of America."

Left: Yoshitaka Imai, Good Fellows Garage

Below: Pontiac and Mercury

page 135: Mr. G painting Krazy Kolor style

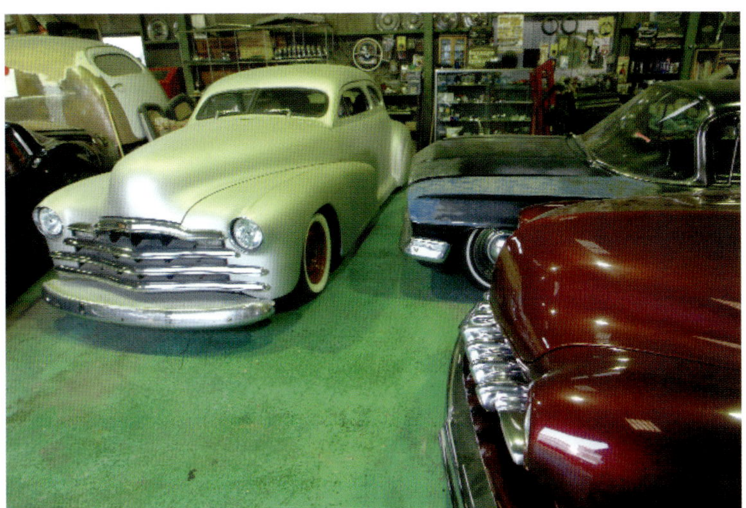

"That whole American lifestyle is a dream life. Like a floating world life. A dream of America. These cars support this dream—the nice lines, the metal and material. Power windows, power steering, power brakes. Everything power. I am very interested in the power of these cars as mechanical objects with a historical past. It is a dream world of power-assisted accessories."

The tarped over, dusty cars in Yoshitaka's shop sit in their dark corners as if asleep. They become a part of his dreamscape—part past, part present, part future. Everything is combined into something both imaginary and real. His aesthetic, skill, ingenuity and imagination are passed into the reconfiguring of these mechanical objects with a loaded past and his role, like that of the other Nagoya builders, becomes one of the reawakeners.

"I remind myself that basically it is the beauty of the cars that creates the power." Yoshitaka explains. "The original skills that went into designing and making the cars are present. People made these cars in factories, on assembly lines. Sixty years ago people had very different ideas about what these cars meant, but I think that these cars were always powerful and beautiful. The '51 Mercury must have been so exciting to see. I am sure it made people stop and point and say, 'Look at that car!' The lines, the materials. Sixty years ago that car changed people. Beauty can do this."

"When I work, the whole car becomes a combination of these impressive elements," Yoshitaka concludes. "Line, style, power, beauty. 1950s American dream culture. Owning a piece of this culture and working on it is very deep. I interact with these powerful elements of time and beauty. It is a really powerful emotional feeling to interact with all these pure elements."

コルベット、トランザム、カマロ…、いわゆるマッスルカーですね。それから1940年代〜50年代の古いカスタム・カーに興味が移りました。ティーンエイジャーのころ、『アメリカン・グラフィティ』という映画を見て、1950年代の文化、ロックンロールとか50年代の車が好きになりました。あれは私と私の友達にとって夢でした。」

「アメリカン・ライフ全部が私にとって夢の生活ですね。まるで浮世の人生です。こういう車のすばらしい線とか金属とか素材が、そのアメリカの夢を見ることを助けてくれます。パワーウィンドウ、パワーステアリング、パワーブレーキ。何でもパワーです。伝統を持つ機械的な物体としての車のパワーにすごく興味があります。パワーアシスト・アクセサリーによる夢の世界です。」

義隆のショップの薄暗い隅には、防水布をかけたホコリだらけの車が何台か眠るように置かれている。これらは彼の夢の情景 — 過去、現在、未来の一部となる。すべては想像と現実を一体化させた何かに組み合わされる。彼の美的感覚、技術、創意、想像力が、過去で満たされたこれらの機械的物体の再構成を通して伝わる。彼の役割は、名古屋の他のビルダーと同じように、それを呼び起こす者の１人となることだ。

「基本的には車の美しさがパワーを生み出すのだということを自分に言い聞かせています」と義隆は説明する。「車を設計・製造した元々のスキルがそこにあります。人々はこれらの車を工場での組み立てラインで作りました。60年前にはこういう車は違ったアイデアを意味するものだったのでしょう。でも常にパワフルで美しいものだったと思います。51年マーキュリーを見ることは、当時もおそらくエキサイティングなことだったでしょう。人々は立ち止まり、指差して『あの車すごいね！』と言ったに違いありません。その線、その素材が、60年前の人々を変えました。美というのは、そういうことができるものです。」

「作業をするとき、これらの印象的な要素は組み合わされていきます」と義隆は結ぶ。「線、スタイル、馬力、美しさ。1950年代のアメリカン・ドリーム・カルチャー…。このカルチャーの一片を所有し、それに作業を施すことには、非常に深いものを感じます。私は時と美というパワフルな要素と触れ合い、これらの純粋な要素と交わることによって、本当に力強い感情をおぼえます。」

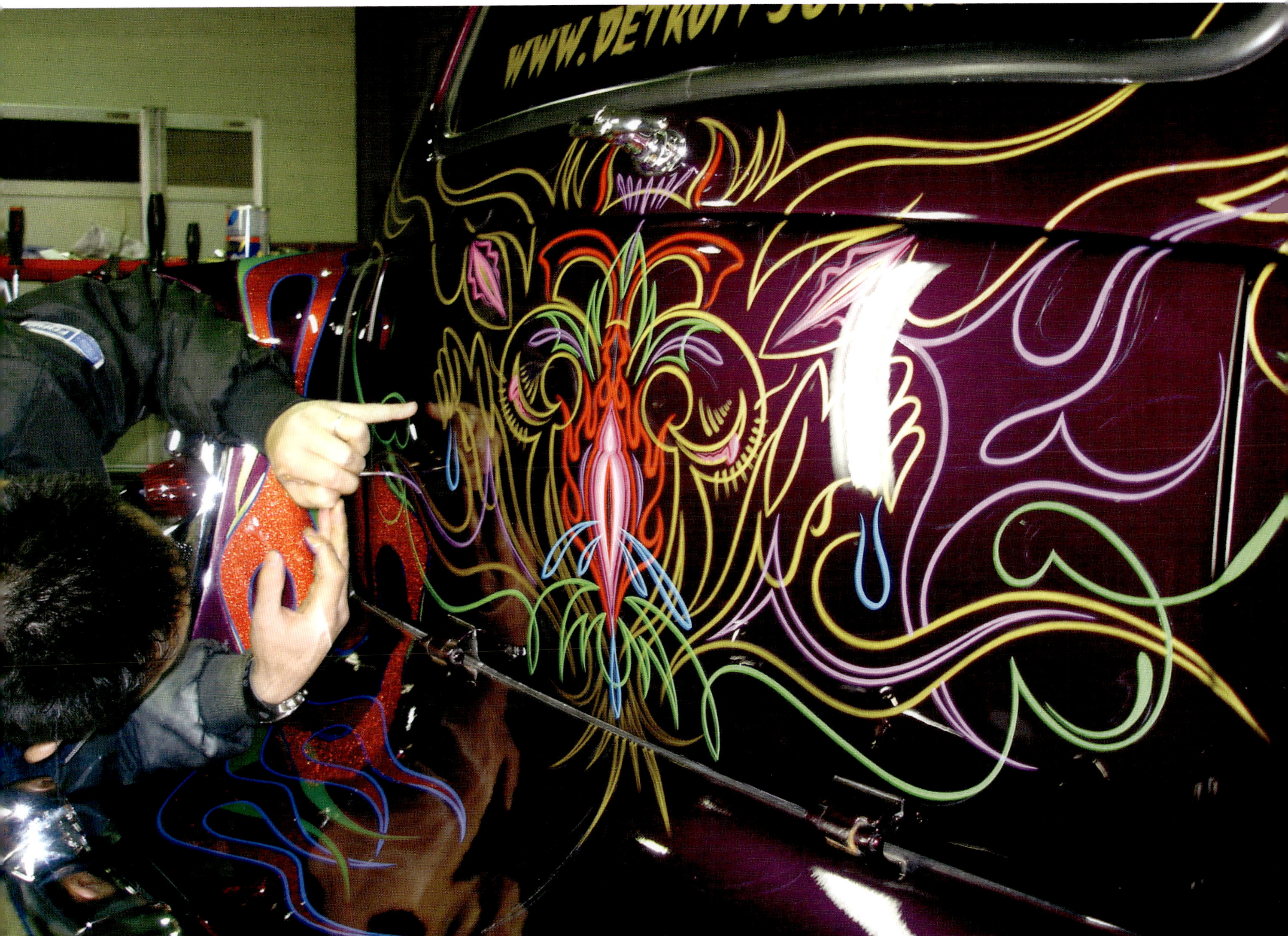
WWW.DETROIT

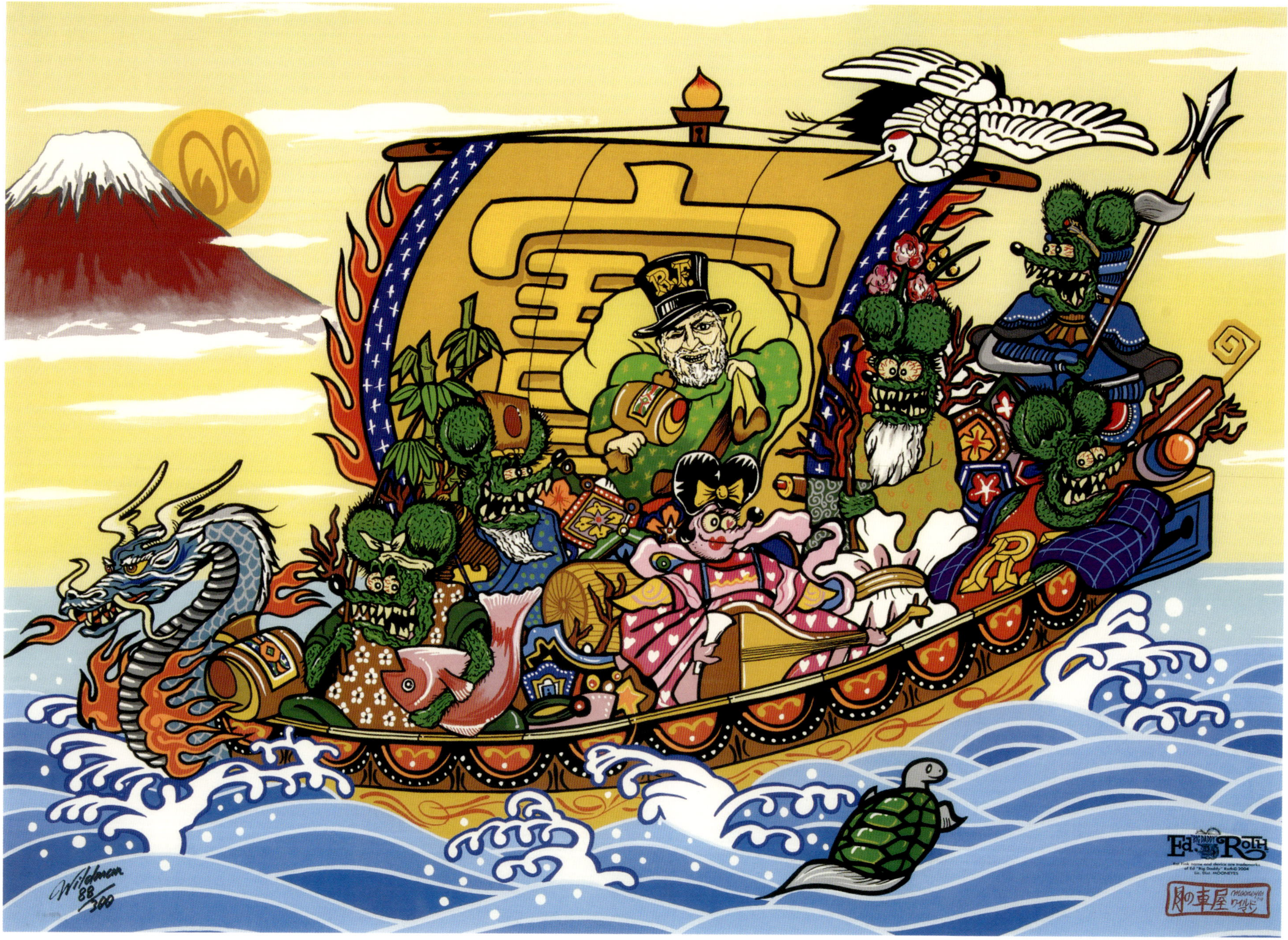
Wildman
88/300
Ed "Big Daddy" Roth
Rat Fink name and device are trademarks
of Ed "Big Daddy" Roth© 2004
Lic. Dist. MOONEYES
月の車屋
ワイルドマン

Chapter Four:
Japan's Kustom Art: Von Dutch, Roth and the Mystique of Difference

"Whenever I looked at that drawing (Rat Fink), I felt I was looking, for the first time, at reality–my reality. The world that my parents, teachers, and responsible type people all around me belonged to wasn't my world. Why did I have to be like them, live like them? I didn't. And Rat Fink helped me realize that."

Ed Roth – *Confessions of a Rat Fink: The Life and Times of Ed "Big Daddy" Roth,* 1980

Takarabune (Treasure Ship)
Traditional theme with Seven Lucky Gods as Big Daddy Roth and Rat Finks, 2004
Wildman
Silkscreen, 16 x 23", edition 300.
Courtesy MOONEYES
Photo: Hal Lum

Today in Japan, symbols of this Kustomized life are gaining momentum. The art of Japan Kustom artists Mr. G, Makoto, Grimb, Psycho and Fudemae is stylized and unique—monsters, dropped cars and stretched bikes, sexy girls, weirdo graphics. The images pick up on a sense of history connected to the early days of the Kustom Kulture movement in California.

Roth and Von Dutch, as founders of this movement, cooked up a soup of associations that created a new language for young people. The importance of Dutch's personal mystique, crazed inventions and sublime symmetrical striping or Roth's Rat Fink was in their ability to act as signposts that reminded young people about alternate routes to life. These showed that one did not necessarily surrender to getting onto the safe, predictable superhighway. Instead, a risky detour down a dark side street might be a better move. Rat Fink's expression is ambiguous—neither smiling, laughing or crying. His bulging, angst-ridden eyes betray the uneasiness of youth.

The "Finkster" became more than a strange looking cartoon character surrounded with buzzing flies; his image represented a new sense of understanding about the world. If you were hip to his nuanced message, Rat Fink helped to codify things and remind young people about important differences between their world and the world of their parents. Roth said, "Whenever I looked at that drawing (Rat Fink), I felt I was looking, for the first time, at reality—my reality. The world that my parents, teachers, and responsible-type people all around me belonged to wasn't my world. Why did I have to be like them, live like them? I didn't. And Rat Fink helped me realize that."

The postwar years in California were marked by profound examples of social change that deeply affected young people. Rapid

日本のカスタム・アート：ヴォンダッチ、ロス、そして相違の美学

日本のカスタム・アーティスト、Mr. G、Makoto、Grimb、Psycho、Fudemaeの作品は、モンスター・アート、ドロップト・カー、ストレッチド・バイク、セクシーガール、奇妙なグラフィックスなど、スタイル化されてユニークである。イメージは南カリフォルニアのカスタム・カルチャー運動の草分け時代の伝統を彷彿とさせる。

もともと1940年代後期、そして50年代、60年代に入ったころのアメリカでは、カスタム・カルチャーは非常にプライベートなものだった。若者たちは、置き捨てられたり廃棄された古い車を見つけては再構築していた。この古いアメリカ文化の象徴は彼らによって再使用され、ルールも塗り替えられた。当時のティーンエイジャーは、車や人生に関する自らの文法を作り出したのだ。

カスタム・カルチャー運動の創始者、エド“ビッグダディ”ロスとヴォンダッチは、若者たちが後に新しい表現を生み出すのに使用するさまざまな論理のつながりを作った。ダッチ個人の神秘的雰囲気、常軌を逸したかのような発明、崇高な対称的ストライピング、また、ロスの創造したラットフィンクの重要性は、人生には別の選択肢があることを若者に教える道標として機能するものだった。

人生の別の選択という道では、安全で予測可能な高速道路を進むために人生を犠牲にする必要はなく、むしろ暗い横道を抜ける危険な迂回路が賢明な場合もある。その道標であるラットフィンクの表情は曖昧だ。 微笑んでも、笑っても、泣いてもいない。飛び出た苦悩でいっぱいの目は、若者の不安を暴露している。

「フィンクスター」は、蠅にブンブンとたかられている奇妙な漫画のキャラクター以上のものになった。彼のイメージは世界についての新たな理解を示すものだった。彼の微妙なメッセージに通じている者にとって、ラットフィンクは物事を体系化することに役立ち、人生には別の選択肢があることや、若者らの世界と彼らの両親の生きている世界の違いの重要性を思い出させた。ロスはこう語った。「あのドローイング(ラットフィンク)を見るといつも、まるで初めて現実を — 私自身の現実を見ているような気がした。私の両親、先生、そして私の周りにいる責任ある人たちが生きている世界は私の世界ではなかった。なぜあの人たちのようでなければならないのか、なぜあんな風に生きなければならないのか。そうする必要はないとラットフィンクは気づかせてくれたんだ。」

カスタム・カルチャー運動が初めて本格的になった戦後のカリフォルニアは、そこに住む若者に深く影響を及ぼした大きな社会的変化の出来事が特色であった。1930年代や40年代、新しい世界を求める多様な人々の集団による急速な流入が、社会的実験のムードを生み出した。そして南カリフォルニアのような場所で開花した自己改革の意識は、急増する若者たちと衝突した。ボヘミアン、ビートニック、ホットロッダーなどのオルタナティブ・サブカルチャーは、この独特の土地に居場所を見つけて繁栄した。特に南カリフォルニアでは、この居場所を車に見出したのだ。

若い日本のカスタム・アーティストらは、この違いの表現をさまざまに試している。ほぼ単一民族、単一文化からなる国として、日本の若者たちは何らかの違いを強く求めている。Mr. G、Makoto、Psycho、Fudemaeらが描くカスタム・イメージも、単にスタイル表現としてだけではなく、その価値の分かる日本の若い鑑賞者が、この新しい表現方法を学び、人生の別の選択肢を追求するための方向を指し示している。

彼らの作品では奇怪な視覚言語が渦巻き、まるで「内情に通じる」人たちだけが解読できるよう様式化された秘密の教義が書かれた古い聖典写本のようだ。この解読プロセスに喜んで参加し、ダイナミックなグループの一員になりたいと思っている日本の若者が今増えている。

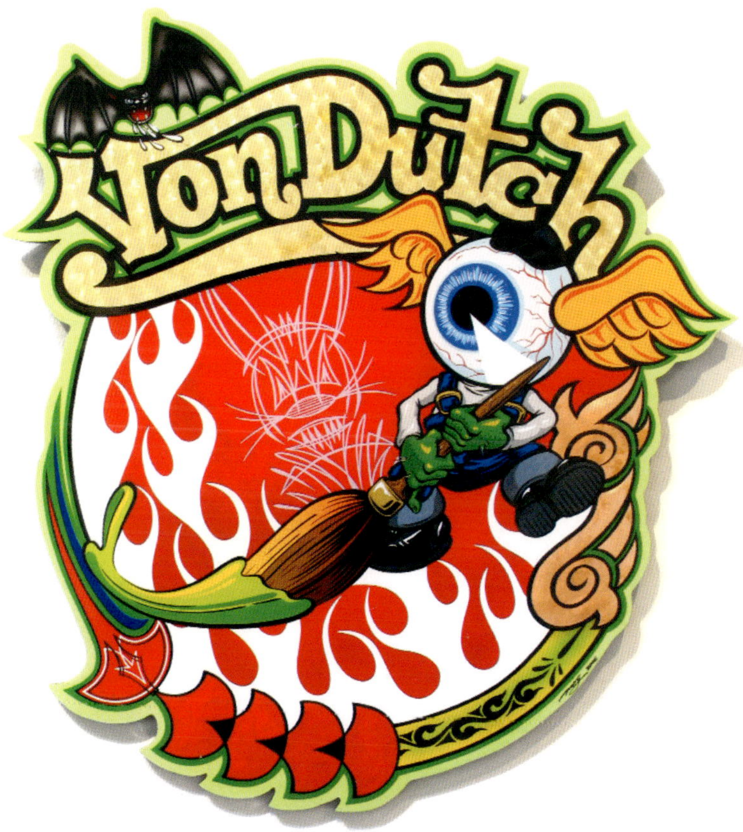

Von Dutch Ism
Painting by Mr. G

immigration into the state during the 1930s and '40s of different groups searching for a new beginning created an atmosphere of social experimentation. A sense of personal reinvention blossomed as it collided with the growing youth populace. Alternative subcultures of bohemians, beatniks and hot-rodders found breathing room in this unique place and prospered. In Southern California, a lot of this breathing took place in cars.

The artwork of young Japanese Kustom artists experiments with this vocabulary of difference. In a largely monoracial and monocultural place, young Japanese crave difference. The art is more than just a style statement as it repeats the process initiated in the U.S. over fifty years ago. The skulls, cars, motorcycles, pinstriping, flames and weirdo monsters spin together like a codex into a secret message to be deciphered by people "in the know."

"At a car show where I was painting, the MC called me to the stage using the name 'Mr. G.'" says Minoru Goto about the origins of his painting name. "Before I got deeper into my painting I was in the business of household electronics. Then in July, 2000, I did some striping and lettering on the side. I guess I'm self taught, I never really studied."

"I saw some striping work of California artist Jimmy C. He did some of the work in the Laguna Art Museum book *Kustom Kulture*. Before I saw this work, I had seen the work of Wildman at the 1990 Mooneyes Street Car Nationals show. He was striping there, so I stopped and watched him for a long time. At the time, I had no idea what it was. It looked complicated to me but something about it intrigued me. I didn't realize it had a history and a significance. In 1989 Ed "Big Daddy" Roth had come to the Street Car Nationals show and spent time with Wildman. I got a video tape of Roth giving demonstrations at the show. I could play and rewind the tape as many times as I wanted to watch Roth work."

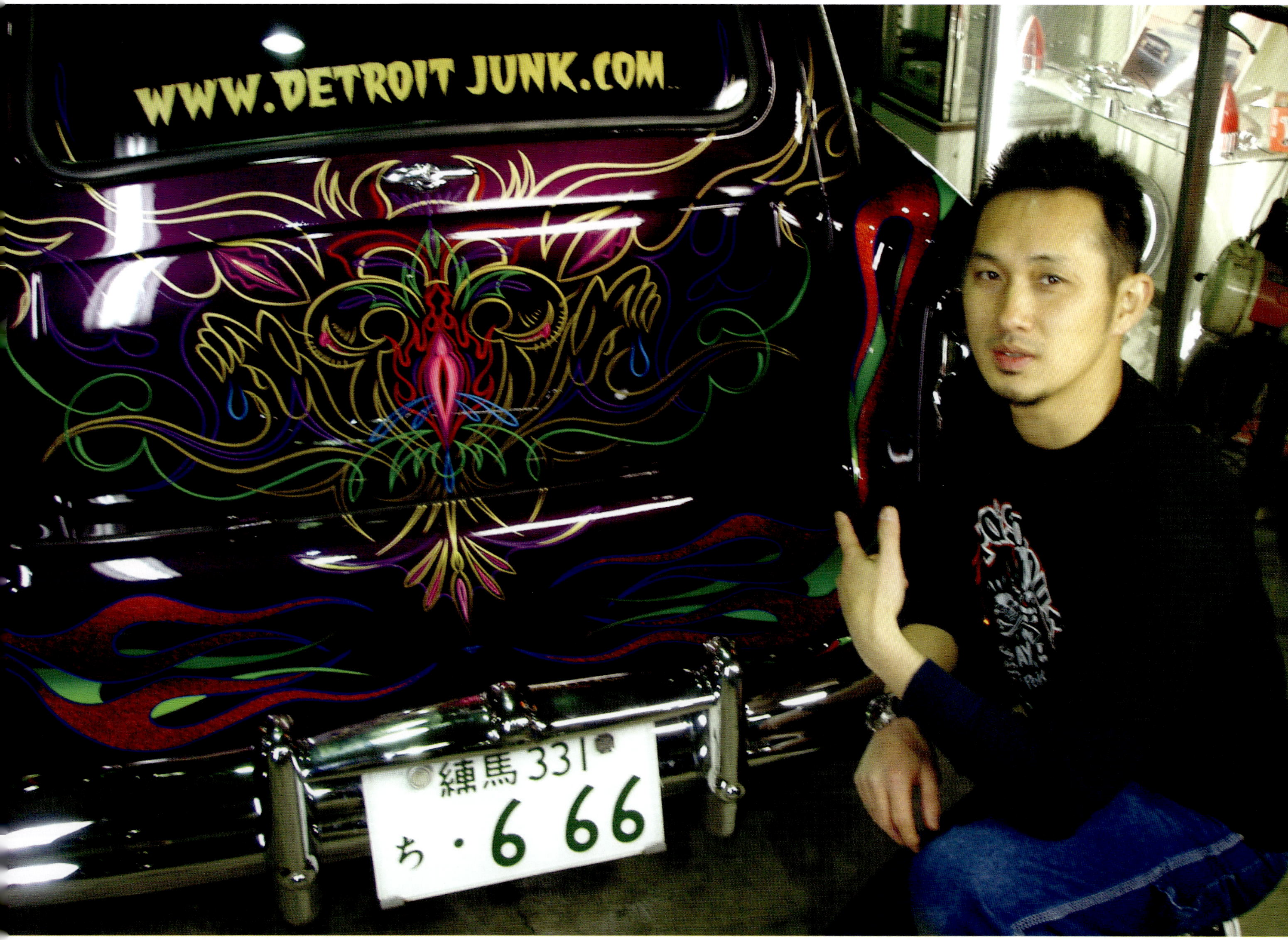
WWW.DETROIT JUNK.COM
練馬 331
ち・666

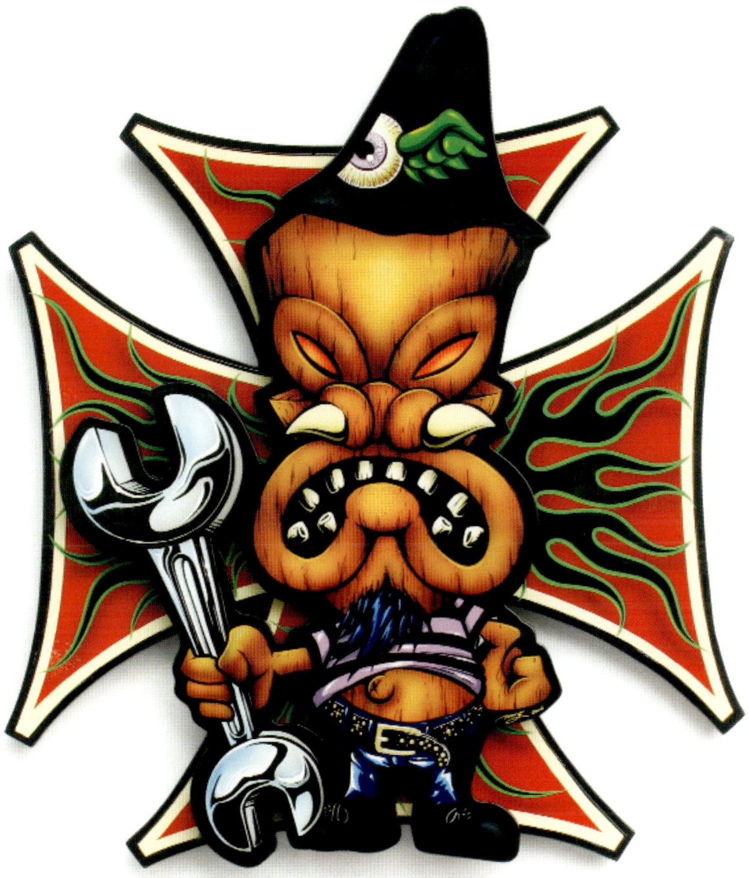

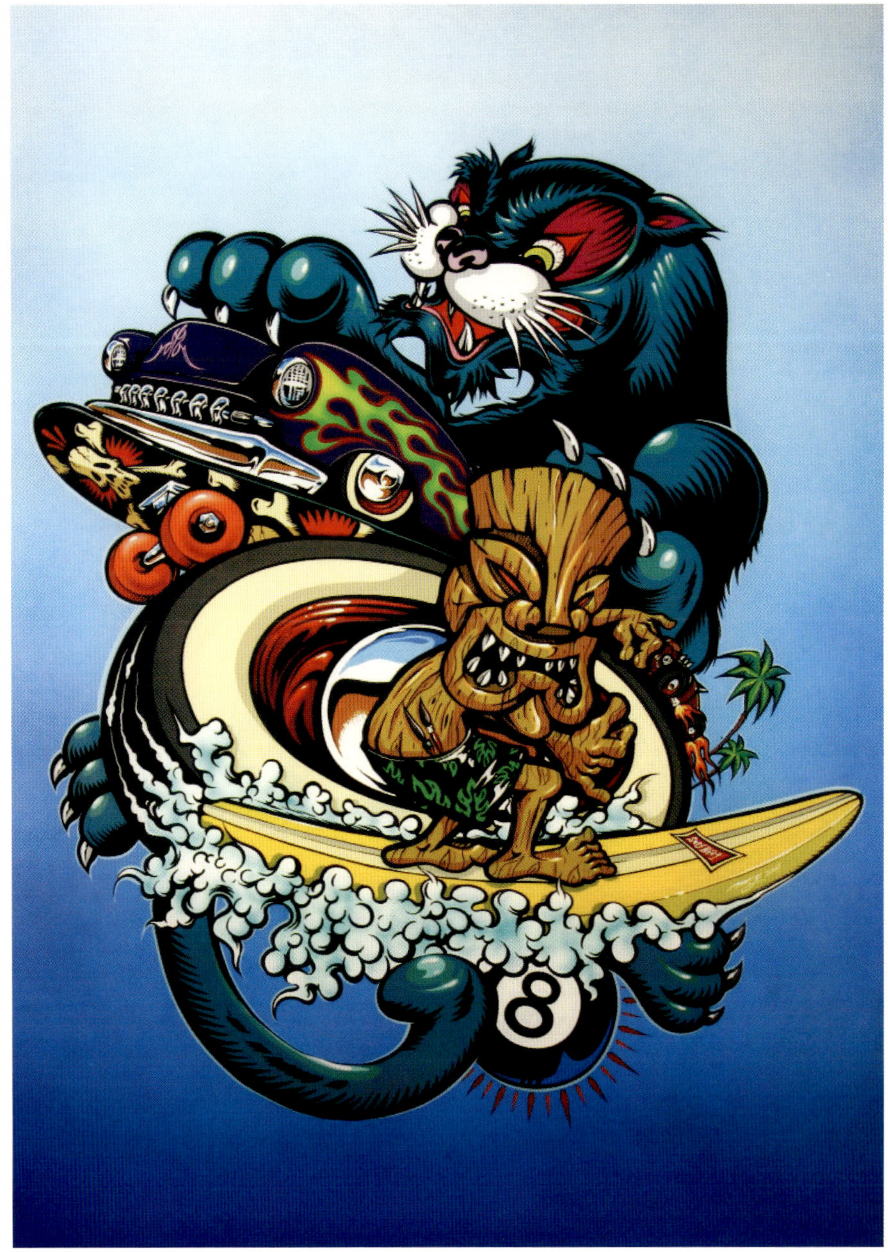

This page: Paintings by Mr. G

Left: Kustom artist Mr. G with his Krazy Kolor style on Nash Yoshii's Nash tailgate

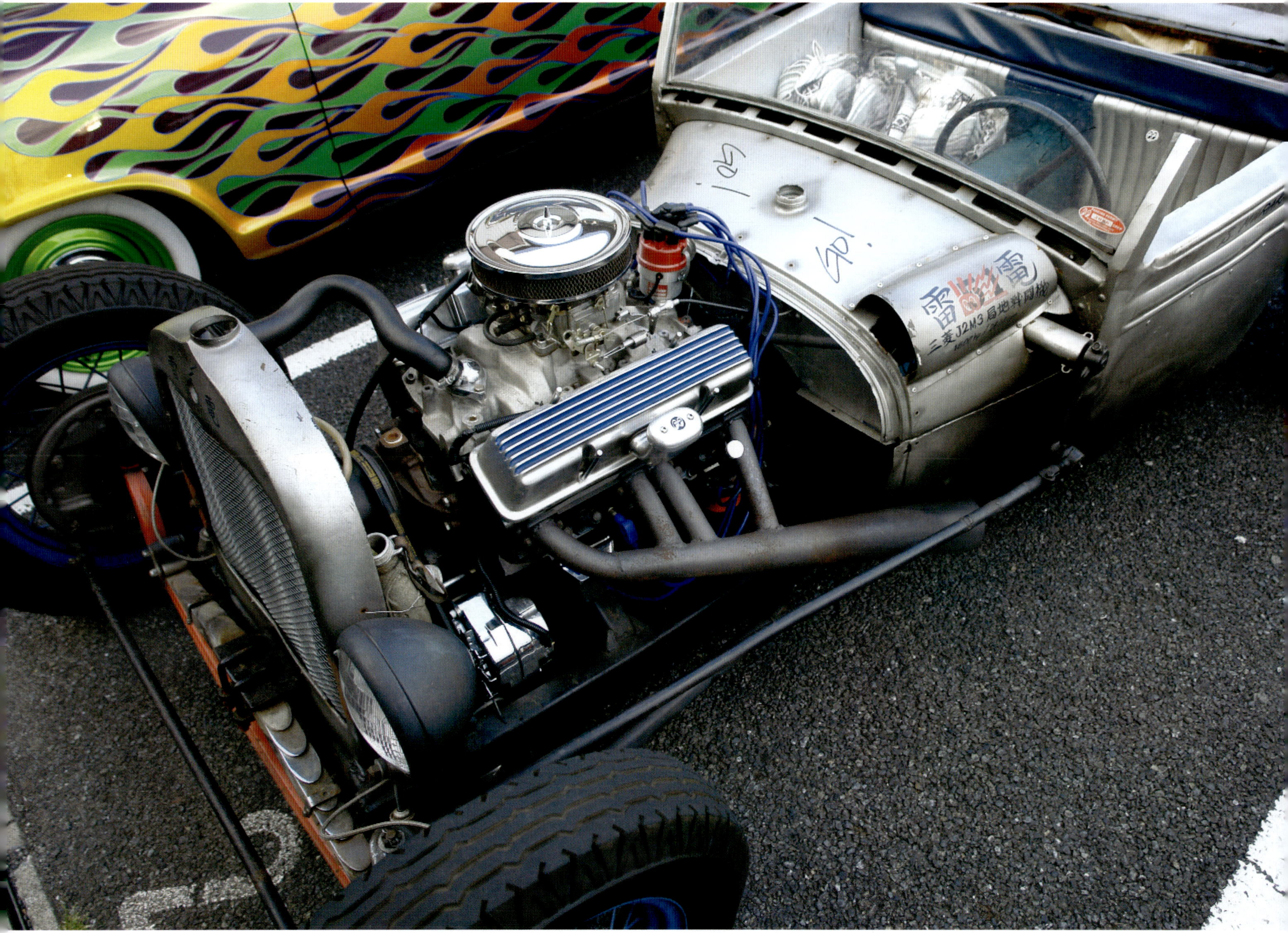
Go!
Go!
雷電
三菱J2M3局地戦闘機

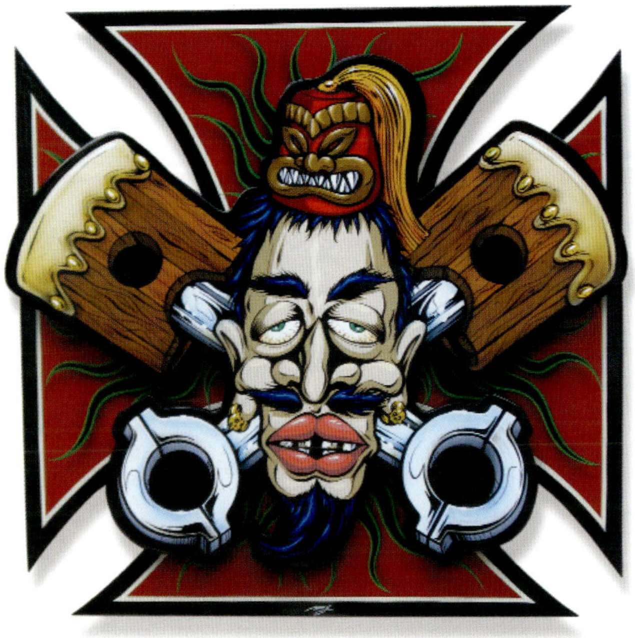

Above: Painting by Mr. G

Left: Classic 1928 Ford Hot Rod, Kustom Kulture Now event

"I watched that tape a thousand times, thought about what I was looking at, and from that I got an idea of what it was all about. This was in 1989, and at that point it was impossible to buy pinstriping materials in Japan. I couldn't find the brushes I needed because nobody did striping. I had to use regular sign painting brushes. I found pieces of plastic and Plexiglas to paint on. I knew I wasn't ready to paint somebody's car. It took me a couple of years to develop my confidence and control my line and flow."

"During those two years I painted through the different seasons. I noticed the paint texture changed depending on temperature conditions. I could see how the brush responded during the different seasons and temperatures. I built my experience with the brush and the paint. In 1989-90 there was little, if any, interest in pinstriping. There was no Internet or DVDs. I liked Mini trucks and bought magazines about them. Some of the photos were from America and I noticed some trucks were striped. I started to learn about different pinstripe designs."

"In 1991 I finally got the right brushes, paint and had some knowledge of the designs. I wanted to start striping vehicles so I moved from Kyushu to Nagoya. I started to go over and visit the Border's car shop there and got a job there. The owner, Mr. Kato, had a bunch of cars for sale, and he said I could practice on them. He was very helpful to me."

"A customer of Border's wanted an entire custom paint job. I gave him a free pinstriping job and the owner was really impressed. After that my reputation expanded quickly. I painted many customers' kustom kars, Mini trucks, hot rods, and lowriders. I had to develop many pinstripe styles. I wondered if I should keep traditional styles on traditional cars or if it was wrong to use New School styles on traditional cars."

「ペインティングを実演していたカー・ショーで、司会者が“Mr. G”という名前で私をステージに呼んだからです」と後藤稔は彼の作家名の由来について語る。「ペインティングに没頭する前は、家電関係のビジネスをやっていました。それから2000年の7月、ストライピングやレタリングの仕事を副業として始めました。まったくの独学で、正式に学んだことはありません。」

「カリフォルニアのアーティスト、ジミー・Cのストライピングの作品を見たことがあります。彼の作品はラグーナ美術館刊の「Kustom Kulture」に数点が掲載されています。彼の作品を見るよりも前に、1990年のムーンアイズ・ストリート・カー・ナショナルズでワイルドマンの作品を実際に見たことがあります。ショーでストライピングの実演をやっていたので、立ち止まって長い間彼の作業を見ていました。そのときは、それが何なのかさっぱり分かっていない頃で、難しそうでしたが何か気になるところがありました。そこに歴史とか重要性があることなど気づきませんでした。1989年にエド“ビッグダディ”ロスがストリート・カー・ナショナルズにやってきて、ワイルドマンと共に過ごしました。そのときロスがショーで実演したビデオを持っています。ロスの仕事ぶりを見たいときに、テープを繰り返し再生・巻き戻ししています。」

「そのテープを数えきれないほど何度も見て、自分が見ている作業について考え、そこから技術を会得しました。1989年のことで、当時は日本ではピンストライピングの材料を買うのは不可能でした。誰もピンストライピングをやっていないので、専用の筆は見つけられず、一般の看板用の筆を使う以外にありませんでした。他人の車に直接描くほどまだうまくなかったので、プラスチックやアクリル板の破片を見つけ、そこに描いていました。自信がつき、線や流れをうまくコントロールできるようになるまで2年くらいかかりました。」

「その2年間、暑いときも寒いときも、春夏秋冬、色々な季節を通してペインティングをやりました。そのときに気温に応じて塗料のテクスチャーが変わることに気づき、違う季節や気温の中で、筆がどのように反応するかが分かりました。一般の看板用の筆とペイントでを積みました。」

「1989年〜90年、ピンストライピングはまだほとんどの一般人の興味の対象にはなっておらず、インターネットもDVDもない当時、私はミニトラックが好きで、雑誌を購読していました。そこに掲載された写真にはアメリカのものがあり、数台のトラックにはストライプが描かれていました。そこから、色々なタイプのピンストライプ・デザインを学び始めました。」

「1991年、ようやく正式の筆とペイントを手に入れ、デザインの知識もある程度ついたので、実際に車にストライピングを始めるために九州から名古屋に引っ越しました。Border'sカー・ショップに何度も通い、そこで仕事をもらいました。オーナーの加藤さんは販売用にたくさんの車を所有し、その車で練習してはどうかと言ってくれました。彼には本当によく助けてもらいました。」

「車全体にカスタム・ペイントを希望された、あるBorder'sのお客様に、無料でピンストライピングをしたのですが、そのときオーナーは本当に感心してくれ、その車の後、私の評判はすぐに広まりました。ミニトラック、ホットロッド、ローライダーなど、たくさんのお客様のカスタム・カーにペインティングしました。多種多様の車それぞれに似合うよう、多くのピンストライプ・スタイルを開拓する必要があり、伝統的な車には伝統的なスタイルを使い、新しい流派のデザインを使うべきではないのではないか、など色々考えました。」

「私は美しいピンストライピングだと思うグリーン、パープル、イエロー、レッドなどの線と色の組み合わせを始め、それに的を絞るようになりました。私はこれを“クレイジー・カラー”スタイルと呼んでいます。異なる色を合わせるとコントラスト感を表現できると感じています。ほとんどの場合、このスタイルでは6色を使います。コントラストと組み合わせがユニークさを生むのです。」

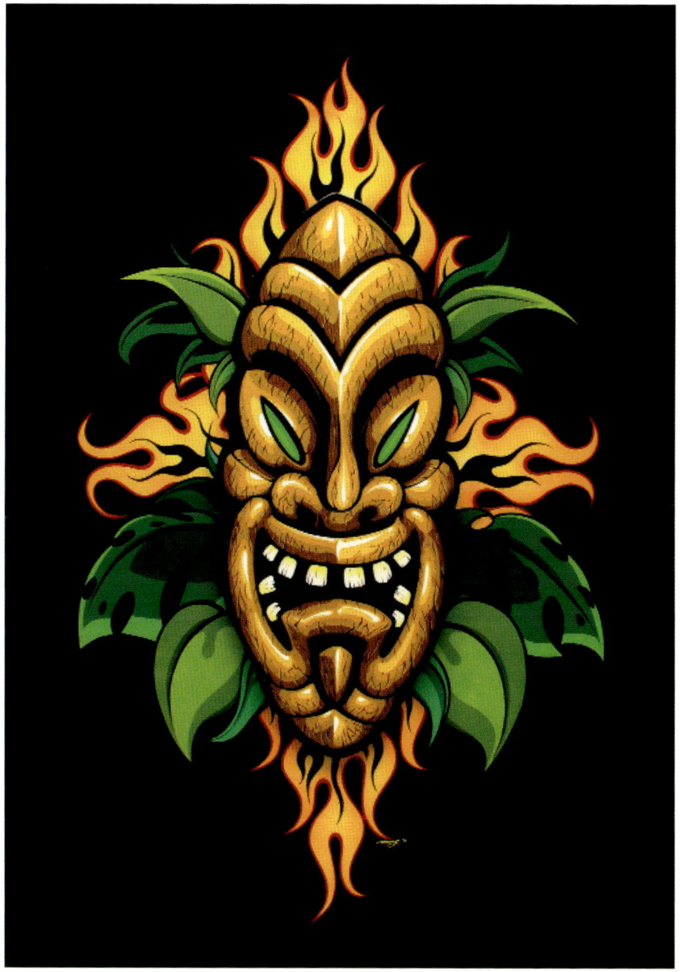

Painting by Mr. G

"I started what I call my Krazy Kolor style and focused on what I think is beautiful pinstriping, using beautiful lines and color combinations like magenta, green, purple, yellow and red. I feel that using different colors contributes to a sense of contrast. Most times I try to use six colors with this style. It is the color contrasts and combinations that are unique. In my work I go back and forth between the abstract and representational. I like to have variety in my work. One painting might be crazy monsters, the next might be purely pinstriping, another might be a combination of my Krazy Kolor style and other elements."

"There are several pinstripers in Japan now and I think about this whole scene. Individuality and personality are very important. I have always wondered what can make my style individual. Tiki art has always interested me. I collect Tiki antiques so I decided to combine Tiki styles with my pinstripe styles, an interesting combination. Individuality is important to me and I always strive to distinguish myself in my work."

At a small art gallery in the Greaser Original Wear store in Toyota City, owner Hiroki Natsume has collected an impressive sampling of Japan's top Kustom artists. The clothes in his shop reflect a sense of curiosity and attachment to specific Kustom Kulture ethnic roots that originated in Southern California, particularly cholo style. Hiroki describes his interest in this style: "Four years ago I went to the Primer National car show (Ventura, CA). I saw the real car clubs and their cars for the first time. When I saw this real emotional attachment to cars and car culture it really impressed me. I saw the Pandilla de Lobos club. I watched some movies, *Blood In Blood Out*, *American Me*, *Boulevard Nights*. I was impressed with the style statements of this culture."

"Chicano culture is impressive. I saw young men expressing things with their clothes. Work, Prejudice, Pride. This pride was associated

「自分の作品では、抽象と具象の間を行き来しますね。作品に多様性を持たせたいので。あるペインティングは奇妙なモンスターで、次は純粋なピンストライピング、それから“クレイジー・カラー”スタイルと他の要素を組み合わせたもの、といった具合にです。」

「今、日本にはピンストライパーが何人かいるので思うのですが、個性と人格はとても大切です。私は何が自分のスタイルを個性的にできるかについてずっと考えてきました。そこで、ティキ・アートに以前から興味があり、ティキ・アンティークを収集しているので、ティキ・スタイルと自分のピンストライピング・スタイルを組み合わせることにしました。これは私にとって面白い組み合わせです。自分の個性を大事にし、作品でいつも自分を際立たせるよう努力しています。」

愛知県豊田市のGreaser（グリーサー）オリジナル・ウェアにある小さなアート・ギャラリー。オーナーの夏目広樹は日本トップクラスのカスタム・アーティストの見事な代表的作品を集めている。

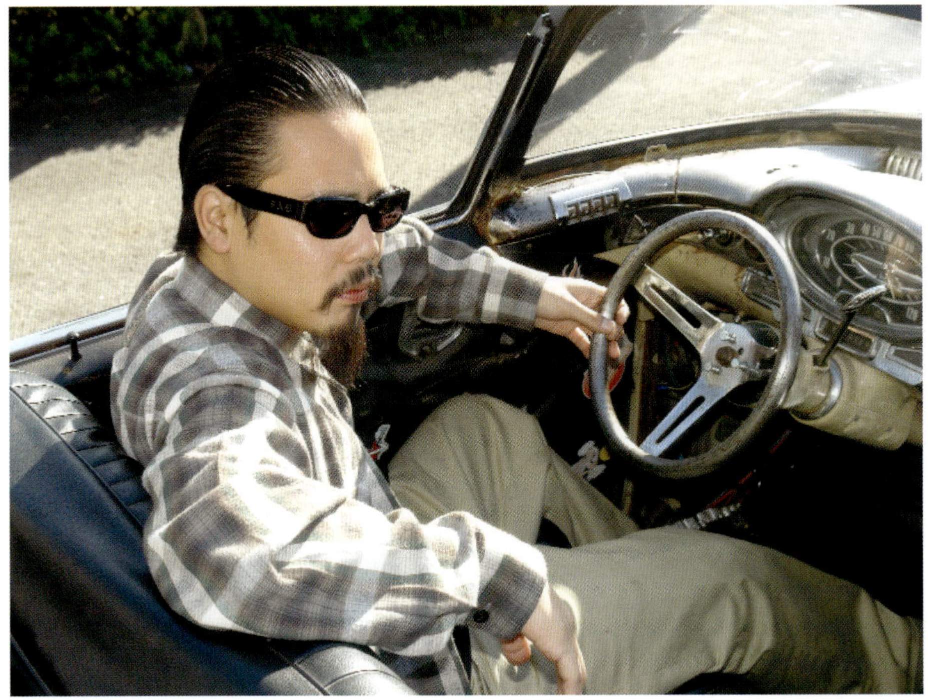

彼の店が扱う服には、南カリフォルニア由来の特定のカスタム・カルチャーの民族的ルーツ、特にチョロ・スタイルに対する好奇心と愛着が見られる。広樹はこのスタイルに対する興味を説明する。「4年前、プライマー・ナショナル・カー・ショー（カリフォルニア州ベンチュラ市）に行き、本物のカー・クラブとその車を初めて見ました。そこで目撃した車とカー・カルチャーに対する本物の愛着にはずいぶん感銘を受けました。そのとき見たPandilla de Lobosクラブのチョロ・スタイルが気に入りました。それから『ブラッド・イン　ブラッド・アウト』、『アメリカン・ミー』、『ブールバード・ナイト』などの映画を見ました。このカルチャーのスタイル表現に感心しました。」

with family, community, language, rebellion and reacting to racially motivated punishment. There was a sense of power that came with their clothes, cars and style. I immediately felt this intense emotion of 'heart.' I think the Kustom artists in my shop are trying to explore this kind of depth and emotion using a combination of images that impress them."

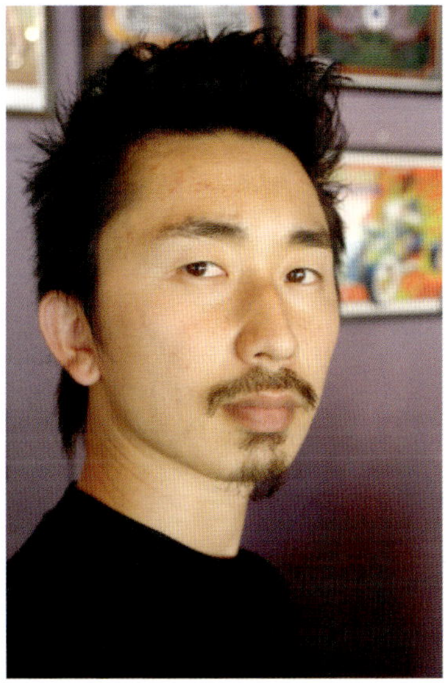

Above: Kustom artist Fudemae

Left: Hiroki Natsume
Greaser Original Wear, Cholo style

The Kustom artist Fudemae paints from his studio in Toyota City. Like his colleagues, he explores the accumulation of visual vocabulary associated with Kustom Kulture. "I had an old Kawasaki, and I wanted to make it into a chopper," he says. "First I fixed the mechanical problems then chopped it, then painted it to customize it. I stared to explore airbrush and pinstripe painting. I had seen a few Japanese car magazines and noticed this phrase Kustom Kulture. I looked for art books about it but there weren't any. But I kept up my interest in painting and striping motorcycles. The business was practical. I painted signage on trucks, or maybe I would stripe a car or bike. Then I thought about trying to paint on canvas."

"Nash Yoshii saw my work and asked if I wanted to be in an art show. I was included in the first California-Japan Kustom Art show. People saw my painting and there was a very good reaction to my style. Nash was very important in terms of putting this all together."

"Interest in Kustom Kulture art is growing in Japan. Particularly the dark images of Frankenstein and skulls. Customers are interested in these themes. I find this interesting but I also explore other styles. I like to add particular details of my own. I look to people like Von Dutch, Roth, Williams and Schorr as teachers. These artists have a different sense of the world, a different way of seeing."

"I love the skull design. I think it is the best design to paint in terms of the depth of thinking about the image. In Japan there is a history

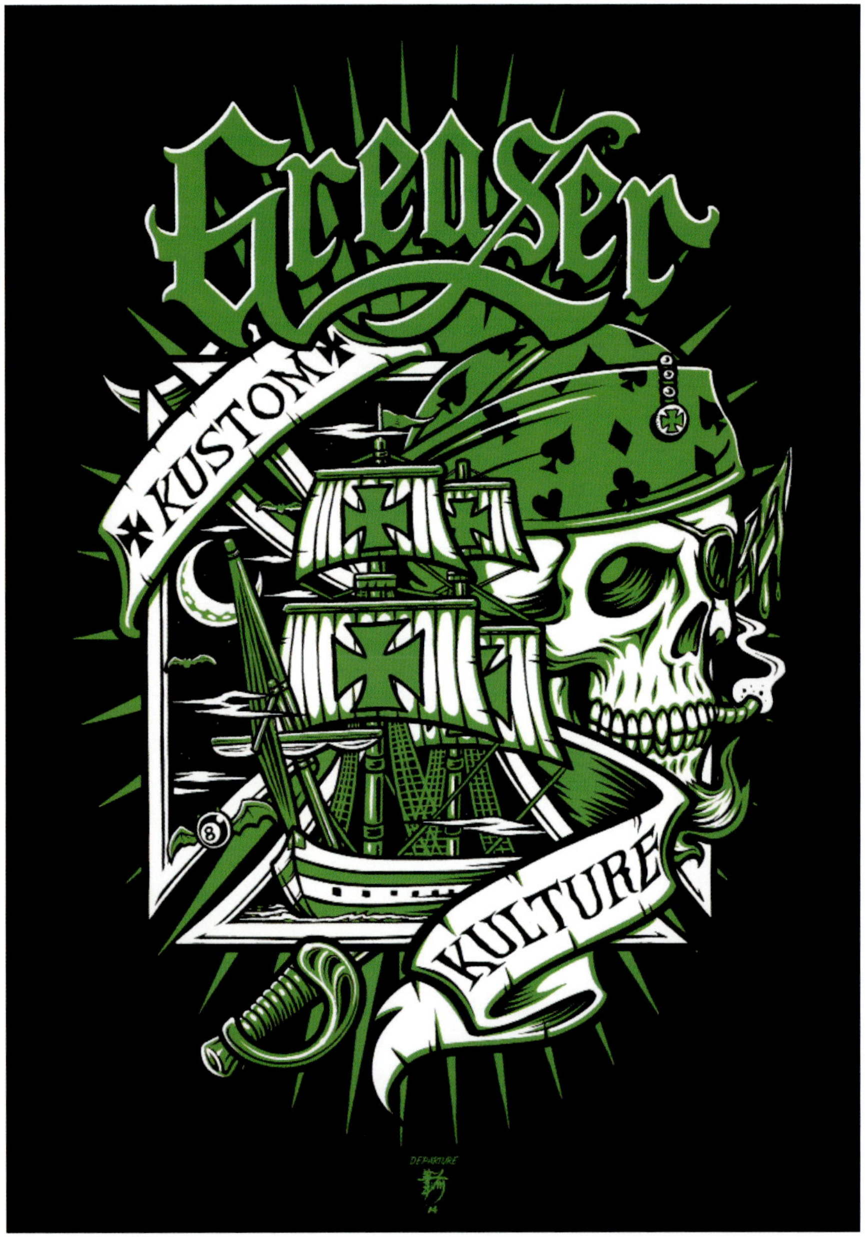
Greaser
KUSTOM
KULTURE

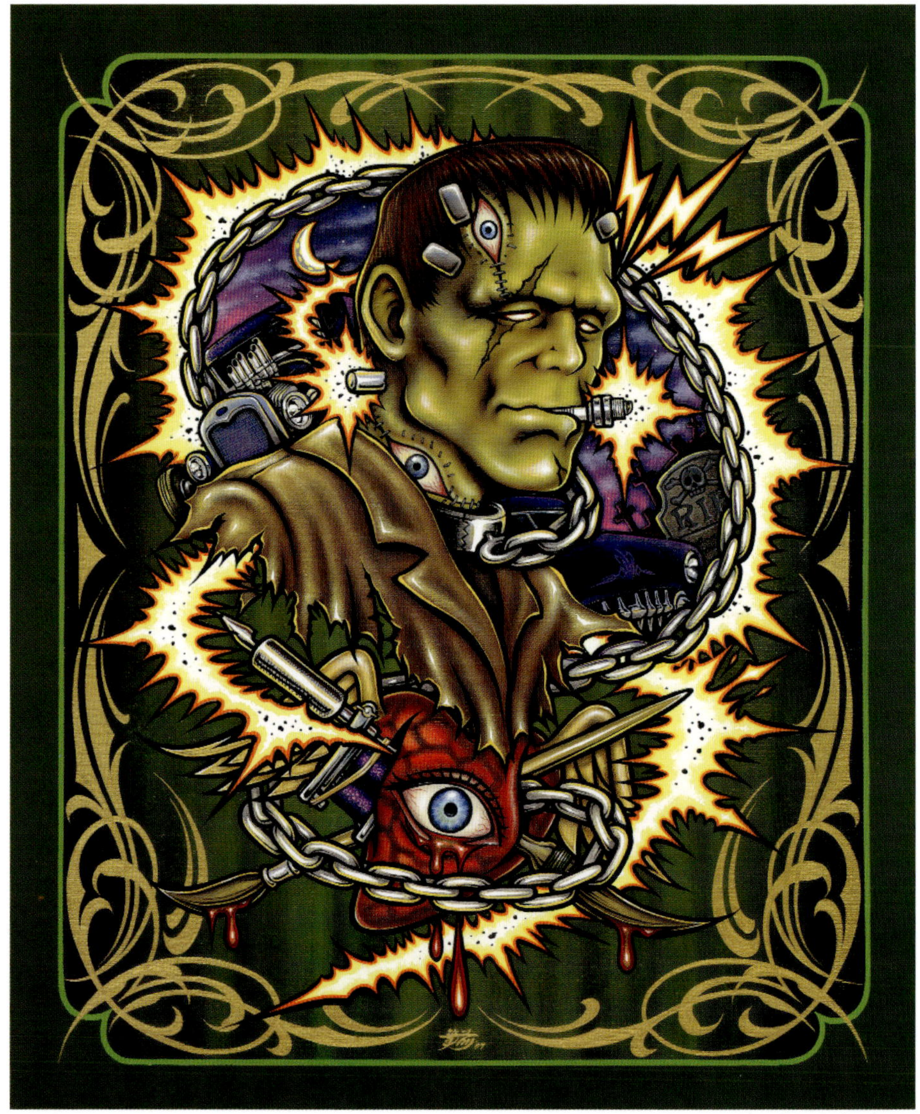

Both pages: Paintings by Fudemae

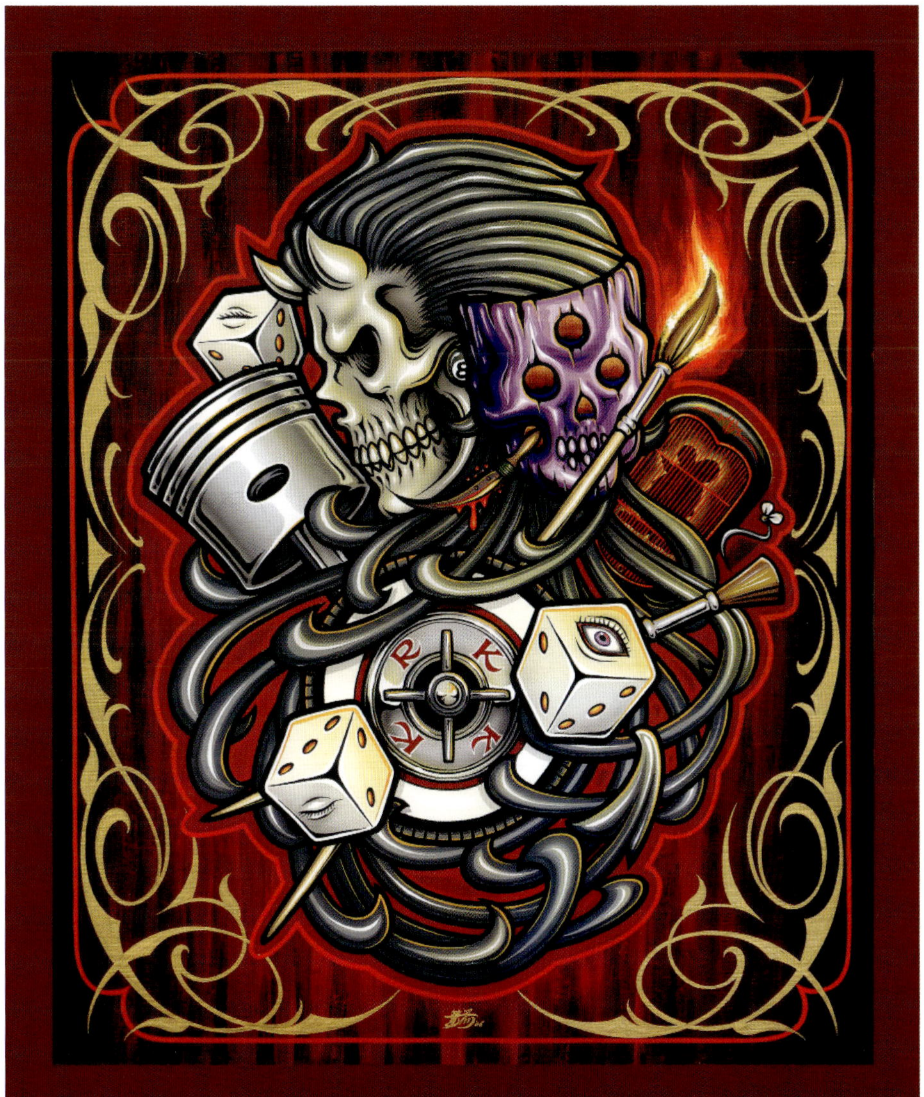

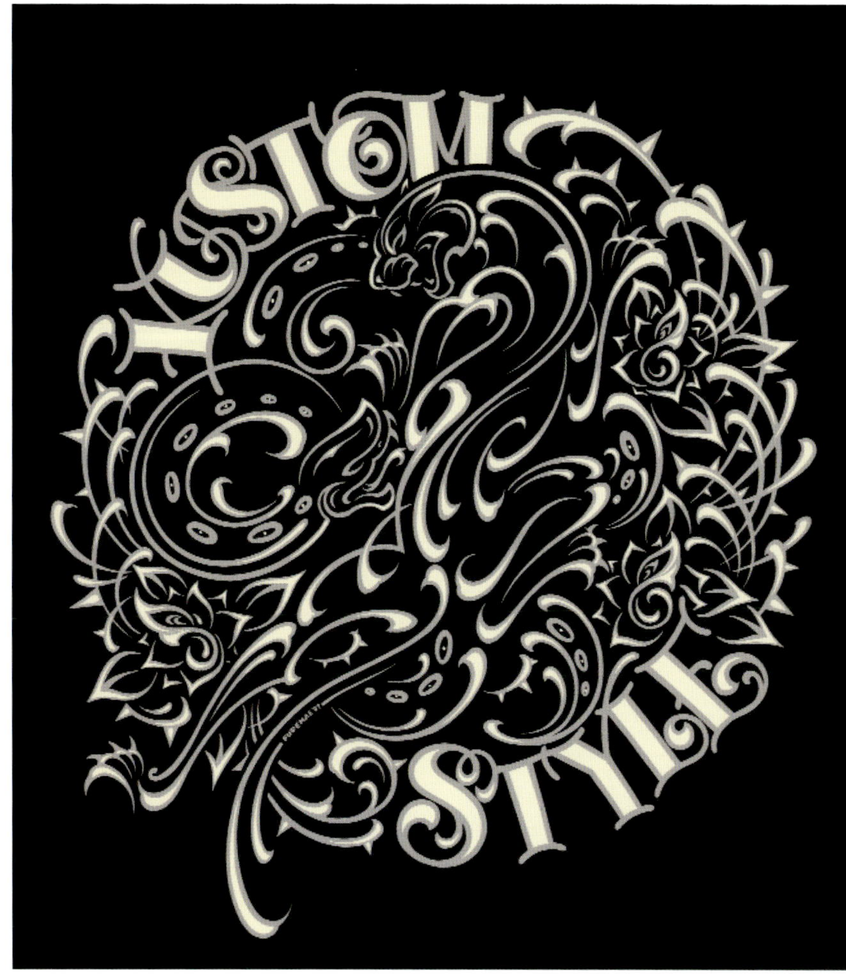

「チカーノ・カルチャーは印象的です。特にチョロ・スタイルです。若い男性が服装を通して何かを表現しているのです。それは仕事、刑罰、誇りを示し、そしてこの誇りは、家族やコミュニティ、言葉、そして人種差別的な刑罰に対する反抗や反応に関連しています。彼らの服や車、スタイルには、パワーが備わっていて、"心" から湧き出る強い感情を直感しました。私のショップのカスタム・アーティストらは、感銘を受けたイメージの組み合わせを使って、このような深さと感情を模索しようとしています。」

カスタム・アーティストのFudemaeは、豊田市のアトリエで仕事をする。彼は同僚と同じく、カスタム・カルチャーに関連のある視覚的ボキャブラリーの積み重ねを模索する。「古いカワサキを持っていましたが、これをチョッパーにしたかったんです」と彼は言う。「まず、機械関係を修理し、それからチョップして塗装しました。カスタマイズのプロセスを私のバイクを通してつかみ、その後エアブラシやピンストライプ・ペインティングについての模索を始めました。日本の車関係の雑誌を見て、"カスタム・カルチャー" という言葉に気づき、カスタム・カルチャーについての本を探しましたが、まったく見つかりませんでした。ですが、バイクのペインティングとストライピングへの興味をあきらめずにいました。当時仕事は実務的で、トラックに屋号を描いたり、ごくたまに車やバイクにストライプをつけることもありました。そのうち、キャンバスに描くのはどうかと考えました。」

「Nash 吉井さんが私の作品を見て、展覧会に出展しないかと声をかけてくれ、そうして第1回カリフォルニア・ジャパン・カスタム・アート展に参加しました。展覧会で私の絵を見た人々から、私のスタイルについてなかなかいい反応がありました。Nash さんは、その展覧会企画で非常に大切な役割を果たしました。」

「現在の日本ではカスタム・カルチャー・アートに対する興味が大きくなってきています。特にお客様はフランケンシュ

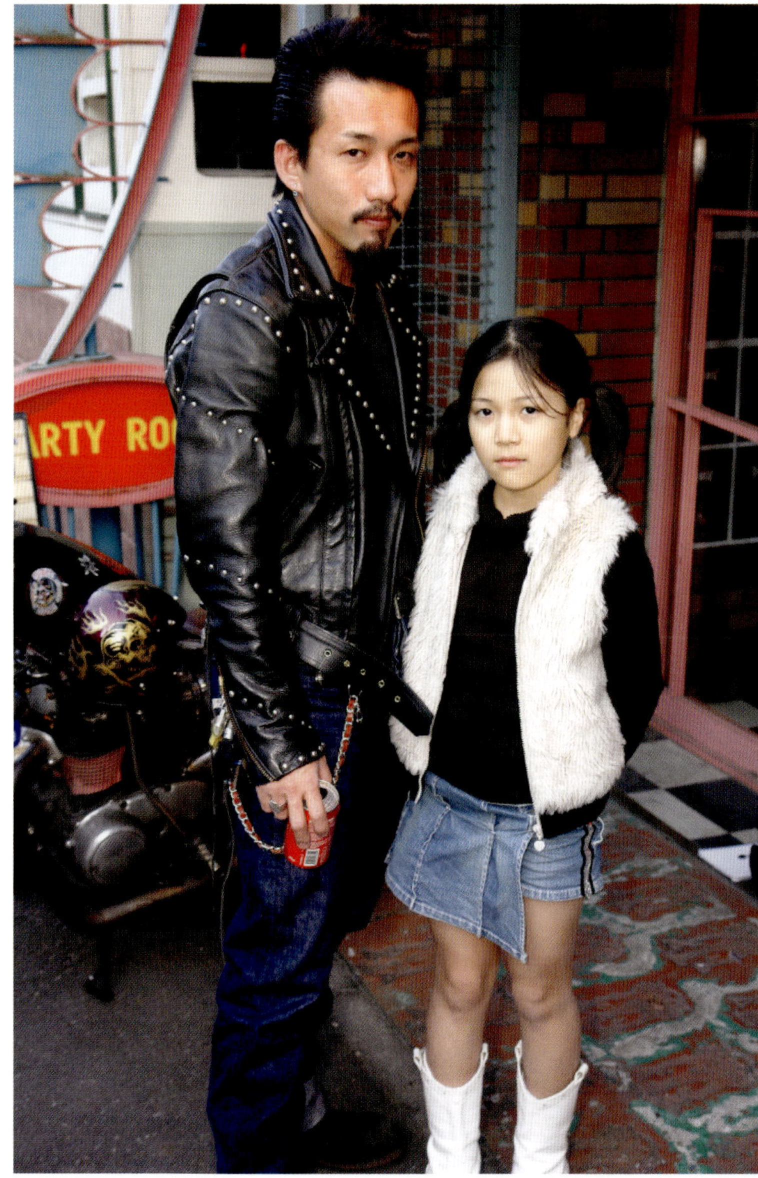

Above: Kustom father and daughter, Atsugi, Kustom Kulture Now event

Right: Dutch

Following pages: Pinstriping by Makoto

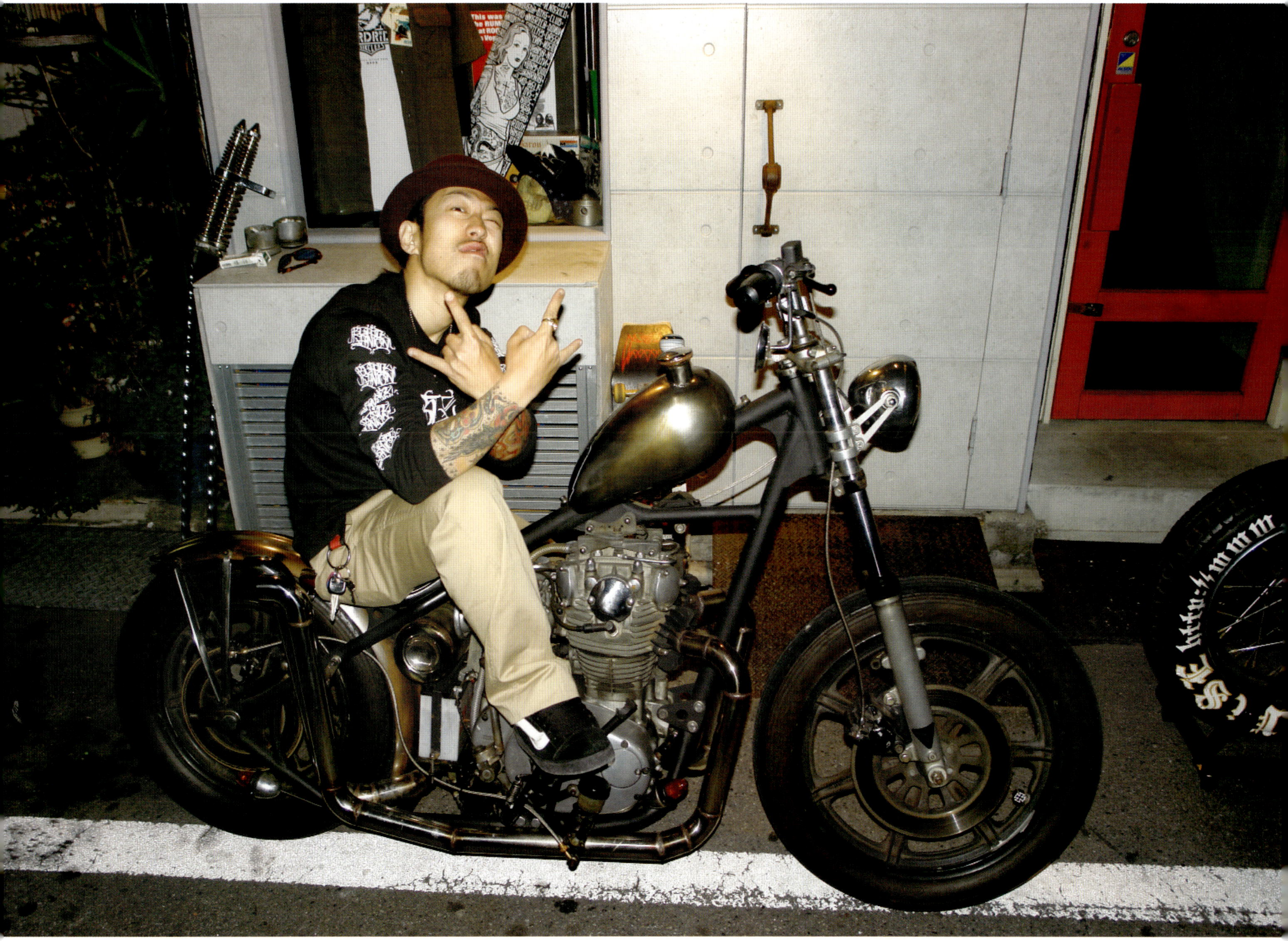

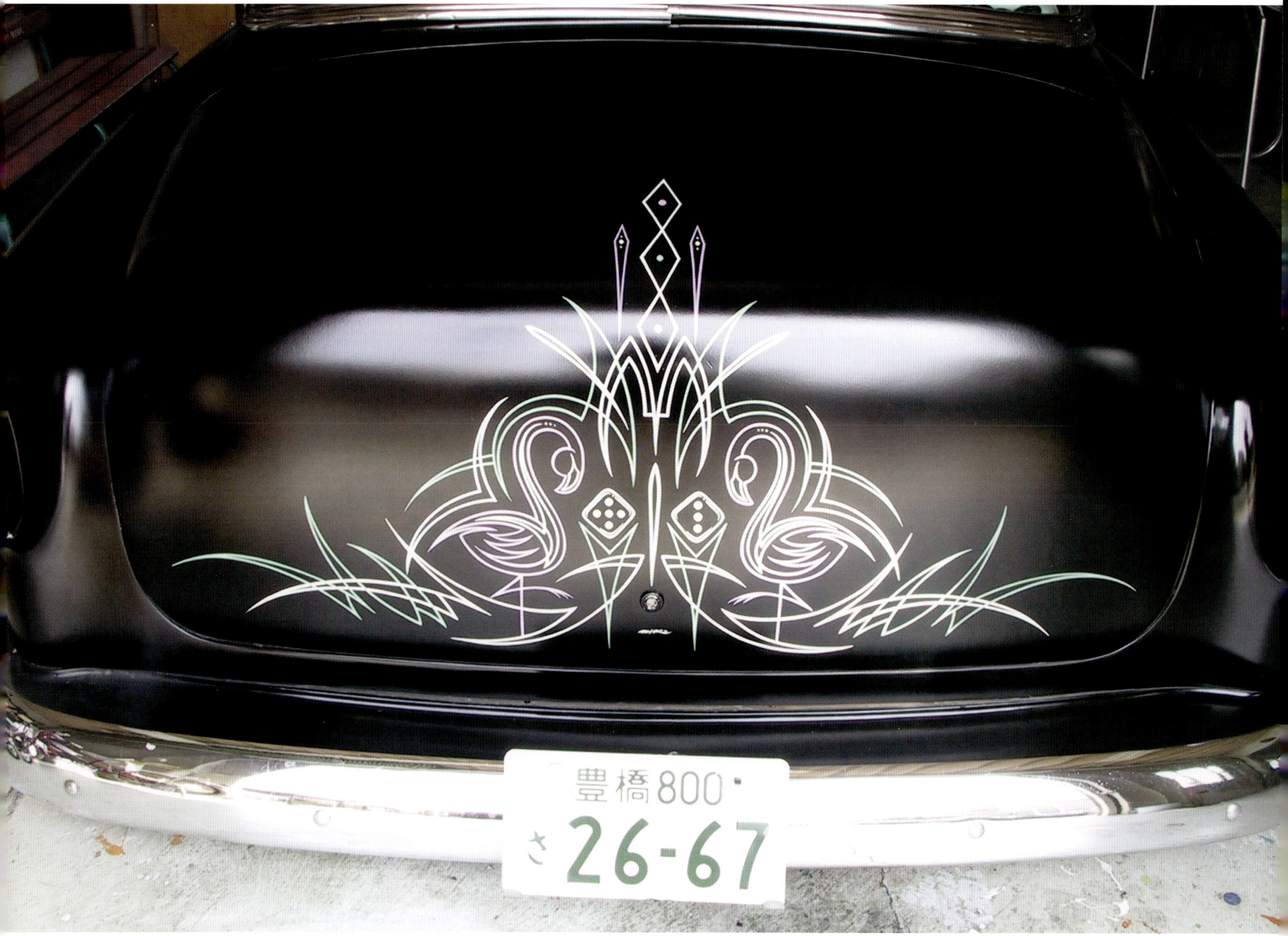
豊橋800
さ 26-67

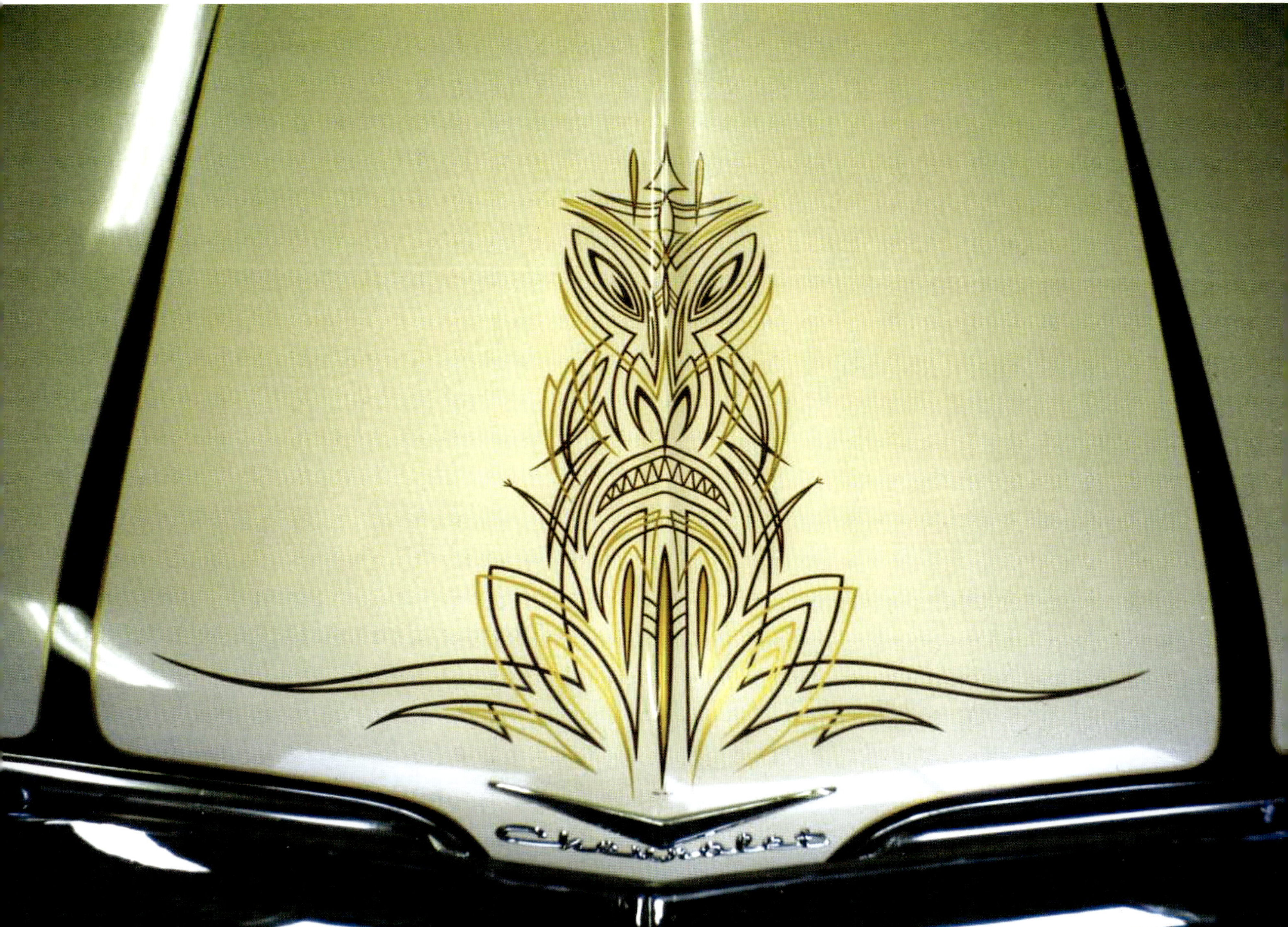

タインとかスカルのような暗いイメージに興味を持たれています。この傾向は面白いと思いますが、私は自分特有のディテールを加えた、これ以外のスタイルも研究しています。ヴォンダッチ、ロス、ウィリアムス、ショアは私の先生であると考えています。なぜなら、このような作家は世界に対して異なる感覚を持っており、世界を違う目で見ているからです。」

「デザインとしてスカルモチーフがすごく気に入っています。イメージに深い考察を与えられるという意味で、スカルはペインティングに最高のデザインだと思います。日本美術には幽霊や鬼の絵の歴史がありますが、日本の伝統的な薄気味悪いイメージと私の作品の間に必ずしもつながりがあるとは思いません。」

「私は自分のアートを壁から取り外し、テールゲートやバイクのタンク、トラックのドアなどにもっと施したいですね。私はペインティングをキャンバスから始めたわけではなく、移動する物体に描くことから始めたんです。私にはそれがすごく大切で、そこにこそ私の心が宿っているのです。移動する物体に描く…。金属の移動する物体に。グラフィティ・アーティストが建物の壁や地下鉄の車両につながりを感じるように、私は車やトラック、バイク、テールゲートにつながりを感じるのです。」

「私は自分を職人だと考えています。物作りには基本的スキルが必要で、スキルはそこから身に付くのです。アートには知性が、クラフトには完璧さとプロ意識が存在します。これらには違いがあり、それぞれがユニークな観点を必要とします。私は作品の制作において、自分はこれら２つの考え方を組み合わせていると思っています。これら異分野の文脈を組み合わせることが、カスタム・カルチャー・アートの力の根源です。Makoto、Grimb、Psycho、Mr. G、そして私は、皆自分の作品でこの２つの分野を組み合わせる課題に取り組んでいます。基本的なスキルとクラフト、そしてヴォンダッチやロスのような他のアーティストとのつながりは、その取り組みから来るのです。」

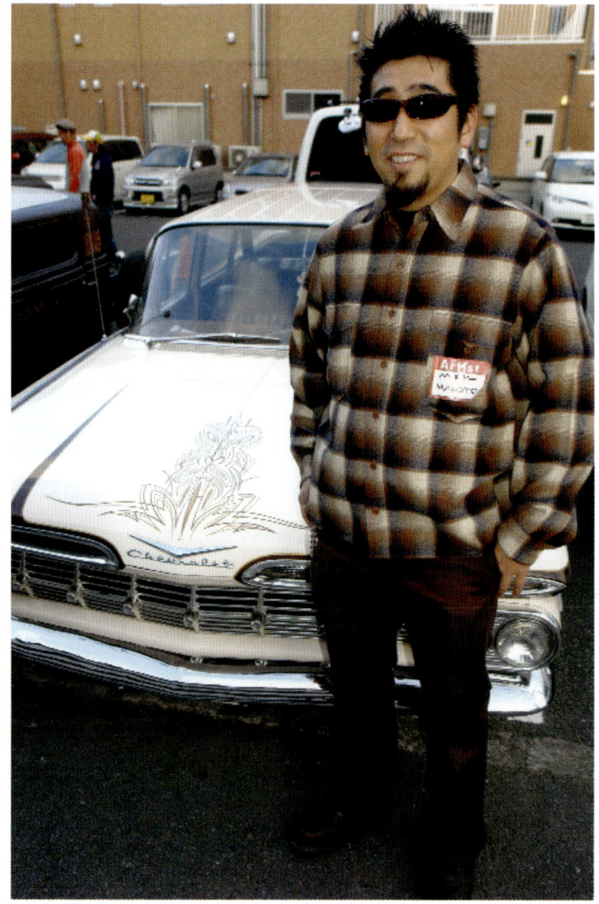

Above: Kustom artist Makoto

Right: Painting by Makoto

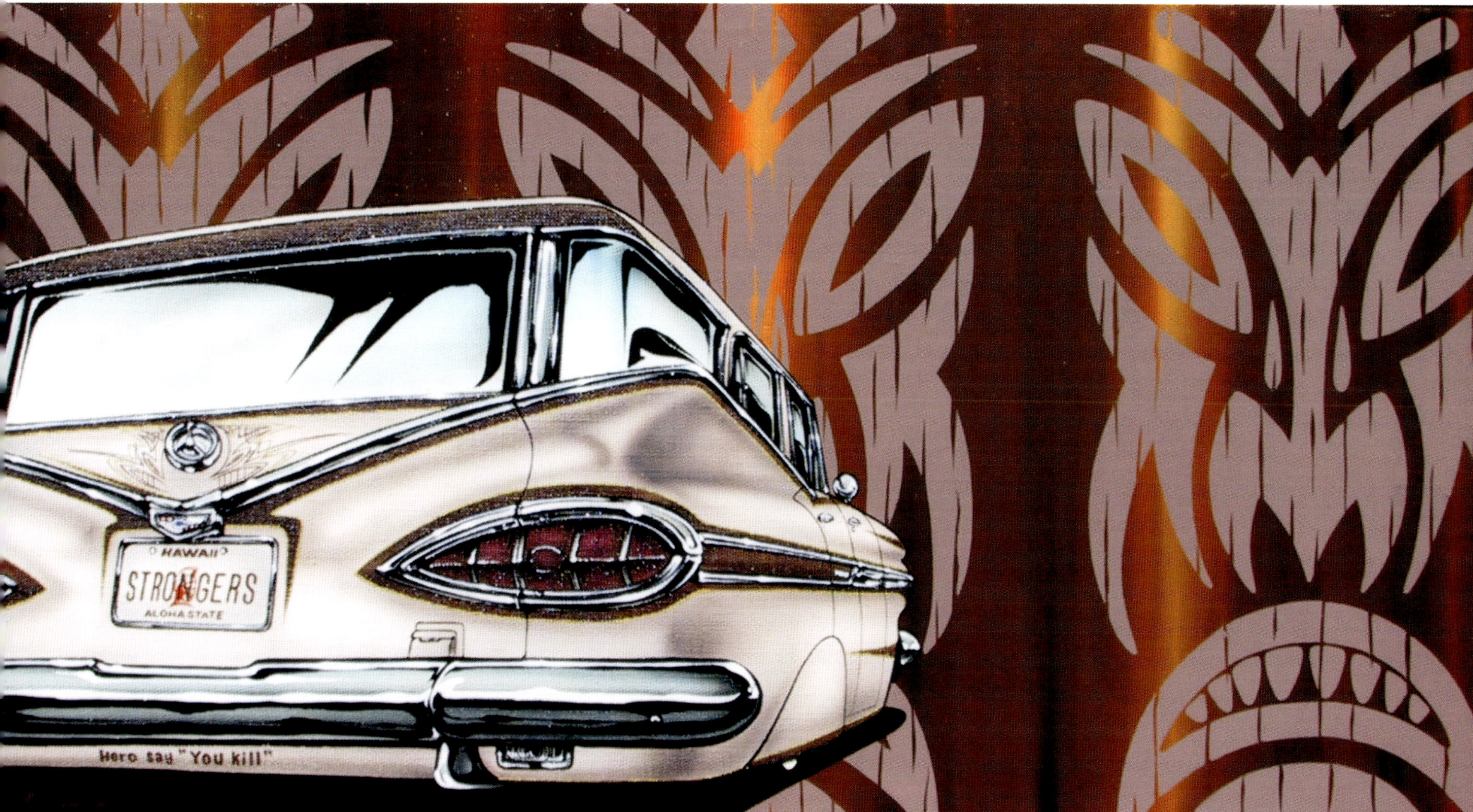
HAWAII
STRONGERS
ALOHA STATE
Hero say "You kill"

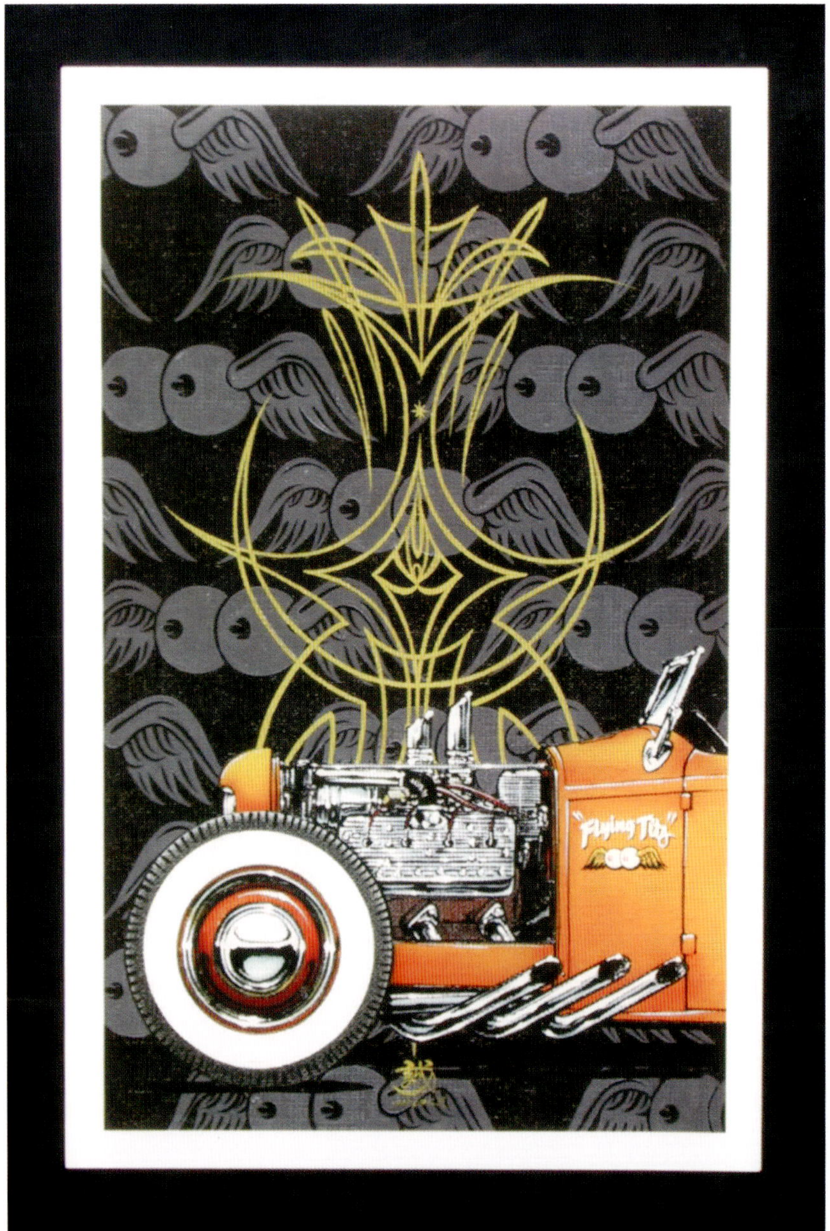
"Flying Titz"

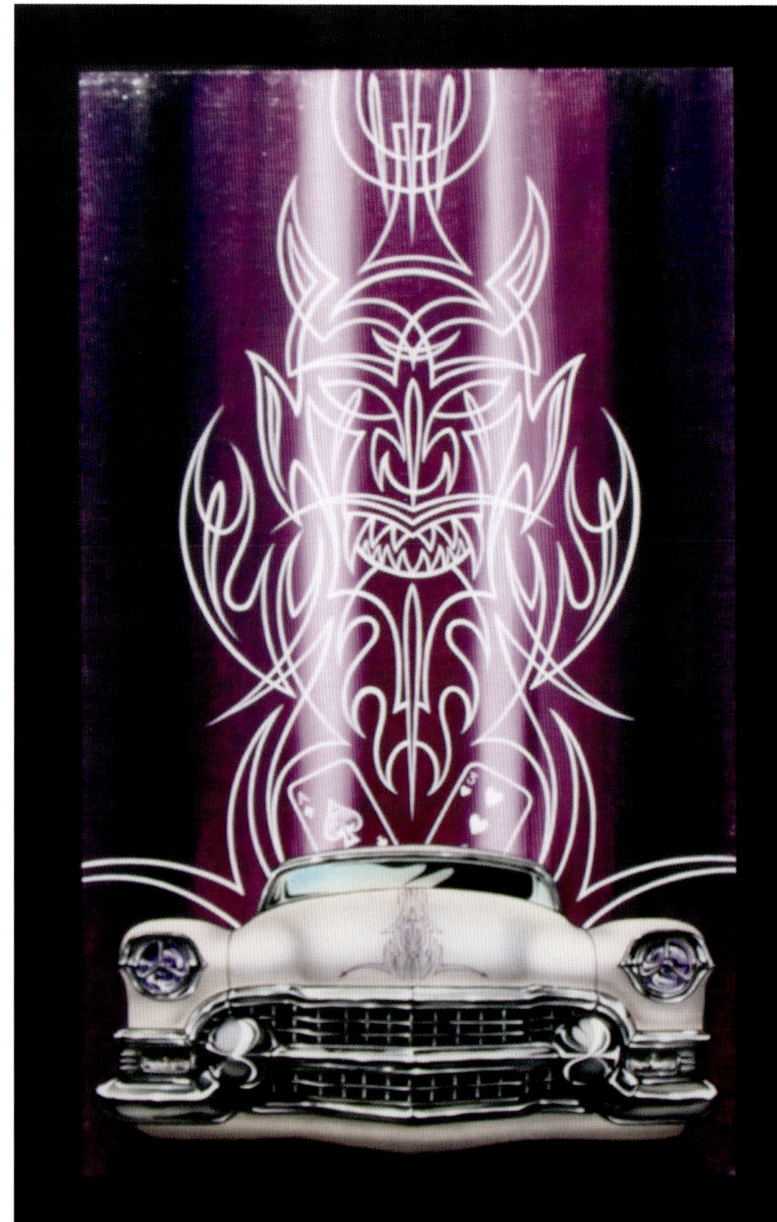

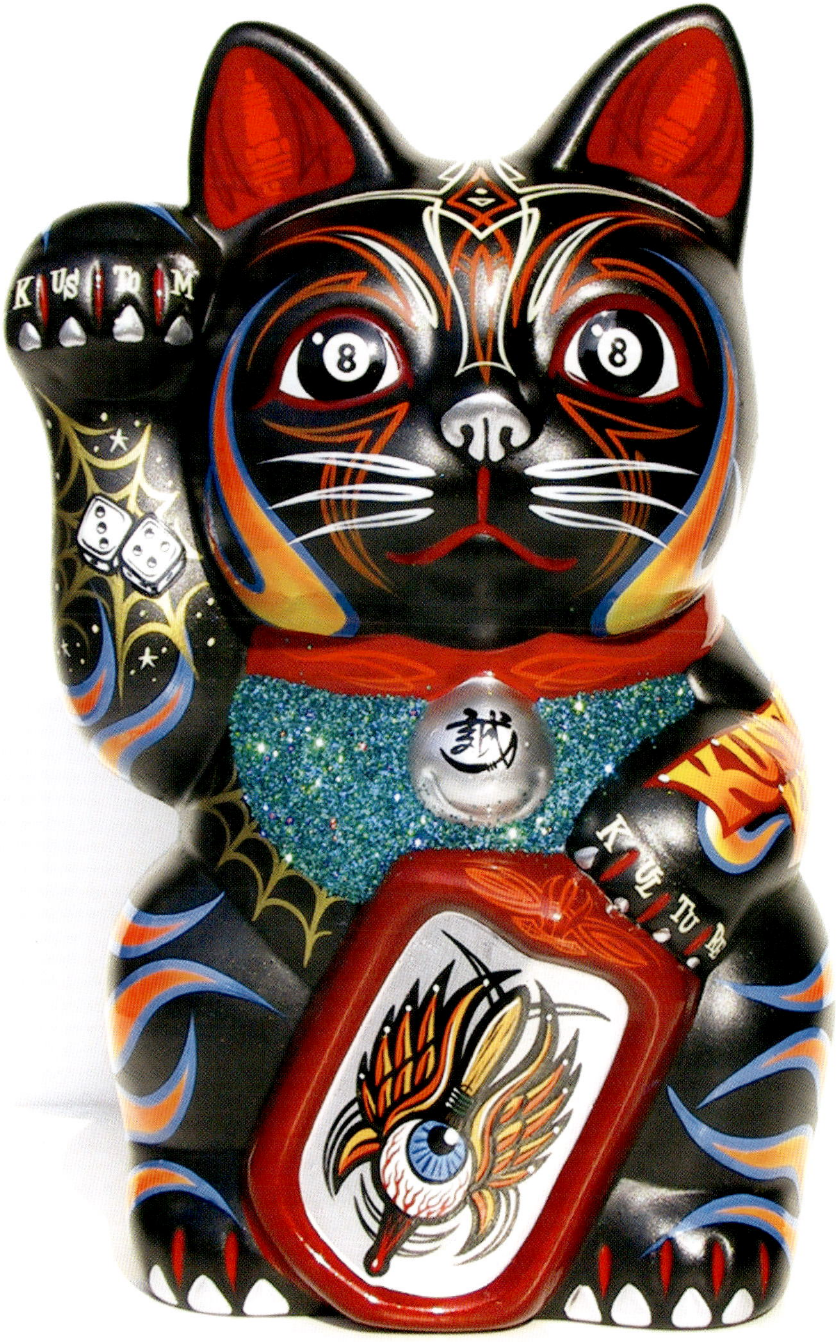

Facing page: Paintings by Makoto

This page, left: Fortune Cat by Makoto

Below: Makoto pinstriping laptop computer, Kustom Kulture Now event

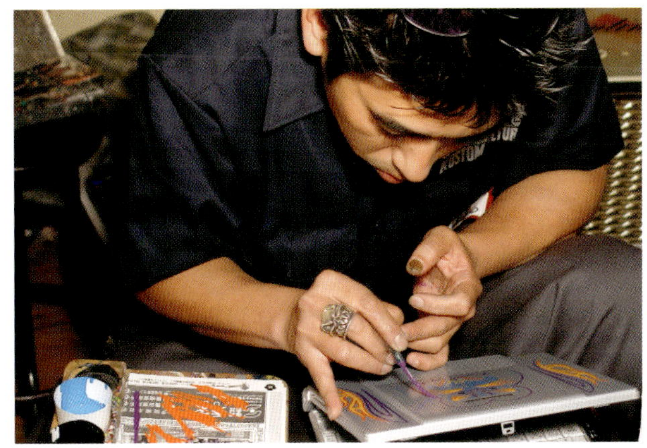

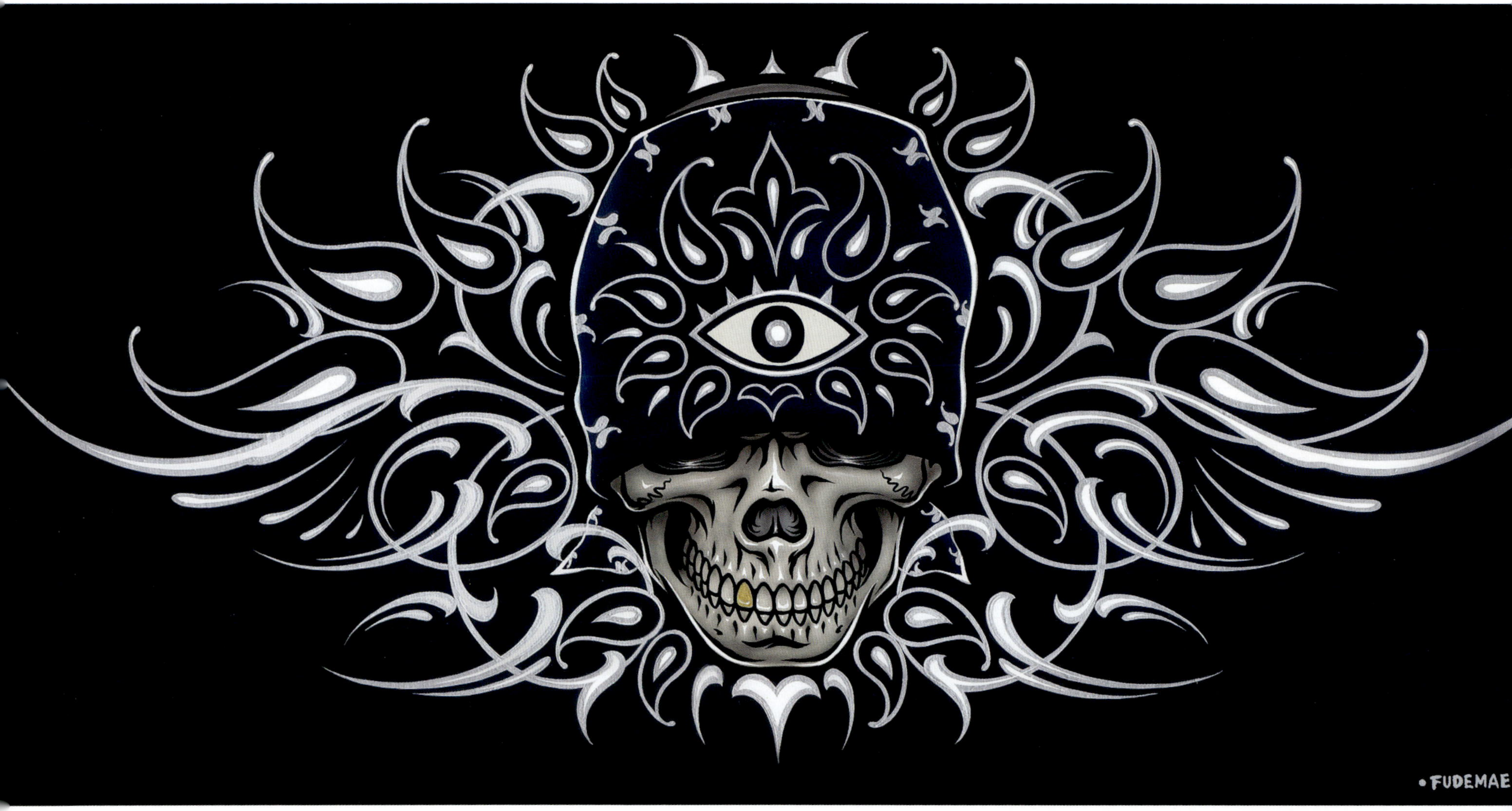
FUDEMAE

of ghosts and demons in art, but I don't necessarily see a connection between traditional Japanese images of the macabre and what I do."

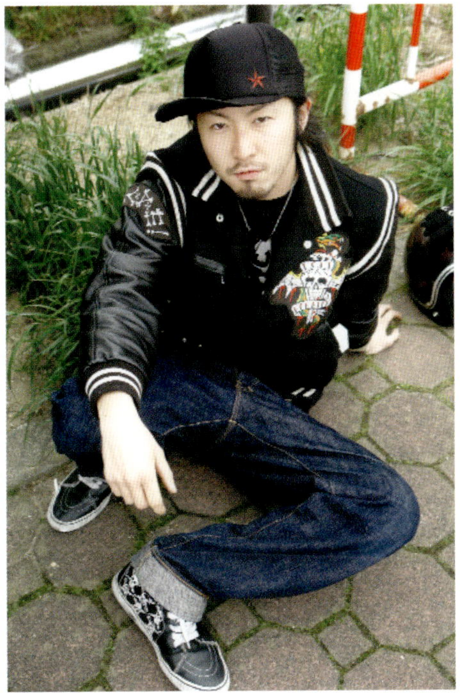

Above: Kustom Style

Left: Painting by Fudemae

"I like to move my art off the wall and onto a tailgate or bike tank or truck door. I did not start with my painting on canvas, I started on moving objects. This is very important, where the heart is, to paint on metal moving objects. It's similar to a graffiti artist who feels connected to the walls of buildings and subway cars; I feel connected to cars, trucks, and bikes."

"I see myself as a tradesman. This is where the skill comes from, the basic skills needed to make things. There is an intelligence in making art and a perfection and professionalism in craft. Each requires a different perspective. I see myself combining these two disciplines of thinking. Combining these contexts is where the power of Kustom Kulture art comes from. Makoto, Grimb, Psycho, Mr. G and myself are all dealing with this issue of combining these two things in our work. The basic skills and craft, the connection to other artists like Von Dutch and Roth. We strive to continue this."

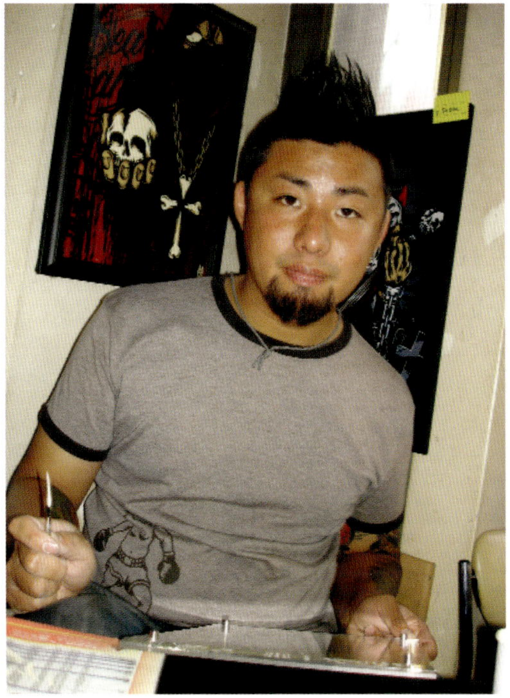

Above: Kustom Artist GRIMB

Near right & facing page: Paintings by GRIMB

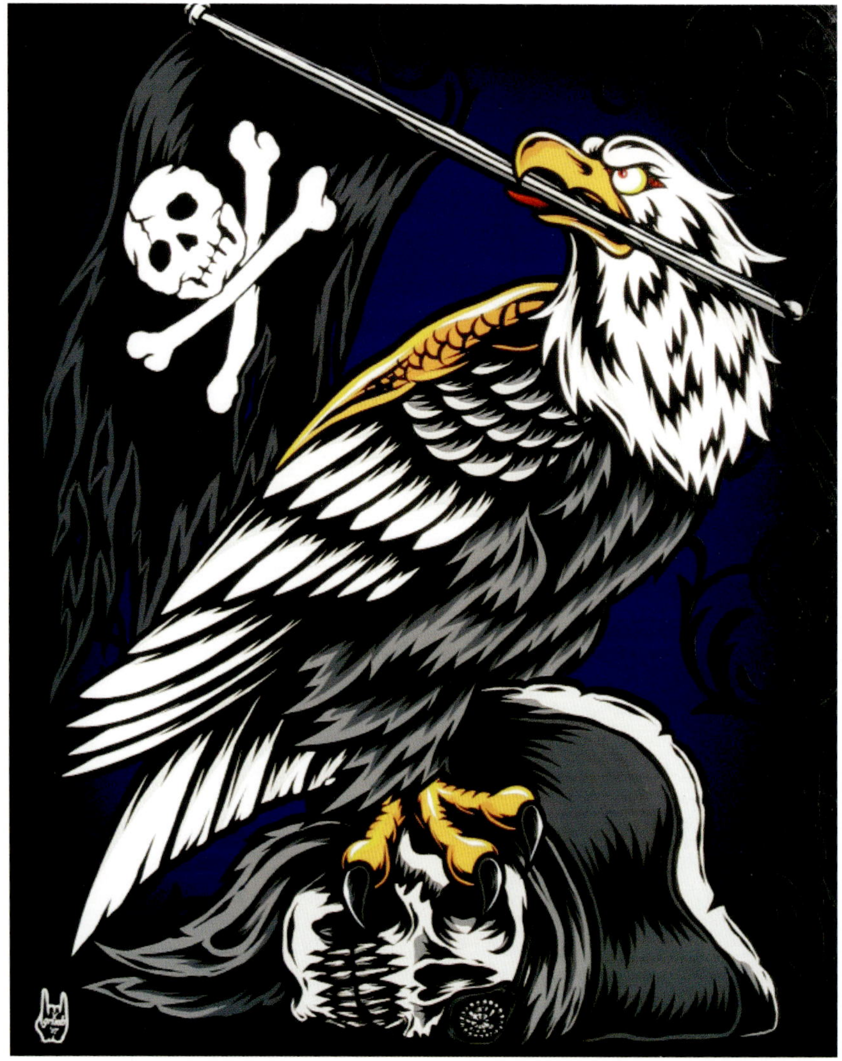

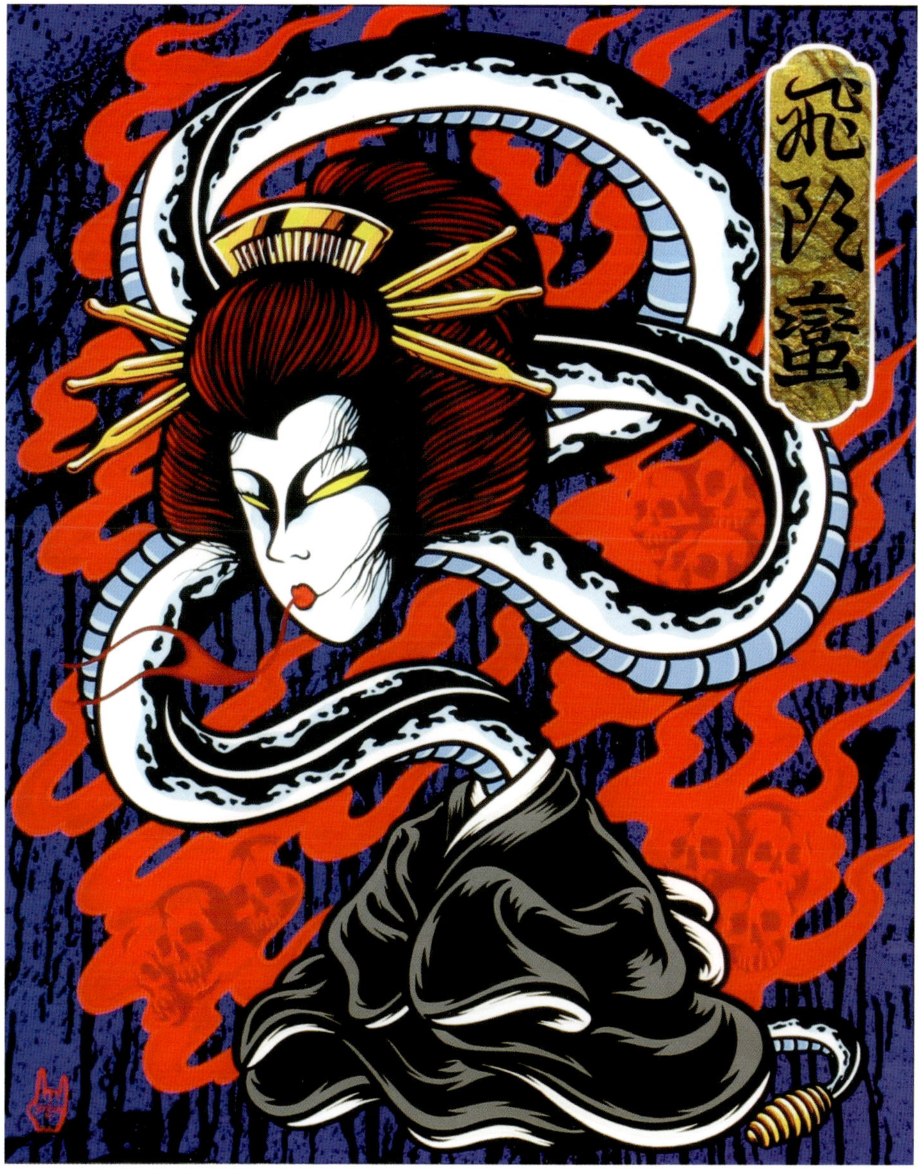
飛頭蛮

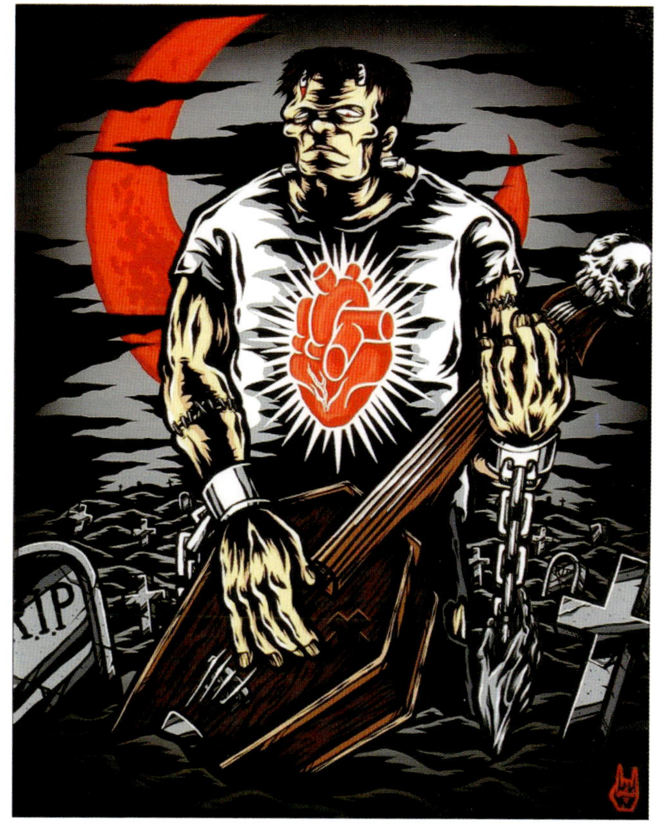
RIP

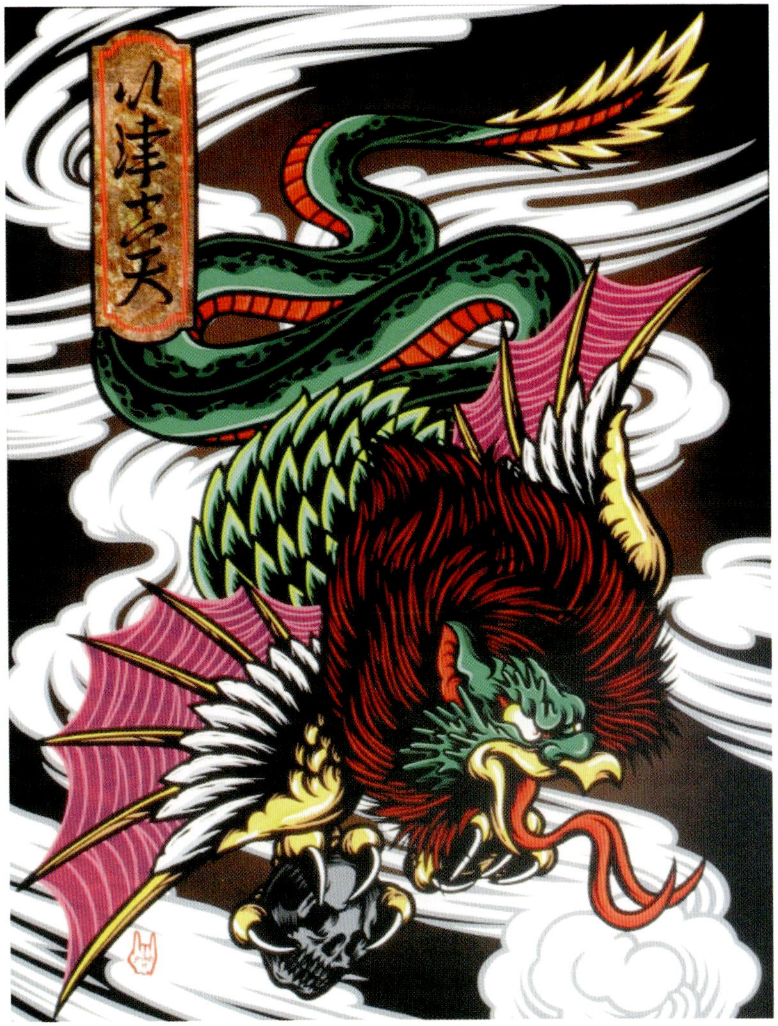
以津真天

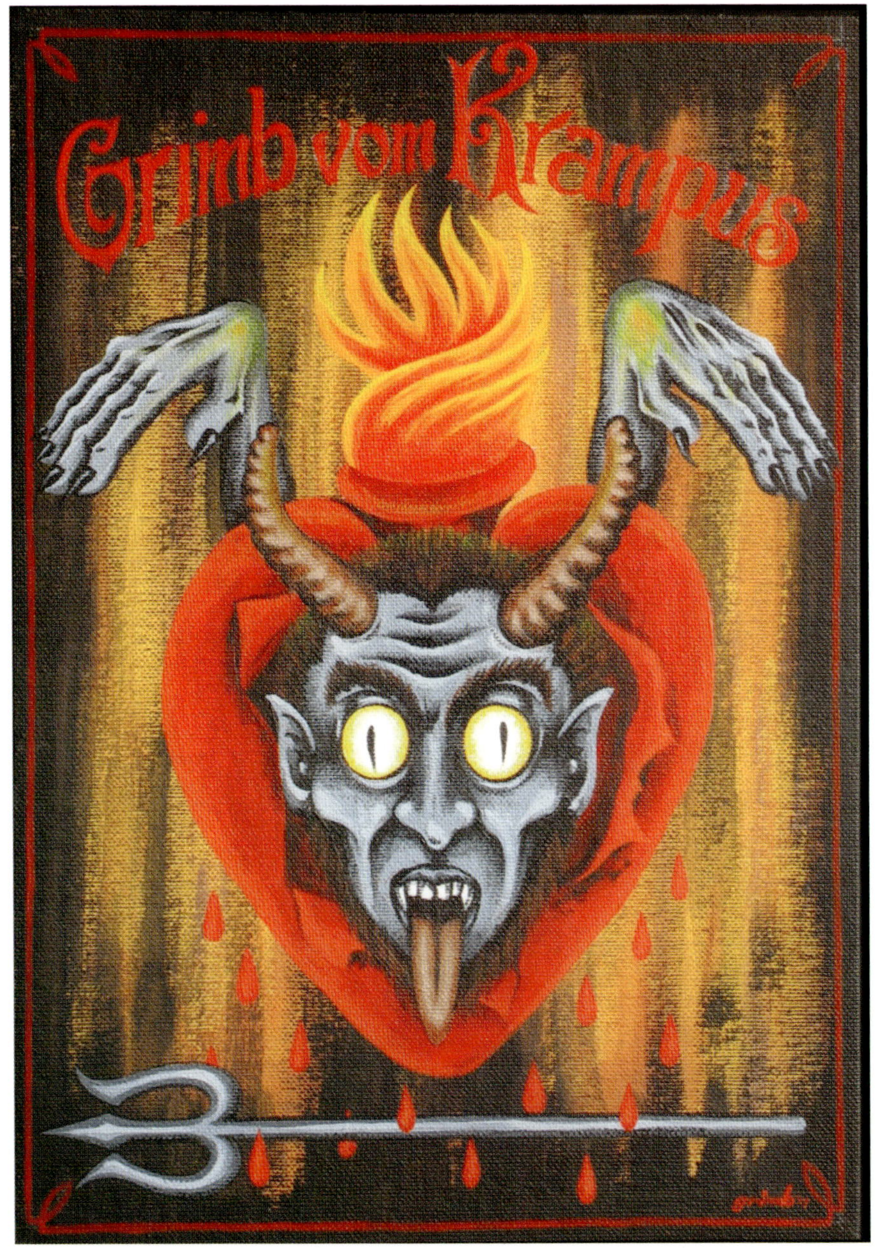
Gruß vom Krampus

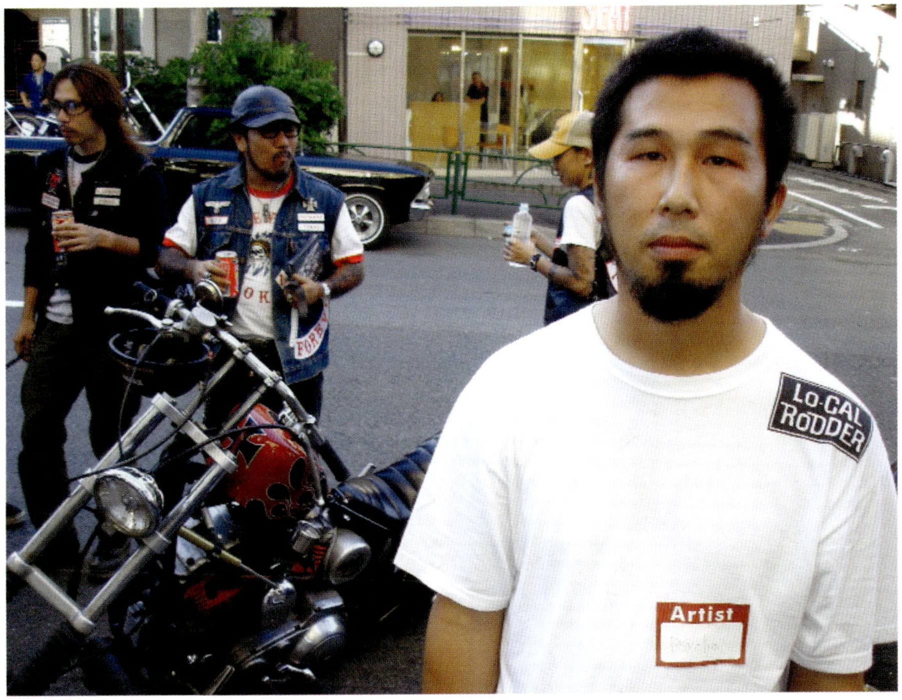

Above: Kustom artist Psycho

Right: Work by Psycho

Left page: Paintings by GRIMB

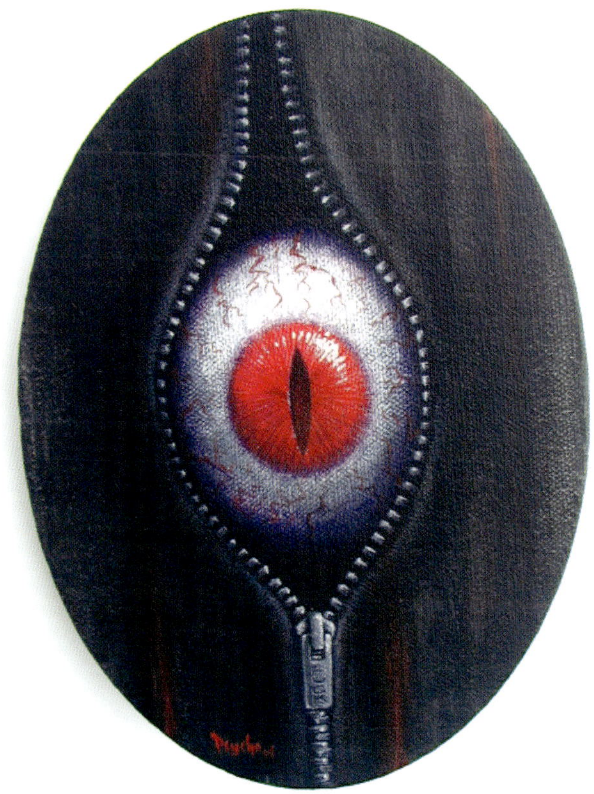

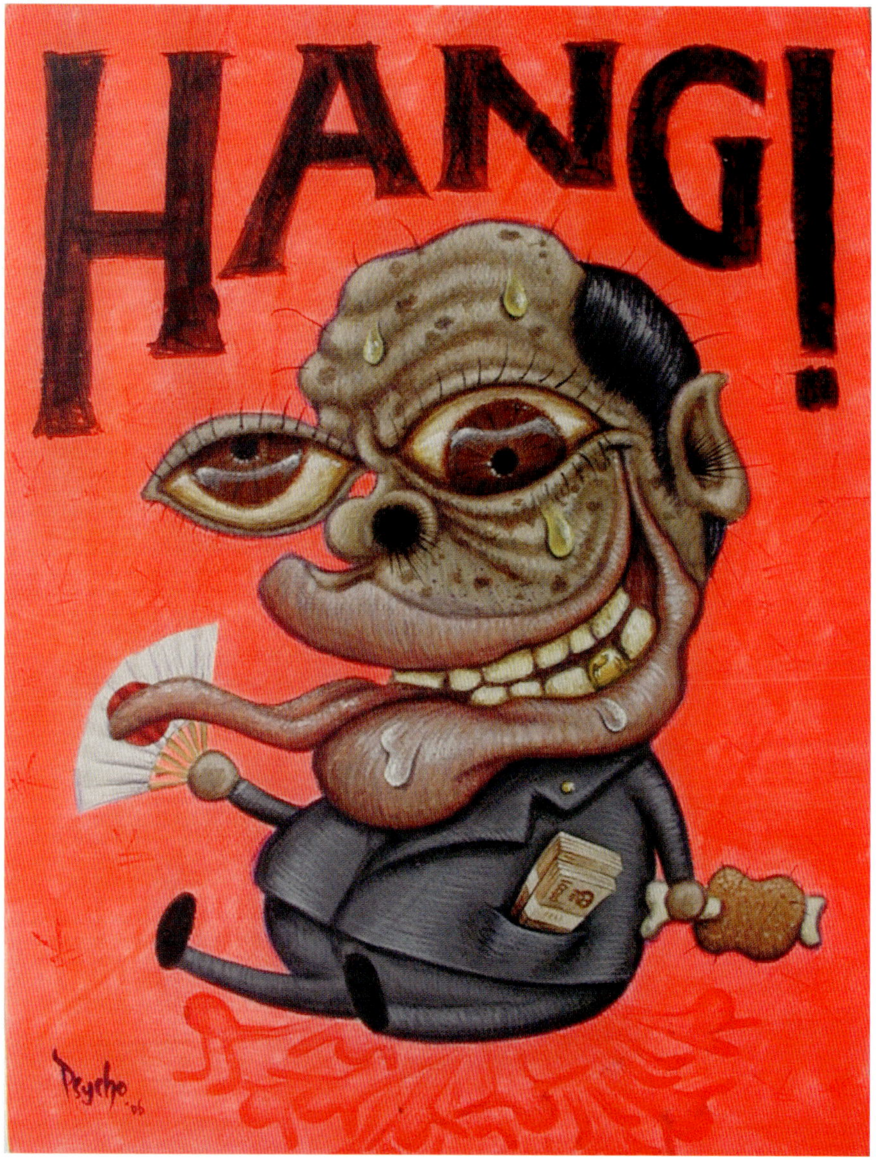

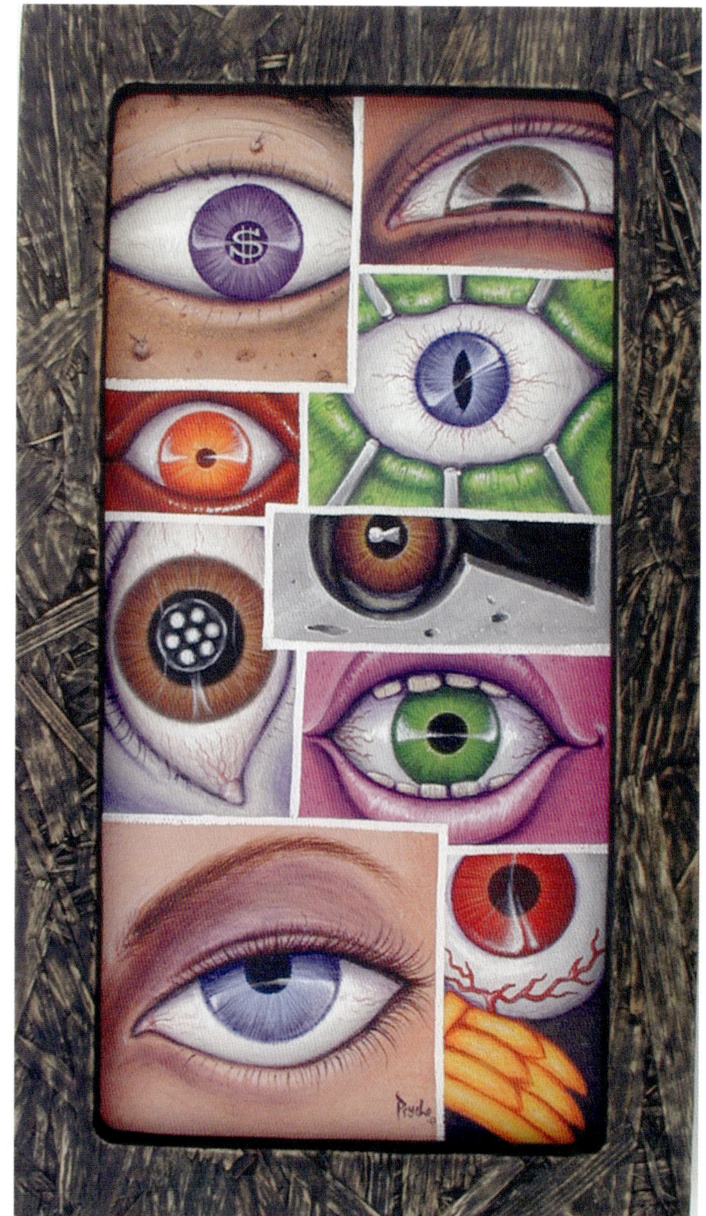

This page: Paintings by Psycho

Facing page: Dead Heat Mikawa

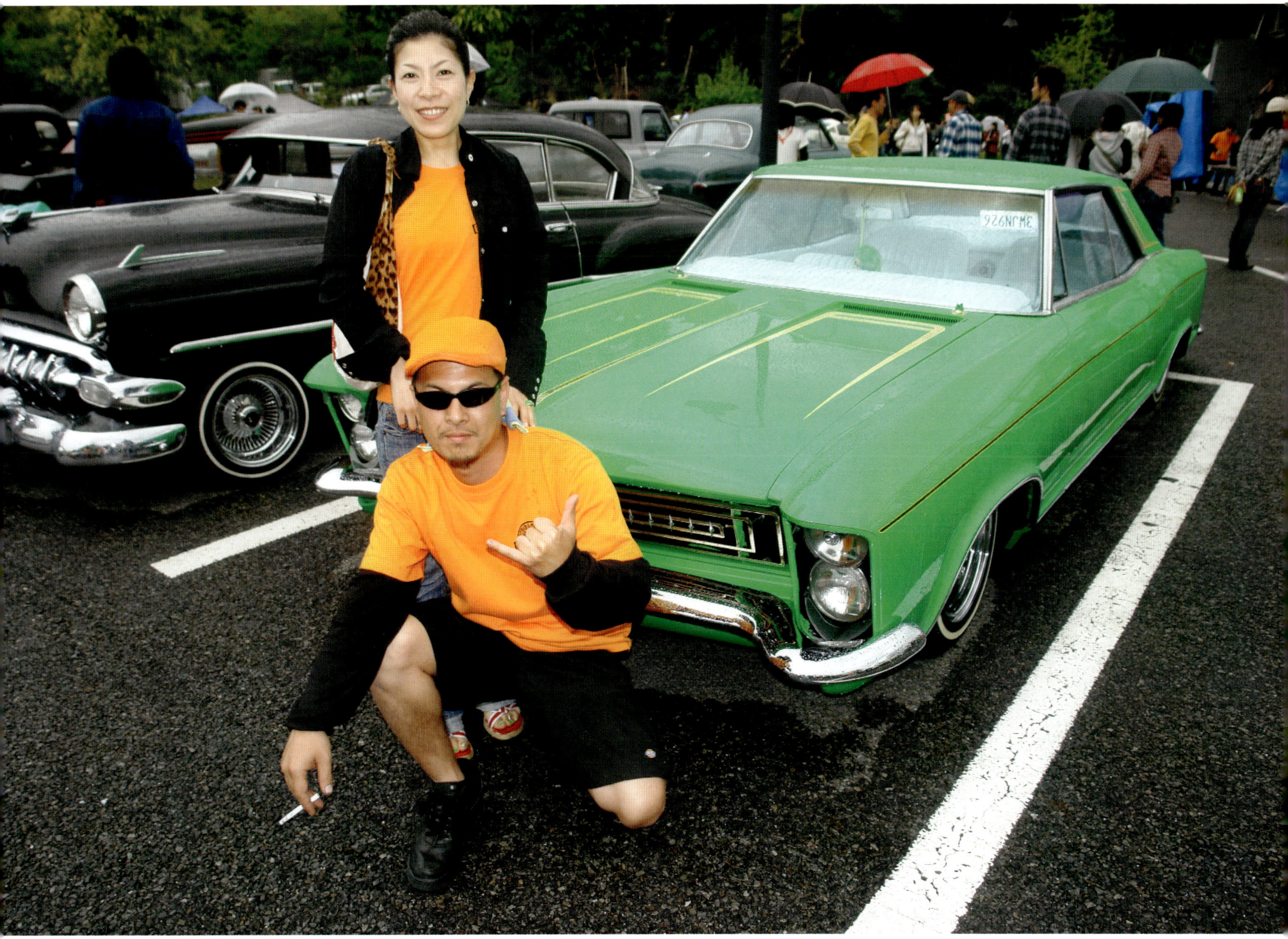

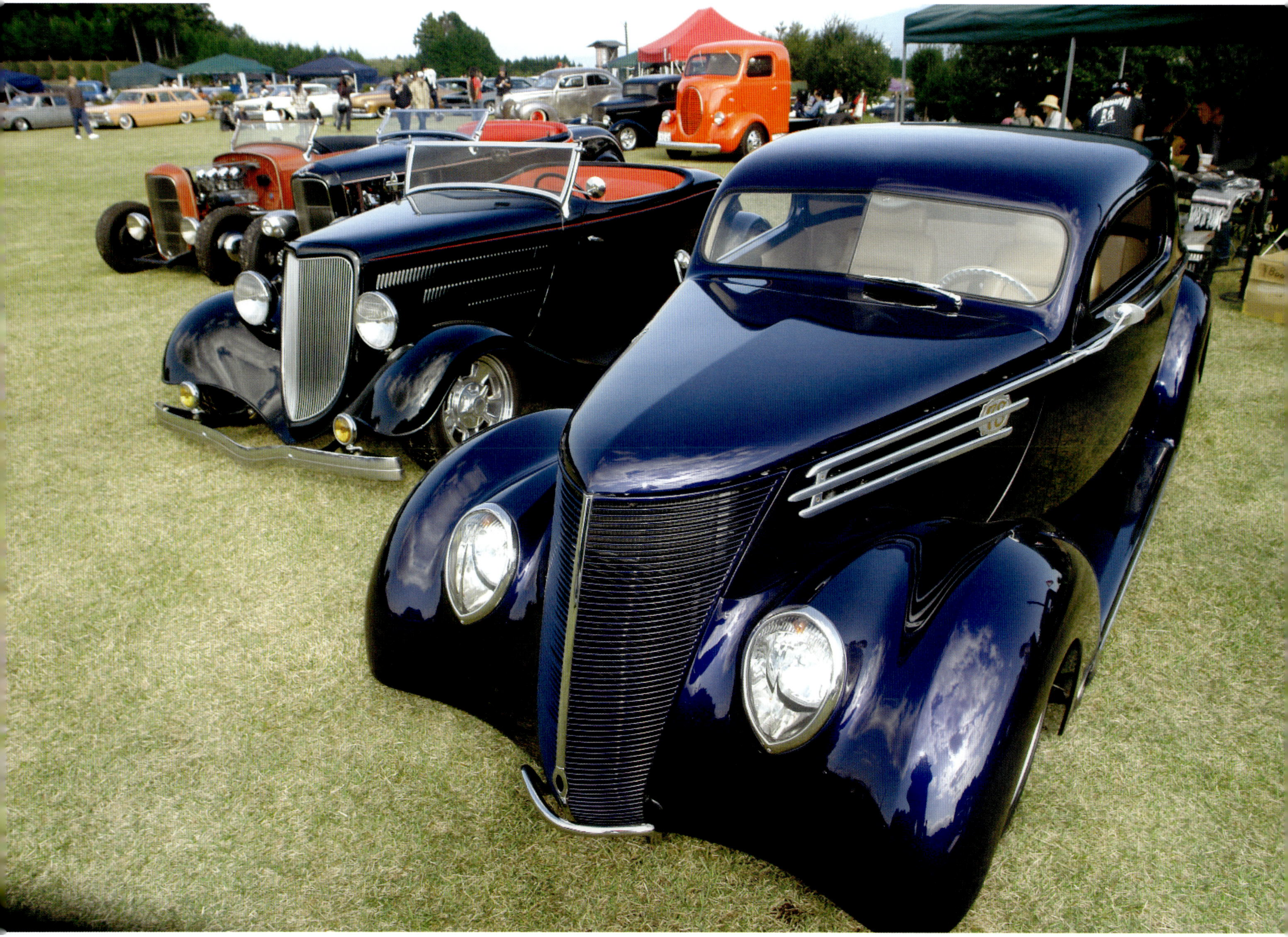

Chapter Five:
Flirting with the Audience–Dead Heat Mikawa and the Custom Hill Get Together

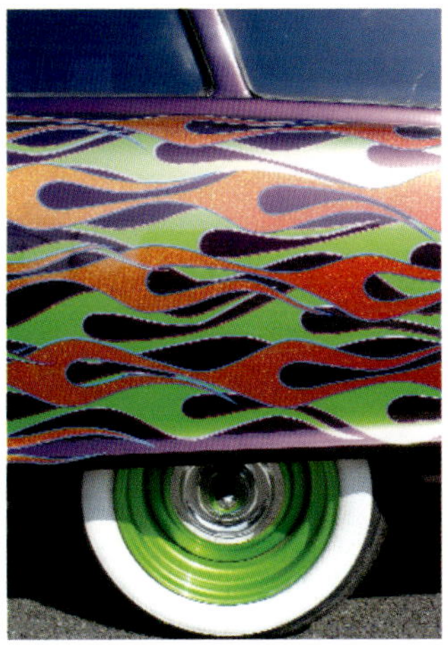

Above: Pussy Wagon, back end

Left: Custom Hill Get Together cars

An intermittent April rain falls in Okazaki City, which is located between the Mikawa hills and the Okazaki plain in Aichi Prefecture. The trees in Okazaki Central Park shield some of the custom cars and people, but there is no avoiding getting wet. Strongers Car club member Dice Kobayashi walks between parking areas and touches base with people who stand next to their cars holding umbrellas and chatting. It takes more than a little water to screw up the positive mood of the day and people cope. The Strongers Club has sponsored the popular Dead Heat Mikawa event for several years, and everyone is happy to be attending. "There's nothing to do about the weather," Dice says. "It rains in Japan during the spring. Everyone is used to it; it's more important for everyone to be here with their cars."

"The Strongers Club is associated with Fellow Kool Garage. They build a lot of different style cars there. I think people bring their cars to events like this for different reasons. They like people to look at the cars and try to figure out what they are saying. What kind of wheels you have, what kind of grill you have, the paint. These choices say something about a person. People buy certain types of cars and then change them because they want to say something. This is like a conversation people are having. I think people read cars like they read a poem. Or maybe like watching a movie. I think this is a big reason why people are here, to see old friends but also to interpret the cars. Many people here really know these cars—the histories, models and styles. They know how the cars have been altered. A lot of these people are very serious about machines."

The warm Pacific current that flows past Japan keeps temperatures comfortable for a good part of the year. Between March and mid-December there are several large annual outdoor car events where people socialize around their cars, and each event might attract 200 or more vehicles. Tokyo Street Car Nationals, Dead Heat Mikawa,

参加者を交えて ― デッドヒイト三河、カスタム・ヒル・ゲットトゥゲザー

岡崎市に４月の雨が断続的に降っている。岡崎市は愛知県の中央部、三河山地と岡崎平野の間にある。岡崎中央総合公園の並木がカスタム・カーや人々を多少は覆っているものの、雨にぬれてしまうことは避けられない。Strongers（ストロンガーズ）カー・クラブのメンバー、ダイス小林は駐車場から駐車場へと歩き、傘をさしながら車の横に立っている人たちと近況などについておしゃべりをする。少しくらいの雨ではその日の明るいムードと熱意は変わらない。Strongers クラブは何年にもわたって人気の高いデッドヒイト三河イベントをスポンサーしてきた。みんなが参加できるのが嬉しくてならない様子だ。「天気は仕方ありませんね」とダイスは言う。「日本では春に雨が降ります。雨にはみんな慣れています。それより、ここへみんなが車を持って参加することの方が大切なのです。」

「Strongers クラブは Fellow Kool（フェロー・クール）ガレージと連係しており、色々なスタイルの車を組み立てています。参加者がこのようなイベントに自分の車を持ってくる理由はさまざまだと思います。他の人が車を見て、それが何を言い表したいのかを考えてもらうのが好きなんです。どんなホイールを付けているか、どんなグリルやペイントを使っているかの選択が、その人となりを表現しています。人は何かを言い表すために、特定のタイプの車を購入し、それを改造します。ちょうど会話のようのものです。詩を読んだり映画を見たりするように、人は車を読み取ろうとしているんだと思います。」

「それが、ここに人が集まる大きな理由でしょう」とダイスは続ける。「馴染みの友達に会うこともそうですが、車の解明もやりますね。ここに来る人たちは本当に車のことをよく知っています。歴史もモデルもスタイルも。そしてその車がどのように改造されたかも知っています。ここに来る人たちの多くはマシンについて本気で取り組んでいます。」

日本列島に沿って流れる太平洋の暖流が１年の大部分で快適な気温を保つ。３月から 12 月中頃まで、いくつもの屋外の年次カー・イベントが開催され、参加者は各自の車の周りで親睦を深める。各イベントには 200 台以上の車が参加することもある。ストリート・カー・ナショナルズ in 東京、デッドヒイト三河、Razzle Dazzle イベント、静岡での Coast to Coast Autumn Nationals、Custom Hill Get Together、ムーンアイズ・ストリート・ロッド・ナショナルズなどは大規模なショーだが、あちこちの地域で地元の人々をひきつけるもっと小さなショーもある。

原ヨシミと妻のチトセ、息子のコウスケは豊橋市からデッドヒイト三河のイベントに参加している。一家はクラシックなターコイズ・ブルーの 283 V8 搭載 1957 年シェビー２ドアの前にしゃがんでいる。チトセはポケットに炎パターンの刺繍があるデニム・ジャケットを、息子はロックバンド「Hysteric Heaven」のトレーナーを着ている。原とチトセはある時代の若者のスタイルに、その息子は別の時代のものに熱中している。車は清水靖が所有する名古屋のショップ、R&B の手によるものだ。原は 1950 年代アメリカのグリーサー・スタイルの髪にくしを通し、髪の形と高さを維持しようとするが、その日の雨でうまくいかない。「私は 40 歳です」と原は説明する。「この車は数年前、R&B で買いました。私たちはずっとこんな車を所有したいと思っていたのです。毎年数回、車のイベントに家族で参加しています。イベントは家族一緒の時間を過ごすのにいいと思いますね。ここでは R&B ショップで車を購入した人たちが集まって駐車しています。同じショップで車を買った縁で、みんな友達です。あの

the Razzle Dazzle event, the Coast to Coast Autumn Nationals in Shizuoka, the Custom Hill Get Together and Mooneyes Street Rod Nationals are some of the larger outdoor shows; but there are smaller shows in different regions that attract local crowds.

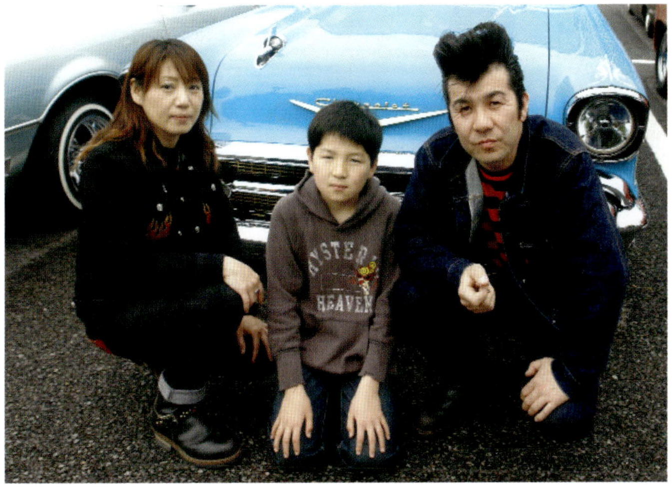

Yoshimi Hara, wife Chitose and son Koske
1957 Chevy, 283 V8 by R&B, Nagoya

Yoshimi Hara, his wife Chitose and son Koske are from Toyohashi and are attending the Dead Heat Mikawa event. The family crouches in front of their classic turquoise blue 1957 Chevy two door with a 283 V8. Chitose wears a denim jacket with embroidered flames over the pockets. Her son wears a sweatshirt for the rock band Hysteric Heaven. Hara and Chitose are caught up in the youth styles of one era, their son in another. Their car was built by the Nagoya shop R&B, owned by Yasushi Shimizu. Yoshimi pushes a comb through his 1950s American greaser styled hair in an attempt to maintain its shape and height but the dampness of the day is working against him. "I am forty years old," he explains. "I bought this car from R&B a few years ago. My wife and I always wanted to own a car like this. We go to a few car events every year. We do this as a family and it is a nice way to spend time together. Many people from the R&B shop park together. We are friends because we bought our cars from this shop. Without this shop we would never have met each other."

Next to the Hara family a young couple chats alongside their 1987 red Chevy C-10 stepside pickup. Tad and his wife Yukie are dressed the part: he wears a sporty black cap and checkered finish flag sneakers and she wears a mini skirt and tall leather boots. They both pose like pros in front of their truck.

"I bought the truck from R&B, and I've owned it for eight years," Tad says with a smile. "I changed the face myself. It has hydraulic air front and rear. I like the stepside style of the pickup box. It is a workstyle truck. I like the style with the large rear fenders. This look has not changed too much over the years." Tad and Yoshimi both talk about their vehicles with a large degree of sentimentality, but it

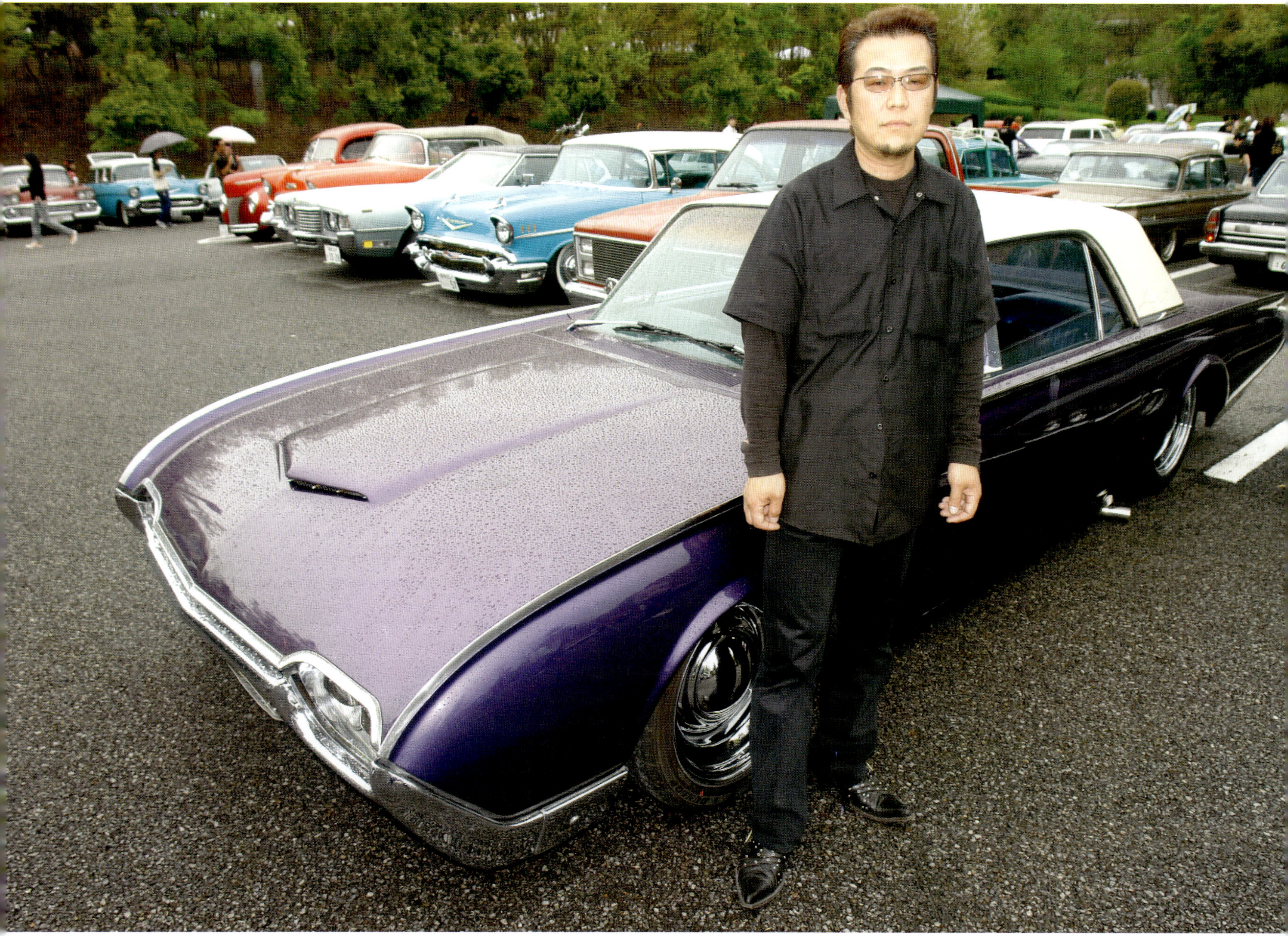

is sentimentality for an imagined time in a foreign place. Cars are large objects that can persevere against the erosion of time, and they become reminders to people of life's transience. For Tad, Yoshimi, their families and the other event car owners, this transcendent significance survives at the intersection of their memory and imagination.

Parked next to Yoshimi and Tad, Tommy holds an umbrella and wipes the beading rain off his highly waxed 1962 purple T-Bird. "My long time dream was to own a T-Bird," he says. "I used to have a Chevy but I never saw any T-Birds. So I bought a kustom T-Bird from R&B. To drive around Japan in this car is very incredible." He opens the trunk to reveal the perfectly carpeted interior and brushed metal hydraulic air tanks. With the toggle of a switch he delicately tilts the T-Bird to one side and encourages the rain water to collect and then run off the car. "See, hydraulics are good with rain," he says with a laugh. "This car has a Ford 390 V8 with a three speed transition. I have owned this car for fifteen years. I never stop working on my car."

R&B owner Yasushi Shimizu talks with his customers and friends who are wiping down their cars. "I have specialized in customizing American cars for more than seventeen years," he says. "I go to America to buy cars and bring them back. I use eBay and Autotrader to find cars, then I ship them back to Japan. I need the Internet to locate and purchase them. I have built maybe 100 cars, mostly sold to people around Nagoya. I have always liked American car culture and always wanted to be a part of it. I saw the movie *American Graffiti* and wanted to have an American car shop. This has always been my dream."

Tommy, 1962 Ford T-Bird, 390 V8, three-speed, full hydraulics

In a different lot, a young man named Tamotsu Mishima stands next to his Volvo Amazon 120 series. It is a two-door saloon model from the early 1960s. The coupe is painted primer black and accented

ショップがなかったら、こうして出会うことはなかったでしょう。」

原一家の隣には、赤い1987年シェビーC-10ステップサイド・ピックアップのそばで話をする若いカップルがいる。タッドと妻のユキエは、その車にマッチした服装だ。彼はスポーティな黒いキャップとチェッカーのフィニッシュ・フラッグ・スニーカー、彼女はミニスカートとロングブーツを着て、彼らのトラックの前でプロのモデルようにポーズを取っている。

「このトラックをR&Bで買って8年経ちます」とタッドは微笑みながら言う。「外観は自分で変えました。前部と後部にハイドロを備えています。ピックアップ・ボックスのステップサイド・スタイルが気に入っています。ワークスタイルのトラックです。大型のリア・フェンダーがあるスタイルが好きです。こういう外観は長年にわたってあまり変わっていません。」タッドと原は2人とも車についてかなりの思い入れを持って話すが、それは想像の中における過去と外国に対する思い入れで、彼らのスタイル、嗜好および車は、このような想像上の過去や場所との関係の認識をあらわにしている。

車は、時間の経過で色あせることに耐え、人生が無常であることを想起させる大きなオブジェである。車は、卓越した重要性を持っており、タッド、原とその家族、そしてイベントに参加した他の車オーナーにとって、この重要性は彼らの記憶とイマジネーションの交わるところで生き残っている。

原とタッドの隣に駐車しているトミーは傘をさし、ワックスで磨き上げた紫色の1962年Tバードから玉のような雨を拭い取る。「Tバードを所有するのは長年の夢でした」と彼は語る。「かつてはシェビーを持っていましたが、Tバードはまったく見かけませんでした。それでR&BからカスタムTバードを購入しました。この車で日本を運転して回るのは本当にすごいことです。」彼はトランクを開けて、隅々までカーペットを敷き詰めた内面と、つや消し金属製のハイドロ・エアタンクを見せる。スイッチを切り替えて、静かにTバードを一方に傾け、雨水が集まって流れ落ちるようにする。「ほら、ハイドロリックは雨にも役立つでしょう」と彼は笑いながら言う。「この車は3速トランスミッション付きフォード390 V8を搭載しています。この車を15年持っていますが、いつも手をかけています。」

R&Bのオーナー、清水靖は、自分の車を拭いている顧客や友人らと話をしている。「アメリカ車のカスタム構築専門で、もう17年以上もやっています」と彼は語る。「アメリカへ行って車を買い、持って帰ります。eBayやAutotraderを使って車を見つけ、日本へ輸送します。車を見つけたり買ったりするにはインターネットが必要です。これまでおそらく100台くらいは製作しました。ほとんどを名古屋近辺の人に売っています。」

「これまでずっとアメリカのカー・カルチャーが好きで、それに関わっていたいと思ってきました。『アメリカン・グラフィティ』を見て、アメリカ車のショップを持ちたいなと思いました。これがずっと私の夢でした。」

別の駐車場では、ミシマ・タモツという名の若い男性がボルボ・アマゾン120シリーズの横に立っている。1960年代の2ドア・サルーン・モデルだ。このクーペはプライマー・ブラックに塗装され、全体にわたって幅の広い炎のアウトラインが赤で描かれている。自分で描いたのだと言う。アウトラインは、車のノーズからフェンダー、側面、テールに流れる形を見ると幅がまちまちで、形状も左右対称ではない。その単純さにアマチュアっぽさが伺えるが、なかなかの効果がある。

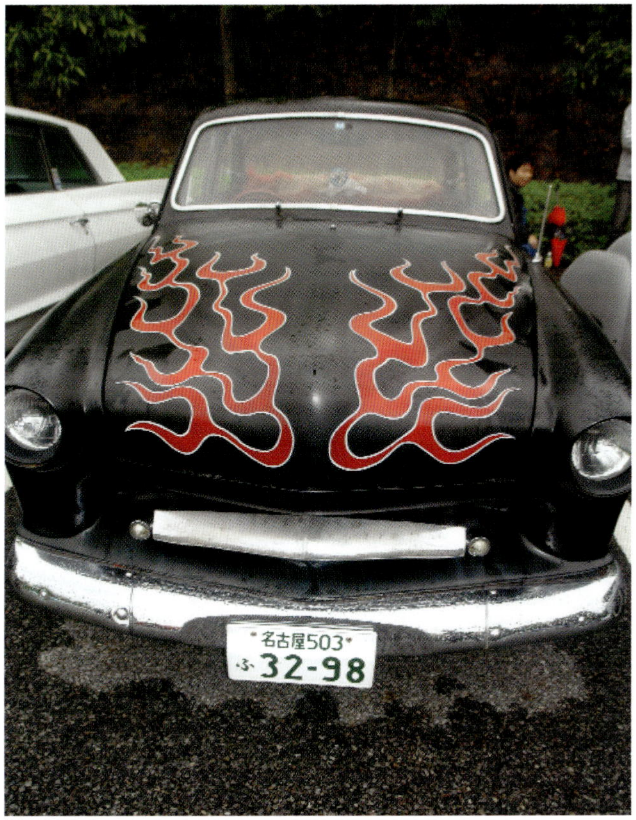

Tamotsu Mishima's phantom
1949 Ford Business coupe

head to toe with a wide red outline flame job he did himself. The outline is uneven in thickness and asymmetrical in shape as it moves across the car's nose, fender, side and tail forms. It looks amateurish in its simplicity but it works. Tamotsu has removed any identifying Volvo name references or logos and has also removed the grill's central column. In its place, he has added a thin piece of horizontal, folded-over sheet metal faux chrome that restyles the car's "face." A few inches have been added onto the fender heads around the headlights, which recesses them. He has intentionally created a phantom car that has no real identity but looks very similar to a 1949 Ford Business "shoebox" coupe.

"I always liked the looks of that style of Ford," Tamotsu says. "I could never afford to buy a real Ford coupe; but I saw this old Volvo, and it had very similar lines and shoebox shape. It was a good price, so I thought I could make my own Ford coupe. This is very close." Tamotsu is aware of the specific history and style; and, for practical purposes, he has re-imagined and manipulated things. For him, the Volvo and its meaning have surrendered to the more powerful form of the Ford coupe; and he sees its recreation as much more fulfilling.

Admirers walk past looking at his car from under their umbrellas. They may or may not be aware of the visual charade; but, if they admire Tamotsu's car, then it really doesn't matter. Ultimately, as machines, cars are more than engine packages and horsepower. They are experienced by most people as expressions of form that create visual harmony or tension. Car makes and models are not necessarily fixed in static time but represent continuums of design rationales that become a part of a culture's consciousness. Tamotsu's phantom shoebox Ford succeeds because the form reflects a fragment of a meaningful continuum.

The outdoor setting for the October 21st Custom Hill Get Together show is impressive. Onoji Campground is located outside the city of

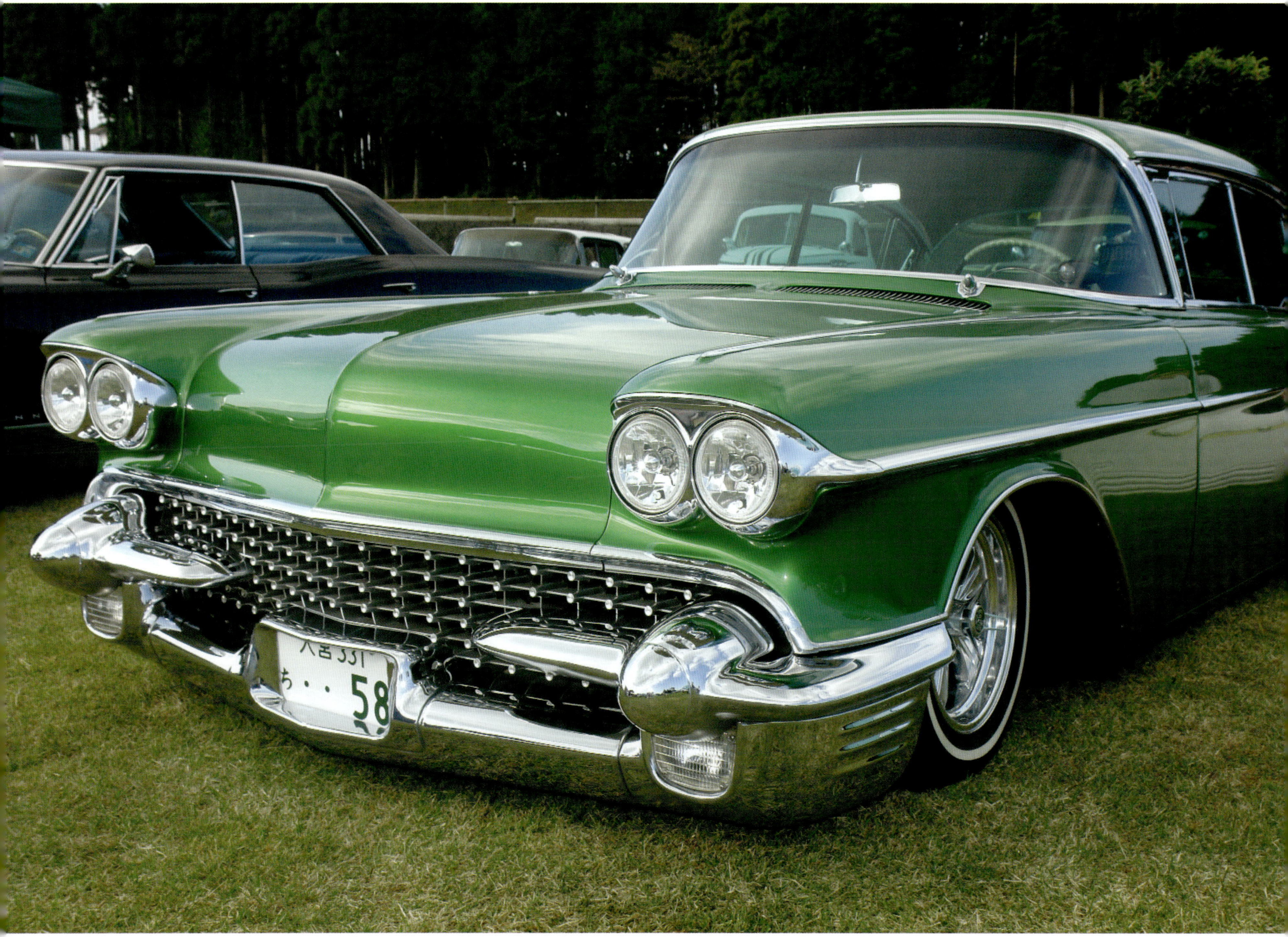
ち・・58

Shizuoka and has a cloud-swept view of Mt. Fuji in the distance. In the foreground there are cars of every description parked in the strong sunlight. The Camshafters Car Club hosts the event, but there are other car clubs attending, including the Pharaohs, the Firecrackers and the Killers. Akira Tokita of Vannuys Automotive in Shizuoka is the organizer and sponsor of this popular event.

"This is the ninth year I have had this event," Akira says. "It started in 1999. I will never forget that first show. There was a serious typhoon that year, but 200 cars showed up. This told me so much about the level of car interest in Japan. People in this area needed to have an event; and everyone was very excited, even with the rain. That first day there was a mix of domestic cars and American makes and models. Today it is the same; more than half the cars here are American. I would say that every car interest and taste is here today."

"Old American culture is fantastic. It's like a dream for people here. This is not Tokyo, not as much English is spoken by people here. But they still have this sense of connection to American cars. These feelings have connections to style and fashion, but they also run deeper. Fifteen years ago I bought a 1948 Fleetline Chevy from California. At that time people in Japan had a limited knowledge of old American cars. Maybe they knew the 1959 Cadillac with the fins, but general knowledge was very limited. People would look at me in my Fleetline and were shocked. Maybe they had only seen old American cars in movies."

Akira is the third member of the original trilogy, with Shige Suganuma of Mooneyes and Junichi Shimodaira of Paradise Road, who have each been key motivators of Kustom Kar Kulture interest in Japan. Their respective shops are the centers of knowledge about the Kustom Kulture sensibility.

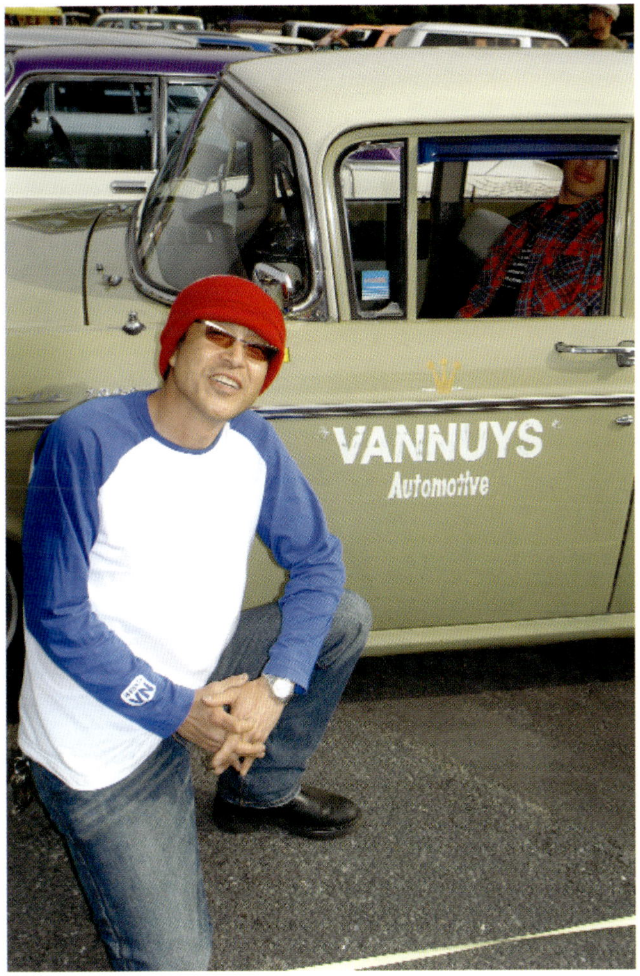

Above: Akira Tokita
Vannuys Automotive, Shizuoka

Left: Custom Hill Get Together Cadillac

タモツはボルボの名称が分かる文字やロゴをすべて取り除き、グリルの中央コラムもはずした。半分に折った薄いクロムめっきのシートメタルをそこに水平に取りつけ、車の外観を変えている。ヘッドライトの周りのフェンダーヘッドに数インチを付け加え、ヘッドライトが奥まるようにした。彼は身元の分からないファントム・カーを意図的に作り出したのだが、それは「シューボックス」のような1949年フォード・ビジネス・クーペによく似ている。

「このスタイルのフォードの外観がずっと気に入ってました」とタモツは言う。「本物のフォード・クーペは高くて買えませんが、この古いボルボを見たとき、シューボックスのような形とラインが非常に似ていて、値段も良かったんで、自分自身のフォード・クーペを作れるんじゃないかと思いついたのです。とてもよく似ているでしょ?」タモツは具体的な歴史やスタイルについては熟知しているが、実用的な目的のため工夫して、あちこちに細工を施した。彼にとって、ボルボとその意義は、もっとパワフルなフォード・クーペという形態のために犠牲にされた。彼はこうして再創造された信憑性から、より多くの達成感を得ている。

傘をさした人たちが歩きながら彼の車を眺めていく。どんな車なのかという謎解きについて全員が気づいているかどうかは明確ではないが、タモツの車を称賛してくれるのであれば、それはどちらでもいいことだ。最終的には、マシンとしての車は単なるエンジン・パッケージと馬力だけではない。ほとんどの人は、視覚的な調和や緊張感を生み出す造形の表現として車を体験する。型式やモデルは必ずしも特定の時代に固定されているわけではなく、文化の意識の一環をなすデザイン原理の連続を表している。タモツの架空のシューボックス・フォードは、彼自身と他の人たちにとって意味のある連続体の断片を反映しているから成功していると言える。

10月21日、Custom Hill Get Together(カスタム・ヒル・ゲットトゥゲザー)ショーの屋外環境はなかなか感動的だ。大野路キャンプ場は静岡市の郊外にあり、遠くには雲の流れる富士山が見える。前景には、強い日差しの中にありとあらゆるタイプの車が停まっている。Camshafters(キャムシャフターズ)カー・クラブがイベントの主催だが、他にもPharaohs(ファラオズ)、Firecrackers(ファイアクラッカーズ)、Killers(キラーズ)などのカー・クラブも参加している。静岡市のVannuys　Automotive(バンナイズ・オートモーティブ)オーナー、時田彰が、人気の高いこのイベントの企画・後援者である。

「このイベントはこれで9回目です」と彰は言う。「1999年に始めました。あの最初のショーは絶対に忘れません…。あの年にはすごい台風が来たのですが、200台の車が集まりました。あれで日本には車に対する興味がどのくらいあるのかが分かりましたね。この地域の人たちにはイベントが必要で、雨が降っていてもみんなとてもワクワクしていました。初日は国産車とアメリカのメーカーやモデルが入り混じっていました。今でも同じです。ここでの半分以上の車はアメリカ製です。今日、ここにはあらゆるタイプや趣味の車が参加していると思います。」

「古いアメリカ文化はとても素晴しいですね。ここの人々にとっては夢のようなものです。ここは東京ではありませんし、ここではそれほど英語は話されていません。それでも、アメリカ車への親近感があります。こういう気持ちはスタイルとかファッションへのつながりですが、それよりもっと深い何かもあります。」

「15年前、カリフォルニアから1948年フリートライン・シェビーを買いました。あのころ、日本人は古いアメリカ車

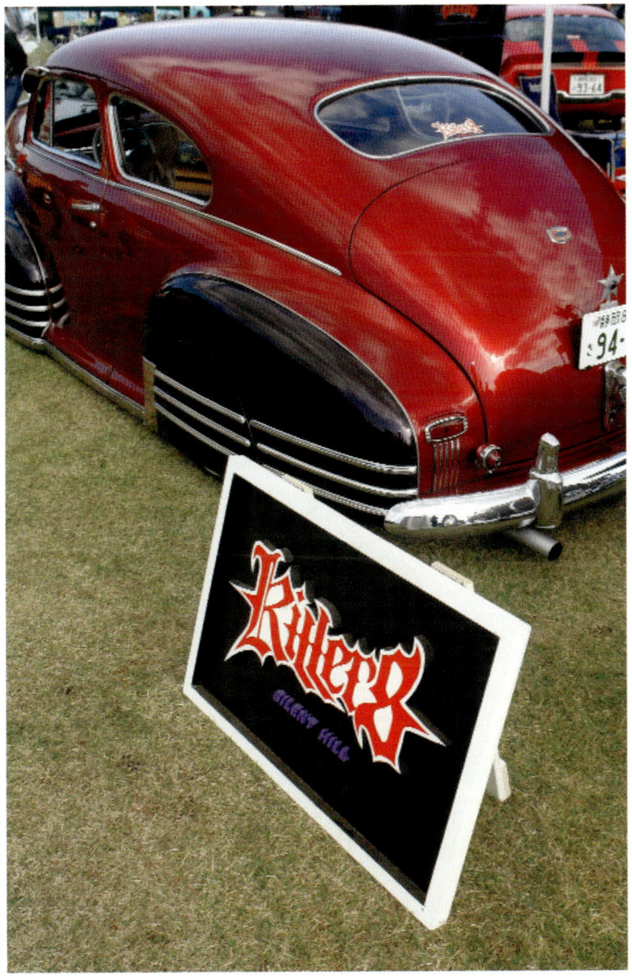

Killers Car Club, Silent Hill

"I went to America for the first time in 1978," Akira says. "I went to L.A. and saw the Van Nuys cruising scene. I bought a 1965 Impala SS coupe and drove it around. Then I came back to Japan; and, in 1979, I opened my Vannuys shop here. I bought a 1959 El Camino, and everyone thought I was crazy. People had never seen anything like it. I met Shige Suganuma around 1984-5, and then we met Junichi. We could see that there was this interest, but originally there were no Kustoms or hot rods. The purpose of this event is to have a get-together where people can share ideas about their cars and interests. It is next to impossible for people to express these kinds of special ideas in Japan. No one understands what it's all about. This kind of car appreciation is seen by most Japanese people as an odd thing to be involved with. Old cars from Japan and America? 'Why?', People ask. 'Buy a new car, it looks better.'"

"In 1997 I kustomized a 1970 Nissan Dream Cruiser," Akira continues. "I changed the tail to open like an American family station wagon with the rear window and tailgate. I painted it a really interesting cream pumpkin color. Ed "Big Daddy" Roth gave me three awards for this car. It is not easy to do this type of kustomizing with a Japanese car. Everything had to be modified. Roth could see this and really liked this car."

"Then I kustomized a 1967 Matsuda; I call this my Hollywood custom job. I learned a lot from this car. I became interested in the balance between the interior and exterior of cars, like two different realities. You are inside the car feeling one way looking out and then you feel different outside the car looking in. I think this is like people; we have an outside and also an inside."

"I worked on a 1974 Toyota in this way. I redesigned the interior into what I call a 1960s 'Galaxy' interior. I redid the seats silver and black. I see 1960s cars as sublime. There is a simplicity that is straight. I tried to explore this feeling with the way I changed the

についてあまり知りませんでした。フィンの付いた1959年キャデラックくらいなら知っていたかもしれませんが、知識はすごく限られていました。みんな私のフリートラインを見てショックを受けていました。おそらく、古いアメリカの車は映画でしか見たことがなかったのだと思います。」

彰は、日本でカスタム・カー・カルチャーを普及させた中心的存在で、ムーンアイズのシゲ菅沼、パラダイス・ロードの下平淳一と共にこの分野における貢献のオリジナル3人衆を成している。彼らのカー・ショップは、カスタム・カルチャー感性についての知識の中核、人々の興味の拠点となっている。

「初めて渡米したのは1978年でした」と彰は語る。「LAに行って、バンナイズ通りのクルーズ・シーンを見て、1965年インパラSSクーペを買って乗り回していました。1979年に帰国したのち、ここにVannuysショップを開店しました。1959年エルカミノを買ったとき、人々は私の頭がどうかしてしまったのかと思ったようです。みんな、当時あんな車を見たことがなかったんですね。1984～5年あたりにシゲ菅沼に会って、それから淳一に会いました。当時すでにこのような興味が一般にあったことは分かりましたが、あのころカスタムもホットロッドもまだ日本には存在しませんでした。知識はありませんでしたが、人が興味を持っていることだけは分かっていました。」

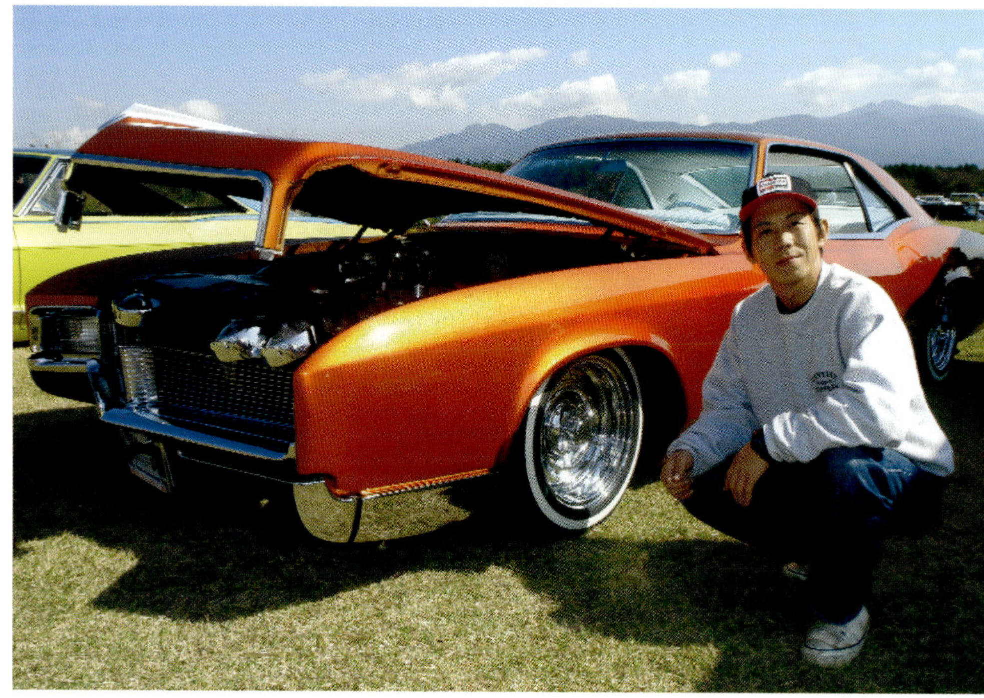

Ando, 1966 Buick Riviera
designed and built by Kyohei Sakuragi,
Wheels Unlimited, Nagoya
425 Buick Nail head V8

page181: Mystery owner
1931 Ford coupe body, 1932 frame
Built/owned by Shiozaki,
Firecrackers Car Club, Fuji City

upholstery of this car—straight silver and black seat upholstery designs."

Akira talks about cars with an artist's sensibility. He sees himself and other serious car people as a special group that experiences a certain brand of obsessiveness. They forget about everything and focus purely on cars. "Humans need food," Akira jokes. "Car people need cars. I don't know why, but there is something between people and cars. This is why I call this event a 'Get Together.' People are talking with each other surrounded by their cars."

Hirofumi Hosono and his son Kousei sit with a massive 1936 Dodge sedan that has been chopped and dropped very low. The car's grill is four feet wide and it must be the biggest car at the show. "This car is from South Dakota," Hiro says. "People cannot believe the size of this car. It has hydraulics; and sometimes, when I raise the car, people jump back. They cannot believe a big car can move like that. My son likes to sit with this car. It's like they are friends. He is still young, and I am not sure he understands about the car. He knows it is different from other cars but maybe not why it is different. That is a complicated thing—this difference."

Japanese car builder Kyohei Sakuragi visits with the owners of two cars he has worked on at his shop, Wheels Unlimited, which is located in Nagoya. "I found this 1966 Buick Riviera in Wisconsin," Kyohei explains, pointing at the copper colored car owned by a young man named Ando. "It has a top mounted 425 Nail-head small block V8. I also built this 1965 Buick Le Sabre." He continues, pointing at the lime green car owned by Hidekuni Hishida.

"I started getting interested in cars when I was sixteen years old. When I was eighteen I rebuilt my first engine. It was a 351 Cleveland Ford V8. This engine has a reputation; it is called the Fire Breathing Dragon by car guys because of its power. It has big block

「このイベントの目的は、人々が車や趣味についてのアイデアや意見を交換できる集まりを持つことにあります。日本のような場所で、このような特殊な考えを表現するのは、ほとんど不可能に近いんです。それが本当にどういうものなのか誰も分かってくれない。このような車に対する認識について、ほとんどの日本人は奇異に思っています。日本とアメリカの古い車？ どうしてって聞かれます。新車買えばいいのに…。その方が外観もいいってね。」

「1997年に、1970年日産ドリーム・クルーザーをカスタマイズしました」と彰は続ける。「テール部分を改造して、リアウィンドウとテールゲイトのあるアメリカン・ファミリー・ステーション・ワゴンのように開くようにし、それから実に面白いクリーム・パンプキン・カラーに塗装しました。エド"ビッグダディ"ロスは、この車に3つの賞をくれました。すべてを変更しないといけないので、日本車でこのようなカスタマイズを行うのは簡単ではありません。ロスはそれを理解したうえで、この車を本当に気に入ってくれました。」

「それから1967年のマツダをカスタマイズしました。これをハリウッド・カスタム・ジョブと呼んでいます。この車から色々学びました。おかげで最近は車の内装と外観とのバランスに興味を持つようになりました。ちょうど2つの別々のリアリティのような感じです。車の中から外を眺めたときの感覚は、外から中を見るときとは、また違う感じを与える。1台の車で2つの観点がある…。2つのリアリティですね。ちょうど人間のように。私たちは外観があって、同時に内面も存在するということです。」

「このコンセプトで1974年のトヨタを改造しました。私が1960年代風"ギャラクシー"インテリアと呼ぶ内装デザインに仕立て直し、座席をシルバーとブラックにしました。私は1960年代の車の、直線の簡潔さを崇高なものと見ています。このフィーリングを模索するため、ストレートなシルバーとブラックの内張りのデザインに変えてみたのです。」

彰は車について芸術家の感性で語る。彼は自分自身および熱心な車のファンを、こだわりという標しのもとに集まる特別なグループだと考える。すべてを忘れて純粋に車だけに焦点を絞る。「人には食べ物が必要なように」と彰は冗談めいて言う。「車が好きな人たちには車が必要です…。なぜだか分かりませんが、人と車の間には何かあるんです。ですからこのイベントを"Get Together"と呼んでいます。車に囲まれて人々が交流を深めるからです。」

ホソノ・ヒロフミと息子のコウセイは、チョップされて非常に低くなった巨大な1936年ドッジの横に座っている。車のグリルは長さ4フィートもあり、おそらくショーで最も大きな車だろう。「この車はアメリカのサウスダコタ州から来ました」とヒロは言う。「みんなこの車のサイズに驚いているようです。ハイドロが付いていて、ときどき車体を持ち上げると、みんな飛びのきます。大きな車がこんなふうに動くなんて信じられないようですが、実際に動くんです。私の息子はこの車と一緒にいるのが好きです。友達同士のような感じなのでしょう。彼はまだ幼いですから、この車のことが分かっているかどうかは知りません。他の車と違うとは分かっていても、なぜ違うのかは分からないでしょう。この違いというのは、複雑なものなので。」

日本のカー・ビルダー、桜木恭平は、名古屋にある彼のショップ Wheels Unlimited（ホイールズ・アンリミテッド）で製作した2台の車のオーナーたちと談話している。「この1966年ビュイック・リビエラをウィスコンシン州で見つけました」と、アンドーという若い男性が所有する銅色の車を

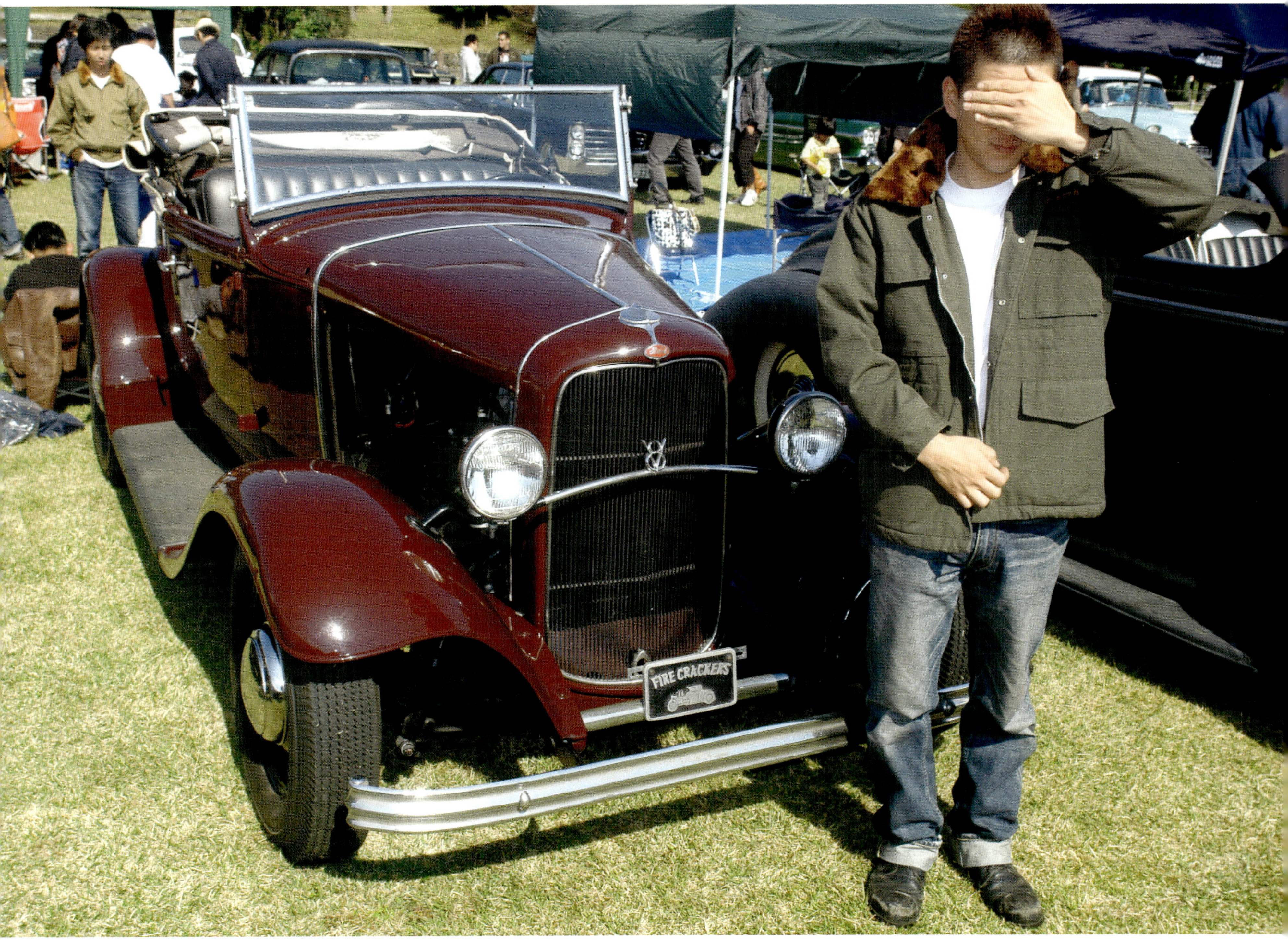
FIRE CRACKERS

指差しながら恭平は説明する。「トップマウント425ネイルヘッド・スモールブロックV8を搭載しています。それから、1965年ビュイック・ルセイバーも組み立てました」と、菱田英邦が所有するライムグリーンの車を指差す。

「16歳のときに車に興味を持ち始め、18歳で初めてエンジンを自分でオーバーホールしました。パワフルさで評判のエンジンで、車愛好家の間では火を吐くドラゴンと呼ばれる351クリーブランド・フォードV8でした。スモールブロック・エンジンにビッグブロック圧縮ヘッドを備えていて、他のタイプのエンジンとは違うので、このエンジンの改造をやりたかったんです。」

「私はジーン・ウィンフィールドの友達で、カリフォルニア州カノガ・パークにある彼のショップを見学したことがあります。2003年、シゲさんがムーンアイズ主催のホットロッド・カスタム・ショーに彼を招き、ウィンフィールドはその後4年連続でショーに参加しました。あれは日本のカー・カルチャーにとって本当に重要で、彼の存在は大きな影響を及ぼしました。私は自分の時間すべてを、車を見つけたり改造することに費やしています。1台の車に7年も8年もかけることもあります。」

風変わりな外観の1950年ナッシュ4ドアセダンがある。暖かい日差しのもとでくつろぐ若いカップルがその横では小さく見えてしまう。バチョは東京のロカビリーバンドでベースを弾き、妻のミナコは1940年代スウィングダンスのファンだと言う。彼女は髪に赤いハンカチを巻き、白いトレーナーを着た「ロージー・ザ・リベター」スタイルだ。その車は3年前、ハリウッドへの旅行で見つけた。「カリフォルニアでこの車を誰かが売ろうとしているのを見て、絶対に欲しいと思いました」とミナコは言う。「このサイズの車を日本で所有するというのは大変なことなんです。こんなに大きいと保管が難しいんですよ。『車、どこに置いてるの？』ってしょっちゅう聞かれます。」

「私たちは西東京の小さなアパートに住んでいます。東京の街中を運転するたびに自己表現をしている事になります。Custom Hillイベントに参加するために何時間もかけて来ました。私はもう何年もの間1940年代のアメリカン・スウィング・スタイルに興味を持ってきました。音楽とか、色々なダンスとか。でも当時のスタイルの服を着ることと、その時代の車を実際に所有することは、まったく別のことなんです。」

イベント主催者の時田彰が手にトランシーバーを持って現れ、バチョ、ミナコ、そして2人が所有するナッシュに近づいてきた。トランシーバーを耳にあて、雑音でうまく通じない日本語に聞き入っている。「今日はトランシーバー、うまくいかないね」と、あきらめた笑いを浮かべて言う。巨大なナッシュを見て、バチョとミナコに会釈をすると、2人は礼儀正しく会釈を返した。

彰は先ほどの会話を続ける。「車はみんなすごいですね…。この車を見てください」と、ナッシュを指差して言う。「この車のサイズと形は、今の私たちとってはとても奇妙な気がします。こんな車は今では絶対に作られる事はありません…。車はシンプルでありながら複雑です。だからこそ人々の間でパワフルなものとなり得ます。このイベントを“Get Together”と呼ぶ理由はそこです。自分たちのこと、自分の車のことを話し合う特別な方法なのです。人は色々な理由でこういう車を買います。これが日本における車に対する理解・認識をどのように変えたかを見るのが面白いですね。国産車が好きな人も、アメリカ車が好きな人もいます。私たちはある種の自己表現としてこういう車を買います。そして人は『おーっ！あの車、すごいね！』って言います。しかしそこにはシンプルながら何か複雑なものがあるのです。」

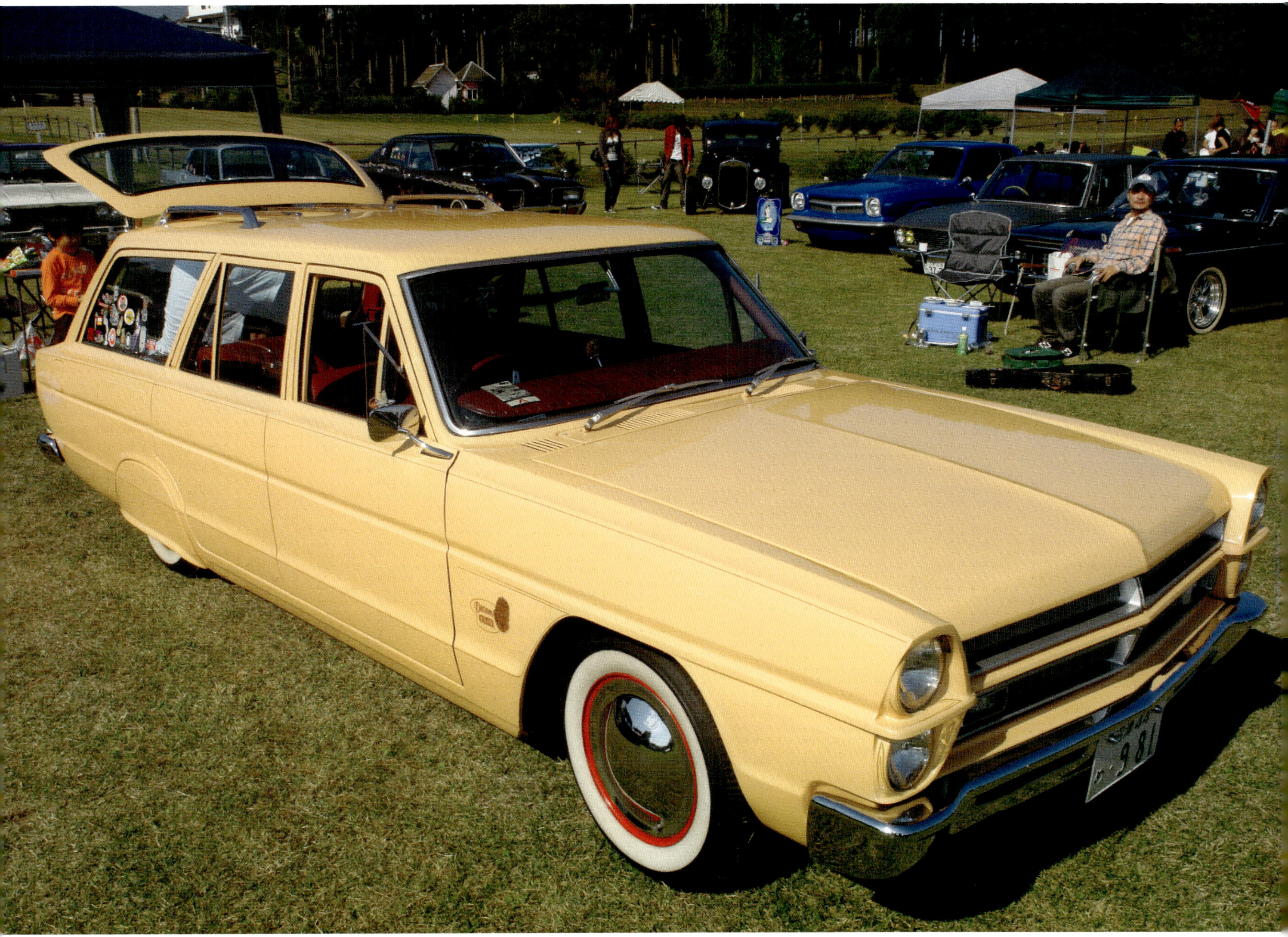

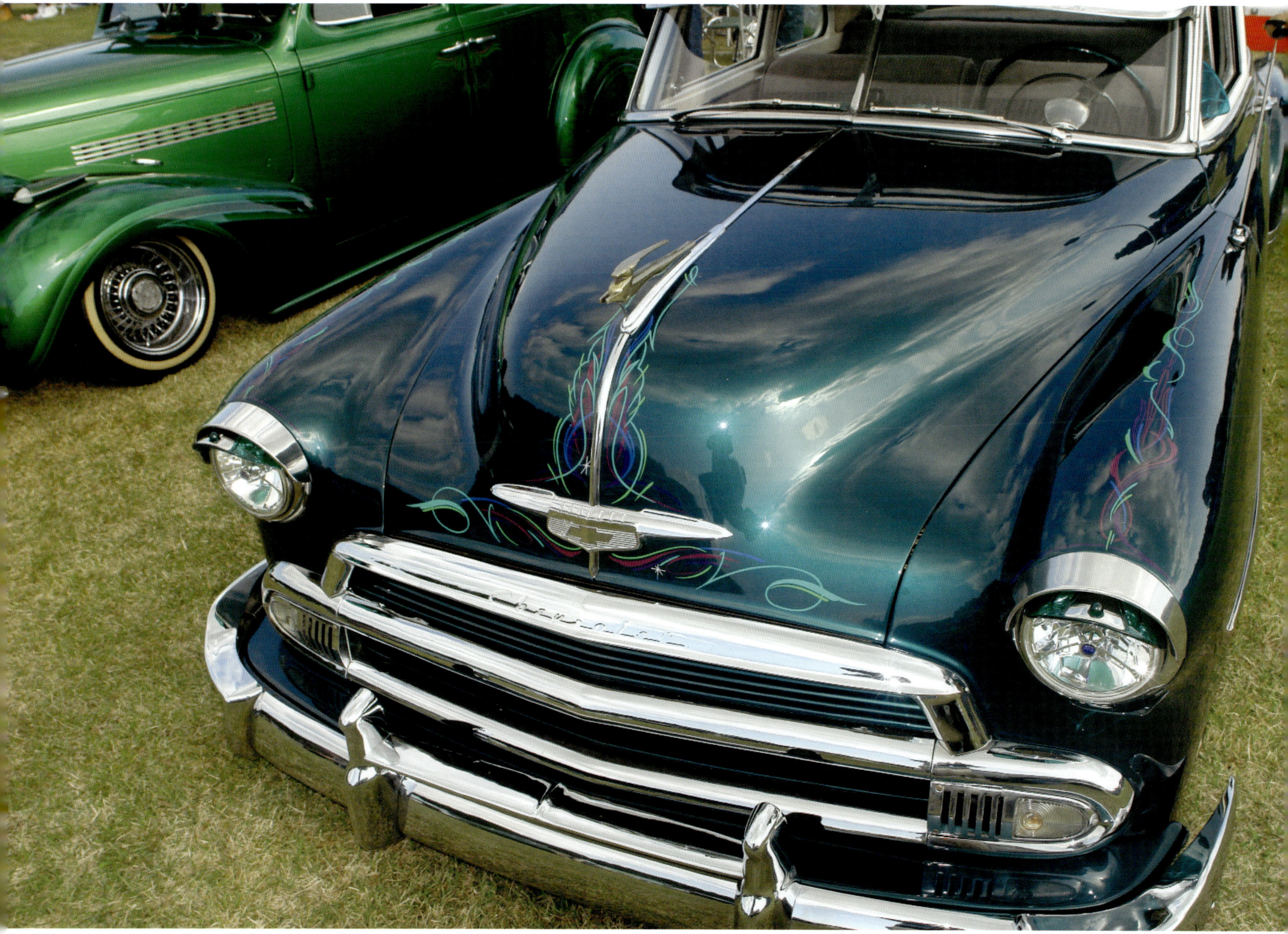

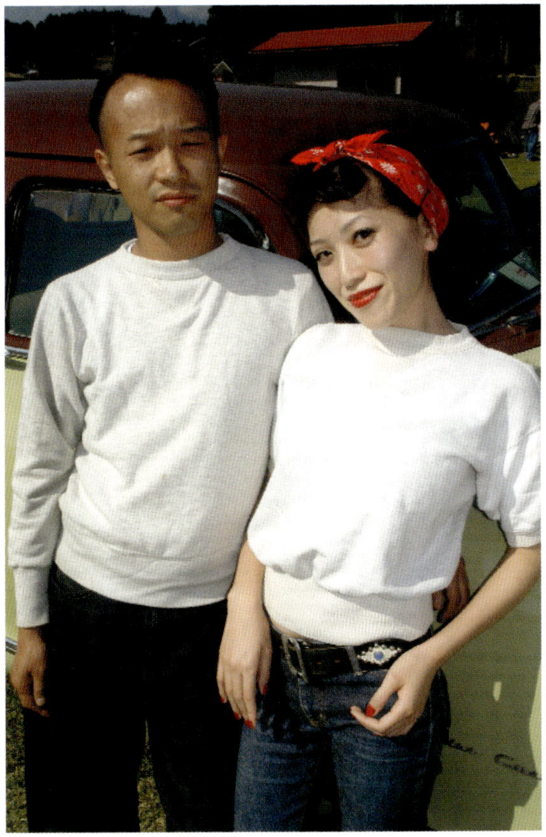

Previous page: 1970 Nissan Dream Cruiser, kustomized by Akira, 1997 awarded three prizes by Ed "Big Daddy" Roth

Above: Bacho (left), Minako (right) with their Nash

Left: Custom Hill Get Together cars

compression heads on a small block engine. It is different from other kinds of engines, and I wanted to rebuild one."

"I am friends with Gene Winfield and visited him at his Canoga Park, California, shop. In 2003 Shige invited him to the Mooneyes Hot Rod and Kustom show. Winfield went to that show four years in a row and it was really important for car culture in Japan, very special that he was there. I spend all my time finding and rebuilding cars. I can spend seven or eight years working on a car."

An odd-looking 1950 Nash four-door sedan dwarfs the young couple relaxing next to it in the warm sun. Bacho plays the bass in a Tokyo rockabilly band; his wife Minako is a 1940s swing-dance enthusiast. She wears a red kerchief in her hair and white sweatshirt, Rosie the Riveter style. They found their car three years ago on a trip to Hollywood. "We saw this car for sale in California and decided we must have it," says Minako. "To own a car this size in Japan is a very big thing. To own anything this big in Japan is difficult. Everyone keeps asking us, 'Where do you keep this?'"

"We live in a small apartment in west Tokyo. Every time we drive around the streets of Tokyo we make a statement. We drove several hours here to be a part of this Custom Hill event. I have been interested in 1940s American Swing style for several years—the music, the different dances. It is one thing to dress in a style; it is very different to actually own a car from that period."

Event organizer Akira Tokita appears holding a walkie-talkie radio as he approaches Bacho, Minako and their Nash. He holds it to his ear, listening to the crackled, broken-up Japanese. "The walkie-talkie is not so good today," he says with a resigned smile. He looks at the huge Nash and bows slightly in greeting to Bacho and Minako, who politely return the gesture.

バチョとミナコは彰の話を聞きながら、同意するようにうなずく。「そう、複雑…」とミナコは言う。「私たちの車が駐車できる場所を探すようなものね。」

このような車やバイクを通して、人々は、歴史、社会的状況、特殊な美的感覚、そして最も大切なこととして、彼ら自身につながる豊富な表現言語を生み出している。日本、そしてそれ以外の場所で、車は表現のオブジェとして利用されている。カスタム・カルチャーは、人が何かを語ろうとする特別な手段として、アメリカで始まった。そして今、スタイル化された会話として、また、車で移動しながらの自己表現の衝動を反映するさまざまな選択肢として、日本で成長を続けている。

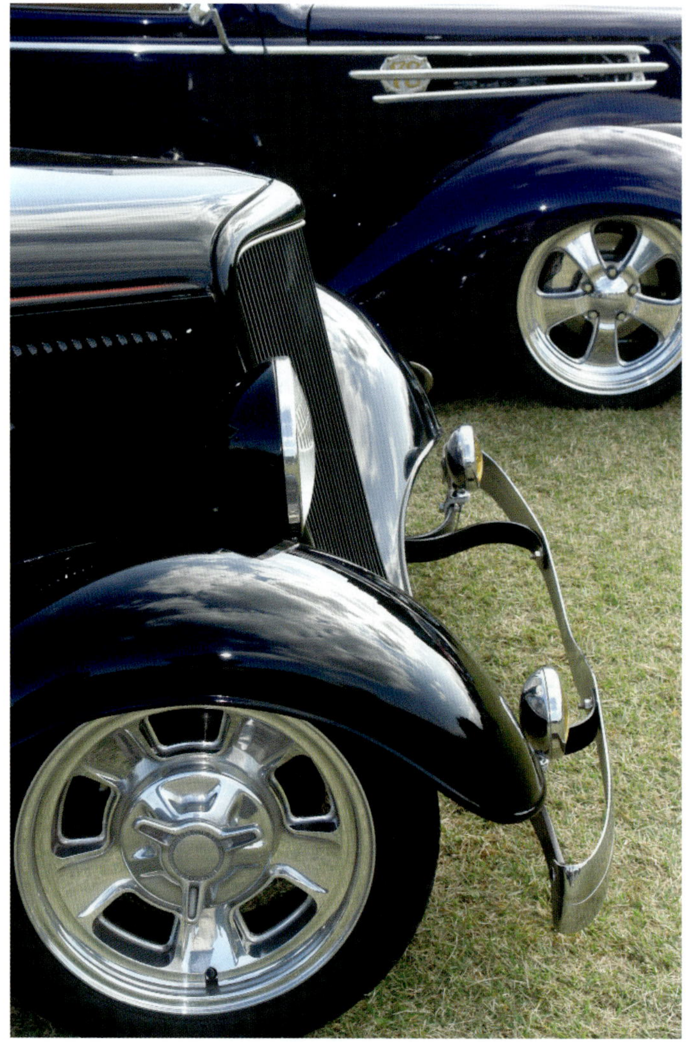

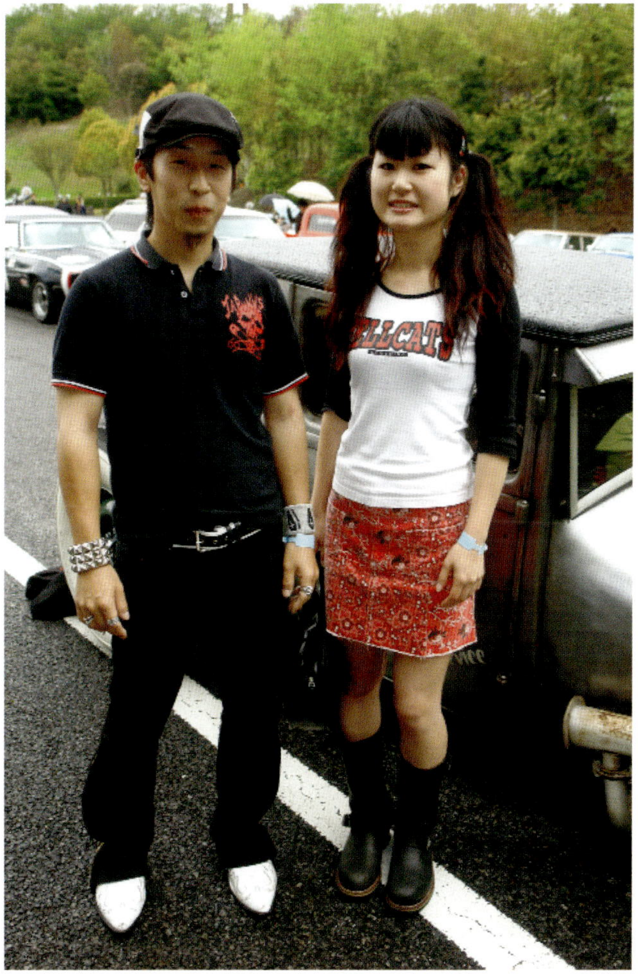

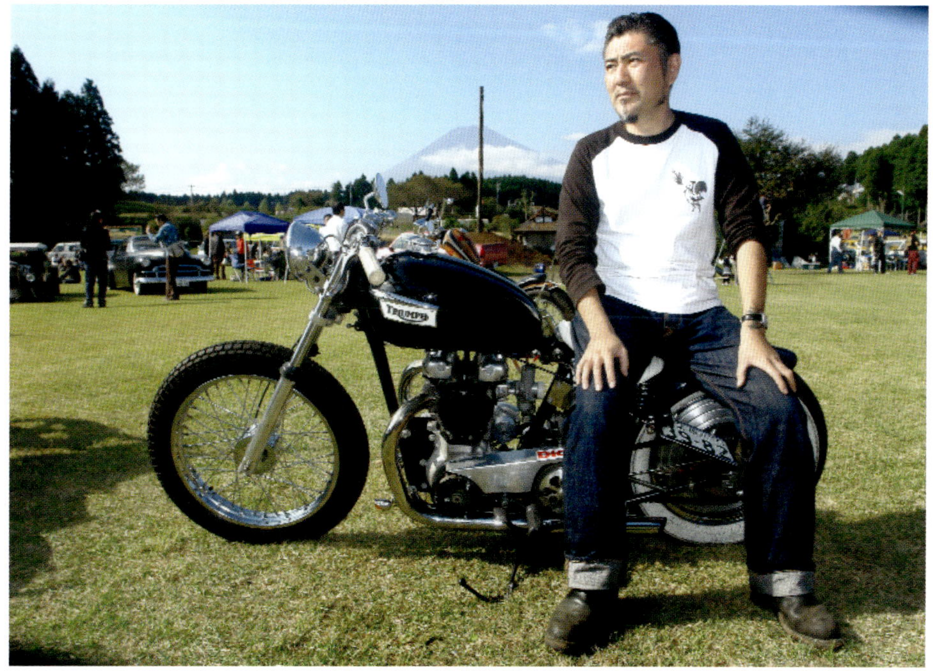

Above: Makoto (left) and Namie

Right: Takada, Kustom chopper builder

Left: Custom Hill Get Together cars

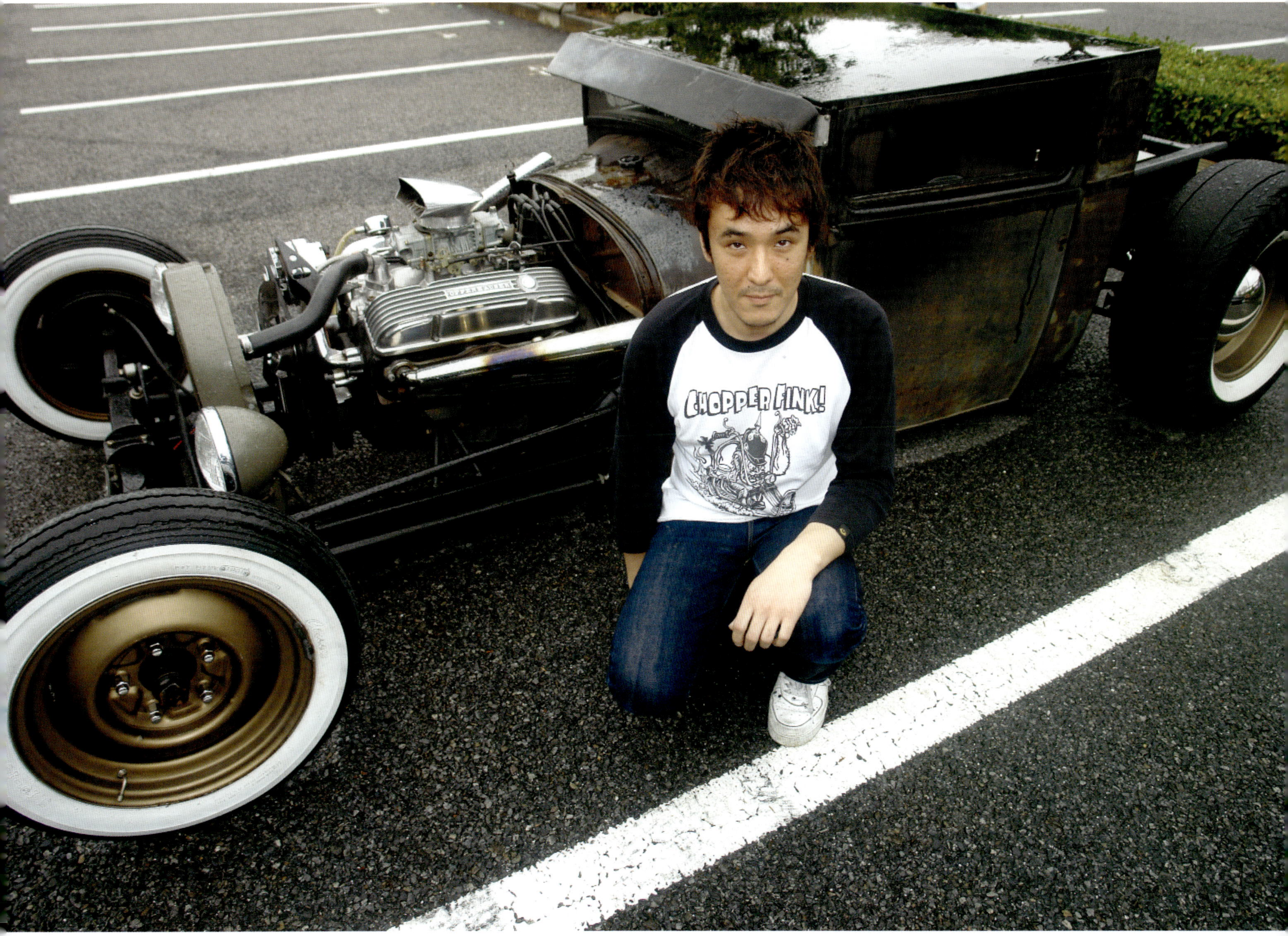
CHOPPER FINK!

Akira picks up with his earlier conversation, "Cars are impressive. Look at this car," he says gesturing toward the Nash. "Its size and shape looks very strange to us today. It could never be made today. Cars are both simple and complicated. They can be a powerful thing between people. People buy these cars for different reasons. It is interesting to see how car appreciation has changed in Japan. Some people like domestic, some like American. We buy these cars to make a type of statement. People say, 'Wow! Look at that car!' There is something basic but also complicated about this." The couple listens to Akira and nod their heads in agreement. "Yes, complicated," Minako says. "Like looking for a place to park our car."

Through these cars and motorcycles, people create a rich vocabulary of associations about history, social context, specialized esthetics and, most importantly, themselves. Kustom Kulture first emerged in America as a special way people chose to say something and continues to develop in Japan.

Left: Oki Masanori, 1929 Ford

Right: Bacho with 1950 Nash bought in Hollywood, CA

Following page: Syu Merk tail, pinstriping by Makoto

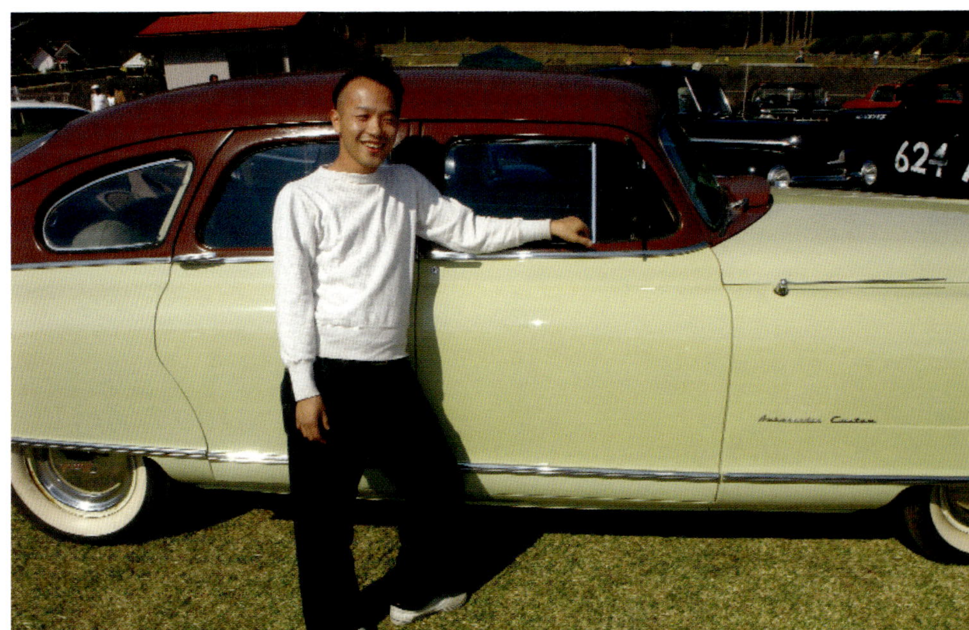

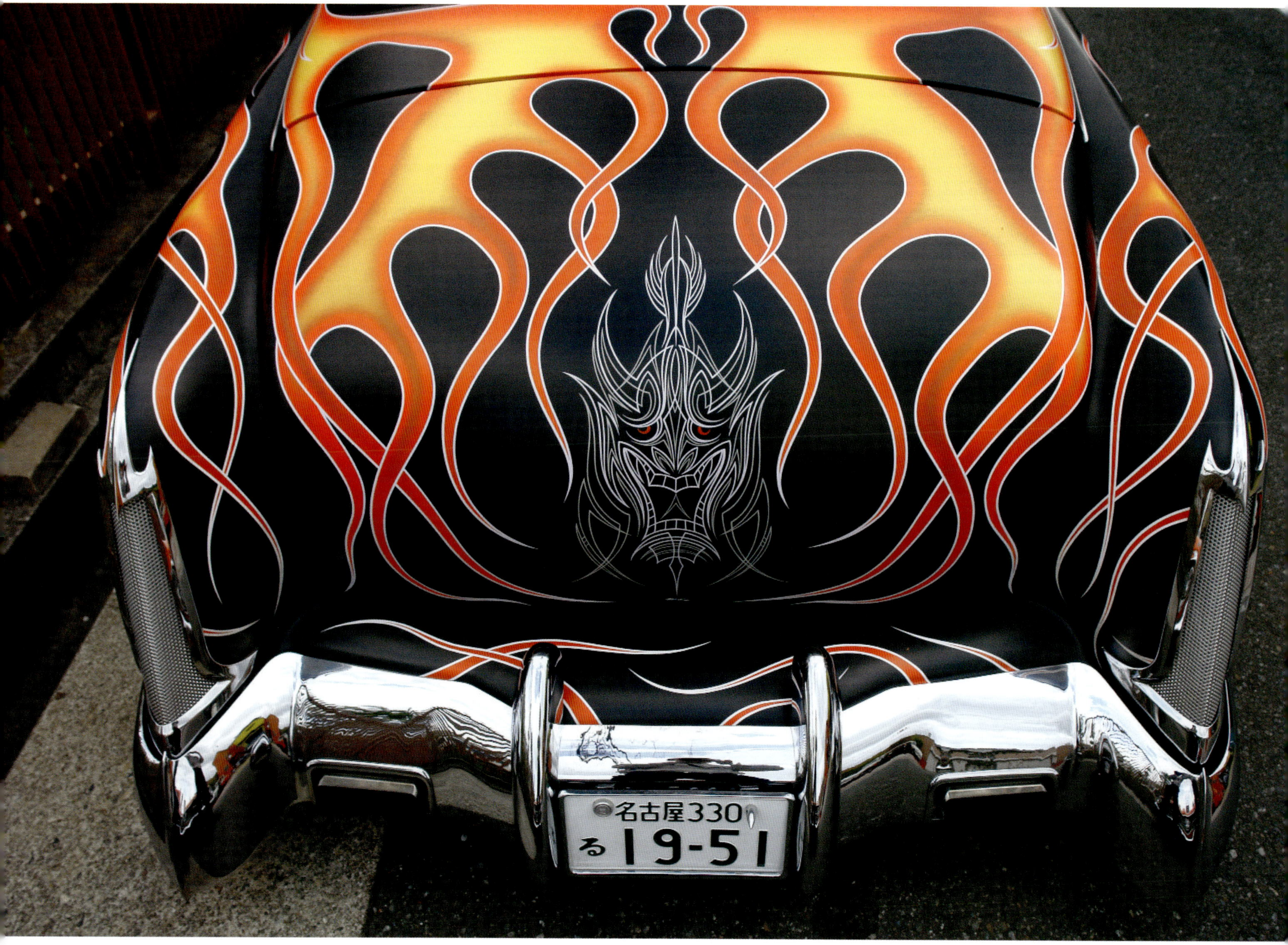

名古屋330
る 19-51

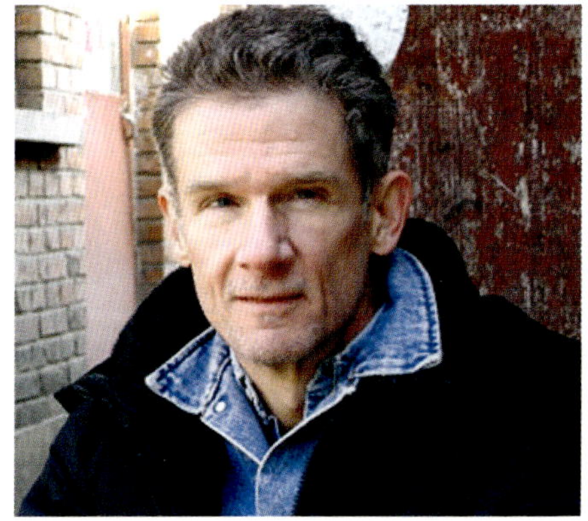

Photo: Tzyy Jye Chang McCabe

Michael McCabe is a cultural anthropologist, writer and photographer who explores the dynamic relationship between tradition and change in a diversity of cultural contexts. He is particularly interested in the exchange of stylistic information, values and behavior among people. For more than ten years he has traveled and lived throughout Asia, documenting the process of cultural influence among young adults there who are increasingly impressed by a rapidly interconnecting world. This is his fifth book. He currently lives in Beijing and New York City.

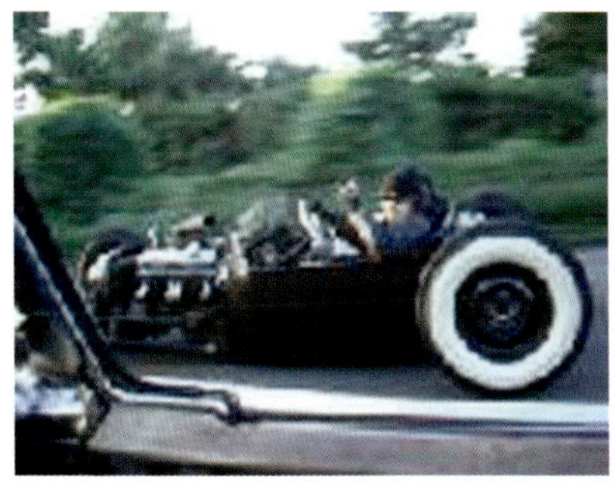

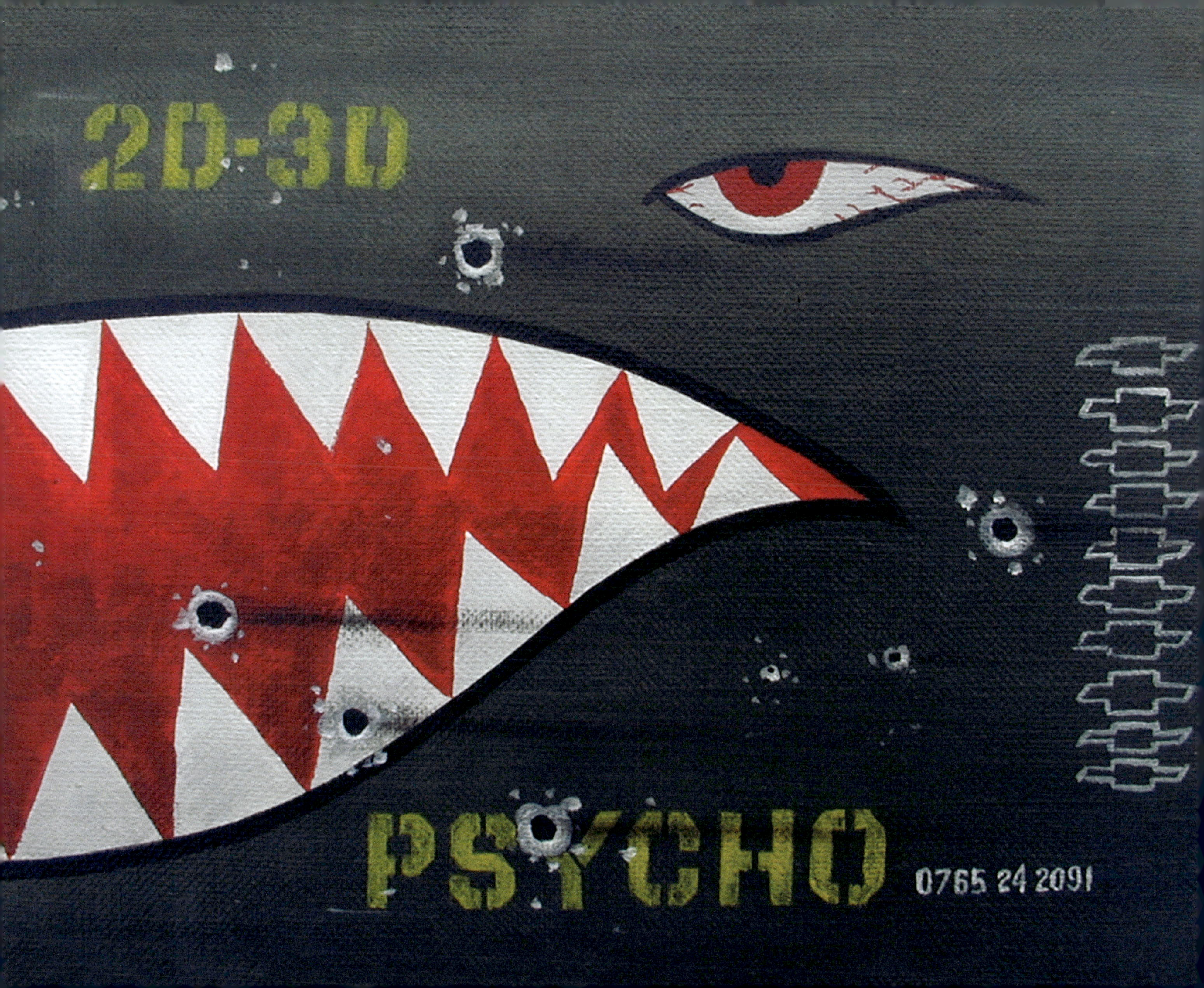
2D-3D
PSYCHO
0765 24 2091